ELEMENTARY PHYSICAL EDUCATION

Growing Through Movement

Robert G. Davis

Virginia Commonwealth University

Larry D. Isaacs

Wright State University

Hunter Textbooks Inc.

Dedicated to my children, Carrie and Rick
—*RGD*

*Dedicated to my family, Brooke and Joy, and
to the loving memories of a best friend — Lucy*
—*LDI*

Photographs by Robert G. Davis
Cover Design by Deborah Dale

© 1983 by Hunter Textbooks Incorporated

ISBN 0-89459-193-2

Printed in the United States of America

All rights reserved. No part of this publication may be reproduced in any form without written permission of the publisher, except by a reviewer who may quote brief passages in critical articles and reviews. Inquiries should be addressed to the publisher:

Hunter Textbooks Inc.
823 Reynolda Road
Winston-Salem, North Carolina 27104

PREFACE

Some substantial changes have occurred in the conduct of elementary physical education over the past ten to fifteen years with the most dramatic being the influence of movement education. Although this approach has shown both gains and losses in various parts of the country, it has basically replaced the game-oriented curriculum prevalent during the fifties and early sixties. Through the influence of movement education, teachers have become concerned with the educational process as well as the product. The process focuses on a nondirective, student centered approach to teaching in which creativity and self-worth are emphasized along with other physical education goals. Borrowed primarily from the British infant schools, movement education has become the major influence in preparing elementary physical educators in most areas of the United States. Accepted by most, but certainly not all, movement education is believed by many to be a replacement for traditional elementary physical education; others, however, view it as an important part of physical education. Those who reject it entirely most likely do not understand its role and importance in the growth and development process. For purposes of this book, movement education is viewed as an essential part of elementary physical education with application at all grade levels although it is emphasized more at the primary (kindergarten through second grade) levels.

Movement education is viewed as a problem solving, student oriented approach to teaching through which children are given the opportunity to explore movement and develop skills, solve problems, develop creativity, and enhance their self-concept in a positive, nonthreatening environment. Through movement education, children are more involved cognitively in the learning process. Children are asked to think through tasks designed to develop the quality of their body movements. This quality of locomotor and nonlocomotor movement is emphasized so children can eventually build on the fundamental base developed through exploration. These movement qualities then form the basis for motor skill learnings.

Movement education, however, is viewed as only one aspect of physical education. Other important considerations are health related fitness, an interdisciplinary approach to curriculum planning, adaptive physical education, and creative dance. Considerable emphasis is given to these areas in this book. There is a separate chapter for adaptive physical education and one for creative dance. A chapter is also devoted exclusively to fitness and includes numerous activities and ideas such as a cooperatively planned fitness program involving the classroom teacher and parents. With declining fitness levels and increases in such areas as obesity and heart disease, health related fitness is viewed as a particularly important aspect of both growth and development. The emphasis in this book is on developing positive fitness attitudes along with fitness levels. Such a combination, hopefully, will foster a healthy lifestyle.

Planning for the best educational experience is done through an interdisciplinary approach in which various academic concepts and information can be reinforced through movement. Subject areas such as language arts, math, social studies, science, art, and music can be successfully integrated with physical education. Such integration can be done without losing the integrity of physical education. Movement activities can also be used to teach and reinforce academic subjects. A separate chapter is devoted to cognitive development. Numerous suggestions and activities for interdisciplinary planning are also included throughout the text.

As can be seen in the introduction to this book, the overall philosophy which guided its development is a commitment to a positive self-concept in all children. This commitment is reflected in the student oriented teaching approach advocated as well as suggested control and discipline techniques. No single educational objective is believed more important than development of positive self-concept. The physical educator and his or her approach to the curriculum can do more to develop either a positive or negative self-concept than any other person in education. Although this is certainly a strong statement, it serves to emphasize the importance placed on self-concept development during physical education.

In order to effectively meet the objectives of self-concept development along with other important physical education goals, one must be able to plan the curriculum using a book which has been effectively organized. Both classroom teachers and physical educators, hopefully, will find this just such a book. Other authors have used various approaches to textbook organization. Some take a game orientation, others provide a variety of activities under major headings such as rhythmics, manipulative skills, and sports, and still others have presented lesson plans for various educational arrangements such as kindergarten through third grade and fourth through sixth grade. The organization used in this text would best be described as a developmental, age group approach. The age divisions are based on growth and development characteristics of students. Data would seem to support an organization of: (1) five year olds (kindergarten), (2) six and seven year olds (usually first and second grades), (3) eight and nine year olds (third and fourth grades), and (4) ten and eleven year olds (fifth and sixth grades). There is a curriculum chapter for each of these divisions. Each curriculum chapter contains growth and development information along with numerous activities organized into developmental categories. Also included are integrated activities for interdisciplinary planning, and finally, each chapter is culminated with a series of example lesson plans covering many of the developmental categories.

Other chapters are designed to assist the reader in planning and conducting the physical education program. The first section, Basic Considerations, deals primarily with organizing and conducting the program and covers such areas as principles of learning, educational domains, styles of teaching, class organization, and class control, to name a few. Fitness is included under Basic Considerations to emphasize its importance. Section II, Curriculum Considerations, in addition to the age group chapters, has a chapter for children with special needs. The chapter includes activities specially designed for handicapped children along with ideas on how to effectively implement Public Law 94-142. A creative dance chapter covering grades three through six is also included. The final section, Other Considerations, is designed to provide supplemental information which should be helpful in implementing the curriculum. The areas of homemade equipment, legal liability, and competition should help the specialists and the classroom teacher. Those interested in using movement for cognitive development will find Chapter 15 useful.

Those students who receive a physical education program taught by a humanistic individual following the guidelines established in this book will be happy, physically fit children who move efficiently and possess numerous motor skills.

CONTENTS

Preface iii

Introduction ix

SECTION I — BASIC CONSIDERATIONS

1. Foundations of Elementary Physical Education 3
   The Educational Domains 3
   Terminology 13

2. Learning 17
   Growth and Development Characteristics and
      Their Importance to Learning 17
   Principles of Learning 20

3. Motor Learning 25
   The Motor Learning Process 25
   Factors Affecting Input: Communicating with the Learner ... 26
   Factors Affecting Central Processing: Decision-Making 29
   Factors Affecting Output: Overt Performance 29
   Principles of Motor Learning 31

4. The Learning Environment 41
   Teacher Behavior 41
   Nonverbal Behavior 45
   Student Behavior 51
   Control and Discipline 51

5. Curriculum Design 61
   Systematic Approach 61
   Unit Planning 68
   Lesson Planning 72

6. Physical Fitness 83
   Children and Exercise 84
   Physiological Fitness 84
   Motor Fitness 99
   Motivating Children to Exercise 100
   Posture 101

SECTION II — CURRICULUM CONSIDERATIONS

7. Curriculum for Five Year Olds 121
   Characteristics of Five Year-Olds and Implications for Instruction ... 121
   Curriculum Emphases 123
   Teaching Approaches 124
   Safety 124
   Goals, Objectives, and Developmental Activities 126
   Integrated Activities 147
   Games 151
   Example Lesson Plans 155

8. Curriculum for Six and Seven-Year Olds **161**

    Characteristics of Six and Seven-Year Olds and
        Implications for Instruction.. 161
    Curriculum Emphases... 164
    Teaching Approaches... 164
    Safety.. 165
    Goals, Objectives, and Developmental Activities......... 165
    Integrated Activities... 177
    Games... 181
    Example Lesson Plans.. 187

9. Curriculum for Eight and Nine-Year Olds **197**

    Characteristics of the Eight and Nine-Year Old and
        Implications for Instruction.. 197
    Curriculum Emphases... 199
    Safety.. 199
    Teaching Approaches... 200
    Goals, Objectives, and Developmental Activities......... 201
    Games... 215
    Example Lesson Plans.. 221

10. Curriculum for Ten and Eleven-Year Olds.................... **229**

    Characteristics of Ten and Eleven-Year Olds and
        Implications for Instruction.. 229
    Curriculum Emphases... 232
    Teaching Approaches... 233
    Safety.. 233
    Goals, Objectives, and Developmental Activities......... 234
    Games... 254
    Example Lesson Plans.. 258

11. Children's Dance **267**
    By Fran Meyer, Hugh Mercer Elementary School, Fredericksburg, Virginia

    Dance Activities for First and Second Grades............. 268
    Dance Activities for Third and Fourth Grades............. 285
    Dance Activities for Fifth and Sixth Grades................ 301

12. Adaptive Physical Education... **319**
    By Mark Runac, Virginia Commonwealth University

    Past, Present, and Future of Physical Education, for the Handicapped.... 319
    Public Law 94-142... 320
    Learning Principles.. 323
    Behavior Modification... 324
    Teaching Techniques for Those with Reduced Mental Capacity 325
    Activities... 325

SECTION III — OTHER IMPORTANT CONSIDERATIONS

13. Physical Education and the Law..................................... **339**

    Potential Hazards.. 340
    Defenses... 343
    Precautions... 344

14. Understanding Competition.................................. 351
　　Competition in School.. 351
　　Competition in Physical Education............................ 351
　　Competition in Athletics... 354

15. The Cognitive Domain and Movement..................... 359
　　Language Arts.. 360
　　Math.. 362
　　Science.. 364

16. Homemade Equipment.. 371
　　By John P. Bennett, George Mason University

APPENDICES

A. Evaluating and Developing Fitness................................. 384
　　VCU Fitness Test.. 384
　　Running for Life... 390

B. Evaluation Instruments for the Affective Domain......... 392

C. The Cognitive Domain... 395

D. Record Sources... 395

Index.. **396**

INTRODUCTION

SELF-CONCEPT

This book is based on the premise that each child should feel good about himself or herself no matter what his or her ability. The way a child feels about himself is termed self-concept. Many educators and psychologists believe self-concept is essential to all other aspects of development. The introduction to this book, therefore, is devoted to the importance of self-concept.

Movement is a major portion of a child's early life; initial learning is of and through movement. A child's first interactions with others are greatly dependent upon movement, and as the child grows, movement becomes increasingly important to interpersonal relationships. During the preschool and elementary years, acceptance in the peer group is dependent somewhat on physical performance, and children are often quite sensitive about their performance in front of peers.

Since self-concept is determined to a great extent on how one feels others view her or him, physical performance which is visible to others can have a marked influence on self-concept development. The physical educator's role, therefore, is to provide success for each child while using techniques which do not embarrass the child. The dynamic and emotional nature of physical education makes the task of self-concept development that much more difficult for physical educators.

The importance of the learning environment to self-concept development cannot be overemphasized. Ways to create a positive learning environment include: (1) using considerable praise while minimizing criticism; (2) treating children with respect; (3) offering activities which give children success with effort; (4) being sensitive to nonverbal communication; and (5) being aware that little things mean a lot.

Praise and Criticism

Probably the most critical element in creating a positive environment is praise and criticism. Behavior which is rewarded (praised) is more likely to reoccur while punishment has variable and uncertain effects on behavior. In many cases, behavior which receives attention even in the form of punishment may be more rather than less likely to reoccur. Praising good behavior while ignoring misbehavior as much as possible, therefore, should help to establish a positive learning environment.

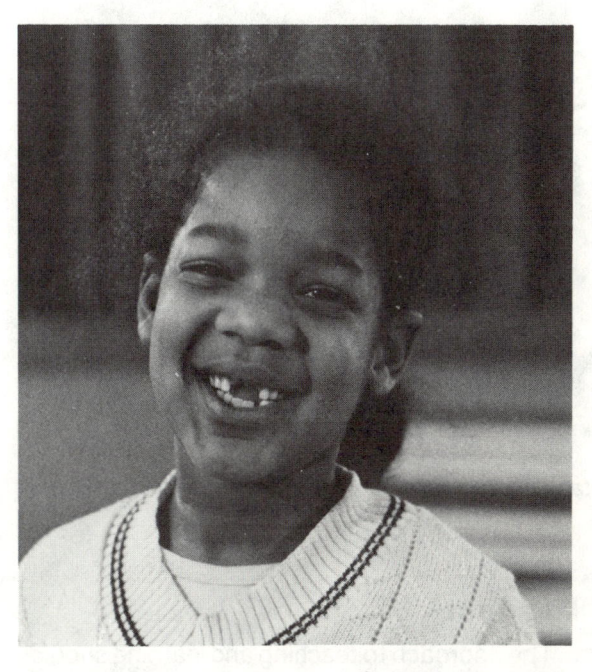

Praise can be given either verbally or nonverbally. Although many teachers rely almost exclusively on verbal feedback, nonverbal techniques may be more effective. Verbal praise often loses its effectiveness from overuse. Children can become desensitized from hearing everyone being praised. Nonverbal praise on the other hand, can be individually directed without the knowledge of other children. This is not to say that children should not receive recognition in front of peers, only that to be most effective, it should not be overdone. Nonverbal feedback complements the verbal and allows for more effective use of praise in general. Nonverbal gestures such as smiles, winks, pats on the back, and approving head nods can be extremely effective in making a child feel good about what he or she has done. Handling inappropriate behavior is discussed in Chapter 4 under "Control and Discipline."

Using instant photographs can help to remember students' names.

Respect

The approach to teaching and learning should be humanistic. Children, after all, are human beings and should be afforded the same rights and courtesies of any other human. Teachers expect children to say "please" and "thank you," yet often do not extend such courtesies to children. Children should listen when teachers speak and vice versa. Sarcasm has no place in teaching nor does belittling children belong in an educational setting.

One way to personalize and thereby humanize education is to call children by name. Names are not always easy to learn or remember, particularly for a physical education teacher who may have 800 or 900 students. One technique for learning names is the use of instant pictures. Children can be photographed in groups of ten or twelve at a time (two rows) and names can be placed above or below the faces. Some of the older style instant pictures had borders on which names can be written. The newer glossy finish does not permit the writing of names, but names can be taped on the picture. This technique is quick and inexpensive. Learning and using names not only aids in developing self-concept, but aids communication with parents and other teachers. It is much easier to discuss a child when a face can be placed with a name.

Selecting Activities

Physical education activities can be critical to self-concept development. Children who are successful at activities which are challenging are more likely to develop a positive attitude about themselves. The key is to present activities which are challenging but not frustrating. In using a student-centered approach, a teacher must consider the growth and developmental characteristics within any age group.

Communicating

Sensitivity to communication is essential if self-concept is to be enhanced. As mentioned, teachers rely heavily on and are most concerned with verbal communication, often overlooking nonverbal communication. A good deal is said through facial expressions, posture, and eye contact. A smile, a touch, distance between individuals, duration of eye contact — all communicate a nonverbal message. Too frequently, teachers unwittingly transmit negative feelings by their actions; and after all, "actions speak louder than words." Other nonverbal factors include room arrangement, decorations, lighting, temperature, and bulletin boards, just to name a few. It is difficult to self-evaluate nonverbal behavior, but a supervisor or videotape machine can be helpful.

Little Things Mean a Lot

Little things which may seem unimportant to a teacher can be extremely important to children. Such things as giving children responsibilities, trusting them, noticing new clothes or hairdos, indicating they are missed when absent, eating lunch with them, and playing with them occasionally during recess can all aid a child's self-concept.

LOVE

If teachers are going to successfully aid children's self-concept development, they must love children. Many well-meaning individuals presently teaching elementary school do not like children or have an obvious disdain for certain children. Unfortunately, such feelings are usually obvious to children. The information in this book is designed for teachers who love children and desire to help children grow through the medium of movement.

ELEMENTARY PHYSICAL EDUCATION

SECTION 1
BASIC CONSIDERATIONS

CHAPTER 1
FOUNDATIONS OF ELEMENTARY PHYSICAL EDUCATION

After completing this chapter, the student should be able to:

1. Describe each educational domain and give at least four physical education goals for each domain.
2. Describe the interrelationships among the domains.
3. Discuss the importance of affective education.
4. Describe ways to improve a child's self-concept through physical education using information from the introduction of this book as well as the chapter content.
5. Describe the ways to evaluate each domain.
6. Define the terms in the chapter.
7. Complete the student activities at the end of the chapter.

Physical education is defined as a planned sequence of activities designed to provide each child an equal opportunity to reach his or her full potential physically, socially, emotionally and, to a certain extent, intellectually. This total child approach is reflected in both activity selection and teaching methods. The process, therefore, is viewed as being as important as the product. The major physical education goal is to produce an individual who moves efficiently, is well skilled, is physically fit, has a positive self-concept, and thinks creatively. This goal can only be accomplished in a positive learning environment in which a variety of activities are presented in a manner which satisfies a wide range of abilities and personalities. No one approach can satisfy these criteria. The prospective teacher, therefore, must experience a number of teaching styles and activities while learning the growth and development characteristics of those children with whom he or she will work.

Although physical growth and development is the emphasis in physical education, it is but one aspect of the total developmental process. It is no more important but, at the same time, no less important than cognitive and affective development. All growth and development factors are, in fact, interrelated and interdependent. An understanding of each including the interrelationships is therefore necessary. This chapter is a presentation of the three educational domains, psychomotor, cognitive, and affective, and some terms necessary for effective educational communication.

THE EDUCATIONAL DOMAINS

The purpose of this section is to familiarize the reader with the three domains, psychomotor, affective, and cognitive. It is not intended as an exhaustive review of the subject, and the reader interested in more detail is referred to Bloom et al. (1) for the cognitive domain and Krathwohl et al. (3) for the affective domain.

The following two examples are offered to clarify the differences among the three domains:

1. An individual is driving a car (the ability to drive falls under the psychomotor domain) when he sees a sign which says stop (the ability to read and understand the sign is covered by the cognitive domain). His decision to stop is determined primarily by his attitude toward safety and his own health (health and safety are attitudes covered by the affective domain).
2. A person is playing tennis (psychomotor ability), and hits an overhead smash near the net. On his follow-through he hits the net, but his opponent does not see the infraction. His knowledge of the rules is covered by the cognitive domain, while his

sportsmanship in telling the opponent of his infraction is part of the affective domain.

Cognitive Domain

Usually, the cognitive domain is most familiar to readers. It deals with thought processes such as problem-solving, evaluation, and comprehension. For purposes of understanding, Bloom and his associates organized this domain into levels of cognitive ability. The lowest level was designated as knowledge, followed in ascending order by comprehension, application, analysis, synthesis, and — the highest level — evaluation. (1) Subjects such as reading and mathematics would fall under the cognitive domain.

Cognitive Goals and Objectives (Examples)

Each of the following broadly stated goals is followed by a more specifically stated objective.

1. The child will learn basketball rules.

Objective: Following the basketball unit, the child will correctly answer at least 80 percent of the questions on a basketball rules test.

2. Students will know the reasons for being physically fit.

Objective: If asked, at least 80 percent of the students will be able to give at least two reasons for being physically fit.

3. Students will develop creativity.

Objective: At least 80 percent of the students will be able to create an original gymnastics routine which includes at least six different stunts.

Physical Education and Cognitive Domain

The major contributions of physical education to cognitive development are: (1) the learning of rules and regulations; (2) the development of problem-solving ability; (3) the development of creativity; and (4) the knowledge of the body — its function as well as its care.

Cognitive development has not been a high physical education priority in the past as is pointed out in Figure 1-1, but the emphasis seems to be changing. Cognitive development was ranked seventh by a sample of physical education professors in 1968. More recently, however, it was ranked second by a group of elementary physical educators who had a strong movement education background.

Ranking cognitive development ahead of organic vigor (fitness) and neuromuscular skills (motor development) as a major purpose of physical education would be questioned by many. There is no doubt, however, regarding the trend toward an interdisciplinary approach to curriculum development within elementary physical education. One must be cautious, however, when planning for more cognitive development during physical education not to lose the integrity of physical education.

Cognitive Testing

The amount of information which has been generated about cognitive testing is staggering. I.Q., achievement, essay, multiple choice, matching, true and false are just a few of the tests and testing styles featured in hundreds of books. The cognitive emphasis which preoccupies American educators is reflected in the sheer numbers of tests which are available. Those interested in finding information about standardized tests should consult Buros Mental Measurement Yearbook, available in most college libraries.

The Psychomotor Domain

The psychomotor domain deals with all physical activity, such as sports and movement, as well as such skills as driving, typing, flying a plane, etc. Many physical education objectives fall into this category. Physical educators can make more contributions to psychomotor development than any other area.

RANKING OF OBJECTIVES

Objective	1967-68 Study	1975 Graduate Curriculum Class
Organic Vigor	1	7
Neuromuscular Skills	2	5 (tie)
Leisure Time Activities	3	4
Self Realization	4	1
Emotional Stability	5	3
Democratic Values	6	8
Mental Development	7	2
Social Competency	8	5 (tie)
Spiritual and Moral Strength	9	10
Cultural Appreciation	10	9

Figure 1-1

Psychomotor Goals and Objectives (Examples)

1. Students will be physically fit.

Objective: At least 80 percent of the students will score above the 50th percentile on the nine-minute run portion of the *AAHPERD Youth Fitness Test.*

2. Neuromuscular skills will be developed.

Objective: By the end of the first grade, nearly all the children will have developed a minimum level of proficiency in perceptual-motor skills as indicated through use of the *Purdue Perceptual-Motor Survey.*

3. Students will learn a variety of leisure time skills.

Objective: By the end of the second grade each child will be able to organize and play at least ten different leisure time games without adult assistance.

Physical Education and the Psychomotor Domain

The physical educator can develop many important components of psychomotor ability through the medium of movement. These include physiological and motor fitness, neuromuscular skills, leisure time activities, and efficiency of human movement. A teacher who carefully designs and properly administers the physical education program will assure the maximum development of psychomotor skills.

Psychomotor Evaluation

Psychomotor testing is usually done individually and it is time-consuming unless efficient methods are used. The best method for obtaining reliable data, of course, is testing one child at a time. This one-to-one testing is important when working with children who have special problems and need extra attention. Such children, however, can usually be singled out through observation, thus eliminating the need to test each child.

Trained Assistants. The second best formalized testing method is the use of trained assistants, usually upper elementary children. It is possible, however, to use parent assistants or teacher's aides who can be pulled from classrooms for short time periods. These assistants can, with little instruction, be trained to administer most tests at the elementary level. Although the data are not as reliable using assistants, they are sufficient for making curriculum decisions and individualizing instruction.

Goals of Physical Education

Psychomotor	Affective	Cognitive
Physiological Fitness	Self-Concept	Creativity

Motor Fitness
   Manipulative Skills
   Locomotor Movement
   Nonlocomotor Movement
   Balance
	Honesty and Sportsmanship
	
	Sharing
	
	Respect for Authority
		Problem-solving
		
		Body Image
		
		Directional terms

Kinesthetic Awareness	Respect for Self and Others	Rules and Regulations
Tumbling and Gymnastics	Leadership	Knowledge of Fitness
Rhythmics	Self-Discipline	Health Safety
Relaxation	Attitudes toward Activity	
Sports Skills	Fitness Health	
Lead-up Games to Sports	Safety	

Figure 1-2

Pairing. Many children can be reliably tested by using a partner arrangement. Upper elementary children — fourth-grade and up — can be paired with peers, while lower elementary children can be paired with older children. In research by Davis and Miller (2), fifth-graders were found to be as reliable as college students in testing first-graders on running tests. Through this pairing arrangement, whole classes can be assessed accurately and quickly in most physical tests.

Self-Testing. The least reliable data are obtained when children test themselves, and although of limited value in terms of curriculum decisions, such data can be motivating to students. This technique is closely associated with learning packets and learning centers (Chapter 5) in which much of the learning and assessing responsibility rests with the students. Tasks are established which do not require any outside observer for evaluation; i.e., "throw the beanbag in the bucket two times in a row from behind the line," or "jump over the stick without knocking it off." These tasks can be self-evaluated and intrinsically motivating when success is accomplished. The teacher's task is to spot-check student progress to see they understand the tasks and in fact did accomplish them.

The Affective Domain

Even though it is potentially the most important, the affective domain traditionally has received the least attention among the three domains. The perpetuation of our society is dependent somewhat upon the values and attitudes covered by the affective domain. Increased emphasis on the cognitive domain seem to have overshadowed more traditional values such as honesty, respect for others, self-respect, respect for authority and interpersonal relationships. These values can and should be taught in school and preplanning is necessary for affective development. Important attitudes such as safety and honesty can be developed through discussion and problem solving. Simulations can be used in more sensitive areas such as interpersonal relationships, i.e., kindness and acceptance of others who are different. Sensitivity, however, must be exercised when working in this area because of the possible harm which can be done to a child's self-concept.

Unplanned opportunities also must be anticipated so they can be dealt with effectively. How will the teacher deal with fighting, cheating, booing, and name-calling? The difference between the average teacher and the superior teacher is often how well these unplanned moments are handled. Merely stopping a fight or telling students not to boo is insufficient educationally. Discovering underlying causes and giving reasons for eliminating certain behavior are important aspects of learning.

Attitudes in general and self-concept in particular are covered under the affective domain. As was pointed out in the introduction to this book, the self-concept — attitude toward self — is vitally important to all aspects of learning. Leaving affective development to chance, therefore, is highly questionable. Most of the lasting effects of education are greatly dependent upon a student's attitude. Good teachers who show enthusiasm, good class preparation, and overall dedication to the job will have a positive influence on a student. So much can be accomplished if teachers make a concerted effort to foster good student attitudes.

Catching two beanbags at one time is a self-testing activity.

How should fighting be handled?

Affective Domain Goals and Objectives (Examples)

1. Students will be good sports.

   Objective: Following a game of basketball, no students will boo the opposition.

2. Students will have a positive attitude toward physical education.

   Objective: Given an anonymous questionnaire, at least 90 percent of the students will rate the physical education program as good to excellent on a scale of excellent, good, average, fair and poor.

3. Students will enjoy participating in physical activity.

   Objective: At least 60 percent of the students will voluntarily participate in some intramural sport.

Physical Education and the Affective Domain. The dynamic nature of physical education provides more opportunities for positive or negative affective development of the child than any other subject in the curriculum. Opportunities for sharing, honesty, fair play, self-discipline and interpersonal relationships occur in nearly every physical education period. How these opportunities are handled will influence the child's development particularly in the area of the self-concept. Unprepared teachers who handle sensitive issues poorly can cause irreparable damage to the child. Physical educators, as well as all teachers, should have a good background in psychology and group dynamics if they are to be effective in the affective domain.

Toffler, in *Future Shock* (5), lends credence to the importance of the affective domain. In his discussion on education, Toffler makes a point about values, an integral part of the affective domain. Students, according to Toffler, ". . . are seldom encouraged to analyze their own values and those of their teachers and peers. Millions pass through the education system without once having been forced to search out the contradictions in their own value systems, to probe their own life goals deeply, or even to discuss these matters candidly with adults and peers." This must be done during the formative years of the elementary school in order to achieve the maximum potential of growth and development for each child.

Affective Evaluation

Most affective evaluation can be done in groups since most instruments require written responses. These formal tests are usually attitude questionnaires or drawing tests to assess body image and self-concept of young children. If properly designed, paper/pencil tests can be given to any grade level, including nonreaders.

Attitude Questionnaire. A great deal can be learned from an attitude questionnaire if it is carefully designed. Information obtained should include: (1) the program — Do students like it? What are their favorite activities? and (2) the teacher — information obtained can be quite specific.

The style and sophistication of the instrument will vary greatly according to the child's age, but the information obtained from various age groups is similar. The range in styles goes from the nonreading four-year-old to children who can handle a six choice descriptor design.

Nonreaders and first-grade children must be given familiar visual cues to keep them on track, along with an easy three descriptor choice. Figure 1-3 is an example of a questionnaire for nonreaders. Children "X" through either of the three faces. The faces should be reversed frequently to avoid a set response. (Checking all smiley faces because they are always first, for example.) To be sure that the children understand the questionnaire, two practice statements should be designed to elicit a specific response, one happy or one sad. If children do not check the desired response on these practice questions, they should be quizzed to find out why before proceeding. All statements must be worked to agreement with the scale — in this case, "happy or sad face."

The neutral face is sometimes difficult for children to understand, but using it can provide information about the statements not understood or those that fail to elicit an emotional response from the children. A circle with a question mark in it has been found to be a useful substitute for the neutral face.

Older children from second grade to sixth grade can handle more sophisticated statements and scales. Figure 1-4 is an example of a questionnaire for older elementary children. The most commonly used scale in research is the Likert or modified Likert Scale. In the modified Likert there is no neutral position, forcing the person to take a positive or negative stand. Figure 1-5 has examples of different scales which can be used on questionnaires. As with primary grade scales, the statements must fit the scale used. For the Likert and modified Likert, declarative statements are made which the student either agrees with, disagrees with, or is neutral towards. In the five scale examples in Figure 1-5, students are asked to rate aspects of the program.

The statements for older children should be worded so the desired response is not always positive. A statement such as "Physical Education should be removed from the curriculum" will, hopefully, receive a "very strongly disagree" response. By wording statements this way, children are forced to read them before responding. Mixing statements in this manner serves as a check against someone recording positive or negative responses for every statement.

Statements should also be included to check for the "lying effect." By pairing two statements which necessitate opposite responses, a further check of honesty is possible. A person responding positively toward the statement regarding the removal of physical education from the curriculum should have a negative response to the statement, "Physical education is an important part of the educational program." By randomly placing such check statements throughout the questionnaire, more reliable data can be obtained.

As can be seen in Figure 1-4, a questionnaire can be used to obtain ratings of activities as well as general statements about physical education. Since all questionnaires should be anonymous, there is no limit to the number of statements or type of information which can be obtained. Fatigue in any test, however, can be a factor, so length must be considered when designing such instruments.

Scoring a questionnaire is not difficult and is necessary for data interpretation. Since collective scores for the entire questionnaire have little meaning, each statement should be dealt with individually. If the test has been properly designed, each statement provides valuable data which are lost in any type of composite score.

The data interpretation is somewhat subjective with the person giving the test determining the acceptable score for each statement. If the tester sought a positive response to a statement, an average score of "5" on a six point scale would seem reasonable with a "2" average on statements designed for negative responses. Anyone failing to meet these standards should reassess that aspect of the program in question and make changes.

Results of the questionnaire should be made available to the children old enough to understand them, and all children should have an opportunity to discuss problem areas in an open forum. The data interpretation may be difficult without such open discussion. An alternative to open discussion would be to administer another questionnaire dealing with one specific problem area. The open discussion, however, will usually be successful with elementary children. (Additional questionnaires can be found in Appendix B.)

Checklists. Another type of affective testing is the checklist. A checklist can be used with groups or individual students, with the latter use being more common. Observation is the normal means for obtaining data. Such areas as pupil interaction, sportsmanship, sharing, respecting other's rights, willingness to listen, and voluntary participation in activities or discussion can be included on the checklist. Figure 1-6 is a sample checklist for determining feelings, attitudes, and other affective domain information. Figure 1-7 is an example of a checklist which can be used early in the year to identify children who may have affective problems.

The Draw-A-Person test. Most would agree that self-concept is an attitude or feeling one has about himself or herself and thus is part of the affective domain. Since the basis for a positive self-concept is body image, the Draw-A-Person (DAP) test can be an important assessment tool. The directions are usually just to ask a child to draw a picture of himself or herself on an 8½ x 11 inch plain piece of paper (see Appendix).

Scoring the DAP can be as simple as giving one point for each body part drawn or as sophisticated as that outlined by Vane in the Vane Kindergarten Test. Psychologists use the DAP as a projective test to determine personality traits such as introversion and extroversion and many teachers who are not properly trained attempt to make psychological data interpretations. Teachers must be cautious about making any inferences from a test such as DAP, and if a problem is suspected, it should be referred to a properly trained individual.

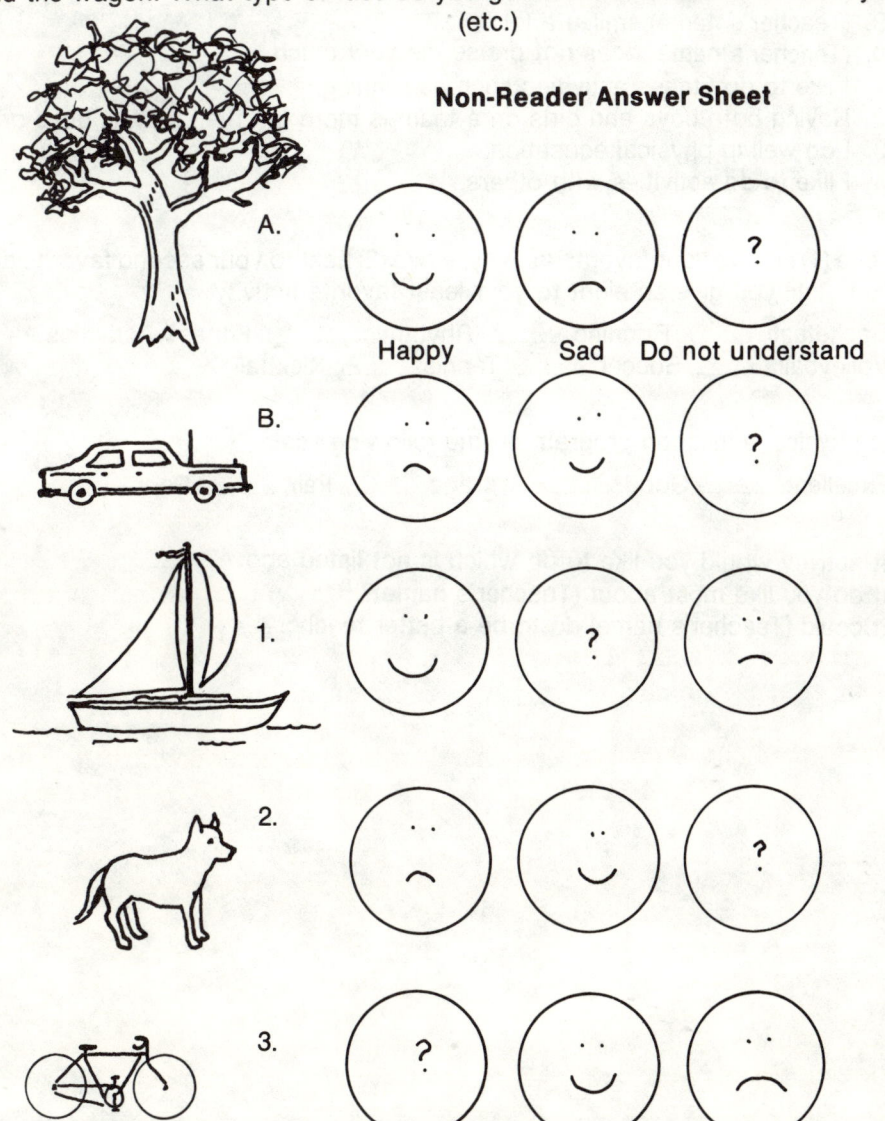

Figure 1-3
Nonreader Attitude Questionnaire
Teacher's Copy

Practice:
A. Find the tree and place your finger on it. When I say I am going to give you ice cream, what kind of face do you have? Mark an "X" on one of the faces next to the tree.
   (Answer: Happy face)
B. Find the car. When I say you have been bad, what kind of a face do you get? Mark one of the faces next to the car.
   (Answer: Sad face)
C. I am now going to read you questions about physical education, and you will "X" either a happy or sad face to each question. Please listen carefully and follow along with me.

1. Find the boat. What kind of a face do you get when I say we are going to physical education?
2. Find the dog. When I say there is a substitute for Mr. Adams (the physical educator) today, what kind of a face do you get?
3. Find the bicycle. When Mr. Adams says find a partner in physical education, what type of face do you have?
4. Find the spoon. What type of face do you have when we dance in physical education?
5. Find the fork. When Mr. Adams says play by yourself, what type of face do you get?
6. Find the wagon. What type of face do you get when other children watch you play?

(etc.)

Non-Reader Answer Sheet

A. Happy   Sad   Do not understand

Figure 1-4
Attitude Questionnaire for Upper Elementary Children

Scale:
1. Strongly Agree
2. Agree
3. Disagree
4. Strongly Disagree
0. No opinion or do not understand

I. Place the number of the response which best reflects your feeling about each statement below:
   _____ 1. Physical education is an important part of school.
   _____ 2. I do not learn much in Physical Education.
   _____ 3. (Teacher's name) likes me.
   _____ 4. I like to dance with a partner.
   _____ 5. Rhythmic activities such as lummi sticks and tinikling are fun.
   _____ 6. (Teacher's name) is patient.
   _____ 7. Physical education should be removed from school.
   _____ 8. (Teacher's name) gets too angry with us.
   _____ 9. (Teacher's name) smiles a lot.
   _____ 10. (Teacher's name) does not praise me very much.
   _____ 11. I like to do fitness activities such as running.
   _____ 12. Having both boys and girls on a team is more fun than just all boys or girls.
   _____ 13. I do well in physical education.
   _____ 14. I like to do activities with others.

II. Place a one (1) next to your favorite activity, a two (2) next to your second favorite activity, and so on, until you give an eight to your least favorite activity:
   _____ Basketball, _____ Running, _____ Rhythmics, _____ Fitness Activities, _____ Volleyball, _____ Soccer, _____ Tennis, _____ Kickball

III. Rate the physical education program on the following scale:
   _____ Excellent, _____ Good, _____ Average, _____ Fair, _____ Poor

IV. 1. What activity would you like to do which is not listed above?
    2. What do you like most about (Teacher's name)?
    3. What could (Teacher's name) do to be a better teacher?

Figure 1-5
Attitude Questionnaire Scales

Likert-type Scale:

    Very Strongly Agree
    Strongly Agree
    Agree
    Disagree
    Strongly Disagree
    Very Strongly Disagree
    Neither Agree or Disagree (No opinion)

Modified Likert:

    Very Strongly Agree
    Strongly Agree
    Agree
    Disagree
    Strongly Disagree
    Very Strongly Disagree

5-Scale:

    Excellent
    Good
    Average
    Fair
    Poor

5-Scale:

    A
    B
    C
    D
    F

4-Scale

    Frequently
    Sometimes
    Seldom
    Never

Figure 1-6
Checklist for Group Observation in the Affective Domain

Record to the right those children (name or number) who exhibit the behaviors listed below.

1. Seems to prefer being alone rather than playing with the group.
2. Does not seem to be liked by other children.
3. Is excessively active during quiet times.
4. Does not share.
5. Argues with other children.
6. Fights with other children.
7. Does not follow safety rules.
8. Does not listen.
9. Seems unhappy or sad.
10. Does not respect the rights of others.
11. Does not follow well.
12. Does not participate.

Although this checklist is negative, it is designed for easy recording. Since most children exhibit positive behavior, it would be difficult to record all those doing the right thing. It is thus easier to identify and record those few who have problems. These problem children are also the ones who will need the most individualized instruction, so their identification is important. This instrument is merely a checklist, not an absolute. The data from it, therefore, should be used cautiously and should not cause a child to be labeled, only helped. Children who are identified should be checked further using the checklist in Figure 1-7. Since most of the evaluation using this instrument is subjective, it is valuable to have someone else observe the class as a check.

Figure 1-7
Checklist for the Affective Domain

Name of Child _____

Period of time data was gathered _____

	ALWAYS	REGULARLY	SOMETIMES	NEVER
1. Plays well with other children				
2. Likes to be by self				
3. Shares				
4. Is happy				
5. Participates in all activities				
6. Argues with other children				
7. Argues with teacher				
8. Gets angry				
9. Fights physically with other children				
10. Strikes out at adults				
11. Sits and listens when asked				
12. Is active				
13. Respects rights of others				
14. Is kind to other children				
15. Is honest				
16. Is a good leader				
17. Is a good follower				
18. Plays safely				
19. Practices good health habits				

As in the case when using any checklist, caution should be exercised when interpreting the data due to the subjective nature of the observation. Children should not be labeled; the purpose is identification and assistance. No far-reaching or conclusive data can be obtained using this checklist.

Know these

TERMINOLOGY

Each profession has its own language and education is no exception. Unfortunately, educators frequently change the language, including the meaning of familiar words. The following definitions are provided to aid communication between the authors of this book and the readers:

Physical Education is a planned sequence of activities designed to give each child an equal opportunity to reach his or her full potential, especially physically, socially, and emotionally.

Self-concept is a person's attitude about himself or herself. It is probably the most important aspect of emotional and social well-being.

Body image is the knowledge one has of his or her body parts and is the cornerstone for the development of self-concept.

Perceptual-motor programs are diagnostic and individualized programs of motor development for children with cognitive learning difficulties.

Physiological fitness is concerned with those aspects of fitness most important to health, such as heart and lung efficiency, presence of body fat, flexibility, muscular strength, and muscular endurance.

Principle of learning is a fundamental truth about how people learn.

Concept, according to Webster, is a thought or opinion.

Learning is a relatively permanent change in observable behavior.

Movement Education is a child-centered approach to teaching as well as an emphasis on the quality of movement and creativity (see Chapter 4).

Educational Gymnastics is an approach to the learning of gymnastics through discovery. The emphasis is on exploration and problem-solving. Although injuries are infrequent, legal complications are associated with educational gymnastics (see Chapter 13).

Kinesthetic Awareness is a knowledge of body parts in space and is important to all movement, especially gymnastics and tumbling.

Goals are general statements about the purpose of a program. The time frame for accomplishment is usually long term — semester or year.

Objectives are specific statements of purpose and are accomplishable in a short time frame — lesson, unit, and/or weekly.

REFERENCES

1. Bloom, B. et al. *Taxonomy of Education Objectives: Cognitive Domain.* New York: David McKay Company, Inc., 1956.
2. Davis, R. and W. Miller. "Relationship Between Field Tests of Cardiovascular Efficiency and a Laboratory Stress Test." Unpublished research paper, Virginia Commonwealth University, Richmond, Va., 1977.
3. Krathwohl, D. et al. *Taxonomy of Educational Objectives: Affective Domain.* New York: David McKay Company, Inc., 1956.
4. "Physical Educator Value Changes." Update. Washington, D.C.: AAHPER, October, 1976, p. 4.
5. Toffler, A. *Future Shock.* New York: Bantam Books, 1970.

— view change w/ 1 of 5 senses —
— visual & auditory —

CHAPTER 2

LEARNING

After completing this chapter, the student should be able to:

1. Discuss the children's growth and development characteristics and indicate their importance to learning.
2. Discuss those factors which make individuals different.
3. Define at least 80 percent of the terms associated with abnormal growth and development.
4. Give the instructional implications for at least 80 percent of the learning principles.

One problem in discussing learning is agreeing on a definition. For purposes of this text, learning will be defined as a relatively permanent change in observable behavior. To bring about this change, certain factors must be considered: (1) What are the child's growth and development characteristics? (2) What principles of learning are most important?

Growth and Development Characteristics and Their Importance to Learning

Although each child is unique, the patterns of growth and development are similar in all children. Development follows a sequence moving from head to feet and from the body's center out to its periphery. Patterns are also apparent in motor development, intellectual development, and social/emotional development. Knowledge of these growth and development patterns is essential to the design and conduct of any educational program.

The following discussion deals only with the general characteristics of children. Specific age group characteristics and their implications for instruction are included in each of the curriculum chapters, seven through ten.

Physical

The child's first learning is of and through movement. This movement development follows an inborn pattern and is a good indicator of developmental age. The pattern also helps in determining normalcy. For example, develop-

Learning through movement should be emphasized.

ment begins with head control and moves toward the lower body. The normal child, therefore, will be able to lift and control the head before gaining any kind of hand-eye or foot-eye coordination. Another important growth pattern is from the center (core) of the body outward. Children, therefore, will be able to be successful with gross motor activities before developing fine motor skills.

The child's locomotor pattern is also sequential. The child first crawls by pulling himself on his belly; this is followed by creeping on all fours which eventually progresses to walking and running. Although some children skip certain aspects of the sequence (usually creeping), normal children enter kindergarten with all the basic locomotor movements which include walking, running, hopping, jumping, and leaping. Combined (learned) locomotor skills such as galloping, sliding, and particularly skipping, do not come naturally and must therefore be taught if there is a need for the child to perform any of these skills.

Intellectual

According to Piaget, a leading cognitive theorist, intelligence develops in five stages: reflex, sensori-motor, preoperational, concrete operational, and formal operational. Piaget's work has been supported by other researchers, and is considered to be the most definitive information on the development of intelligence (7).

It is interesting to note that Piaget stresses the importance of movement particularly in the reflex and motor stages. Although usually completed by two years of age, these stages have been used to justify motor development programs at the elementary level. Perhaps such perceptual-motor programs would be beneficial to those who had not fully developed during the sensori-motor stage.

There is little evidence, however, that motor development programs affect the innate intelligence of children. Perceptual-motor programs are predicated on the notion that by participating in motor activities designed to improve perceptual skills, such as visual and auditory perception, a child will improve his or her other intellectual ability. Such a premise has little support in the research literature.

Movement can be used successfully as a medium for teaching academic concepts. This approach to teaching has nothing to do with developing an individual's intellectual ability. See Chapter 15 for more information on cognitive development.

Social/Emotional

Although social and emotional development are often dealt with separately, it is difficult to consider one without the other. For educational purposes and understanding the normal child's development, it is more meaningful to consider them together. As in the case of any growth and developmental process, outside influences have a great effect. A child's social and emotional development, however, are much more dependent on outside influences than physical and intellectual development.

Even with this outside influence, a pattern of social/emotional development is still discernible. From birth through early childhood, the focus is on self. Children seek attention in both positive and negative ways. Temper tantrums, misbehavior, and fighting are a few negative ways children seek attention. Constantly calling for the teacher's attention during movement activities ("Watch me! Watch me!") and doing as they are told are ways children seek positive attention from teachers. Young children like to do individual activities in which they receive individual attention ("I like the way you do that, Anne") rather than group or team activities. The team concept does not develop until third or fourth grade.

Self-centered behavior is followed by a gradual transition toward a peer-centered, group loyalty phase most evident in the 10-12 year old age group. These older children are influenced more strongly by peer values than adult imposed values; cliches are numerous. Most children will do nearly anything to save face in front of the peer group, and teachers who confront children in the presence of the peer group are asking for trouble. The child will either be defiant and maintain status, or with excessive pressure, will break and lose face, which has negative implications for self-concept development.

In all phases of social/emotional development, however, normal children seek adult approval. Most children also seem to like some order and discipline in their lives.

Individual Differences

Although growth and developmental patterns are similar among individuals, many factors influence the process, thus creating unique individuals. Heredity, sex, nutrition, family size, the home environment, and culture all modify the basic developmental sequence.

Heredity. Eye color, hair density, shape and size of head, hands and feet, handedness, and

Group activities involving movement can aid social and emotional development.

to a certain extent, intelligence are largely determined by heredity. According to authorities, approximately sixty percent of an individual's intellectual capacity is determined by heredity. Other aspects of growth and development such as protection from and susceptibility to diseases are also linked to heredity.

Sex. Sexual differences are also apparent. Boys tend to develop slower than girls in almost all aspects of growth and development. Boys, however, ultimately tend to be faster and stronger than girls. During the elementary years, child-rearing practices seem to influence the skill and interest differences between the sexes. Parental attitude is a major factor in shaping the behavioral differences between the sexes.

Nutrition. Diet plays a major role in growth and development, and affects a person's size, weight, looks, and health. Strength, endurance, and speed, as well as other fitness components, are dependent upon a proper diet. Poor nutrition can cause many problems and has been found to reduce functional ability.

Family Size. The family size and the birth order influence a child's personality. Researchers have found similarities between the order of birth and children's behavior. Single children, for example, have similar personality characteristics, even when other environmental and social factors among families are quite different. Older brothers and sisters appear to have a marked influence on the behavior of their younger siblings.

Home Environment. Closely linked to family size is home environment. Such factors as discipline in the home, absence of the father, mother, or both, and socioeconomic level play important roles in a child's development.

Cultural. Difference in the society has one of the most marked influences on behavior. Societies throughout the world vary greatly. Some place high priority on competition while others do not. In certain parts of the world, the female is the dominant individual. Communist countries are very state-oriented, while capitalistic societies are based more on individual effort rather than group achievement.

Abnormal Development. All children, unfortunately, do not develop normally. Following is a brief discussion of problems which children can encounter during the growth and development process:

Perceptual-motor problems are associated

mainly with the sensory mechanisms such as eye-hand and eye-foot coordination, auditory discrimination, balance, touch, and kinesthetic awareness (a knowledge of the body parts in space). Body image, self-concept, laterality, and directionality are closely associated with perceptual-motor development. Children who experience perceptual motor problems may also have learning difficulties, although the correlation between these two areas is low.

Mental retardation can be caused by genetic factors or by trauma. Inheritance is a major cause of retardation with disease and injury also taking their toll. Mentally retarded children are usually divided into three categories: (1) educable with an I.Q. of 60-80, (2) trainable with an I.Q. of 25-60, and (3) custodial with an I.Q. below 25. Until recent years, retarded children were usually institutionalized, but are now receiving increased attention due to an influx of federal money for their education and increased public concern for their welfare.

Autism is a disease characterized by withdrawal from reality. The child lives in a personal world which demands order; any change in surroundings can trigger a violent response by the child. For the most part, however, time is spent in a catatonic state. Only recently have means been found to assist the autistic child's learning.

Aphasia is a failure of the child to obtain meaningful spoken language by the age of three. The cause is not fully understood.

Schizophrenia, like autism, is a withdrawal from the world. Both diseases have many similar characteristics. The autistic child, however, is born withdrawn, whereas the schizophrenic child is often normal at first, and then withdraws over a period of time.

Maternal Deprivation Syndrome, as the name implies, is a condition caused by a lack of maternal care. Abandoned children, particularly babies, can experience this condition, which is characterized by a withdrawal from life. Many such children simply die for lack of affection. Substitute mothers who can give a lot of tender loving care have been successful in saving these children.

Fetal Alcohol Syndrome has only recently been described, and is characterized by retarded development including learning difficulties. Children of alcoholic mothers often exhibit these tendencies, and all children who have this syndrome exhibit facial features similar to Downs Syndrome (Mongolism)(1). Researchers have also suggested that only two heavy drinking episodes during pregnancy can be sufficient to produce this condition.

Minimal Brain Dysfunction (MBD) is a catch-all term for children who exhibit behavior for which no known cause can be found. It is hypothesized that there must be an undetectable problem in the brain causing such behavior. Hyperactive, as well as hypoactive children, are often classified as MBDs.

Hyperactive children are so active as to interfere with the normal learning process. At their worst, these children can be both destructive and disruptive in the typical classroom. Unable to sit still for even short time periods, the hyperactive child is constantly on the move, and extreme hyperactive periods can be accompanied by destructive tantrums. These children are usually hostile to authority and constantly want to "do their own thing." Severe cases are treated with tranquilizing drugs which usually stupify the child. Such drugs do not aid the child's learning, but help to improve the learning environment for other children. Since some teachers may confuse normal active behavior and general misbehavior with hyperactivity, authorities must exercise extreme caution in drug usage.

Principles of Learning

A principle of learning is a fundamental truth about learning. It has been studied and researched, and if properly applied, will assist in promoting learning. A principle which is violated, of course, has the reverse effect. Too often principles are stated without a discussion of their practical implications. In this section, some, but certainly not all, of the principles of learning will be discussed. A thorough understanding of these principles is essential to teaching and learning.

1. **It is more efficient to learn concepts than facts.**

    Implication • Although facts are important, particularly in the early stages of learning, concepts should be emphasized for the most efficient cognitive development. Most children nine years and older are capable of conceptual learning. For physical education, movement concepts and physiological concepts can be learned. Specific concepts such as balance, propulsion, fitness, and efficiency of movement are among those which can be learned at the upper elementary level. As mentioned, one example of a concept is balance. The children can be taught about widening the base of support or lowering the center of gravity to improve balance. Thus the child can apply the concept to a variety of activities requiring balance.

2. **Learning is facilitated when the child is motivated.**

    Implication • Set up a positive learning environment (Chapter 4) in which each child gains success. Extrinsic motivators, such as stars or ribbons, can be used initially, but should give way to intrinsic (internal) motivation generated by success. Intrinsic motivation, according to learning theorists, is much stronger than extrinsic and has longer-lasting effects.

3. **Children who help make decisions about their learning will be more motivated to learn.**

    Implication • All grade levels from kindergarten up can participate in the decision-making process through use of anonymous questionnaires (see Appendix). By taking time to design and administer these questionnaires, feedback can be gained on the children's attitudes toward activities and the teacher. This information can be valuable in making program or behavioral changes.

    Within each class of upper elementary children and, to a certain extent, lower elementary, the rules and regulations as well as some curriculum content can be cooperatively determined by the teacher and children. When children participate in the program design, they are much more willing to follow, as well as enforce, the rules and regulations. By giving children some choice of activities, the teacher can negotiate participation in other less favored activities which are also important to growth and development. It is particularly helpful to find out the children's favorite activity and use this as a positive reinforcer to insure good behavior.

4. **Children who are not afraid of making mistakes learn more rapidly.**

    Implication • Eliminate comparative grading in which children are punished by low grades. Using contracts and learning packages which give the child unlimited opportunity to learn while moving at his or her own pace. Encourage student efforts through praise and avoid criticism whenever possible. Reward improvement rather than only perfect performance. Let children explore movement in the early years with a minimum emphasis on perfection.

5. **Undue pressure on students may result in negative behavior such as fear, lack of participation, or psychosomatic illness.**

    Implication • See the discussion under principle 4. Also, ask specific questions on the questionnaire mentioned in principle 3 dealing with this principle. It is possible that the children's perception of the teacher is not consistent with the teacher's self-evaluation. This may be particularly true when a male is working with young children. The young child's world is usually dominated by women and a man may create anxiety in children.

6. **Rewarded behaviors are more likely to recur.**

    Implication • Be ready to reward good behavior either verbally or nonverbally. Do not assume that since children are supposed to be good, reward for such behavior is unnecessary. If you want good behavior, thank children for doing the right thing. "Please" and "thank you" can go a long way toward bringing about good behavior. Negative behavior which gets attention reward is also more likely to recur.

7. **To be most effective, rewards must be closely connected to the behavior exhibited.**

    Implication • The teacher should use a style that allows for a lot of personal contact with children. Self-testing activities should also be used to provide immediate feedback to the child.

8. **Threats and punishment have uncertain effects on learning.**

    Implication • Every attempt should be made to create a positive learning environment. Rewards are more effective than threats or punishments in this regard. Children should know the rules and reasons for them. The rewards for following these rules should be emphasized and the consequences for violations minimized.

9. **Children learn best when the task is challenging, but not overwhelming.**

    Implication • Activities should be selected which challenge the children's ability, but can be accomplished with effort by a majority of the children. For a lesson plan, at least 80 percent of the children should be able to successfully accomplish the objectives by the end of the class. By assessing the children's incoming ability, it is possible to select challenging activities which interest the children.

10. **Overstrict discipline may produce anxiety, shyness, and acquiescence in children while more permissiveness is associated with initiative and creativity.**

    Implication • As stated previously, discipline is absolutely essential to successful teaching and learning, but what is overstrict discipline? Most people see discipline as very static control of children with each child afraid to move without a teacher's permission; fear is often the order of the day. In a more dynamic approach to discipline, children feel free to move and be creative while staying within established guidelines which they helped design. There is, however, a clear cut line between dynamic discipline and lack of control. In a dynamic approach, the teacher is able to have the children stop, look, and listen at any time. A teacher who uses dynamic discipline is aware that children learn best by doing, particularly in the psychomotor domain.

11. **Criticism, failure, and discouragement will damage a child's self-confidence, level of aspiration, and sense of worth.**

    Implication • Too often the incompetent teacher is guilty of applying this negative principle. Such teachers should not be hired and those in the system should be removed. For some reason, however, it is nearly impossible to fire even nontenured teachers. Something must be done to protect children from the sadistic incompetence of some teachers. Teachers and administrators have been observed belittling and physically abusing children frequently enough to call the practice a major problem. There is no easy answer to this problem, but it must be addressed more forcefully by educators.

12. **People learn in different ways.**

    Implication • No one teaching style is going to satisfy every learning style, so teachers must be well versed in both teaching and learning styles. Children should also be evaluated to determine how they learn best. Perhaps one child likes to be off by himself with a book while another likes to interact with others. Still others may look to the teacher as the primary source of instruction. Teachers should design their classrooms to account for these individual differences. A good open education classroom will include individual learning centers as well as areas for group activities.

13. **An intermittent reinforcement schedule will produce behaviors which are different to extinguish.**

    Implication • This principle has both positive and negative implications. On the positive side, rewards for positive behavior should be spaced to bring about the most lasting effects. Negative behavior which gets attention, particularly on an intermittent schedule, will also be hard to eliminate. Teachers should avoid giving undue attention to negative behavior unless there is a chance the behavior will result in injury. Most children who misbehave do so for attention, when given, will cause the behavior to recur.

14. **Learning cannot be observed, but can be inferred when there is relatively permanent change in observable behavior.**

    Implication • In specifying the outcomes of the teaching/learning process, objectives should be expressed in behavioral terms.

REFERENCES

1. AAHPERD, Basic Stuff Series I. *Motor Learning.* Vol. 3. Reston, Virginia: 1981.
2. "Alcohol and the Fetus." *Time.* June 13, 1977, p. 56.
3. Arnheim, D.D. and W.A. Sinclair. *The Clumsy Child.* St. Louis: The C.V. Mosby Co., 1975.
4. Biehler, R. *Psychology Applied to Teaching.* Boston: Houghton-Mifflin Co., 1971.
5. Combs. A. *The Professional Education of Teachers.* Boston: Allyn & Bacon, 1965.
6. Corbin, C. *A Textbook of Motor Development.* Dubuque: Wm. C. Brown Co., 1973.
7. Drowatzky. *Motor Learning: Principles and Practices.* Minneapolis, Minnesota: Burgess Publishing Co., 1975.
8. Madden, P. "A School Psychologist's View of Learning." Unpublished Handout, Virginia Commonwealth University, 1973.
9. Magill R. *Motor Learning: Concepts and Applications.* Dubuque, Iowa: Wm. C. Brown, 1980.
10. Marteniuk, R. *Information Processing in Motor Skills.* New York: Holt, Rinehart, and Winston, 1976.
11. Piaget, J. *The Psychology of the Child.* New York: Basic Books, 1969.
12. Singer, R. *Motor Learning and Human Performance,* (3rd ed.), New York: Macmillan Publishing Company, Inc., 1980.
13. Watson, G. "Principles of Learning." *NEA Journal,* March, 1963.
14. Werner, I. and D. Elkind. *Child Development: A Core Approach.* New York: John Wiley and Sons, Inc., 1972.

CHAPTER 3
MOTOR LEARNING

After completing this chapter, the student will be able to:

1. List and describe each of the four stages of the motor learning process.
2. Describe the advantages and disadvantages of teacher versus student performed demonstrations.
3. Describe a technique for locating student demonstrators.
4. Describe three types of visual aids which can facilitate the presentation of motor skills to children.
5. Describe the instructional implications for at least 80 percent of the motor learning principles.

One of the primary goals within the elementary physical education curriculum is to teach new motor skills to children as well as to refine and expand upon existing motor abilities. The first step toward accomplishing these goals requires the teacher to be sympathetic toward the children's feelings of clumsiness which may accompany the initial learning of a new motor task. To refresh one's memory of this sometimes awkward feeling, try several of the following tasks: serve a tennis ball with the nondominant hand, shoot a basketball with the nondominant hand, juggle three tennis balls, now four tennis balls. Most individuals will experience a feeling of awkwardness as well as frustration and anxiety because of their inability to perform as precisely as desired. Now keep in mind that each time a new task is presented to young children, they too may experience some of these same feelings. Obviously, if these frustrations and anxieties are allowed to continue and build during the practicing of new movement tasks, it is highly probable that many youngsters will give up or lose interest. To be a successful teacher, it is imperative at the onset to have an understanding and working knowledge of principles which govern the teaching and learning of motor tasks and the factors which inhibit skilled performance.

It is also important to realize that the stages which comprise the motor learning model to be discussed hold true, regardless of the teaching method utilized — command, problem-solving, guided discovery, etc. This is because as soon as a motoric task is introduced, whether it be to learn a specific skill (dribble a basketball) or just to freely explore the many ways to manipulate a ball, both psychological and physiological factors begin to influence one's performance. The purpose of this chapter is to identify and discuss these intervening factors. Only when these factors are controlled or trained, will the physical skills of students blossom.

The Motor Learning Process

The act of learning a new motor skill can indeed be a difficult task for the novice performer. The chain of events leading to skilled motor performance is a complicated one which contains many variables. If one thinks of the learner as a processor of information, the motor learning process can be viewed as consisting of four stages: input, central processing, output, and feedback.

Input

The process of receiving environmental stimulus through one or more of the senses is termed input. For example, someone throws a ball; the visual sense of seeing the ball coming initiates the information processing.

Central Processing

The decision-making process involves the central nervous system (brain and spinal cord). Using the example above, once the learner realizes that the ball has been thrown in his or her direction, the learner, on the basis of inputted information, prior experience, and knowledge of the task, must make various decisions about

26 *Motor Learning*

```
┌─────────────────┐      ┌──────────────────────┐      ┌─────────────────┐
│     INPUT       │─────▶│  CENTRAL PROCESSING  │─────▶│    OUTPUT       │
│ SENSORY RECEPTORS│      │ (BRAIN-DECISION MAKING)│      │ OVERT PERFORMANCE│
└─────────────────┘      └──────────────────────┘      └─────────────────┘
         ▲                          ▲
         │                          │
         └──────────────────────────┴──────────────────────────┘
                                 FEEDBACK
```

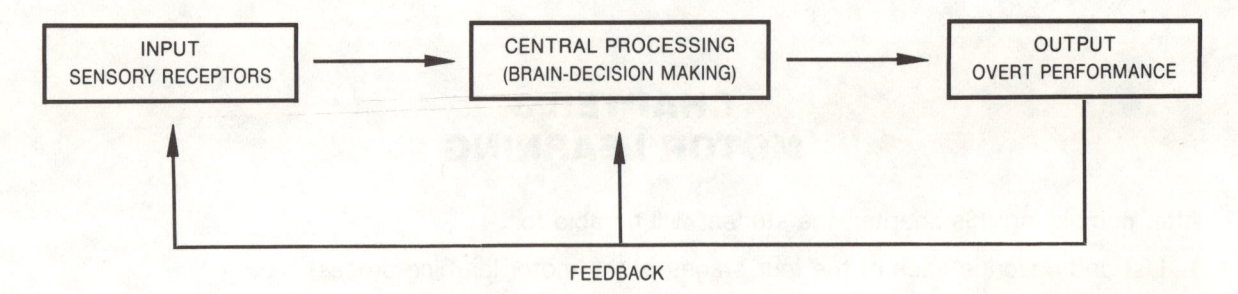

Figure 3.1 The Motor Learning Process

the ball's path in order to catch it. These decisions would include: (1) how fast the ball is traveling and (2) where the ball will land.

Output

Once a decision has been derived concerning the body adjustments needed to successfully intercept the ball, the brain must direct nerve impulses to the appropriate muscles which then make the plotted adjustments.

Feedback

Once the task is completed, the learner will receive immediate feedback as to the correctness of his or her actions. Figure 3.1 illustrates the motor learning process.

Thus the simple act of catching a ball requires seeing the ball (input-sense organs), making a decision as to where the ball will land, adjusting the body position to catch the ball (central processing-brain), and finally the muscles must be positioned according to plan (output-muscles). A breakdown in any part of the process can result in undesirable performance.

Correcting Motor Performance

Obviously, the first time a new motor task is presented to the students, it is not realistic to expect everyone to perform correctly. It then becomes the teacher's duty to analyze why a particular student was not successful and modify instructions and provide additional information to facilitate learning.

Unfortunately, many instructors attempting to correct faulty performance concentrate on requiring the students to make adjustments in their movement patterns (output), when the inability to accomplish the task may be caused by a breakdown in another part of the system (input and/or central processing). When a batter in baseball, for example, consistently swings too late at the pitched ball, he or she is generally instructed to choke-up on the bat to accomplish the swing quicker. Such an analysis generally tends to treat the symptom rather than the true cause. It is highly probable that the batter who swings late may not be receiving the appropriate visual information needed to make correct decisions. When analyzing performance, all stages of the motor learning process must be considered.

Factors Affecting Input: Communicating with the Learner

To be a good motor skills teacher, it is important to communicate effectively with students. The section to follow explains (1) the role of the perceptual senses in conveying information, and (2) how to use demonstrations and visual aids as media sources to improve communication skills.

Sensory Systems

The motor learning process is initiated by providing input through one or more of the following sense receptors:

1. Visual Perception — seeing
2. Auditory Perception — hearing
3. Tactile Perception — touch
4. Kinesthetic Perception — feeling
5. Olfactory — smell
6. Gustatory — taste

The perceptual senses of smell and taste are obviously less important in motor skill learning. The remaining perceptual senses, however, are all used extensively in the learning of motor tasks. The following are simple examples of how one may rely upon the senses in physical performance situations.

Visual attention — keeping your eye on the ball

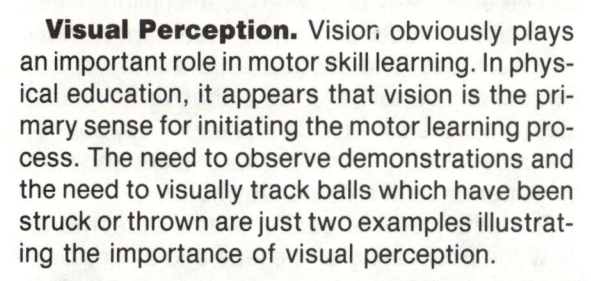

Utilizing tactile perception to dribble the basketball

Visual Perception. Vision obviously plays an important role in motor skill learning. In physical education, it appears that vision is the primary sense for initiating the motor learning process. The need to observe demonstrations and the need to visually track balls which have been struck or thrown are just two examples illustrating the importance of visual perception.

Auditory Perception. The sound of a ball hitting a bat or racquet can provide auditory clues to indicate how hard a ball has been struck and thus how fast the ball is traveling.

Kinesthetic Perception. An internal "muscle sense" which allows one to determine the body's position in space without utilizing visual cues is referred to as kinesthetic perception. The novice tennis player, for example, must learn to make a preparatory backswing at or below waist level. Since the performer must be looking at the oncoming ball, he or she is unable to look back at his or her arm to affirm its position. Instead, feedback from the muscle must be relied upon to determine its location.

Tactile Perception. The sense of touch is used extensively in many sport activities. When dribbling a basketball, for example, the performer must confirm the ball's position in space by utilizing tactile perception — not visual perception. The performer who constantly looks at the ball is not able to spot teammates who may be free to take a shot at the basket.

Demonstrations

Educators have traditionally attempted to teach using the auditory and visual senses. Due to individual differences in students' intellectual abilities (vocabulary), however, the teacher is often faced with the task of "speaking down" to young children. Such futile attempts often lead to confusion about the tasks to be performed. To avoid this dilemma, it is suggested that demonstrations accompany verbal explanations. The demonstration presents to the learner an entire picture of the skill to be learned, thus lending the student a sense of direction. The old saying, "a picture is worth a thousand words," appears to be especially true when teaching motor skills to young children.

Since the primary purpose of utilizing a demonstration is to present to the learner a visual illustration of the task, care must be taken in selecting demonstrators. While many teachers feel an obligation to perform all demonstrations, ideally, the individual who is the most proficient at performing the selected task should be selected to perform. One primary advantage of the teacher demonstration appears to be the earning of students' respect. There are inherent disadvantages, however, to teacher performed demonstrations. Students who experience difficulty in performing the selected tasks generally give up too early and, when reminded of the teacher demonstration, they will frequently alibi,

"Sure you can do it because you are the teacher." Such problems can be avoided by utilizing student demonstrations. The added peer influence from student demonstrations encourages more desire and determination in practice sessions.

To find a suitable student demonstrator, the teacher can simply ask the students, for example, to find the best method to dribble a basketball. While the children are participating in this self-discovery process, the teacher should be on the lookout for students who utilize acceptable techniques. After a short period of time, the teacher can point out those who are utilizing the best methods so that other classmates may watch their performance.

A word of caution: while demonstrations may be an influential factor in skill development, their use does not guarantee improved rates of learning. For demonstrations to be effective, the following conditions must be present.

1. **Condition: The learner must be attentive to the demonstration.**
   Implication: Before allowing the demonstrator to perform, care must be taken to ensure student attention. The teacher should eliminate external distractors such as looking into the sun and the loud noises which accompany passing trucks or low-flying airplanes. If distractions occur during the demonstration, the teacher should wait until the disturbances have passed.

2. **Condition: The learner must know in advance the key elements to look for during the demonstration.**
   Implication: Since most skills contain more than one key element, the ability to model behavior can be facilitated through multiple demonstrations. During each performance, the teacher can direct the students' attention to different aspects of the task (one cue at a time). In demonstrating the forward roll, for example, the students' attention should first be directed toward the initial hand position. During the second demonstration, the student should focus on the chin. Following three to five demonstration trials, students will have been exposed to the key components. Thus multiple demonstrations tend to be more effective than the single demonstration.

Visual Aids

A close examination of many curriculum guides from local schools leads one to suspect that instructors tend, for the most part, to teach only skills in which they have expertise and can physically perform; this is truly unfortunate. Teachers should realize that they are not superhuman, and that it would be nearly impossible for one to have expertise in all physical skills. The fact that an instructor does not possess the ability to demonstrate a specific skill and does not have a student who can do the demonstrating does not justify deleting that skill from the curriculum. The dedicated teacher has at his or her disposal other alternatives. Recall that the purpose of a demonstration is to present to the learner a visual representation of expert performance in hopes that the learner will in turn model the behavior. With this in mind, it should be clear that any type of visual media may be utilized to present this visual representation of the task. Common sources of visual media which can be effectively utilized to teach children motor skills include filmloops, videotapes, flow charts, slides and pictures. Furthermore, researchers support the view that using visual aids (other than live models) is especially beneficial in developing complex motor skills and may be superior to live demonstration.

For instance, the teacher wants students to view the positioning of the legs and ankles during the execution of cartwheel-round off. Nature, however, requires that this task be performed at a high rate of speed — a speed so fast that the novice performer is not likely to see clearly the body regions specified by the instructor. In this case, it would be more appropriate to utilize a filmloop or motion picture showing someone performing this task. These sources of media can then be shown in slow-motion and stop action replay. The utilization of these special projection features will allow the learner to stop and follow the desired regions of observation through the entire range of the activity. For schools with budgets that do not support an extensive film library, a viable alternative is to either make or purchase a series of inexpensive flow charts. Flow charts are actually frame-by-frame pictures or illustrations of someone performing a specific task. Illustration 3.2 is an example of a flow chart depicting the cartwheel-round off.

Figure 3-2. Flow Chart Depicting Cartwheel Roundoff

Factors Affecting Central Processing: Decision-Making

The primary task of the performer during the central processing (decision) phase of the motor learning process is to devise an appropriate plan of action that will suit the task at hand. Following is a brief discussion of several factors which may influence this decision-making process.

Memory

Perhaps the most important component of the central processing mechanism is memory. To perform a specific task efficiently, the performer must process incoming information and then rapidly retrieve information from memory to solve the problem.

Past Experience

One reason novice performers tend to experience difficulties in plotting strategies for solving problems is their inexperience with the task. The skilled performer, however, needs only to select the appropriate strategy from memory. Students can effectively acquire appropriate strategies by experiencing a wide variety of movement tasks under varying environmental conditions. Through trial and error, the learner will soon realize which strategies work. This explains, in part, why correct practice generally improves performance.

Factors Affecting Output: Overt Performance

A multiple of physical, emotional, and social factors can have an influence in accounting for individual differences in children's motor performance. Following is a presentation of some of these selected factors.

Physical

General Development. The sequence of a child's movement patterns is a good indicator of developmental age and provides information on the normalcy of the child. Since development is from the head toward the feet, the child will gain control of the head and upper body before the lower portion can be controlled. With development from the center of the body outward, gross motor movements using the large muscles of the arms and legs will develop before fine motor coordination requiring such things as finger dexterity. One can witness this pattern while watching a young child attempt to catch a ball. In the early stages of developing this skill, the child will tend to hug or trap the ball against the body (using large muscles of the shoulder). Not until several years later can the child catch the ball by utilizing the small fine muscles of the hands. Thus maturation is a factor influencing performance.

Body Build. There are basically three body types: ectomorph (thin), mesomorph (muscular-athletic), and endomorph (fat). Body types are not usually well defined at the elementary level but become more obvious after puberty. To a great extent, body build is influenced by heredity. Since children will differ greatly in ability according to their body type, individualized instruction is a must.

Weight, Height, and Limb Length. Height and weight charts have been the traditional criteria for determining obesity. Unfortunately, such charts are nearly useless in all but extreme cases. The important factor in determining obesity is a person's percentage of body fat. The determination of body fat is easy and inexpensive (see Chapter 6). The myth that body fat will go away is just that, a myth. Fat cells developed in early childhood, it is believed, will remain forever, and are a leading cause of obesity in later life. Even those who were fat babies and are now thin, find it more difficult to keep their weight down due, it is thought, to the large number of fat cells which they possess.

Height and weight also affect performance in such things as balance, running, and fitness. Closely linked to height and weight is the center of gravity, which is influenced by the relationship between height and weight. The center of gravity is in the chest area in young children and in the pelvic area at maturity. Young children, therefore, experience difficulty in balance activities, including locomotor tasks.

In addition, closely associated with height and the center of gravity are the differing lengths of body segments. Children with long limbs have an inherited advantage in performing many motor skills. For example, young children with long legs have a potential for a greater stride length, usually an advantage in running. Children with long arms have an inherited lever advantage which gives them the potential to throw harder and farther than children with shorter arms.

Physical Fitness Factors. Strength, muscular endurance, cardiovascular endurance, and flexibility are all components of physical fitness which can obviously account for individual differences in motor performance. Generally, children who possess advanced degrees of these fitness components will excel over less fit children in most sport activities. For a complete discussion of these fitness components, refer to Chapter 6.

Sex. There are very few physiological differences between boys and girls at the elementary age. Interests, however, vary based on background experience and parental attitude toward activities. There should be no separation of children based only on sex. Children should be separated according to interests and/or ability.

Age. Age and performance are directly related, with older children being superior to younger children. Motor learning is progressive and should build on previous skills. Children who miss a certain stage of learning may have difficulty catching up at a later time.

Social/Emotional

Personality. Most studies on sports participation and personality have been done using college students as subjects. Whether the findings are applicable to elementary children is unknown. Researchers have found that those with aggressive personalities are more likely to participate in contact sports. The researchers believe that the student selected the sport based on his personality rather than the sport creating the personality. It is possible, however, that the personality development of the young child is influenced by participation in certain sports.

Self-Concept. The way a child feels about himself or herself will influence performance. Those who have had poor experiences in physical endeavors tend to shy away from activity; the physically handicapped often experience problems in this area. Achievement will do much to improve self-concept, so every opportunity should be taken to select activities and present them in a manner that will ensure more success than failure. The physical educator can do more good or harm to a child's self-concept than perhaps any other teacher.

Motivation. Performance is dependent somewhat on motivation. The strongest motivation is usually the intrinsic reward the student feels from a satisfactory performance. Entrinsic rewards such as stars, trophies, ribbons, etc., can also motivate, particularly in this society which has an extrinsic reward system in almost everything. Threats and punishment will do little to motivate performance or learning.

Anxiety. Stress and anxiety are closely linked to motivation and are important to performance. A certain amount of stress in the form of motivation is required for optimum performance. When the stress is excessive, however, performance drops off sharply. Figure 3.3 shows this relationship between performance and stress.

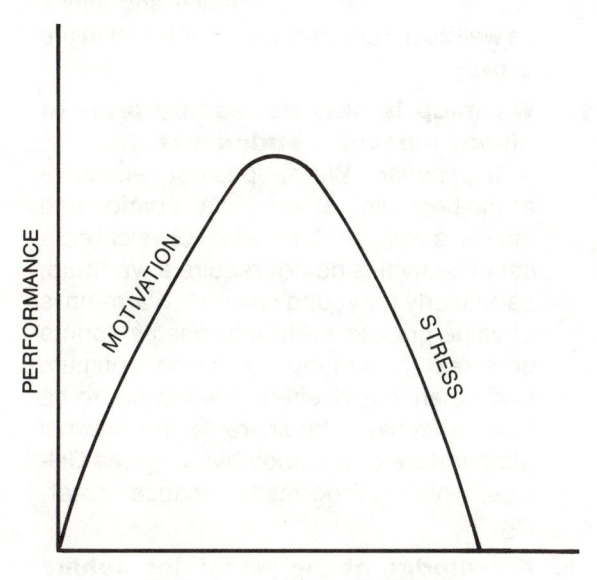

Long relay lines provide children with little activity.

Figure 3-3. Stress & Performance

PRINCIPLES OF MOTOR LEARNING

1. **Motor learning begins with movement exploration and experimentation.**

   Implication • The teaching styles used in preschool, kindergarten, and much of first grade should be free exploration and guided exploration (Chapter 4). A positive learning environment in which children are free to explore through movement and equipment should be established. The teacher's role is to plan the environment, motivate, and guide the children through a variety of experiences. The primary goal should be the development of the movement qualities and establishing a broad base of physical abilities upon which to build more specific movements and skills.

2. **Demonstrations should be minimized during exploration, but are important in formalized skill learning.**

   Implication • A command style of explanation/demonstration has limited value in the early childhood curriculum except where individualized instruction is necessary for a child with motor development problems. Normal children will progress satisfactorily if the right environment and guidance are provided.

3. **There are critical learning periods during which the chances of success will be optimum.**

   Implication • Motor development progresses in a sequential pattern common to most individuals. Practice before the child has matured will have little effect on learning, and there is some evidence to suggest that behaviors not learned at the proper time will be difficult to learn later. This has given rise to the theory of critical learning periods. Researchers lend support to the importance of a carefully planned movement program to insure optimum growth and development.

4. **Motor learning goes from simple to complex.**

   Implication • A sequential program must be planned to develop prerequisite abilities for later success.

5. **Practice does not necessarily make perfect.**

   Implication • Incorrect practice can lead to poor skill development. Such habits make later skill learning more difficult. Incorrect skill performance, therefore, should be corrected during the initial learning phase.

32 Motor Learning

6. **There is a wide variance in skilled performance.**
    Implication • Although a number of principles of physics are common to sports skills, various forms can be used to apply these principles. One need only watch the different golf swings or tennis strokes to see the variety. The emphasis in teaching, therefore, should be on the application of principles rather than a perfection of form.

7. **Success fosters more success.**
    Implication • Provide a curriculum in which children can achieve success.

8. **Visual cues are more important in the early phases of specific skill learning.**
    Implication • Demonstrations can be helpful, but keep explanations to a minimum.

9. **Whole learning is more effective than part.**
    Implication • Children should practice the whole activity wherever possible. It should be broken into parts only when the skill is complex. If teaching the tennis serve, for example, it is better to teach the whole racket motion rather than beginning the stroke from behind the head.

10. **A skill has three parts: preparation, execution, and follow-through.**
    Implication • If skilled movement is desired, all three phases of the skill must be taught.

11. **Only one cue at a time should be given.**
    Implication • When teaching, have the child focus on only one aspect of the skill at a time. The cue might be keeping the eyes on the ball or keeping the feet together. Excess cues will cause the learner to freeze (paralysis by analysis).

12. **Motor learning is extremely specific with transfer occurring only where the skills are nearly identical.**
    Implication • There is no such thing as a natural athlete. Some persons are able to learn different sports more quickly, but they must practice. A good wrestler, for example, may not be able to swim and a good swimmer may be a disaster on the basketball court. Even activities which look similar, such as badminton and tennis, are high specific. In fact, playing one may adversely affect performance in the other. Some general abilities are common to most sports, such as eye-hand coordination, strength, and endurance. Even these factors, however, are skill specific; e.g., strength in wrestling will not aid strength requirements in basketball.

13. **Practice of skills should be spaced rather than massed.**
    Implication • Practice sessions should be interspersed with rest periods to reduce the adverse effects of fatigue on skill performance. Long practice sessions may lead to incorrect performance and injury, as well as boredom or loss of interest in the activity.

14. **Warm-up is only necessary prior to all-out muscular endeavors.**
    Implication • Warm-up is not necessary at the beginning of every class period and may be a waste of time. Most physical education activities do not require a warm-up, particularly for young children. Warm-up is of value prior to such activities as sprints or a testing situation in which optimum performance is desired. A warm-up, to be most effective, should raise the internal temperature of the body two degrees Celsius, which will normally produce sweating.

15. **Knowledge of the principles behind skills helps children to transfer information to similar skills.**
    Implication • Skill instruction should be accompanied by an explanation of the principles involved when dealing with upper elementary children capable of understanding such information.

REFERENCES

1. Drowatzky, J. *Motor Learning: Principles and Practices*. Minneapolis: Burgess Publishing, 1975.
2. Magill, R. *Motor Learning: Concepts and Applications*. Dubuque: Wm. C. Brown Company, 1980.
3. Marteniuk, R. *Information Processing in Motor Skills*. New York: Holt, Rinehart and Winston, 1976.
4. Singer, R. *Motor Learning and Human Performance* (3rd Edition), London: The MacMillan Company, 1980.

STUDENT ACTIVITIES

1A A juggling experiment.
    Purpose: The purpose of this activity is to demonstrate the effects of practice on learning a new motor task.
    Task: Hold two tennis balls in your dominant hand. Attempt to juggle the two balls, keeping one ball in the air at all times. Place your nondominant hand behind your back. You are to practice this juggling routine five minutes per day for five days.
    Scoring: Count the number of balls which you are able to catch without missing; record that number as the number of successful catches for trial number 1. Then perform trial number 2, etc. After five trials your scores may be as follows: 0-2-1-3-4. Record your scores on the table provided.

TABLE 3.1

NAME: _____ DATE: _____ Day 1

Trial	Score	Trial	Score	Trial	Score
1		11		21	
2		12		22	
3		13		23	
4		14		24	
5		15		25	
6		16		26	
7		17		27	
8		18		28	
9		19		29	
10		20		30	

Compute the following:
Total number of trials for each of the five days.
Average number of trials per day for each of the five days.
Total number of successful catches for each of the five days.
Average number of catches per day for each of the five days.

TABLE 3.1

NAME: _____ DATE: _____Day 2_____

Trial	Score	Trial	Score	Trial	Score
1		11		21	
2		12		22	
3		13		23	
4		14		24	
5		15		25	
6		16		26	
7		17		27	
8		18		28	
9		19		29	
10		20		30	

TABLE 3.1

NAME: _____ DATE: _____ Day 3

Trial	Score	Trial	Score	Trial	Score
1		11		21	
2		12		22	
3		13		23	
4		14		24	
5		15		25	
6		16		26	
7		17		27	
8		18		28	
9		19		29	
10		20		30	

TABLE 3.1

NAME: _____ DATE: _____ Day 4

Trial	Score	Trial	Score	Trial	Score
1		11		21	
2		12		22	
3		13		23	
4		14		24	
5		15		25	
6		16		26	
7		17		27	
8		18		28	
9		19		29	
10		20		30	

TABLE 3.1

NAME: _____ DATE: _____ Day 5

Trial	Score	Trial	Score	Trial	Score
1		11		21	
2		12		22	
3		13		23	
4		14		24	
5		15		25	
6		16		26	
7		17		27	
8		18		28	
9		19		29	
10		20		30	

Discussion.
1B. What effects did practice have on your learning this motor task?

2. While observing an elementary physical education class, locate a representative member from each of the three body types (endomorph, ectomorph, mesomorph). Watch each member while they perform identical tasks. Discuss differences in their overt motor performance as a possible function of body build.

3. Observe a young male and young female of approximately the same size and weight while they perform various movement tasks. Contrast the differences in their performance. What possible factors might account for these differences?

CHAPTER 4
THE LEARNING ENVIRONMENT

After completing this chapter, the student should be able to:
1. Discuss the importance of objective evaluation of the teaching/learning environment, and list four teacher behaviors and four student behaviors which can be evaluated objectively while observing a physical education class.
2. Explain the similarities and differences among the teaching styles discussed and give a physical education example for each of the various styles.
3. List the four levels of questions a teacher can ask and discuss the importance of each level.
4. List at least seven important nonverbal factors which affect learning.
5. List four nonverbal gestures used to praise a child and four which can be helpful in controlling children.
6. Describe how the nonverbal learning environment can be modified or changed to improve success and thus enhance a child's self-concept.
7. Discuss ways in which a teacher can control the learning environment.
8. Discuss both rules for the children and rules for the teacher, being sure to mention how rules are determined and presented to the children.
9. Discuss procedures to follow when disciplining a class including which principles of learning apply.
10. Outline the steps to follow when disciplining an individual in a class being sure to mention the principles of learning which apply.
11. Complete the student activities at the end of the chapter.

The learning environment is a key to successful teaching and learning. The first learning environment is said to be inside the mother when the unborn child begins to respond to stimuli. A child's first learning outside of the mother is of and through movement which is influenced by the environment. Children reared in an "enriched" environment, which includes affection, stimuli and movement, seem to develop more rapidly and reach a higher level of development than those reared in a "deprived" setting. What constitutes the best learning environment is not known. It is known, however, that learning is fostered in a positive nonthreatening environment where reward rather than punishment is consistently used.

It is not easy to evaluate objectively the effectiveness of a learning environment. In the past, administrators and supervisors have often evaluated teachers on their ability to control students rather than on how much learning was taking place. Control was usually determined by the noise level in the room, the number of students in their seats, and whether the teacher was dispensing information to the entire class. Too frequently, these criteria are still employed.

A more objective evaluation could be done by focusing on the teacher, the students, the teacher/pupil interaction, and the physical environment. If meaningful changes are to be made in the learning environment, this kind of objective evaluation must be done. This chapter will focus on those factors which are important to learning.

TEACHER BEHAVIOR

By far the most important part of any learning environment is the teacher. The teacher must first love children, but love alone is not sufficient to bring about learning. Other factors such as dedication, respect for students, and enthusiasm are just a few ingredients necessary for successful teaching and learning. Unfortunately, none of these factors can be objectively evaluated. How can love be measured? Enthusiasm? Or respect? Worthy as they may be, truly objective evaluation is not possible without further delineation of the words. Granted, if a teacher is constantly beating children to the point of injury or calling children unkind names, his or her love for children could be questioned.

42 Learning Environment

Such extremes, however, are fortunately the exception rather than the rule.

One way to objectively evaluate the teaching/learning environment is to express important learning factors such as love and enthusiasm in observable behavior. Then there should be agreement by a number of individuals that any behavior listed is an indicator of the factor in question. Coming up with such a list would be difficult but not impossible.

Some things which can be objectively evaluated follow. These teaching behaviors would seem to be important to learning and should be a part of any learning environment evaluation.

Amount of Talk

One of the easiest aspects of teacher behavior to evaluate objectively is the amount of time spent talking. Since children remember ten percent of what they hear, twenty percent of what they see, and eighty percent of what they do, talking should be kept to a minimum and participation, particularly in the psychomotor domain, should be maximized. If a large percentage of class time is dominated by teacher verbalization to the entire class, it is safe to say that little learning is taking place. On the other hand, a low percentage does not necessarily indicate a positive environment. Many people may have experienced a physical education program in which the ball was rolled out by the teacher who then disappeared into an office until the class was over. In physical education, the emphasis should be on giving individual instruction. Thus, when evaluating the amount of teacher talk, there should be a differentiation between individual instruction and talking to the entire class.

Styles of Teaching

Figure 4-1 is a continuum of teaching styles. The continuum is from teacher-centered at the command end to child-centered at the free exploration end. Teachers should know how to use all styles of teaching.

Command Style. This style is totally teacher-centered with no student involvement in any phase except practice. The teacher determines the goals and objectives to be taught, the class organization, and the pace of the class. The command style is typical of physical education instruction at most levels, including elementary. Teachers who use command for large group instruction do not take into account variance in

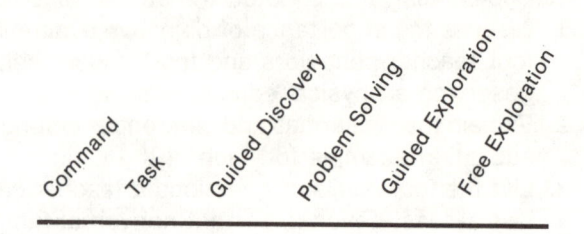

Command   Task   Guided Discovery   Problem Solving   Guided Exploration   Free Exploration

Figure 4-1. Continuum of Teaching Styles

rate and style of student learning. In this regard, a teacher is less humanizing and, therefore, less effective.

The command style can be used with some individuals who respond well to this approach, particularly mentally retarded children. It can also be effective for small groups or in one-on-one situations. For the teacher, it is both easier and less time-consuming than other methods.

The command style can be effective, but should not be the initial teaching style when working with a large group of normal children. After some method has been used to determine the ability level of the various individuals, a command style can be used to assist certain students. The poorly-skilled student tends to respond well to the specific explanation/demonstration/manipulation type approach which characterizes the command style. This style is particularly good when teaching a specific skill to an individual or very small group of individuals who have nearly identical abilities and learning styles.

Task Style. The task style is also teacher-dominated. Most of the decisions about learning are made by the teacher and the students are responsible for carrying out the teacher's directives. Children work in pairs or small groups, aiding each other in the learning process. This method is helpful in getting peer interaction, and the children do have some cognitive involvement in the process. An example of this learning style would be the station approach in which tasks are specified at each station. The group works together to help each member accomplish the task and determines when to move to the next station. This teaching style is effective when specific skill development or social interaction are desired.

Learning Environment 43

Guided Discovery Style. In this style, a specific objective is established by the teacher, and children are guided toward accomplishment of this objective. This style requires careful planning, including determining the developmental sequence of a skill from simple to complex. Questions must be developed in advance to get children involved in accomplishing the objective, and teachers must think carefully about how to keep the children on track. Since the possibility of wrong answer exists, the teacher must be careful not to discourage or embarrass children who respond incorrectly. A simple "no" can be harsh, and may cause the child to withdraw from the process.

Guided discovery is characterized by questions asked by the teacher which guide the children toward the goal. It is traditionally used with an entire class, but can be used with one student or a small group. The questions are more open ended (multitude of possible correct responses) at first, but gradually become more specific (only one or two correct responses) as children near the objective.

Example:
1. How many ways can you dribble a ball?
2. Can you dribble it just using one body part?
3. Can you dribble it like Johnny? (Johnny is using only one hand.)
4. What is Johnny doing with his hand to make the ball bounce better?
5. Is Johnny letting the ball touch the palm of his hand?
6. Who else can dribble the ball without looking at the ball?

The guided discovery style is probably the best method for teaching specific athletic skills where there is little danger of injury. Caution must be exercised, however, when solutions may involve physical attempts which might lead to injury. This is particularly true in gymnastics. A question such as, "How many different ways can you roll on the mat?" could lead to an injury. The *educational gymnastics* approach where children are asked to explore equipment through a questioning technique can also be dangerous and is discussed more thoroughly under legal liability, Chapter 13. Children should be thoroughly briefed on rules and spotting prior to participation in any form of gymnastics. For most skills, questions can be posed and children can respond by trying different methods. The correct behavior can then be reinforced. This method takes more time than either the task or command style, but is more educationally sound because of the child's cognitive involvement.

Problem-Solving Style. Although questions are used in both the guided discovery style and the problem-solving style, they are quite different. Many people feel they are using problem-solving anytime they ask questions, but in problem-solving, the questions must be open ended (have more than one answer). Through problem-solving, children are encouraged to explore movement by solving problems which have a multiple of correct responses. Questions are presented in such a way that each child, regardless of ability, will be able to find a solution. In any problem-solving situation, however, there is always a possibility of an incorrect response, but since the accomplishment of a specific skill is not desired, an incorrect response is unimportant as long as the child tries. Perhaps unimportant is too strong a term since a teacher who observes any child having difficulty should work with that child on an individual basis. By using problem-solving, the teacher is free to interact with some children while others work on a solution. This is in sharp contrast to the command style in which all attention is focused on the teacher and little individualized attention is possible.

Problem-solving can be used at all levels but has more applications in the early learning stages, particularly when working at the primary grade level. Young children should be given the opportunity to experience all types of movement while using different body parts. By using the problem-solving style, a teacher is better able to provide these experiences.

Typical problem solving questions are:
1. How many ways you can move across the floor?
2. How many different body parts can you use to hit the ball?
3. Can you move different body parts to the music?
4. Can you play with two pieces of equipment at one time?
5. How many things can you and your partner do with the jump rope?

Guided Exploration Style. Since it provides many experiences through exploration, guided exploration, like problem-solving, is more useful during the early stages of learning. Compared to the styles already described, there is less teacher involvement and more child participation. An important consideration in this

Children work to solve a problem.

method is the environment. Careful planning is needed to establish an atmosphere which encourages participation. This atmosphere is dependent upon the teacher's enthusism, the equipment available, lighting, temperature, noise, and the number of students.

As in problem-solving, the teacher attempts to encourage students through questions and praise. The teacher helps the children get started with a question. For example: "What are some things you can do with this equipment?" or "How would you move to these different sounds?" The teacher then makes individual contacts with the students to praise, assist and encourage. The teacher says very little to the group when using this method but interacts extensively with individuals. The teacher's role also includes evaluation. He or she must be constantly observing both the group and individuals within the group. Considerable time is spent "thinking on one's feet."

The major differences between problem-solving and guided exploration is in the time students must focus on the teacher. Very few questions are asked in guided exploration, and thus the focus is on the task and the objects in the environment. Some children respond well to guided exploration while others have difficulty without more teacher direction.

Free Exploration. The environment is a key element in free exploration. Equipment selection and placement, room conditions, and student attitude will determine the success or failure of this method. The method borders on free play and only the children's attitude will determine how much learning will take place.

The use of this method is important since it fosters the development and use of creativity. The less teacher intervention, therefore, the better. Since the development of creative thinking is so important to a child, situations which require its use should be established at all grade levels.

Examples for young children would be exploring movement or exploring different equipment. Older children can create their own games or rhythmic routines. All elementary children can design and conduct their own physical education shows. Teachers should look for opportunities to allow children to use their imagination.

To use free exploration, the teacher must establish an environment which stimulates participation. No pressure is placed on those who do not wish to be involved. With the right situation, however, most (if not all) will participate. Those who elect not to take part can be encouraged, but not forced into activity. The question or task posed by the teacher can be as open as, "What would you like to do in this room?"; "Can you think of something to do with this equipment?" or "What can you create in here?"

Children explore ways their bodies can move.

Safety is important when turning children loose with so little guidance. Some safety ground rules have to be established prior to activity. This style is *not* recommended for tumbling or gymnastics. Although some teachers have successfully used what is being termed "educational gymnastics" for years, recent court cases lost by teachers make this a legally questionable teaching approach.

Question Analysis

As was seen in the discussion on teaching styles, questions can play an important role in the learning environment. By asking questions, a teacher can involve the child in learning process. The use of questions can be evaluated objectively by determining the number and type asked. It is easy to determine the number asked, and the teacher can do a self-evaluation by audio-taping a lesson and then listening to the tape. The type of question asked is also important, since closed questions (only one right answer) may inhibit discussion while open-ended questions (more opinion-oriented) will foster discussion and get children thinking. Four levels of questions suggested by Humphrey et al. are: (1) those requiring simple recall of facts, (2) those which require higher cognitive ability such as classifying or evaluating, (3) questions which bring out students' attitudes and feelings, and (4) those which require creative student thinking. Levels one and two are for closed-end questions while open-ended questions would be categorized under levels three and four. (4)
Examples:
Level 1 — How many points are scored on a touchdown?
Level 2 — What is a good way to shoot the ball?
Level 3 — How do you feel about jogging?
Level 4 — What would be some ways we could promote our physical fitness program?

To develop creative thought a teacher should use questions primarily from levels two through four.

Nonverbal Behavior

The teaching/learning process is dependent upon communication. The effectiveness of this interaction is determined by both verbal and nonverbal teacher behavior. Eye contact, facial expressions, posture, and gestures all influence the message being sent. To be effective, an individual must know what the listener is receiving, both verbally and nonverbally. Even values can be transmitted nonverbally. As Toffler points out in *Future Shock*

> Today it embarrasses many teachers to be reminded that all sorts of values are transmitted to students, if not by their textbooks then by the informal curriculum — seating arrangements, the school bell, age segregation, social class distinction, the authority of the teacher... All such arrangements send unspoken messages to the student, shaping his attitudes and outlook. (6)

A good deal of attention is paid to what a teacher says, but often little to a teacher's nonverbal behavior. The latter, however, is as important if not more so, than the former. The adage, "a picture is worth a thousand words," applies. A look, or a gesture, can say so much, and can be used to praise or control a class as well as to distort a message.

Praising Gestures. A smile, a pat on the back, clapping the hands, a wink, and the thumb and first finger together to make an "O.K." sign are all gestures of praise. Such gestures are very helpful in praising individual students even when the teacher is some distance away. By catching the child's eye and smiling, the teacher is able to make many contacts with students during a class period. This individual contact is much better than verbal praise to the entire group, although both techniques should be em-

46 Learning Environment

The OK sign is a gesture of praise.

ployed. By smiling, a teacher is giving approval for behavior. The smile also makes a frown much more meaningful when undesired behavior occurs.

Control Gestures. Gestures which help to control children include a glance or stare, pointing a finger, facial expressions, closing the gap between the teacher and the student, or shaking the head. When using nonverbal control gestures, the teacher must first make eye contact with the deviant child and then show dissatisfaction with the child's behavior. This nonverbal form of discipline does not call as much attention to the child as a verbal reprimand. This quiet approach does not embarrass the child in front of peers nor does it cause undue attention to the behavior which might cause it to recur. Since negative behavior, if reinforced by attention, may be more likely to happen again, every attempt should be made to control it with the least possible disruption to the class.

Message Distortion. Communication is enhanced when there is agreement between verbal and nonverbal behavior. A teacher who verbally professes love for children must be willing to physically be close to them. So often a teacher is isolated by room arrangement. It is also difficult for the students to accept a talk on fitness and weight control from an overweight, unfit individual. Similar problems are caused when a teacher smokes, does not follow good health habits, uses incorrect English and generally does not practice what he or she preaches.

Increasing Openness. Openness of communication and learning go together. Galloway makes a number of suggestions on how openness and awareness can be fostered:

1. Do not overlook students. Use eye contact and smiles to encourage students as well as praise them.
2. Look for nonverbal cues from students who may be seeking help. A child's expressions, posture, and mannerisms communicate a great deal.
3. Listen attentively when a student is talking.
4. Keep verbal and nonverbal behavior consistent.
5. Resist the temptation to talk; use nonverbal behavior whenever possible.
6. Use meaningful gestures and body movements which support verbal behavior.(3)

The Science of Nonverbal Communication. Some writers have attempted to express nonverbal behavior as a science. In this science, it is suggested that certain nonverbal behaviors are indicative of some personality or character trait. Folding the arms across the chest during communication is supposed to be a closed gesture which indicates rejection of the ideas being discussed. The speaker whose arms are folded across the chest is said to be lying or hiding the truth. Sitting postures, eye contact, distance between individuals, and other gestures communicate, it is theorized, certain underlying, unspoken messages.

A science has as one of its characteristics predictability, i.e., when certain chemicals are mixed a known substance will be produced. A science is also exact. Nonverbal communication, no matter how fascinating, does not meet the criteria for a science. It is just too easy to fake.

This lack of scientific quality is not to say nonverbal communication is unimportant. On the contrary, a teacher, as has already been pointed out, must be sensitive to what is known about communication including the nonverbal aspect. Listed below are some aspects of nonverbal communication germane to American society which should help a teacher.

1. Eye contact should be maintained for about three seconds before any glance away. To maintain less than three seconds indicates a certain lack of interest in what is being said and if a constant stare is maintained, the other person usually be-

gins to feel uncomfortable. So when having a conversation, eye contact is a series of three-second stares interspaced with momentary glances away from the other person.

2. The distance from another person is a factor. Unless the individual is a child or intimate friend, distances closer than three feet will usually cause tension and hinder communication. This problem can be seen in elevators — when people are forced together, communication usually stops. The cone of security surrounding individuals usually develops with age. Sensitivity to this distance factor, therefore, is more important when communicating with adults. Maintaining too much distance from a child, however, can indicate rejection which might be sensed by the child.

3. Sitting posture can also indicate interest or lack of it. Slumping posture supposedly shows a lack of interest or rejection of what is being said, while sitting up and leaning forward has the reverse effect.

4. Placing an object such as a desk or podium between two people can hinder communication. The desk is said to be an island of security, a protective barrier which may indicate an air of superiority in many situations.

5. Gestures also communicate:
   a. Finger around the nose indicates doubt.
   b. Steepling — hands together and first fingers raised to form steeple which is near the chin or mouth — by a speaker indicates confidence (sureness) in what he or she is saying.
   c. Arms open in chest-baring gestures indicates truthfulness or openness.
   d. Turning slightly away from the speaker or crossing the legs so as to turn away from the speaker can communicate rejection and vice versa.

All the above may not constitute a science, but they are important to fostering communication.

Praise and Criticism

As stated earlier, children learn best in a positive, nonthreatening environment. Such an environment is fostered by maximizing praise and minimizing criticism. An observer can record the number of praises — verbal and nonverbal — as well as the number of criticisms or corrections. Corrections are necessary for learning, but are recorded as negative teacher behavior when they are the initial teacher response following student performance. An example would be when a student does a forward roll which is immediately followed by the teacher saying, "Next time keep your chin on your chest." Student performance should be followed by some sort of positive statement such as, "That was very good." The teacher could then ask, "What do you think might happen if you kept your chin on your chest?" This approach of praise and then correction would be recorded as a praise only and nothing would be recorded in the criticism and correction column. A teacher can do a self-evaluation on verbal praise or criticism by tape recording a lesson and analyzing the replay.

Teachers in general and physical educators in particular are quick to find fault with student performance, i.e., a ten-question math worksheet is presented to a teacher for evaluation: "These three are wrong. Do them over." Why not: "These seven are very good; check these three again." The student throws a ball: "Step forward with the opposite foot next time." Why not: "That was a good throw. Can you throw it farther by stepping forward with the opposite foot?"

Both verbal and nonverbal praise are important, but emphasis should be placed on praising nonverbally. Teachers who are conscious of praising often accomplish it by verbal means only. Frequent praise heard by the entire class often loses its effectiveness from overuse. Nonverbal praise, on the other hand, can be more individually directed by eye contact and gestures. The other children are less aware of the praise so when they receive some, it may have more meaning. Verbal praise should be used primarily for class recognition ("This certainly has been a nice class today!") or to give special attention to children who need or deserve it ("Look at the nice job Judy has done!").

The number of praises should be much higher than criticisms. Being conscious of the tendency to criticize or correct will help teachers change their behavior. Teachers should put themselves in the students' shoes and say, "What would I want to hear first?" A little empathy can go a long way.

NONVERBAL ENVIRONMENT

A number of environmental nonverbal factors are important to enhancing communication. They include room color, lighting, temperature,

Bulletin boards communicate and decorate.

decoration, room size, number of people in the room and equipment and facilities. The environment established by a teacher is a factor in getting children to move. Bright colors usually stimulate activity, while dark colors inhibit movement; cool temperatures are usually better than hot; and carefully-designed bulletin boards can add to a positive learning environment. These are just a few examples of nonverbal factors which must be considered when attempting to foster activity and communication.

Bulletin Boards

Of the factors just mentioned, the teacher has considerable control over room decorations of which bulletin boards are a part. The following criteria should be considered when designing a bulletin board:

1. The message must be short and simple.
2. Neatness counts.
3. Use good color contrasts.
4. The message should be positive.
5. Creativity helps.
6. Check English.
7. Mount pictures from magazines on construction paper before attaching to board.
8. Use a 3-D effect when possible.
9. A quick glance should be sufficient to receive and understand the message.
10. Titles should be no more than three to five words.
11. Keep all the letters in one word the same color.
12. Keep all the colors in the title one color except when highlighting a key word.
13. Avoid vertical lettering.
14. Avoid using pictures of professional athletes. (They are usually not good role models.)
15. Design so key elements are the focal points of the board (Figure 4-2).
16. Do not clutter the board with too much information.

To determine focal points, draw a diagonal between opposite corners; then draw a line perpendicular to the diagonal line. The intersection of the two lines is the focal point.

The opaque or overhead projector can be used to project images for tracing. Little artistic ability is required to produce nice figures. Elementary children like cartoon characters on bulletin boards.

A colorful entrance starts each day on a happy note.

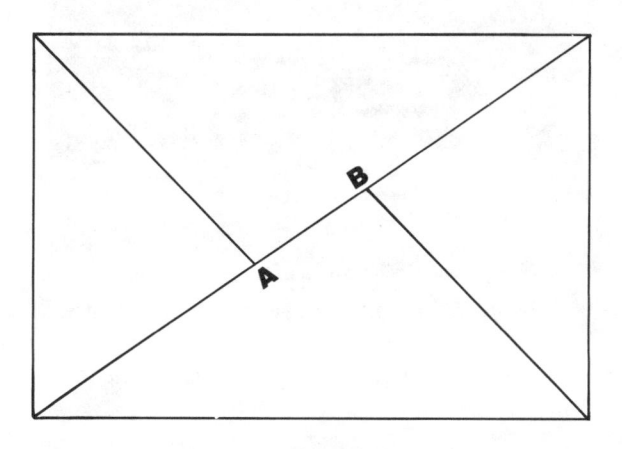

Determining focal points for bulletin boards: Draw diagonal from any corner and perpendicular line; intersection is focal point — A and B.

Figure 4-2

Indoor Instructional Facilities

Gymnasium/Cafetorium. The ideal indoor teaching facility is a gymnasium which is used primarily for physical education instruction. Since the facility is designed with a movement environment in mind, it generally has incorporated in its design special safety features. Such features may include nonskid flooring, protective mats on walls, high ceilings, and protective screens around windows, just to name a few.

A common practice in many school districts is to combine the gymnasium, cafeteria, and auditorium all into one structure usually called a cafetorium. While such a facility generally has many of the advantages offered in a gymnasium, working schedules around lunch hours and special functions tends to be a problem.

Unfortunately, not all elementary schools have gymnasiums or cafetoriums. In fact, many physical educators note that they must work their schedules around special functions and lunch schedules. Thus, even physical educators working in schools with a gymnasium or cafetorium must find alternative teaching stations. The two most frequently utilized alternative teaching stations include the (1) stage and the (2) academic classroom.

Stage. Due to a limited amount of space, conducting physical activities on the school's stage is less than ideal. Active running games are to be avoided. Many physical educators have found that tumbling skills can be effectively taught in this small area. Care, however, must be taken to insure that children do not accidentally fall from the stage. It would be wise to rope off and mark with bright colored cones the edge of the stage.

Academic Classroom. Physical activities conducted in the academic classroom are usually passive in nature. In other words, running games and games involving throwing, kicking, or striking a ball are to be avoided. Some teachers, however, have been successful in conducting some types of ball games when a light sponge ball or yarn ball was utilized. All classroom activities, however, do not necessarily have to be passive. Many of the active, physical fitness activities presented in Chapter 6 can be effectively presented in the classroom.

Outdoor Instructional and Playground Areas

Grass Play Area. Grass is the primary outside teaching area. It should be used for most activities including running, chasing, and tagging. In fact, an outdoor activity which by its nature may result in children falling or running into one another should be conducted on a grass area.

Blacktop. Every school playground should be equipped with a paved or blacktop area which can be used following inclement weather. For instance, after periods of rain the ground

50 Learning Environment

may remain damp and unplayable for several days, while a blacktop may dry in several hours. Since children have a small base of support and high center of gravity, they can be expected to fall quite often. Tag and other running-chasing activities, therefore, should not generally be conducted on hard paved surfaces. Instead blacktop activities should include ball and hoop manipulative skills and jumprope activities. Other appropriate, but passive, blacktop activities include four-squares and hop scotch. The advantage here is that the lines needed to play these activities can be painted on the paved surface.

Sand and/or Sawdust Pits. Some activities require children to propel themselves through space with loss of contact with the ground. Unfortunately, a safe two-foot landing is not always accomplished or, in some cases, desirable. Examples include track activities such as the high jump and running long jump. If children are allowed to perform these activities without some special type of cushioning, injuries are likely to occur. Allowing children to utilize gymnastic matting outdoors is not the answer. Instead, sand and/or sawdust pits can be constructed. Both products can absorb shock, thus reducing the likelihood of injuries.

Apparatus Area. A special area should be set aside for the erection of playground apparatus. Playground apparatus can be divided into two types, developmental and nondevelopmental. Developmental apparatus is that type which tends to foster both organic and skill development, two of the objectives of physical education. Developmental apparatus which contribute to strength development include the following: (1) horizontal ladder, (2) jungle gym, (3) chinning bar, (4) climbing pole, and (5) parallel bars.

Apparatus labeled as nondevelopmental contribute little to the physical objectives of physical education. Nondevelopmental apparatus include: (1) swings, (2) sliding boards, (3) merry-go-rounds, (4) seesaws, and (5) spring animals.

High injury risk and low developmental value

Developmental apparatus contributing to strength development include (left to right) the horizontal ladder, jungle gym, and chinning bar.

Learning Environment   51

STUDENT BEHAVIOR

Another component of the teaching/learning environment which can be evaluated objectively is student behavior. The amount of activity, student interaction, skill performance, misbehavior, and verbal and nonverbal behavior can all be assessed.

Amount of Activity

One of the easiest components to analyze is the amount of time students are active. All the teacher needs is a cumulative stopwatch and a regular watch. A student is then randomly selected and watched for a period of time which is recorded using a regular watch. Each time the child makes some purposeful movement associated with the lesson, the stopwatch is started; whenever the child stops to listen to directions, is misbehaving, or doing nothing educationally productive, the watch is stopped. Following the lesson, the teacher will have two times: (1) the total observational time and (2) the total time spent in meaningful psychomotor development; the percentage of movement time should be high (75-80 percent). This technique, of course, is only effective when the learning is in the psychomotor domain. Many teachers are quite surprised to see how much time they spend talking and how little activity takes place, particularly in circle games, relays, many team games, and games requiring waiting for a turn. Most such activities should usually be avoided when psychomotor development is the objective.

Student Interaction

Extensive social development, either positive or negative, can take place in physical education. Determining the number of encounters is easy — just count. Each time two students interact, record it. Again it is usually best to select a student at random and record her or his interactions. By using a plus (+) and minus (-) system, it is also possible to indicate the positive or negative nature of these encounters. By frequently observing the class over a period of time, the social climate can be accurately determined. This knowledge is important to activity selection — those activities to bring the class together and others to set up situations which will allow for a discussion of interpersonal relationships. Social development is covered by the affective domain, which is an important part of physical education.

Skill Performance

The effectiveness of a physical education program can also be determined by the student's skill level. By pretesting and posttesting the children on skills, improvement should be evident if the program is effective. Behaviorally stated objectives such as those in Chapters 7-10 can be used to determine progress as well as to gather data on teaching effectiveness.

Misbehavior

Children misbehave. The causes are many: need for attention, poor home life, illness, lack of ability, the teacher, the environment, and others. Misbehavior is, therefore, a complex problem which must be handled carefully. Causes of misbehavior should be determined prior to taking actions other than those designed to protect the child or other children from injury. Dealing with behavior problems is one of the more difficult and time-consuming tasks in teaching; each case is different. Nothing is more rewarding, however, than helping a child overcome a problem which is causing his misbehavior.

Nonverbal Behavior

A student can communicate a great deal to a teacher nonverbally. Facial expressions, posture, movement, and closeness all say something. Many children have learned to manipulate both parents and teachers by nonverbal means. Looking interested to get something from a teacher or throwing a tantrum to impress a parent are just two examples of manipulation. Fortunately, most young children are not sophisticated enough to use nonverbal language as skillfully as adults, thus making it possible for the teacher to gain valuable information from student nonverbal behavior.

CONTROL AND DISCIPLINE

Control and discipline are not synonymous, but they are interdependent in an educational setting. In the case of control, the emphasis is on designing a program in which every child participates willing and enthusiastically most of the time. Even in the best of programs, however, there will be discipline problems. If a teacher spends time thinking through those factors necessary for control, the number of problems can be kept at a manageable level. This section will focus on control factors and how to handle problem children humanistically.

52 Learning Environment

Misbehavior has many causes.

Control

Principles of Learning. For best control, the teacher must adhere to the principles of learning mentioned in Chapter 2. Violating any of these rules will lessen the chances for success.

Positive Program. This discussion on control and discipline is based on the premise that the physical education program is positive. In other words, it is geared to the child's developmental level; children experience success; it is individualized; children enjoy the activities; and the teacher uses praise more than criticism. An inadequate program poorly-conducted will be difficult to control and will create many discipline problems which will be nearly impossible to handle humanistically.

Student Input. Students who are given an opportunity to help design and evaluate a program will be more likely to participate willingly in it. Student input can be achieved informally through discussion and formally by administering anonymous questionnaires. Examples of such questionnaires can be found in Chapter 1 and Appendix B. Students should have a part in curriculum development but should not control it; the teacher must be the final authority. A prudent teacher, however, will listen to students.

Rules. Any learning environment requires rules and reasons for those rules. Such rules should be worked out with the student. In the lower grades (K-2), the teacher should take most of the responsibility for determining the rules, but can have the children think through the reasons for each rule. During the first class period of the year, the teacher should sit with the children and discuss the rules. The teacher can ask, "Why can there be no pushing and shoving during class?" or "Why should we stay inside the line?" Most rules should focus on safety, and any rule that cannot be justified should not be established. As children become older, the teacher can use a problem-solving approach by asking, "What are some rules we should have in physical education?" or "What should we do if a rule is violated?"

Student rules are those which should be adhered to by the children. Below are some of the more important ones:

1. Stay inside established boundaries. This is particularly important indoors where such objects as chairs, tables, piano, drinking fountains, and door handles may be present.
2. No sliding on the ground or floor. This is a favorite childhood activity which can lead to personal injury or injury to others who may fall over another sliding child. (A child knows when he or she is going to slide, but others do not.) Clothes also take a real beating when children slide, and ripped clothes will not help a public relations campaign.
3. No pushing or shoving, particularly during gymnastics.
4. Always have a spotter for tumbling.
5. *Stop* when the whistle blows. The whistle should be used sparingly and should have only one meaning — *stop*. Since it can be used to stop behavior before someone is injured, the whistle is a safety device. The teacher can also spread children over a large outdoor area and still maintain control. Indiscriminate usage causes the whistle to lose effectiveness.
6. No talking while the teacher or someone else is talking.
7. Rules for specific sports must be established prior to play. Such things as not standing behind a batter in baseball, no

Learning Environment 53

sliding tackles in soccer, etc., should be established to avoid injuries. Prior to conducting any activity, the teacher must think through all the injury possibilities and modify the activity to minimize danger.

Rules for the teacher are just as important as rules for the children.

1. Keep the number of rules short, but follow through with every one.
2. Have a reason for a rule.
3. Objects should be placed on the ground while the teacher is talking. This will avoid the tendency to play with them and not pay attention.
4. When talking to children, keep the sun at their backs — a teacher's facial expressions and other body movements can communicate a great deal, but children blinded by the sun are unable to see them.
5. Do not wear sunglasses outside. Eye contact is important to good communication and increases the chances for praise as well as control. Such eye contact is not possible through sunglasses.
6. Establish a rule for who goes after a ball. Four or five people chasing a ball can lead to injury and can completely destroy a game.
7. Keep extra equipment (such as balls) handy when playing a game — while one child is retrieving the errant ball, another one can be used to keep the game going.
8. Use a grass area whenever possible. The next best area for physical education is a gymnasium, followed by a hardtop area. Classrooms or hallways are least desirable.
9. Never use solid objects as safebases or turning points in a race. Safebases should be marked-off areas, and turning points in a race should be marker cones or lines. Children running toward a tree or wall could easily trip or be pushed, which could lead to a serious head or neck injury.
10. Provide eyeglass guards or have children remove glasses if there is any possibility of a ball or other object hitting them hard enough to cause an eye injury.
11. Do not allow gum chewing during gymnastics and tumbling.

Sun in the eyes hinders communication between teacher and student.

Placing equipment between feet while the teacher is talking helps get student attention.

12. Do not allow young children to blow up balloons. Children could get a piece stuck in the throat if a balloon broke during filling.
13. Insist on proper footwear and clothing. Sneakers are desired but not a must. Sandals and other loose footwear should not be allowed. Be careful not to set up a situation where good clothes could be damaged. Bare feet can be used indoors, but children should not be allowed to play in socks.
14. Minimize teacher talk and keep students active as much as possible.

Praise and Criticism. Teachers should apply the praise and criticism information discussed earlier in order to control the learning environment.

Success. Children who are successful tend to be happier. Physical education programs, therefore, should be designed so that every child experiences success during every class period. Use of a problem-solving approach will help to achieve this goal. One must keep in mind, however, that children like to be challenged; success must be possible, but not too easy. Failures should be minimized, but in any challenging program there will be children who will be unable to achieve certain tasks. Providing a variety of activities during each class period will increase the chance of some success for everyone.

Student Rights. Humanistic teachers recognize the rights of their students. Children are, after all, human beings with all the rights and privileges afforded any other person. Many adults have misinterpreted the student rights movement as student control. Students taking advantage of newfound freedom have violated the rights of others, including their peers and adults. The guidelines must be clearly established and no administrator, adult, or child can arbitrarily make rules which violate the rights of another human being, including students. Recognition of this fact by both adults and students will go a long way toward success in classroom control.

Discipline

Even in the best of situations, problems requiring disciplinary measures will occur. How a teacher handles such problems may mean a program's success or failure. For individual children, it can be an influential factor in the development of self-concept. Discipline, therefore, should be handled as humanistically as possible. Children, however, want and need discipline.

Group Disciplining. The beginning teacher usually experiences more group or whole class problems than the experienced teacher. Children of any age will see how far they can go with a new teacher.

A stop signal must be established and adhered to if for no other reason than safety. Being able to get the students' attention could be critical in certain situations when their safety is threatened. Since the whistle is easy to carry and has such a good range of sound, it is suggested as an outside stop signal. The rule of stop, look, and listen when the whistle blows is for safety and should be adhered to strictly. Not as many dangerous situations occur indoors, so some nonverbal signal such as a raised hand can be used. Teachers should avoid the use of the voice as a stop signal. Terms, therefore, such as "freeze" or "quiet" can be ineffective outside as well as hard on the vocal cords.

Wait until everyone has become quiet after the stop signal is given. No attempt to talk should be made if even one person is talking. Nonverbal gestures such as folding the arms across the chest and facial expressions can communicate displeasure. If silence is not forthcoming, children should understand the consequences. Although negative reinforcement should be avoided, children must realize that they are in a learning environment which requires their cooperation, and without it, the teacher will not go on. Such a tactic is only meaningful if the children really like the program being offered. A way to use positive reinforcement in this situation is to use a favorite activity as a reward for positive behavior; i.e., "If you stop, look, and listen every time I give the stop signal, we will play basketball at the end of class."

Group discussion can be used to determine the underlying causes of misbehavior. By bringing children into a close circle and sitting with them, communication can be enhanced. Try to problem-solve with them regarding causes; i.e., "Do they dislike the activity?" If they like the activity, "What should be done with those who

Learning Environment 55

Group discussions help to solve class problems.

disrupt the class?" (peer pressure); "How can the problem be solved?"; and "How can we keep from wasting your fun time?" When working in this group setting, try to discover ways to give positive reinforcement and avoid any tendency to make threats or deal out punishment.

The steps to follow in a group discipline situation are:

1. If a significant number of students are causing a problem (usually five or more in a class of 25), remind all the children of rules which they may be violating without singling out any child or group of children; i.e., "Remember to stay inside the boundary lines."
2. If little behavioral change takes place after the reminder, bring the children together for a problem-solving discussion.
   "What can happen if you go outside the lines?"
   "What should we do with those who do not follow the rule?"
3. If only a few continue to violate the rule, remove them from the activity.
4. If a large number are at fault, stop again. The second discussion can be more forceful:
   "We cannot continue under these unsafe conditions."
   "You are wasting your time."
   "Why are so many unable to follow the rule?"
   "If you are willing to cooperate we will play Crab Soccer before the class ends."
   "If you do not follow the rule, we will return to the classroom."
5. If little change takes place, there must be follow-through by taking them back to the classroom. The physical educator, however, must remain with them until the class period ends. Classroom teachers need their break and do not want the responsibility for the children because the physical educator had trouble with them.
6. Work with the classroom teacher to design a program to gain the required rapport with the children.
7. As a last resort, a physical educator can refuse to teach children who are not sufficiently controlled in the classroom. It is nearly impossible to control a class seen only once or twice a week if they are under little control in the classroom. This approach, however, rarely wins friends and is considered drastic.

Fortunately, few classes every reach step 7. The problem children are usually identified early, and a more individual approach to discipline is possible.

Individual Problems. The majority of discipline problems involve one or two children and not always the same children. When dealing with individuals rather than groups, the possibilities for harming a child's self-concept are magnified. Extreme caution, therefore, must be exercised. The behavior should be stopped in a manner that draws the least amount of attention to the child. By getting the children into activity quickly, the teacher can make contact with a problem child or children without undue fuss. Fortunately, most children need only subtle reminders about their conduct, which can be accomplished quickly and easily through nonverbal means.

Steps to follow in disciplining an individual are:

1. Ignore as much misbehavior as possible unless safety is a factor or a child is disrupting the entire class. Most children misbehave as an attention-seeking device. After identifying problem children, seek opportunities to praise them when they do something correctly.

56 *Learning Environment*

Disciplining child in front of peers can harm a child's self-concept.

Discussing problem behavior with students in a non-threatening manner gets results.

2. Eye contact and facial expressions are usually sufficient to correct most misbehavior.
3. Closing the distance between the teacher and child is also effective but may draw unwanted attention to the child.
4. While the other children are engrossed in activity, take the problem child aside to discuss the problem. The discussion should focus on self-evaluation. A non-threatening environment which fosters communication should be established. "Do you feel O.K. today?"; "Did you understand the rule?"; "Why do you think I brought you over here?"; "What should we do about this problem?"; "When you feel like you can follow the rules, you may come back to the activity." Some would argue there is no time for such a discussion. On the contrary, if a teaching style such as problem-solving, guided discovery, or the task approach is used, a teacher should be free to individualize instruction. A child who is a discipline problem is just as important as a child who has a hand-eye coordination problem, maybe more so.
5. Removing a child from the activity should be viewed by the child as the severest penalty for misbehavior. Such an attitude will only occur if the child likes physical education and wants to participate. Such action also focuses attention on the child, which may be exactly what the child wants. Judgment must be used as to which is the stronger motivator, the negative reinforcer of getting attention while on the sidelines, or the desire to behave and stay in the activity. When it is obvious that a child relishes the spotlight while standing on the side it may be necessary to remove the child entirely from the learning environment. For legal purposes, it is necessary to send the child to a supervised area such as the office. In light of a Supreme Court ruling regarding suspension without due process, some school systems will not allow a child to be placed in the hallway since this is viewed as a form of suspension. The child, therefore, must be supervised and in a learning environment, even if it is self-study. Children in hallways also receive a lot of reinforcement when peers and other teachers see them and want to know why they are there. Such reinforcement could lead to a repeat of the negative behavior.

6. The principal should be a last resort reserved only for cases in which the teacher admits defeat. No other individual, including the principal, can create discipline for someone else. The ability to discipline is an individual skill which must be developed. If the principal is good and the child is extremely difficult, a teacher may be justified in sending the child to his or her office. Passing problems to someone else, however, is not the solution. A teacher must strive to find the causes of misbehavior and seek remedies.

Principles of Discipline

In his book, *Building Positive Self-Concept*, Felker (2) lists the following principles of discipline:

1. **Seek ways to avoid having the child feel that failure is typical of him.**

   Implication • Avoid such expressions as "Not you again?" "Can't you do anything right?" and "You are the biggest problem in this class." Each new instance should be treated as if it were the first. Seek every opportunity to praise the child for positive behavior in front of his peers. Children so often are labeled early in their educational career, causing teachers to look for misbehavior before thinking about praising positive behavior. Fortunately, teachers are no longer allowed to place negative comments on cumulative folders to be passed on with the child from year to year. A teacher should seek information on a possible problem child only as a way to aid the child.

2. **A child must learn to accept the responsibility for his behavior.**

   Implication • Many children are quick to give excuses for behavior or pass the blame onto others. If the child is ever to accept the responsibility, the teacher must handle such behavior carefully. To do this a teacher must be certain the child is at fault. The worse thing to do is punish a child or even accuse a child unless there is no question as to blame. Accusations by other students should also be ignored. An attempt should then be made to have the child admit guilt and determine his or her own just punishment. Students who accept responsibility for their behavior should be praised for coming forward, but must nevertheless experience some consequence for their misbehavior.

A discipline strategy suggested by Felker (2) has seven steps which, although time-consuming, have been judged successful.

1. The child describes his or her behavior.
2. The child then assesses his or her behavior in terms of its helpfulness to others and self.
3. The child then develops an alternate plan for governing his or her behavior.
4. The plan is then signed by the child.
5. After a period of time the child reassesses his or her performance.
6. The teacher provides reinforcement for those aspects of performance which were successful.
7. The child is also encouraged to make positive statements about his or her performance.

New teachers seem to have more problems with control and discipline than any other area. Negative approaches such as yelling, grabbing, and hitting may seem to be easy ways to solve problems. Unfortunately, this approach seems to work and thus reinforces the teacher's behavior. What is unseen, however, is the psychological harm to the child's self-concept. The physical approach can also lead to a suit (see Chapter 13).

A behavior modification program may be necessary for the truly emotionally disturbed child. A thorough discussion and an example behavior modification program is included in Chapter 12.

The positive approach to control and discipline is a little slower but so much more effective. The following are some statements which help to win rapport with children.

1. "I like the way nearly everyone is following the rules."
2. "Who can bounce the ball as well as Judy?"
3. "I like this class."
4. "Thank you for putting your equipment down when the whistle blew."
5. "You have been so good today. What game would you like to play?"
6. "Mrs. Smith, you have a very nice class. I have enjoyed working with them today."
7. "Susie, isn't that a new dress?"
8. "We missed you yesterday, Bob."

No matter how bad a class has been, try to make some positive statement about them before they leave.

REFERENCES

1. Biehler, R. *Psychology Applied to Teaching.* Boston: Houghton-Mifflin Co., 1971.
2. Felker, D. *Building Positive Self-Concept.* Minneapolis: Burgess Publishing Co., 1974.
3. Galloway, C. *Teaching is Communicating.* The Association for Student Teaching, 1970.
4. Humphrey, J. et al. *Principles and Techniques of Supervision in Physical Education.* Dubuque: Wm. C. Brown Co., Publishers, 1972.
5. Mosston, M. *Teaching Physical Education.* Columbus: Charles E. Merrill Publishing Co., 1966.
6. Toffler, A. *Future Shock.* New York: Bantam Books, 1970.

STUDENT ACTIVITIES

1. Design a bulletin board in miniature on a piece of poster board about 2' x 3'. Use a physical education promotion theme following the guidelines established in this chapter.

2. While holding a conversation with someone outside your class, note his or her nonverbal gestures and behavior. See how he or she holds eye contact; try to see how close you can get, and otherwise experiment with your knowledge of nonverbal communications.

60 *Learning Environment*

3. Observe an elementary physical education class or, better yet, watch the videotape of a lesson. Using this sheet, record the objective data indicated. Watch the tape and check your accuracy.

Grade Level _____   Name _____
                                    Date _____

Total time children were in class _____
Total time a randomly selected child was active _____
   Comments:

Number of Praises _____ Total _____
Number of criticisms or corrections _____ Total _____
   Comments:

Number of questions asked: Open _____ Total _____
                          Closed _____ Total _____
   Comments:

Primary style of teaching used _____
   Comments:

CHAPTER 5
CURRICULUM DESIGN

After completing this chapter, the student should be able to:
1. List and describe the components of a systematic approach to curriculum design.
2. Write three properly stated behavioral objectives — one for each of the three education domains.
3. Determine if objectives are properly stated in behavioral terms.
4. Classify objectives into their appropriate domain.
5. List and describe the components of a unit plan.
6. List and describe ways to individualize instruction.
7. List and describe the components of a unit plan.
8. List the three phases of a lesson plan and give two criteria for each phase.

SYSTEMATIC APPPOACH

The purpose of education is to provide for the total development of each child — physically, socially, emotionally, and intellectually. This can be accomplished by systematically planning and conducting the curriculum. Since it is so closely associated with the computer age, many people look upon any systematic approach as dehumanizing; perhaps the word system is a poor choice. Contrary to the fears of some, a systematic approach is far more humanistic than other methods of curriculum design. In the systematic approach, each child's ability is evaluated and teaching methods are used which truly individualize instruction. A system for curriculum design includes the following parts:

1. **Goals** — Stated in general terms
2. **Objectives** — Behaviorally stated
3. **Pretest** — Using behavioral objectives
4. **Methods** — To individualize instruction
5. **Evaluation** — To make changes

Goals

Educational goals are usually expressed in broad terms; i.e., "The children will develop perceptual-motor skills" or "Children will develop coordination." Such generally stated goals can be useful in public relations as well as establishing the basis for more specifically stated objectives.

Objectives

Educational objectives have been expressed in terms ranging from nebulous to so specific as to be useless. As with most things in education, the way objectives are stated varies with time. Many believe, for example, that behavioral objectives (specifically stated and measurable) are new, when in fact such expressions of purpose were very much a part of education as early as the 1930s. Mager (6) is credited with the revival of instructional (behavioral) objectives, and numerous other writers have since promoted behavioral objectives.

The use of behavioral objectives has several advantages: (1) accountability is possible, (2) programs can be based on competence rather than time; (3) contracts can be developed; (4) instruction can be individualized; (5) curriculum decisions are easier to make; and (6) pretesting of students is possible.

Components. A behaviorally stated objective consists of three basic components: (1) *the observable behavior;* (2) *the criteria or level of performance;* and (3) *the conditions under which the behavior must be exhibited.*

The behavior must be such that it can be perceived by one of the five senses — seeing, hearing, smelling, touching, or tasting — or a combination of any of the five. Although teachers normally rely on their eyes or ears, the other senses could come into play under certain circumstances. The industrial arts teacher, for example, may use touch to determine the smoothness of finish while the home economics teacher could specify a good taste and smell. Traditionally, however, objectives are expressed in some behavior which the teacher can see or hear.

1. The student will do a forward roll from a stand to a stand using the hands only once.
2. If asked, at least 80 percent of the students will be able to verbalize two reasons for doing exercises.

The behavior in "1" is the "forward roll," while in "2" it is the "verbalization."

The criteria of acceptability is how well the child must perform. In the previous example, the child had to go "from a stand to a stand using the hands only once." In the second objective, the criterion was "two reasons" for doing exercises.

The conditions can be important to expressing a behavioral objective but are not always critical. Neither of the two examples discussed above has conditions included. See if you can pick out the conditions in the two examples below:

1. Given a junior basketball, the student will be able to make three out of five shots in an eight-foot basket from a distance of ten feet.
2. Following a unit in basketball, the student will be able to correctly answer at least 80 percent of the questions on the rules of basketball.

The conditions in "1" are quite specific and extremely important to evaluation of the student's performance. The first part "given a junior basketball," and "eight-foot basket from a distance of ten feet" are all part of the conditions. In number "2," the condition is "following a unit in basketball." It is often difficult to differentiate between condition and criterion. Picking out and labeling parts is not as important as being specific enough in the objective that anyone can use it for evaluation purposes.

Specificity. How specific must a behavioral objective be? The teacher must be specific enough to clarify the behavior to be elicited from the student. Thus for an advanced tumbling group, a forward roll objective could be stated this way:

The student will demonstrate a forward roll from a standing position using the hands only once. The head may not touch the mat and the feet must be kept together.

The forward roll is the observable behavior, but now the criteria of acceptability is much higher.

For individual lesson plans, this following objective, although shortened, is perfectly acceptable:

The student will demonstrate the forward roll observing the four-points discussed in the demonstration phase of the lesson.

This abbreviated objective is acceptable since it can be assumed that specific points of the forward roll will be covered during the demonstration phases of the lesson. No matter how the objective is shortened, however, it must clearly convey the intent of the instruction.

Look at these two objectives and decide which is a properly stated behavioral objective.

A. The student will demonstrate the one hand jump shot.
B. The student will run the quarter mile in less than 100 seconds.

"B" is the properly stated objective. Although "A" states an observable behavior, it does not establish a criterion of acceptability. In "B," the observable behavior is "running the quarter mile" and the criterion of acceptability is "less than 100 seconds."

Try these two:

A. The student will know the drive shot in hockey.
B. From a distance of 15 feet, the student will be able to hit the hockey ball into the net two out of three times using the drive shot.

Obviously "B" is the properly stated objective. Words such as *know* which appears in example "A" along with *understand, comprehend,* etc., all too often appear in educational objectives. Although such words may be effective for public relations, they do not allow for the measurement of learning. In "B," criteria are established so both the teacher and the student know what is expected, and the evaluation of the student will be objective rather than subjective.

Here are two more:

A. From a distance of 20 yards, the student will attempt to kick five footballs between the goal posts using the instep kick.
B. Using an instep kick, the student will kick a slowly rolling soccer ball. The student

Curriculum Design 63

must kick two out of four balls into a goal area 22 feet long by eight feet high.

Actually, both "A" and "B" qualify as behavioral objectives. The acceptable criterion in "A" is merely to "attempt." "B," however, is not only more specific, but requires a higher level of performance for acceptability — "two out of four balls going into the goal area."

Evaluation and Revision. Evaluating objectives and revising them is one of the most important phases of the objective writing process. Behavioral objectives can be evaluated by the teacher, co-worker, or a supervisor. No matter who evaluates, however, each person should see the same thing if the objective is properly stated in behavioral terms. In other words, after observing the lesson, a supervisor or co-worker should be able to determine the degree to which the objective was met without further clarification from the teacher. Failure to meet this criterion of clarity will necessitate the revision of the objective.

Although evaluation is absolutely essential to improving the learning process, it need not consume an exorbitant amount of valuable activity time. Clearly written behavioral objectives frequently can be evaluated through systematic observation during the skill practice phase of the lesson and do not necessarily require specially allotted time in the lesson.

The Verb. A key to expressing objectives behaviorally is the verb. Figure 5-1 is a listing of verbs which can be used in stating behavioral objectives. Verbs for each of the three educational domains are included.

Psychomotor Domain

1. bends	11. holds	21. rides
2. bats	12. jumps	22. tosses
3. chases	13. kicks	23. somersaults
4. climbs	14. leaps	24. stretches
5. crawls	15. pitches	25. swims
6. catches	16. pulls	26. swings
7. grabs	17. rolls	27. tosses
8. grips	18. runs	28. twists
9. hits	19. skips	29. walks
10. hops	20. slides	

Cognitive Domain

Knowledge Level:
1. arranges	7. gives	13. positions
2. checks	8. identifies	14. says
3. circles	9. labels	15. shows
4. copies	10. lists	16. states
5. defines	11. matches	17. tells
6. describes	12. names	18. writes

Understanding Level:
1. applies	6. differentiates	11. interprets
2. computes	7. distinguishes	12. plans
3. contrasts	8. evaluates	13. proves
4. defines	9. explains	14. solves
5. demonstrates	10. formulates	15. uses

Processing Level:
Analysis:
1. breaks down	6. extracts
2. disassembles	7. investigates
3. dissects	8. separates
4. divides	9. simplifies
5. examines	10. takes apart

Synthesis:
1. assembles	6. develops
2. builds	7. produces
3. completes	8. puts together
4. constructs	9. reorganizes
5. creates	10. structures

Classify:
1. arranges	6. places
2. chooses	7. regroups
3. grades	8. sequences
4. groups	9. sorts
5. orders	10. tallies

Evaluate:
1. appraises	6. tallies
2. assays	7. ranks
3. assesses	8. rates
4. decides	9. weights
5. grades	10. determines value of

Affective Domain

1. accepts	15. criticizes	29. permits
2. advocates	16. defends	30. promotes
3. argues	17. disproves	31. proposes
4. asks	18. disputes	32. praises
5. assumes	19. enjoys	33. questions
6. attempts	20. evaluates	34. recommends
7. attends	21. initiates	35. rectifies
8. berates	22. involves	36. rejects
9. bothers	23. joins	37. suggests
10. challenges	24. likes	38. supports
11. chooses	25. loves	39. sustains
12. completes	26. obeys	40. tolerates
13. consoles	27. offers	41. volunteers
14. consults	28. participates	42. watches

Figure 5-1. Verbs for Writing Behavioral Objectives

Curriculum Design

Behavioral Objectives and the Educational Domain. Objectives can be stated in behavioral terms for any of the three educational domains:

Psychomotor:
1. By the end of the unit, the child will be able to demonstrate at least three of the following five skills (as outlined in Cochran's book): (1) forward roll, (2) backward roll, (3) headstand, (4) handstand, and (5) cartwheel.
2. By the end of the lesson, the child will be able to catch the beanbag with either hand when the beanbag is thrown from a distance of ten feet by a partner. At least 80 percent will accomplish this objective before a more difficult skill is introduced.

Cognitive:
1. If asked, at least 80 percent of the students will be able to give at least two reasons for being physically fit.
2. By the end of the year, at least 90 percent of the students will be able to touch all the body parts listed in the curriculum guide for grade one.

Affective:
1. At least 60 percent of the students will voluntarily participate in an after-school volleyball program.
2. At least 80 percent of the students will rate the physical education program as good to excellent on a scale of excellent, good, average, fair, poor. Ratings will be done using an anonymous questionnaire.
3. During a fifteen minute game of basketball, there will be no fights between players.
4. No player will argue with an official over his call during a game of basketball.
5. Win or lose, each player on the team will offer to shake hands with the opponents.

Pretest

The third part of a systematic approach is determining the incoming ability of the students through use of a pretest. Since the objectives specify the outcome of the instructional process, they are the most logical foundation for the development of a pretest. The objectives thus become the pretest. It is not necessary nor would it be feasible to test the children on all objectives at the beginning of the year. No instruction should take place, however, until the child's incoming ability has been assessed. Certain growth and development areas, such as fitness levels, basic competencies, body images, and attitudes should be measured at the beginning of the year while specific skills can be evaluated before presenting a unit or even at the beginning of a lesson.

The pretest can be either formal or informal depending upon the data desired. Formal testing in the psychomotor domain usually requires assessing children individually as is the case in fitness testing where specific data are required. Anytime the teacher wants to make a comparison of pretest scores with posttest scores for the purpose of gathering data, formal testing is required. Informal testing is done through class observation to get a general assessment of ability. By playing Simon Says — Body Image, Chapter 7, for example, the teacher can gain a general idea of the children's body image. This information can then be used to determine those parts which need work, how much time should be spent on this aspect of development, and which children need special attention. Part of a teacher's job is to be a keen observer, using the eyes and ears as instruments for observation; behavioral objectives can be used to calibrate these instruments.

Formal testing requires observing one child at a time.

Methods

After objectives have been established and used to pretest the children, methods must be determined to aid the growth and development of the children. Such techniques as ability grouping, stations, contracts, etc., are all methods which can be used to help accomplish objectives. No matter which method is used, however, the teacher must keep in mind varying entrance levels of students as well as their differing learning rates. Any method which does not account for these factors is doomed to failure.

Various media can be employed to assist in the process of individualization. Too often teachers view themselves as the only medium for dispensing information. Records, movies, tapes, posters, and books can all be used in the instructional process. Although some commercial materials are available, the best aids are those developed by the teacher. Who knows each child's level of ability and style of learning better than the teacher?

Individualized Instruction. Some strides have been made toward individualized instruction in education. The open classroom, open school, teaching machines, learning centers, and computer-assisted instruction are just a few ways to personalize instruction. There is no question about the need for individualized instruction. Many researchers have pointed out the wide variance in children's abilities, even within the same age group. Teachers, therefore, must seek ways to individualize instruction in physical education.

Learning centers are one way to individualize instruction. In physical education the use of learning centers in the form of stations has been confined primarily to circuit training and gymnastics. These stations, however, have been used more for the purpose of grouping children than for individualizing instruction. A true learning center has instructional material, practice items, and evaluation instruments, all of which can be used by students for self-pacing and self-testing. Merely placing four or five pieces of gymnastics equipment around the room and dividing up the class cannot be considered individualized instruction or learning centers.

The effect of a well-planned learning center environment or psychomotor and affective development are dramatic when compared with a more traditional approach. A case in point is the following description of an actual situation which occurred in an elementary school:

Using media at a learning center

Four classes of sixth grade children, two all-girl classes and two all-boy classes, were meeting simultaneously in a gymnasium and a large hallway. The hallway was covered with mats and thirty boys in one class were tumbling one at a time across a section of the mats while being evaluated by the teacher. Inside the gym were two all-girl classes, one on each side of half of the gym. Each class was divided into four squads of approximately seven girls. One girl at a time came up to the mats, which were in the front of the class, performed, and was evaluated verbally for all to hear.

In the other half of the gym a group of boys was divided into four learning centers of tumbling and apparatus. Each center included written instruction and students were told in advance how to work and help each other. A great deal of interaction was taking place among students and nearly everyone was active. The teacher in this case was stationed at the vaulting box and was providing instruction, encouragement, and spotting, all the while maintaining a position so that he could see the other centers.

It was quite obvious that the chances for psychomotor learning were enhanced in the learning center approach. The participation level was nearly nonexistent in the other three classes. Performing in front of one's peers while a teacher finds fault with the performance can also damage a child's self-concept (mostly criticism was given to the children in the three low participation classes). The use of learning centers will not guarantee learning, but having children sit and watch others perform will insure that little psychomotor learning will take place.

66 *Curriculum Design*

In addition to individualizing instruction, learning centers or stations have other values, including: (1) large group instruction; (2) social interaction; (3) integration of language arts with physical education; (4) ability grouping of students; and (6) offering activities even though there is an equipment shortage.

Large group instruction is not normally a problem in physical education, but through a learning center approach the organizational principles in the following example can be applied with any size group. In this example, fifty students are in a basketball class and there are only ten basketballs. Under the old physical education organization, ten teams would probably be formed and five half-court games would be played. This game-oriented approach is a poor way to learn basketball skills, particularly for children with little experience. In a stations approach, seven stations with seven people at a station could be set up. Station one could be just general shooting using three basketballs. Instruction could be provided using a series of still pictures or through use of loop films which can be homemade. Station two could be for running forward and backward in a limited space. Instructions (or commands) could be given by audiotape or videotape recording. The third station could be passing and shooting using partners and would require three basketballs. The teacher could take the main responsibility for conducting this station. Station four could be different types of passes in which soccerballs would substitute for basketballs. As long as students knew they would get to use the basketballs as they rotated to the other stations, they probably would accept the substitution of soccer balls at one station. The fifth station could be guarding and dribbling, which would require three basketballs, and some form of media could be used to instruct the students. Station six could be actual play using three-on-three with a substitution of the seventh child after every basket. The last station could be a basketball calisthenic area. So with ten basketballs, three baskets, and three soccerballs, fifty students could be actively involved in learning. The teacher could remain at one station or could circulate among the stations, giving assistance and encouragement as needed.

Socially, the station organization allows for more peer group interaction than the more teacher-centered approach. After establishing tasks to be accomplished, children can be encouraged to assist each other in learning. The better students learn by helping the less skilled to learn. This child-centered approach places more responsibility for learning on the student. Students begin to develop leadership skills as well as self-discipline. Everyone participates, and this can minimize the chance for misbehavior generated by the boredom of inactivity. If opportunities for social interaction are not provided by organizational patterns such as stations, there probably will be little opportunity for development of interpersonal relationships.

Language arts can be integrated into physical education through stations by using written instructions or a combination of pictures and words when working with young children or nonreaders. Vocabulary must be selected carefully, although new vocabulary words can be introduced if used in combination with pictures. The better readers in the class can also assist those children having trouble. For physical educators, the best source for determining the children's reading level is the classroom teacher, who can also provide new vocabulary words which can be included in physical education. This interaction with other teachers outside physical education should improve the image of physical education as well as the rapport among teachers. Figure 5-2 has examples of written instructions for use as stations by various age groups.

Ability grouping is another way to individualize instruction using learning centers; caution however, should be exercised in its use. In several areas, including gymnastics, tennis, and swimming, ability grouping can facilitate instruction. The number of groups which can be handled realistically is about three. Although three is not an absolute, it is difficult to plan and conduct a class with more than three groups at one time. Although ability grouping is common in such areas as reading and math, it has been used sparingly in physical education. The danger in its overuse is the possible harm to the slower child's self-concept. There is, however, no doubt that ability grouping is an efficient way for students to learn.

Children can be grouped using objective or subjective evaluation. Although there are few if any standardized tests of skill for elementary children, it is not difficult to group children according to their performance on certain objectives. Teachers can also group children based on observational data. Once grouped, children should be constantly reevaluated to see if they should move to another level.

> **Figure 5.2. Example of Instructions at Stations**
>
> **First Grade**
>
> Station 1: Hand-Eye Coordination
>
> > Can you throw and catch the beanbag?
> > How many ways can you throw and catch with a friend?
> > Can you hit the triangle while standing on the square?
>
> **Third Grade**
>
> Station 4: Hand-Eye Coordination
>
> > How many ways can you throw and catch two beanbags with a friend?
> > Can you throw the beanbag through the swinging tire while standing behind the line?
> > How far back can you get and still throw it through the tire?
>
> **Fifth Grade**
>
> Station 8: Hand-Eye Coordination and Lead-up Skills to Basketball
>
> > Working with a partner, see how many different ways you can get the ball from one person to another.
>
> Station 9:
>
> > Play "Monkey in the Middle" with one person on the inside and three people passing the ball. If the middle person touches the ball, someone must take his place. Use the passes learned at Station 8.

When using groups, teachers must make prudent use of media for instructional purposes. The media include: (1) audio and videotape, (2) loop films, (3) slides or a slide-tape presentation, (4) posters on charts, (5) books and other handouts, (6) peer group assistants, (7) older children working with younger ones, (8) teacher aides or parent helpers, and (9) learning packages.

Gymnastics example: Fifth and sixth grade children are grouped into three levels of tumbling ability. The advanced group is assigned a section in *Gymnastics and Tumbling* by Price et al. (8) and told to use the pictures and descriptions to learn the different partner activities. The middle ability group is provided some basic tumbling skill loop films and instructed to work together on them. The teacher works with the poorly-skilled group giving individual attention. As the low group practices, the teacher circulates among the three groups giving assistance, praise and encouragement.

More participation by students is a characteristic of the learning center approach. Children can move along at their own pace and need not wait for the teacher or other children. More activities can be offered in learning centers even when equipment is in short supply. When a school has only two mats, for example, it is poor planning to teach tumbling with 15 children to a mat. By setting up stations, the mats can be placed at one station, and children can rotate to that station, where they receive individual attention from the teacher who remains at the station until all children have had a chance. Other centers can include hand-eye coordination activities, sports skills, or rhythmic activities. By using learning centers, children get tumbling experience, but are not forced to stand or sit waiting for a turn. Needless to say, this is not the best way to learn tumbling, but with a shortage of equipment, it is better than not having it at all.

Self-instructional materials. According to Young and Noonan (9), self-instructional materials consist of packages or modules in which students interact with various media. Examples of such material include programmed texts, computer-assisted instruction, and audiovisual workbook programs. The purpose of these packages is to permit student self-pacing.

Learning packages are complete educational kits with all the necessary material to allow for self-evaluation, instruction practice, and learning. Although they are suited more for readers, they can, through use of pictures and audio or videotape, be designed for nonreaders. A good package should have each of the following:

1. An explanation of the kit.
2. Means by which students can determine where to begin in the package (self-testing items).
3. A sequence of activities from easy to more difficult (usually stated in behavioral terms).
4. Instruction either in writing or on audio or videotape for each skill in the sequence. (Other media could also be used for instruction.)
5. A progress chart.

Packages can be designed for any skill such as hand-eye or foot-eye coordination, for a sport such as gymnastics, tennis, soccer of hockey, or for fitness.

By using learning packets, instruction can truly be individualized. Students do not have to be working on the same skill or sport. Pacing is determined by the student, and the student is constantly aware of his progress, which fosters intrinsic motivation. The teacher is free to give individual assistance.

Figure 5-3 is a learning package in miniature. Packages are most meaningful when designed by the teacher for a specific group. Each curriculum chapter (7-10), contains standards for skills and sports which can be used as foundations for learning packets.

Evaluation and Change

Any system must be constantly evaluated and changed when appropriate. As is the case in pretesting, the behavioral objectives are used to make curriculum decisions. Questions such as "Was the method effective?" and "Were the criteria too demanding or the objectives unrealistic?" must be asked. The number of children accomplishing a particular objective is typically used to answer such questions. The standard is usually 80 percent of the children retaining 80 percent of the information. This 80/80 criterion is for curriculum decisions only, and is used to determine when to move on with the majority of the class. For example, let us assume that approximately 20 percent of the children accomplished a particular objective. Such a low figure is indicative of an objective which is beyond too many children. The objective, therefore, must be eliminated or changed. On the other hand, if 70 percent of the children meet the objective, perhaps only a method change may be necessary to bring other children up to standard. Since children need to be challenged, striving for a 100/100 criteria would be nearly impossible as well as boring to the vast numbers of children ready for new goals. This is not to suggest that the other 20 or so percent be neglected. If individualized methods are used, these slower children will continue to work on skills while others move on. A teacher must always be aware of the general level of the class while not ignoring the slower learners.

For those phases of the program in which an individualized method such as a learning package is utilized, the percentage are used in a different way since all children are moving at their own pace; the 80/80 criterion is not as important. It is not necessary for every child to learn everything taught. The interests as well as the capabilities of children must be considered when determining how much time or stress is placed on learning. If the skill is a prerequisite skill for others, perhaps more attention is justified. On the other hand, children can live very effectively without many of the more specific sports skills.

Unit Planning

Unit planning is an outgrowth of a systematic approach to curriculum development. Although units may vary in length, they should all reflect the careful thinking required in a systematic approach. Almost any aspect of growth and development can be put into a unit format although it is difficult to specify a time frame in some cases. Sports activities lend themselves well to unit planning in which time can be specified. Units of four to six weeks are common for upper elementary sports, gymnastics, and rhythmics. Units in basic movement competencies, on the other hand, are difficult to specify in terms of time. Even though time cannot be determined, a unit plan is not only possible, but necessary.

A unit should include each of the following:
1. Goals
2. Objectives
3. Evaluation Methods
4. Content
5. Teaching Methods
6. Media
7. Equipment

Figure 5-3
Miniature Gymnastics Learning Package for Children Age 9-11
Rules and Procedures for Using This Packet

1. Spotters are required for all stunts.
2. Some of the more advanced stunts have special requirements for safety listed beside them. No stunt in Section 3 may be attempted until permission is received from the teacher.
3. No horseplay will be tolerated.
4. Read all instructional information before attempting any stunt.
5. Handle film and tapes carefully.
6. When you are not sure of something, check with your teacher.
SPOTTERS REQUIRED FOR ALL STUNTS.

The tumbling skills on page 2 of the booklet are arranged from those that are easy to those requiring a good deal of skill. As you can see, a space is provided for your teacher to sign when you have correctly demonstrated the skill. No new skill in any one section should be attempted until the one above has been initialed. Section 1 and 2 must be completed before going on to Section 3.

Beginning on page 4, instructions, including pictures, are provided to help you. Some skill instruction also includes films and/or tapes; if so, a number for the film or tape has been placed in the appropriate column. These materials can be found in the learning centers located around the gymnasium. You are free to use these materials at any time.

SPOTTERS REQUIRED

Section 1. Tumbling Skills Checklist
1. _____ Squat forward roll
2. _____ Standing forward roll
3. _____ Running forward roll
4. _____ Dive forward roll
5. _____ Fish Flop
6. _____ Standing backward roll
7. _____ Straddle backward roll
8. _____ Straight backward roll
9. _____ Backward roll, extension and snapdown

Section 2.
10. _____ Tripod
11. _____ Tip up
12. _____ Headstand
13. _____ Mule kick
14. _____ Handstand
15. _____ Walk on hand
16. _____ Turn while balancing on hands
17. _____ Cartwheel
18. _____ Round-Off
19. _____ Front walkover
20. _____ Kip Up

Section 3:
21. _____ Front headspring
22. _____ Front handspring
23. _____ Back handspring (spotters required)
24. _____ Back somersault (belt required)
25. _____ Round-off, back handspring (belt required)
26. _____ Round-off, back somersault (belt required)
27. _____ Front somersault

Instructions

Skill I — Squat forward roll. Get into a squatting position as shown in Figure 1, placing arms on outside of knees. Fingers should be pointed straight ahead and should be right next to feet. The chin should be touching the chest. Push off with the feet while holding your weight up on your arms which should be slightly bent. Only the back of your head should touch the mat. Roll forward, reaching the hands out in order to come up on your feet; see Figures 2 and 3.

Skill II — Standing forward roll. Begin in a standing position. Squat and roll forward all in one motion following the rules established in Skill I for chin position, hand placement, etc.

Descriptions for each skill would follow in order.

Performance Standards

Skill I — The forward roll must be done in a continuous motion in a straight line from a squatting position to a squatting position. The hands may touch the mat only at the beginning of the roll. Only the back of the head may touch the mat.

Skill II — Must be done from a stand to a stand observing all the criteria of Skill I above except for the squat starting position.

The objectives should be specified in behavioral terms and be used as part of the evaluation process — pretest and posttest. Other evaluation tools such as standardized tests can also be included. It is possible to specify these formal tests in the objective: "At least 80 percent of the students will score in the 50th percentile or better on the *AAHPERD Youth Fitness Test.*"

The content should agree with the objective. For every objective specified, there must be some activities included in the content which will aid in the accomplishment of that objective. All activities which are part of the developmental process should be included.

Teaching methods and media should be specified along with the content. Certain activities lend themselves better to different approaches, and the methods and media, therefore, will vary. If only one style such as contracting will be used, it should be specified.

Equipment requirement should come after the content. This approach allows for a quick cross-check between equipment needs and availability. Some content might have to be altered if there is a shortage of materials, so this is an important part of the planning process.

A Motor Development Unit for Five Year Olds

Goals:
Psychomotor
1. To develop the quality of movement, both locomotor and nonlocomotor.
2. To develop manipulative skills.
3. To develop kinesthetic awareness.
4. To develop balance.

Affective
1. To develop a positive attitude toward movement.
2. To develop a positive self-concept.

Cognitive
1. To develop problem-solving ability.
2. To develop creativity

Psychomotor Objectives:
1. Each child will be able to do all the basic locomotor movements at varying speeds, in all directions, at various levels, and with various force without losing his or her balance.
2. Children will be able to move all body parts capable of nonlocomotor movement with varying speed and force while keeping time to a tom-tom or music.
3. Children will be able to throw and catch a seven-inch sponge ball with two hands and a four-inch beanbag with one hand at least four out of five times.
4. Children will be able to kick a stationary seven-inch sponge ball and hit a four-foot target ten feet away.
5. Using six-inch beanbags, the children will be able to throw it to a partner 10 feet away without looking. The child can look to see the distance, but must close his or her eyes before throwing. The receiving child should not have to move to catch the beanbag.
6. Each child will be able to walk forward and backward on a four-inch balance beam six inches off the floor for a distance of eight feet without falling off.

Affective Objectives:
1. The children will respond positively to statements on a questionnaire dealing with the physical education program and the teacher.
2. All children will actively participate in all the activities.

Cognitive Objectives:
1. Most children will be able to think of various ways to solve movement problems and every child will be able to find at least one solution.
2. All children will think of unique ways to move to music and will be able to combine three different locomotor movements into a routine.

Assessment:
Evaluation of the child's incoming ability should always precede instruction. This evaluation can be at the beginning of a short unit or just prior to a lesson when a lot of material is included in the unit. For this unit the assessment should be broken into smaller segments and come just prior to each lesson:
1. The objectives will be used as evaluation criteria for this unit. If properly stated, the objectives are always used to assess incoming ability.
2. Activities to be used for assessment:
   a. Busy Bee
   b. Brothers
   c. Simon Says
   d. Can You?
   e. Moving to music
   f. Verbal questions
   g. Moving to tom-tom
   h. Statues

Content:
I. Quality of Movement
   A. The emphasis will be on developing the ability to do all the movements in various directions, at different levels, speeds, and with varying force.

B. Basic locomotor movements
 1. Walk
 2. Run
 3. Hop
 4. Jump
 5. Leap
C. Combination movements
 1. Skip
 2. Gallop
 3. Slide
D. Nonlocomotor movements
 1. Bend
 2. Stretch
 3. Twist
 4. Turn
 5. Swing
 6. Bounce
 7. Curl
 8. Shake
 9. Push
 10. Pull
E. Activities
 1. Moving to tom-tom and music
 2. Creative activities
 3. Story plays
 4. Some maximum participation games
F. Teaching techniques
 1. Free and guided exploration
 2. Problem solving

II. Body Parts to Be Covered
A. Head
 1. Forehead
 2. Eyebrows
 3. Eyes, nose, mouth
 4. Ears
 5. Cheeks
 6. Jaw
 7. Lips
B. Neck
C. Shoulders
D. Chest
E. Elbows
F. Abdomen
G. Waist
H. Wrists
I. Hips
J. Thighs
K. Legs
L. Ankles
M. Feet and Toes
N. Hands, Fingers, and Thumbs

III. Directionality Concepts
A. Front, back
B. Right, left
C. Upper, lower
D. Beside
E. Over, under
F. Near, far
G. Around
H. Up, down
I. Between

IV. Activities for Learning Body Parts and Directional Terms
A. Simon Says
B. Busy Bee
C. Brothers
D. Hula Hoops
E. Hokie Pokie
F. Bean bags
G. Story Plays

This format would be continued until all the content had been included.

Equipment:
There would always be enough equipment to give one piece to every child unless otherwise specified:
 Hoops
 8 ½" Playground balls
 7" sponge rubber balls
 6" Beanbags — two for every child
 1 Record Player
 1 Tom-tom
 Scoops
 Plastic balls (softball size)
 Tennis balls
 Etc.

Touch Football Unit for Fifth and Sixth Grades

Goals:
1. Perform at least 80 percent of the skills.
2. To learn the rules.
3. To develop sportsmanship.

Objectives:
Psychomotor:
1. Using a junior football, at least 80 percent of the students will be able to demonstrate each of the following skills.
 a. Throw a forward pass and hit a target three feet in diameter from a distance of 15 years three out of five times.
 b. Center a ball between the legs hitting a three-foot target seven yards away three out of five times.
 c. Run three pass patterns as discussed in class.
 d. While running, catch three out of five balls thrown from a distance of 15 yards.

72 *Curriculum Design*

e. Punt a ball 20 yards.
f. Place kick a ball 30 yards.

Cognitive:
1. Pass a written test of football rules with an 80 percent or better score.

Affective:
1. There will be no arguing with an official over a call.
2. There will be no booing.
3. There will be no physical fights.
4. At least 60 percent of the students will voluntarily participate in intramural football.

Evaluation:
Use objectives as criteria to measure incoming ability.

Content:
I. Skills
   A. Passing
   B. Centering
   C. Catching
   D. Punting
   E. Kicking
   F. Pass patterns
II. Lead-up Games
   A. Kick over
   B. Punt over
   C. Two-on-two
   D. Field goal
   E. Flicker ball
   F. Six-on-six
   G. One-hand touch
III. Rules
   A. Kick-off
   B. Blocking
   C. Tagging
   D. First downs
   E. Offsides
   F. Out of bounds
   G. Touchdowns
   H. Safety
   I. Unnecessary roughness
IV. Equipment
   A. Pinnies — one for every two children
   B. Footballs — one for every two children
   C. Marker cones — 16

Lesson Planning

One of the more important phases of the planning process is the lesson plan. A carefully designed lesson plan will not guarantee success, but the lack of one will probably insure failure. Frequently the lesson plan is neglected altogether or is a rush job done just before the class. This is unfortunate since the lesson plan can help focus the teacher's attention on class organization, purpose, pitfalls, equipment needs, and safety. Preplanning will also aid in individualizing instruction, using facilities properly, and determining alternatives due to inclement weather.

The particular philosophy behind lesson planning presented here is based on scientific knowledge about children's growth and development characteristics and how they learn. The starting point and key is the goal, i.e., "What does the teacher want to accomplish?" This goal is followed by a behaviorally stated objective and activities to help accomplish the objective.

The organization of activities usually follows the format of an opening, middle, and closing phase of the lesson. This approach to lesson planning is based on a half-hour lesson with varying times being allotted for each phase of the lesson. Frequently, the three-phase lesson format will vary according to the lesson's objective.

Opening

The teacher should get the children into activity quickly during the lesson's opening phase. Most children are coming from a classroom environment in which there is little movement — often a frustrating experience. Children, are therefore ready to move when it is time for physical education. This opening activity should take only 10 to 15 seconds to explain and should have 100 percent participation; it should last around five to seven minutes. For early childhood, activities such as story plays, creative activities, and rhythms are good. Activities such as relays, circle games, or games which require waiting for a turn have no place in this opening phase. Although not essential, the activity selected should help to accomplish the objective of the lesson. The more closely related the activity is to the objective, however, the more time it can receive.

Opening activities for upper elementary children should also allow for maximum participation. Traditionally, upper elementary lessons begin with exercises called "warm-up." Not only is warm-up unnecessary for all activities, but beginning every lesson the same way can lead to boredom and poor attitudes toward exercise. Upper elementary lessons can begin with combatives, rhythmics, tag games, circuit or station activities, gymnastics, etc. Variety is just as important at this level as it is with lower elementary children.

Middle

The middle phase of the lesson is most directly related to the objective. Although in an ideal situation, all segments of the lesson should be addressed to the objective, it is not always possible. During this part of the lesson, new information can be presented which is both challenging and interesting. Since children learn best by doing, however, any talking by the teacher should be kept to a minimum. As in the opening phase, activities should allow for 100 percent participation. Sufficient time should be allotted so nearly all the children (80 percent or more) can be successful.

Closing

The final phase of the lesson should be, but does not have to be, closely related to the middle phase. The key to this final phase is fun. If some new skill has been learned in the middle phase, for example, it can be used in a game situation. For the younger children a low organizational game or activity will usually guarantee success for everyone, thus ending the class on a high note. In selecting a game, care should be taken to find one which has a high amount of participation and some developmental value. This would be the phase, however, in which activities such as relays and circle games could be played. Such activities usually have low participation, but are enjoyed by children. The lower the activity's developmental value, the less time it should receive. A fun concluding activity will help develop a positive attitude toward physical education.

Flow

A good lesson should flow from one activity to the next without a distinct break in action, but this is not always possible. Moving from one organizational pattern to another with minimum confusion can be accomplished with careful preparation. Formal lines and military-style formations should be replaced with free formations in which children scatter over the designated area seeking personal space. Since lines and circles, however, are a part of the physical education curriculum, time should be spent early in the year on efficient ways to form these patterns.

Timing

Timing a lesson is also important. Since most teachers are tied to a schedule, time planning is necessary if the objectives are to be accomplished and the lesson is to end on a high note. Typically, the opening phase of a 30-minute lesson will last five to seven minutes and the closing likewise. The majority of time should be allotted to the middle phase. Keeping to a schedule will also help develop rapport with classroom teachers who expect the specialist to arrive on time.

Safety

The final consideration, but the most important, is safety. Safety determinations are made after the lesson has been designed, so that the best organizational patterns, which has maximum participation will be utilized. If this pattern is not considered safe, it can be slowly scaled down in light of restricting factors such as space and number of children. If safety were considered first, a weak organizational pattern might be selected to guarantee safety. For example, one ball per 30 children may be safe, but so might one ball per child. Safety is important, but all organizational patterns should be explored before selecting the best.

The above approach to lesson planning provides a logical and valuable organizational pattern to follow in developing children through physical education. It should be kept in mind, however, that children learn best by direct, purposeful experience and lessons which provide as much participation by the children as possible.

REFERENCES

1. Blake, H., J. Fleischut, and R. Westervelt. "Open up." JOHPER, April, 1975, p. 49.
2. Conrad, M., V. Seefeldt, and P. Reuschlein. "Relationship between Grade, Sex, Race, and Motor Performance in Young Children." Research Quarterly, 47:726-730.
3. Davis, A. "Station Teaching." JOHPER, April, 1975, pp. 49-50.
4. Grandgenett, R. "Individualizing P.E. in the Primary Grades." JOHPER, February, 1976, p. 51.
5. Herrold, L. "Individualizing the Physical Education Program in the Elementary School." MAHPER Newsletter, 25:8, Spring, 1973.
6. Mager, R. Preparing Instructional Objectives. Palo Alto: Fearon Publishers, 1962.
7. Perrigo, R. "Individualizing P.E. for Intermediate Grades." JOHPER, February, 1976, pp. 51-52.
8. Price, H. et al. Gymnastics and Tumbling. Annapolis: United States Naval Institute, 1959.
9. Young, R. and J. Noonan, "Strategies I, Overview of Instructional Strategies." Unpublished paper, Virginia Commonwealth University, Richmond, Virginia, 1977.

Example Lesson Plans

Kindergarten

1 — 1:30

22 children

Goal: To develop creativity

Objectives: By the end of the creative activities, each child will have participated in each of the activities, and will react appropriately to the music, i.e., fast motion with lively music and slow motion with slow music.

  At least 80 percent of the class will think up some original activity in the opening phase of the lesson.

Activities:	Formation:

I. Statues — using whistle
  A. Animals
  B. Sports
	I. Free

II. Moving creatively to different kinds of music
  A. Free movement about room
  B. Axial movements
  C. Moving different part of body and different number of parts (problem solving approach)
	II. Free

III. Growing like trees
  A. Water, sun, soil
  B. Roots
  C. Limbs and leaves
  D. Wind — light and strong
	III. Free

Area: Large Open Area

Equipment: Record Player, and assorted records
Safety: Remind children of rules if necessary.
Evaluation: (To be filled out after the lesson)

2nd Grade

10:00 — 10:30

25 Children

Goal: To develop manipulative ability and non-dominant side.

Objective: Following individual instruction and practice, at least 80 percent of the class will be able to throw and catch a beanbag at least four times in a row with the nonpreferred hand and will be able to catch two beanbags at one time, one in each hand, at least two out of four times.

Activities: Formation:

I. Moving freely in a confined space   I. Free
   to the beat of a tom-tom
   A. Different directions
   B. Different levels
   C. Different speeds
   D. Different force

II. Manipulative Activities using Beanbags   II. Alone, one beanbag per child

   A. Problem solving approach
   B. Exploring ways to throw and catch
      1. How many ways can you throw and catch one beanbag?
      2. Can you get low and still catch?
      3. Can you move and catch?
      4. Can you throw and catch with a partner?
      5. How many ways can you throw and catch the beanbag?
      6. Can you throw and catch two beanbags with your partner?   II. 6. Partners, and 2 bean bags
      7. Can you throw and catch a beanbag in each hand at the same time?

III. Progressive Tag — using sponge rubber balls (7" diameter)   III. Free

   Special Rule — Must throw with the nondominant hand.

   Area: Large open space

   Equipment: Beanbags, sponge balls, and a tom-tom

   Safety: No hard throwing of beanbags

   Evaluation: (To be filled out after the lesson)

5th Grade

30 minutes

27 Children

Goal: To develop volleyball skills

Objectives: By the end of the class the children will be able to bump and set a volleyball to a partner 5 consecutive times using the technique discussed in class.

Activity: Formation:

   I. Problem Solving Exercises   I. Free
      A. What are some exercises for developing flexibility? Show me!
      B. What are ones for developing strength?

  II. Volleyball Skills   II. One ball per person
      A. Bump ball to self — Guided Discovery
        1. Explore ways to keep the ball in the air without catching it.
        2. How does one hand only work?
        3. How about two hands?
        4. I am looking for the person who can keep it up best.
        5. Watch Sue.
        6. What is she doing?
        7. Can you do it like her?
      B. Bumping with a partner.

      Practice

 III. Bumping Game   III. 2 games — 6 or 7 on a side
      A. Bump over the net even if it bounces — can only use bump
      B. Four balls at once
      C. Points are scored when ball cannot be returned or is returned out of bounds
      D. Games goes continuously until all balls stop and then it begins again with all balls in play.

Area: Gym or Outside

Equipment: Volleyballs and Nets

Safety: No hitting the balls with one hand during game.
Keep space between each other during phase II.

78 *Curriculum Design*

STUDENT ACTIVITIES

1. Using a piece of paper, cover question 2 until you have answered question 1. You can then immediately check your answer. Continue to use the paper to cover subsequent questions as you progress through the test.

A Programmed Test on Writing Behavioral Objects

1. A BEHAVIORAL objective describes: (choose one)

    a. What the instructor does in teaching the student.
    b. What the student does to learn something.
    c. What behavior the student exhibits as a result of the learning experience.

    Answer___

2. The correct answer is c. Behavioral objectives describe behavior. Label each of the following objectives as behavioral (B) or non-behavioral (N).

    a. Teach the student to do a forward roll.
    b. Learn to write behavioral objectives.
    c. Write objectives in behavioral form.
    d. Differentiate between behavioral and non-behavioral objectives.

    Answer___

3. "a" is non-behavioral since it focuses on what the teacher is doing — not student behavior. "b" moves the focus to the student, but describes the learning experience — not the outcome. "c" and "d" describe outcomes — things the student can do as a result of the learning experience — so they are behavioral.

4. Behavioral objectives are like blueprints for instruction. A builder's blueprint specifies:

    a. The shape and dimensions for the final structure.
    b. Procedures required to build the structure.

    Answer___

5. The first answer is correct. The blueprint is similar to the curriculum.

6. Curriculum design begins with:

    a. The student's prior knowledge.
    b. The entering behavior of the student.
    c. The instructor's experience of what a student knows at this grade level.

    Answer___

7. "a" and "b" mean the same thing, and are correct. "c" is subject to error, however qualified the instructor. The entering behavior is best determined by:

    a. Pretest.
    b. Personal knowledge of the student.
    c. The student's performance on standardized tests.
    d. The student's performance record from previous classes.

    Answer___

8. Since we want specific information, the pretest is best, but obviously all sources of information are helpful. Incidentally, should:

    a. The pretest be administered separately, or
    b. It be incorporated into the learning experience?

    Answer___

Curriculum Design 79

9. Either is appropriate, and can be left to the discretion of the teacher.

10. Let's write a behavioral objective. You are shooting an arrow at the target. Your object is to_____the bull's-eye. Check your answer. Are you describing what the teacher does? Or how you learn? Or the outcome?

11. Hit the bull's-eye or (some similar action word) specifies the objective. The action or performance must be observable and measurable. Check objectives in the following list which meet the criterion.

    a. Understand physiology.
    b. Know about rhythmics.
    c. Compute federal tax using form 1040.
    d. Like gymnastics.

    Answer___

12. All, except "c," are too vague to be "Observable and measurable." Objectives such as "a" would be improved by a more specific action like "interpret or communicate." Change the action word in the following to something more specific:

    a. Know basketball rules._____
    b. Understand zone defense._____
    c. Like sports stories._____
    d. Appreciate gymnastics (limit yourself to one minute on this one!). _____

13. Perhaps many action words suggest themselves. We could write or recognize basketball rules; construct or play zone defense; read or write sports stories. The fourth objective needs to be broken down into many specific behaviors. A specific action or performance is a good start. In some objectives, the thing acted upon is also vague. To know about birds raises many questions. How do birds fly? What species? Bird migration? Behavioral objectives must be SPECIFIC, and we may need to write a number of objectives to specify the outcome. Rewrite the objective "draw pictures" to make it more specific.

14. Be your own judge on this last one. You may have said "draw boxes" or "sketch trees." Sometimes specification assumes 100 percent performance.
    For example:

    a. (Safely) land an airplane, or
    b. (Correctly) add whole numbers less than ten.

    In other instances, we should specify level or performance, such as:

    c. Spell 100 words with not more than five errors, or
    d. Run 100 meters in less than 15 seconds.

    Add a "level of performance" specification to the following:

    e. Throw a ball_____
    f. Translate five sentences into sign language _____

15. "Level of performance" tells us how well the student will perform. It might include time, distance, direction, quantity, number and kind of errors, and so on. So far we have described:

    a. Outcome (what does the student do).
    b. Level of performance (how well), to what we must add:
    c. Conditions (under which performance is demonstrated).

    Underline the phrase describing the conditions for each of the following behavioral objectives.
    For example:

    Run 100 meters in less than 20 seconds, <u>carrying a ten pound sack of flour.</u>

80   Curriculum Design

   a. Using a junior basketball and an eight foot basket, the student will make 3 out of 5 baskets from less than 15 feet.
   b. Run a cross country course in 15 minutes or less.
   c. Answer at least 15 out of 20 questions on a test of basketball rules without using a book.

   O.K., see if our answers agree:

   a. <u>Using a junior basketball and an eight foot basket.</u>
   b. <u>a cross-country course</u>
   c. <u>without using a book</u>

16. For each of the following objectives, identify:

    1. Outcome
    2. Level of performance.
    3. Conditions under which performance is demonstrated.

       a. ( ) Using the task force approach
          ( ) To identify five major problems
          ( ) In the area of curriculum
       b. ( ) To increase cost/effectiveness
          ( ) By a factor of two
          ( ) Utilizing educational technology
       c. ( ) In thirty minutes or less
          ( ) Analyze (and express) the causes
          ( ) In outline form

   Now check your answers:

       a. 3 - 1 - 2
       b. 1 - 2 - 3
       c. 3 - 1 - 2

17. Arrange the following learning behaviors as a learning hierarchy starting with 1 for the most general behavior:

    ( ) Solve chemical equations
    ( ) Write the names of chemical compounds in symbol form
    ( ) Analyze an unknown chemical compound containing only group 1 metals

    Answer: 2,1,3. While analysis is the most complex of the three behaviors, it represents a higher level on the learning hierarchy (taxonomy). Let's try another:

    ( ) To devise solutions to learning problems resulting from low motivation and disadvantaged background.
    ( ) To analyze social causes of student militancy
    ( ) To define "the disadvantaged student."

                HINT: *Devise* means *synthesize*

18. Answer: 3,2,1. Synthesis is the most complex learning outcome, and occurs higher in the taxonomy than analysis, which is more complex behavior than reciting or writing a definition.

2. Write one physical education behavioral objective for each of the three educational domains (the objective cannot appear in this book).

Psychomotor:

Affective:

Cognitive:

3. Design a physical education learning center for upper elementary children which will help them to learn one of the psychomotor activities listed on the *Section Outline* in Chapter 10. Use the miniature format included in this chapter.

CHAPTER 6
PHYSICAL FITNESS

After completing this chapter, the student will be able to:
1. List and describe each of the physiological and motor fitness components discussed in the chapter.
2. Describe ways that each fitness component can be evaluated.
3. Describe ways that each fitness component can be developed.
4. Describe some of the after-effects of maximum effort testing.
5. Describe an efficient means by which postural data can be obtained.
6. Describe the team approach to good postural development.
7. Describe ways good posture can be developed in children.

What does a teacher usually want to know about a child who walks into his or her room at the beginning of the year? How intelligent is the child? Is he or she a behavior problem? Such concerns are important, and to be successful, a teacher must know the answers to such questions. The unasked questions regarding the child's physical growth and development, however, are just as important. Is the child growing and developing normally? Is he or she overweight? What about his or her cardiovascular efficiency? Is the child physically fit? The answers to these questions should be vigorously sought. The "whole child" or "total personality" approach to education seems to have lost favor in the educational community, due perhaps to "the return to basics" movement.

With the gradual reduction of academic proficiency among high school graduates, a new emphasis is being placed on reading and math achievement. Educators' concern over minimal academic proficiency is legitimate. What has been overlooked is the data regarding the steady physical fitness decline. These declining fitness scores are dramatic evidence of the need to rethink educational priorities (10).

No one specific factor seems to be responsible for this decline, but rather a combination of factors, including: (1) a changing life-style dominated by the automobile and television; (2) a reduction of fitness emphasis during the 1960s as a result of preoccupation with space travel and the sciences; (3) physical education specialists who have been concerned primarily with gifted athletes; and (4) a lack of federal and state government commitment to physical education.

What we are left with is a standard which rates the overweight, poorly-skilled, and unfit individual as the norm. Children, especially babies, are sometimes thought to be unhealthy if they do not possess abundant adipose (fat) tissue. On the other hand, people on weight-reducing exercise programs are often considered ill when they finally reach a good proportion of body fat.

Given these declining fitness levels, what does the future hold? We are currently experiencing what has been termed a heart attack epidemic and heart disease is the leading killer among adults. Although the death rate among males is considerably higher than among females, the gap is narrowing due, it is theorized, to the changing life-styles of women. Many persons discount the significance of heart disease, citing increased longevity as evidence of improved fitness. Unfortunately, longevity says little about the quality of life.

Fitness contributes to this quality of life, and programs should begin early if they are to be of real value. Since it is in childhood that the problem begins, cardiologists generally agree that the next major breakthrough in the understanding of heart disease will be found in children. Many people advocate vigorous fitness programs for elementary children which emphasize cardiovascular efficiency activities as part of an overall physiological improvement program. These early involvement programs, it is hoped, will improve fitness levels as well as establish good fitness habits and attitudes.

The term "physical fitness" is difficult to define. In fact, there are as many definitions of physical fitness as there are fitness programs.

One point of consensus, however, is that physical fitness is a multidimensional quality. For instance, individuals with big muscles are not necessarily physically fit. Strength is but one of several physical fitness components. For purposes of this text, an individual is considered physically fit when he or she has obtained a miminal degree of efficiency in each of the critical areas of physiological fitness. The specific components of both physiological and motor fitness will be discussed later in the chapter.

Children and Exercise

The benefits of exercise have long been known. Improved bone and muscle growth, more efficient use of the body, cardiovascular improvement, a feeling of well-being, better acceptance by the peer group, improved looks, and a generally healthier body are all by-products of a well-planned physical fitness program. Exercise should begin as early in life as possible. Very young children can and should participate in vigorous play activities involving large muscle movement. Such exercise will result in a number of positive gains.

Growth

Growth is facilitated by exercise and retarded by sedentary life-styles. Vigorous exercise by children has caused no ill effects, although trauma such as that associated with contact sports may affect bone growth. Although exercise will not have a marked influence on the genetically determined body size and somatotype (body proportions), it is necessary to reach the optimum level determined by heredity. As changing life-styles reduce an individual's exercise, the need for planned exercise programs increases. Children no longer must do field work, walk to school, or do vigorous daily chores. Current life-styles include riding everywhere, hours of television, and electronic gadgetry to ease life's "burdens." Lacking these natural exercise requirements, artificial programs such as jogging and calisthenics must become a daily part of one's life if optimum growth and development are to occur.

Strength

Muscles will grow if exercised and weaken if a sedentary life-style is pursued. Although large bulging muscles are not necessary for daily functioning, a minimal strength level is required to earn a living, to perform household chores, to respond in emergencies, and to perform motor tasks. It is well known that active children make strength gains as they grow.

Body Fat

Fat reduction through exercise has been found by a number of researchers. Although exercise alone is insufficient as a primary means of weight loss, it is a significant dietary complement. The combination of these two programs, exercise and diet control, is considered the most efficient fat reduction approach.

Bone Growth

Most forms of exercise have a positive effect on bone growth. Vigorous exercise even for young children is beneficial.

Cardiovascular Efficiency

Appropriate endurance exercises at any age will significantly increase cardiovascular efficiency. These gains are most dramatic at the elementary level when children participate in vigorous fitness programs. The long-term effects of these endurance programs on heart disease are unknown since no longitudinal studies have been conducted.

FITNESS CLASSIFICATION

As previously mentioned, there are two major classifications of physical fitness components, physiological and motor. The physiological components are those most important to an individual's health and well-being, while motor fitness components are essential to movement and sports activities. The various physiological and motor fitness components are presented in Figure 6.1.

Figure 6-1. Components of Fitness	
Physiological	**Motor**
Cardiovascular Efficiency	Speed
Flexibility	Power
Muscular Strength	Agility
Muscular Endurance	Balance
Body Composition	Coordination
	Reaction Time

Physiological Fitness
Cardiovascular Efficiency

Cardiovascular efficiency is the single most important fitness factor for all ages. This physiological fitness component is a specialized form of muscular endurance involving the heart, lungs, and blood vessels. Reasons for developing and maintaining an efficient cardiovascular system are:

1. The ability to resist fatigue is directly related to the system's ability to supply oxygen and remove waste products.
2. Developing cardiovascular endurance

tends to lower resting heart rate which allows the heart more rest. While average heart rates range from 72-80 beats per minute, it is not uncommon for conditioned individuals to possess resting heart rates as low as 40-45 beats per minute.
3. Many researchers believe cardiovascular training keeps the body's blood vessels free of fatty buildup which could eventually block the flow of blood to the heart.

Evaluating Cardiovascular Efficiency. Field tests utilized to measure cardiovascular efficiency in children generally take one of two forms. One form is a timed run for distance. The object of this test is to determine how far a child can run in a specified amount of time. Commonly employed times are six minutes, nine minutes, and twelve minutes. The decision as to which time to use is determined largely by the facilities available, time limitations, and the age of the children to be tested.

The other technique of measuring cardiovascular efficiency is a distance run for time. Here the object is to run a specified distance in the least amount of time. Commonly employed distances are one mile and one and a half miles. (Norms of performance for the VCU Fitness tests can be found in Appendix A.)

Effects of Cardiovascular Testing. There are some possible negative after-effects which can occur following fitness assessments. While a few individuals may exhibit some of these symptoms following flexibility and/or strength assessments, these uncomfortable feelings are more frequently manifested following cardiovascular evaluations.

1. Discomfort: Any prolonged stress will cause discomfort. If the child is aware of the changes which will take place, there will be less anxiety. Running or other cardiovascular activities seem to cause the most discomfort among children, and it is difficult, therefore, to motivate young children to maximum efforts. At first sign of pain, children (usually six to eight years of age) will tend to cease activity or significantly curtail efforts. Extrinsic motivators as well as stressing the test's importance do help.
2. Nausea: Highly motivated children may experience nausea following maximal tests, particularly running tests. This is not unusual, but can be diminished by having children cool down (continue moving) after the test, and by avoiding testing immediately after eating. Morning resting is better than afternoon.
3. Muscle Soreness: Children will often experience short-term muscle soreness after a distance run test. The poorly-conditioned child, however, may have soreness for a day following the test. A preconditioning program of three to four weeks will greatly diminish the incidence of this residual pain.
4. Headache, Dizziness, and Fainting: Some poorly-conditioned children who are highly motivated may experience headaches or dizziness, and some may faint, although this is unusual. First aid should be administered.
5. Injury: Muscle pulls and strains are not uncommon. Proper warm-up and preconditioning should precede testing.
6. Loss of Sleep: Interrupted sleep the night after a test is common and should not be a cause for concern.

The residual pain experienced by some children following maximum effort testing (distance running) can be upsetting to both parents and students. Parents have spent hours as well as money in emergency rooms fearing their child had some serious ailment only to learn that the pain was a result of running too far the day before. The teacher's understanding of the points just presented could have helped avoid this problem.

Developing Cardiovascular Efficiency. To develop cardiovascular efficiency, one must employ the training principle of overload, which is working the system at a higher level than it is used to. The overload placed on the system can be varied by manipulating the intensity of the workload, the amount of time spent in exercising (duration) and the number of days per week the exercise routine is conducted (frenquency).

The key to determining the amount of overload (intensity) placed on the cardiovascular system is heart rate. Since there appears to be a direct relationship between heartrate and workload, intensity of exercise can be self-monitored by taking periodic heart rate counts during the exercise period. Children as young as first grade can be taught to determine their heart rate. The rate is best determined at the carotid artery in the neck area, but may also be felt at the brachial artery at the wrist.

During any given exercise period the goal is to elevate the heart rate to a specific level and maintain this target heart rate for a predetermined amount of time, usually 15-30 minutes (duration). The intensity of the workout can be

86 Fitness

TARGET HEART RATES

Age	Max. HR	Intensity					
		60%	65%	70%	75%	80%	85%
5	215	129	140	150	161	172	183
6	214	128	139	150	161	171	182
7	213	127	138	149	160	170	181
8	212	127	138	148	159	170	180
9	211	126	137	148	158	169	179
10	210	126	136	147	158	168	178
11	209	125	136	146	157	167	178
12	208	124	135	146	156	166	177

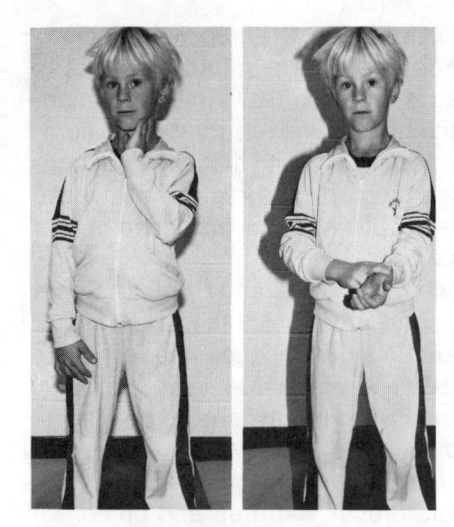

Taking pulse: left, at carotid artery; right, at brachial artery

Figure 6-2. Target Heart Rates

expressed as a percentage of maximum heart rate. Most individuals should start their program at a 60 percent intensity level. To obtain a training effect, it is important to increase the intensity of the program by 5 percent per week until one reaches 75 percent intensity (overload principle). To determine maximum heart rate, use the formula below. Let an example serve to illustrate the point: Mary, a 10-year-old female, wants to start a cardiovascular training program for the first time. What would be Mary's target heart rate?

.6 [(220-Age) − Resting Heart Rate] + Resting Heart Rate
.6 (220-10) − 75 + 75
.6 (135) + 75
= 156 Target Heart Rate

Thus, Mary should perform some physical activity that would elevate her heart rate to 156 beats per minute and maintain this intensity for 15-30 minutes. Since Mary has not exercised in a long time, she should initially start her program for a duration of 15 minutes. This duration should be gradually increased (5% per week) until Mary is capable of maintaining her target heart rate for 30 minutes, four times per week.

Selected Cardiovascular Development Activites. There are a number of ways to develop the cardiovascular system. *Remember any activity which will elevate to, and maintain one's target heart rate for a minimal period of 15-30 minutes is an accepted activity.*

Walking and/or running is one of the cheapest but yet most effective means of developing the cardiovascular system. While it is not the purpose of this text to present a detailed description of correct running technique, a few precautions concerning running are warranted:
1. Exercise routines should be conducted on soft surfaces such as grass or a cushioned track. Running on pavement is to be avoided.
2. It is important to purchase a good pair of running shoes. These special shoes are designed to absorb much of the impact that otherwise would be transferred to ankles, knees and hips.
3. Prior to jogging, take the time to walk the course to inspect for large rocks or potholes which may cause twisted ankles.

Fartlek training (speed play) is an exercise method which was first made popular by the Swedish. Moving at various speeds (walk, run, jog, sprint) on different surfaces (grass, soil, etc.) characterized this training method. This "play on speed" tends to excite most elementary school children. A portion of a Fartlek routine would go something like this:

Jog for 2 minutes
Run for 15 seconds
Jog for 30 seconds
Sprint for 5 seconds
Walk for 30 seconds
Jog for 1 minute
Jog backwards for 20 seconds
Run backwards for 15 seconds
Turn and sprint for 10 seconds
Walk for 30 seconds

Fitness 87

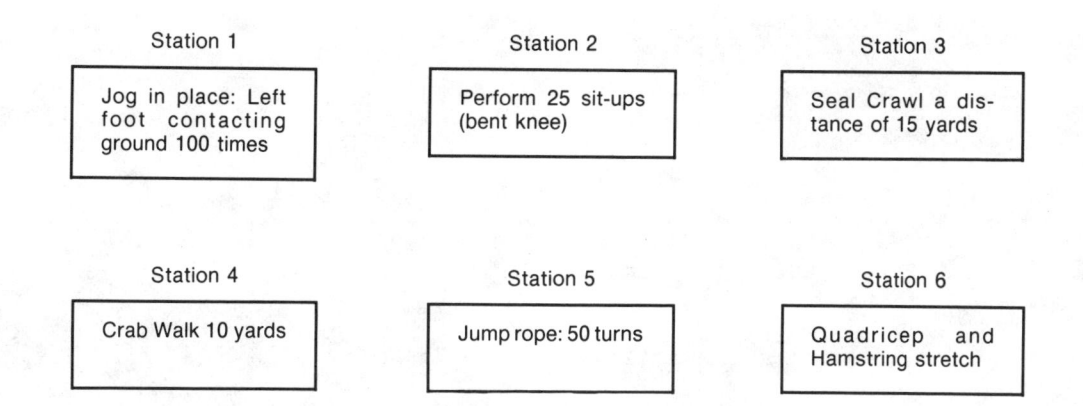

Station 1	Station 2	Station 3
Jog in place: Left foot contacting ground 100 times	Perform 25 sit-ups (bent knee)	Seal Crawl a distance of 15 yards

Station 4	Station 5	Station 6
Crab Walk 10 yards	Jump rope: 50 turns	Quadricep and Hamstring stretch

Figure 6-3. Sample Circuit Training Course

Children will enjoy composing their own routines.

Circuit training requires the children to perform individual tasks at stations which are placed throughout the playground. The idea is to complete an assigned exercise at a given station, then quickly move on to another station. Progression can be determined by recording the number of stations completed in a given time period, usually 15-30 minutes. While participating in the circuit, heart rate checks are encouraged to determine the intensity of the workout. A sample playground circuit is presented in Figure 6-3.

Aerobic Dance is quickly becoming a popular form of cardiovascular training. Essentially, the activity requires children to perform various motor tasks (running, jumping, hopping, leaping, turning, etc.) to musical accompaniments. Music in 4/4 time (School fight songs, Star Wars, etc.) is an excellent accompaniment. While commercial records are available, children are urged to develop their own routines. A sample routine appears in Figure 6-4.

Myths Associated with Cardiovascular Development

Myth: Young children who perform strenuous exercises will develop a dangerous condition known as "Athletic Heart" (an enlarged heart).

Fact: It is true that strenuous exercise will cause the heart to enlarge. The heart muscle, like skeletal muscle will grow bigger and stronger when overloaded. The misconception of exercise and an unhealthy heart is a result of doctors detecting that some individuals with large hearts are not healthy. It was later discovered, however, that this enlargement was caused by a diseased heart muscle. Enlargement of a healthy heart is a desired by-product of cardiovascular training.

Myth: Females should not participate in jogging programs because the pounding of the body can jar and damage the reproductive organs.

Fact: It was once believed that jogging could jar and damage the uterus. Recent evidence indicates, however, that this organ, suspended in a fluid environment, cannot be damaged by jogging.

Figure 6.4. Sample Aerobic Dance Routine

#1: 16 beats
Slide 4 steps to the right
Jump forward, jump in place, jump back, jump in place
Slide 4 steps to the left
Jump forward, jump in place, jump back, jump in place

#2: 16 beats
Scissor jump with right foot forward
Scissor jump with left foot forward
Jumping jacks — do 2

#3: 16 beats
Skip forward — 4 skips
Jog back — 8 steps

#4: 16 beats
Hopscotch — 4 times
Hop on right foot — 4 times
Hop on left foot — 4 times

#5: 16 beats
Rocking horse kick — 4 times
(Rocking horse kick: Rock forward on right foot, rock back on left, rock forward on right foot, kick left foot forward. This is one "rocking-horse kick." The next rocking horse kick starts rock forward on left foot, back on right foot, forward on left foot, kick right foot forward.)

88   Fitness

Developing flexibility

Myth: Females should not participate in vigorous physical activity during menstruation.

Fact: No evidence exists which suggest that physical activity is harmful during menstruation. In fact, for some, menstrual cramps have been relieved following bouts of exercise.

Flexibility

Flexibility refers to the range of motion in a joint such as the shoulders and hips. The degree of flexibility you will be able to attain in a given joint is determined by the nature of the joint (bone structure) and the condition of the ligaments and muscles which surround the joint. Although the bony structure cannot be changed, the range can be increased through exercises which stretch the muscle fibers.

While flexibility has not been a major problem in normal children, it is fast becoming one. It is important, therefore, to stress this often neglected component of physiological fitness. It appears that flexibility is important for the following reasons:

1. Strenuous demands are placed on the body when executing selected motor tasks. Being limber tends, therefore, to be one means of preventing muscle injury.
2. In order to exhibit "correct form" in movement tasks, flexibility is a must. Many believe the lack of flexibility is a major contributor to poor performance. For instance, a lack of shoulder flexibility can hinder one's throwing performance if joint stiffness will not permit an acceptable backswing of the arm.
3. Flexible individuals are able to conserve energy since their limberness allows them to perform muscular movements with minimal resistance to both tissue and joint.

Evaluating Flexibility. Flexibility is joint specific; flexibility in one or two joints is not a good indicator of total body flexibility. For example, many individuals who possess a limber upper body may have a stiff lower body. The first step in a flexibility program is to determine which major body regions need work. Figure 6-5 depicts the major regions which should be subjected to flexibility evaluation. Listed below are simple activities which can be utilized to evaluate the degree of flexibility in each of the major body regions.

A. Shoulders
B. Lower Back
C. Hamstring Muscles: Muscles of the back portion of upper leg.
D. Quadricep Muscles: Muscles of the front portion of upper leg.
E. Calf Muscle: Muscles of the back portion of lower leg.

Figure 6-5. Major body regions to be stressed in a well-rounded program of flexibility.

A. Shoulders: Have child lie face down on a mat with chin touching mat and arms reaching forward. While keeping the elbows and wrist straight and chin in contact with the mat, have child attempt to raise palms of hands as high off the mat as possible. Utilizing a yard stick, measure the distance between the mat and palms.
B. Lower Back: Child should be seated with knees slightly bent. Child attempts to touch nose to knee. If child cannot accomplish this task, a simple yard stick can be utilized to measure the distance between the child's chest and his knees.
C. Quadriceps: Have child lie on the stomach and bring heels toward buttock. The angle formed between the upper and lower leg should be approximately 130 degrees or, roughly speaking, the heel should be about 1-2 inches from the buttock.
D. Hamstrings: Have the child lie on the back. While keeping the knees straight, have the child attempt to raise each leg, one at a time, keeping the other leg straight, and attempt to have the child's heel point straight at the ceiling (i.e, 90 degrees).
E. Calf Muscle: Child should be seated on floor with knees extended and locked. Child attempts to move the foot toward the shins until a 20 degree angle is achieved.

Test batteries such as the VCU Fitness Test also contain flexibility evaluation procedures (see Appendix A).

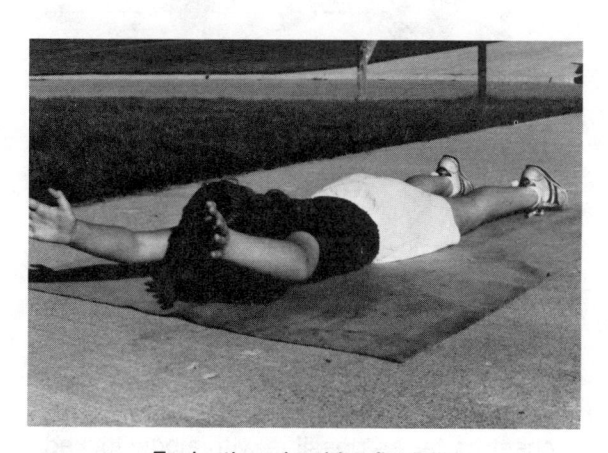

Evaluating shoulder flexibility

Evaluating quadriceps flexibility

Evaluating hamstring flexibility

Evaluating lower back flexibility

90 Fitness

Developing Flexibility. There are basically two types of flexibility development techniques, dynamic and static. While both are usually safe for children who are already fairly flexible, the static technique tends to produce less muscle soreness and is, therefore, recommended. The following are characteristics of these two techniques:

Dynamic. The common and possibly harmful flexibility development method is quick repetitions of the exercise, such as bouncing down to touch the toes. Those with poor flexibility, and particularly adults, may find the dynamic approach harmful to muscles. Rapid muscle stretching, which is common in dynamic flexibility exercises, can cause the activation of stretch receptors in the muscle. These receptors can trigger a reflex muscular contraction which, under the stretching condition, may cause injury.

Static. Unlike the forced bouncing movements of the dynamic method, the static method requires gradual easing into the stretch until a burning sensation (not pain) is felt in the exercised muscle. This position should be held from 30-60 seconds. During this period the burning sensation will ease thus allowing farther stretching.

Flexibility Exercises. The key to becoming flexible is persistence and patience. By faithfully performing the following exercises, flexibility will increase within 4-6 weeks. When time permits, best results are obtained when these exercises are performed twice daily.

Shoulder Stretch:

a. While standing, rotate shoulders backwards attempting to touch both shoulder blades (scapulae) together. Repeat 10 times.

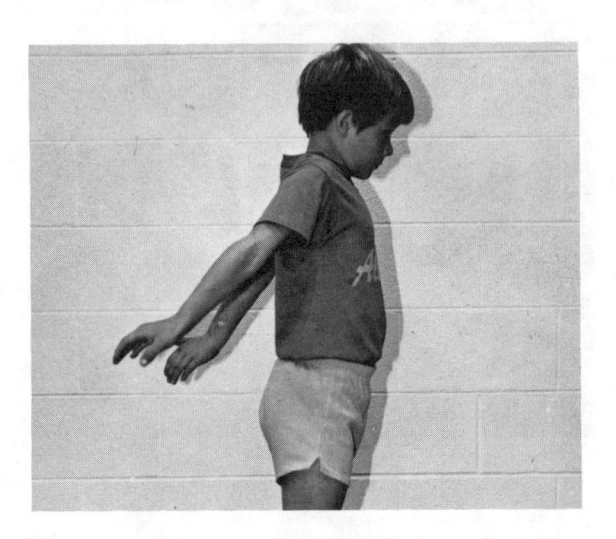

Extreme flexibility

b. While standing with arms extended from the side, rotate arms in large circles, decreasing to smaller ones for 30 seconds. Repeat 10 times.

c. While standing, bring arm across upper chest as far as possible with elbow locked. Use the other arm to assist in the stretch. Work both arms, one at a time. Repeat 10 times for each arm.

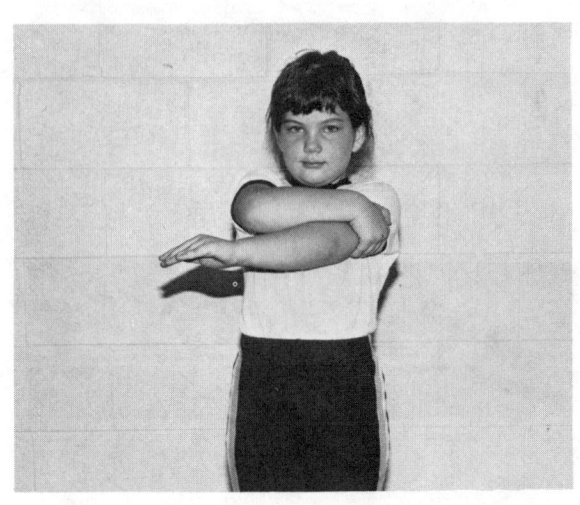

d. While standing, bend elbows and attempt to reach as high as possible behind the back. Alternate arms and repeat 10 times.

Lower Back Stretch:

a. While lying on back, raise right knee to chest, pull and hold. Opposite leg is kept straight. Alternate legs and repeat 5 times.

b. While lying on back with knees bent, press lower back forcefully downward, tilting pelvis. The object is to flatten the lower back area against the floor. Repeat 20 times holding each trial for six seconds.

Quadriceps Stretch:

a. Lie on stomach and bend knees. Reach back and grasp ankles and pull toward buttocks. Repeat 10 times.

b. While seated on floor with knees bent, grab right ankle with left hand and slowly pull right leg up towards head. Repeat 5 times with each leg.

Hamstring Stretch:

a. While standing, bend at knees and grab toes. Slowly extend knees until a locked position is achieved. Repeat 10 times.

92 Fitness

b. While sitting with legs extended and locked and toes pointing up, attempt to put nose first to right knee, then to left knee. Each stretch should be done slowly with locked knee position maintained at all times. Repeat 5 times.

Calf Stretch:

a. Stand approximately 1½ feet from a wall. Lean forward attempting to touch chest to wall while keeping the knees and back straight, and heels flat on the floor. As flexibility is gained you gradually start by standing farther from the wall. Repeat 15 times.

b. Attempt to walk on heels while trying to point toes toward ceiling. Remember, keep the knees locked and straight while attempting the heel walk. Walk 15 yards.

Muscular Strength

The amount of force which can be exerted by a muscle or muscle group for a brief period of time is referred to as muscular strength. Selected reasons outlining the importants of developing and maintaining muscular strength are presented below:

1. Physical educators agree that a minimal level of muscular strength and endurance is needed to perform all motor skills.
2. A strong muscle is able to absorb shock and is, therefore, capable of resisting injury.
3. Deficiencies in back and abdominal strength are a leading cause of poor posture and lower back pain.
4. Individuals possessing high degrees of strength are capable of performing motor tasks with greater ease and efficiency than weaker individuals.

Muscular Endurance

The ability to hold or perform repeated trials of a muscular contraction, which is an indication of the muscle's ability to perform work for an extended period of time, is referred to as muscular endurance.

Reasons for developing and maintaining muscular endurance follow:

1. Most sports activities require many repetitions of the same movements. For instance, in a tennis match one may hit as many as several thousand forehand groundstrokes. Muscular endurance is needed to accomplish this feat.
2. A muscle which is easily fatigued is more likely to sustain injury.

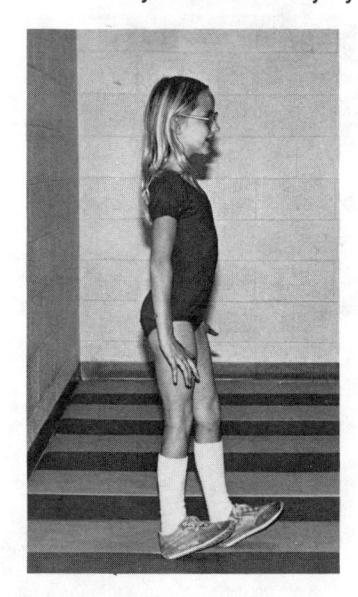

Evaluating Muscular Strength and Endurance. The shoulder girdle and abdominals (stomach) are the body regions most often subjected to muscular strength and endurance evaluation during the elementary school years. Refer to the appendix for strength norms established by the VCU Fitness Test. Other evaluative techniques follow:

Abdominal Strength and Endurance. The most frequently utilized activity to measure abdominal strength and endurance is the bent-knee sit-up. The child being tested lies on his/her back with knees bent so heels are six to eight inches from the buttocks. With arms folded across the chest, child attempts to sit up so arms contact the upper thigh. Criterion norms of performance vary according to the source of validation.

Shoulder Girdle Strength and Endurance. The likelihood of detecting deficiencies in shoulder girdle strength and endurance are great, for research suggests that American children are among the weakest in the world in this area of physical fitness. Schurr (16) recommends a timed Seal Crawl walk to evaluate this fitness component in children in grades one to three. This activity requires the child to assume a push-up position. On the signal "Go" the child walks on hands while dragging feet for a distance of 20 feet. For girls greater than 9 years of age, the flexed arm hang has been commonly employed to measure upper body strength and endurance. Only recently have norms been established for both boys and girls between six and nine years of age. Procedures for administering this test and accompanying norms can be found in Appendix A.

Techniques for Developing Muscular Strength and Endurance. There are basically two types of exercise techniques which can be utilized to promote increases in muscular strength and endurance. The first, isotonic, requires the performer to place resistance against a moving muscle. The most frequently employed isotonic activities are lifting weights and calisthenics. While weight training is an effective method for improving muscular strength and endurance, the major disadvantages lie in the cost of equipment and of danger, both in terms of muscle injury as well as having weights fall on children. High resistance exercises (very heavy weights) are not recommended for the developing child. Calisthenics, however, are highly recommended and will be discussed later.

The other strength training technique is isometrics. Isometric means the length of the exercised muscle will remain the same throughout the contracting phase (*Iso* the same; *metric* length). To perform an isometric contraction, the child attempts to push, pull or lift an immovable object, exerting as much muscular tension as possible and holding it for a period of 5-8 seconds. To avoid muscle injury, tension should be gradually increased up to 3-4 seconds before attempting a maximum effect. A word of caution, *breathholding is to be avoided.* The advantage of the isometric method is that it does not require a lot of space and equipment. Children can, for instance, perform these exercises while sitting at their desks. The major drawback associated with isometrics is that since the exercising muscle does not change in length, isometrics will only strengthen the muscle at one point. To insure strength improvement through a whole range of motion, each excercise should be performed at 5-8 different angles.

General Principles of Muscular Strength and Endurance Development

The following are principles of strength development.

1. Overload Principle: Placing the muscle or muscle group under a workload greater than what it is normally accustomed to will increase muscular strength.

2. Principle of Progressive Resistance: Gradually increase the resistance applied to the exercised muscle. Too much too soon can cause injuries.

3. Principle of Specificity: Exercise tends to be task specific. For instance, if one trains for maximum muscular strength, significant gains in muscular endurance will not be accomplished. Muscular endurance is best acquired by performing many repetitions with a reduced amount of resistance, while the reverse holds true if the development of muscular strength is the goal.

Following these principles of strength development will increase muscular strength and endurance as well as muscle size (hypertrophy). Once training stops there will be a decrease in muscular strength accompanied by a decrease in muscle size (atrophy).

Selected Muscular Strength and Endurance Activities. The calisthenics and playground activities presented below utilize the isotonic technique for developing muscular strength and endurance. Selected isometric activities are also described.

94   Fitness

Calisthenics are essentially isotonic exercise which are a way to develop strength and muscular endurance. Almost any calisthenic can be modified to increase or decrease the degree of difficulty. As a general rule, once a child can repeat a given exercise twenty times without a rest, he or she should move on to a more difficult exercise for the muscle group in question. Before moving on, however, the child should be able to do the twenty repetitions correctly. Exercises performed incorrectly are of questionable value. These same calisthenics, when repeated many times, are valuable for developing muscular endurance. Anytime a muscular activity is repeated while in an overload situation, endurance will be enhanced. Low resistance exercises repeated many times will have an effect on muscular endurance.

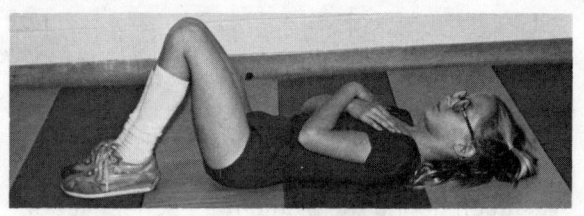

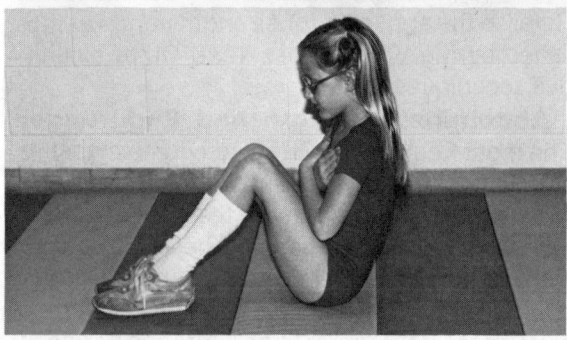

Developing abdominal stretch utilizing the bent sit-up

Calisthenics

Purpose: Abdominal Strength
Equipment: Mat
Task: Lie on back with arms resting across chest and knees bent so heels are about 4 inches from buttocks. Attempt to sit up so that shoulder blades come off the mat. Return to starting position and repeat.

Variations:
a. Place hands behind the head.
b. For children not capable of performing a sit-up, allow them to place arms straight over head and swing them forward to aid in accomplishing a sit-up.

Purpose: Arm and Shoulder Strength
Equipment: None
Task: Assume a push-up position. Slowly bend arms and attempt to touch chest to ground. Maintaining a straight back, return to starting position.

The basic — push-up

Variations:
a. To make the task easier, the push-ups can be done from the hands and knees instead of hands and feet.
b. To make the task more difficult, place hands about three inches apart.

Push-ups are easier if done from the knees.

Purpose: Arm and Shoulder Strength
Equipment: None
Task: Assume a push-up position. Allow partner to grasp ankles and hold at partner's hip level. Now walk forward on hands, being careful not to overarch back.

Push-up with partner

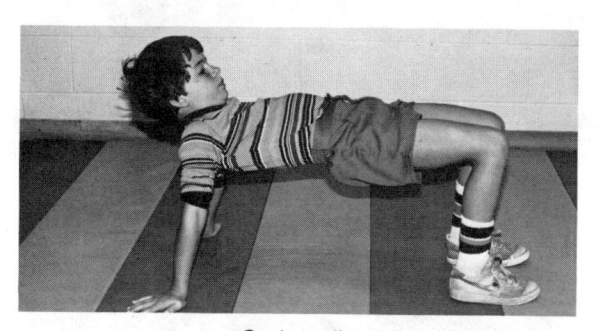

Crab walk

Seal crawl

Equipment for developing strength

Purpose: Arm and Shoulder Strength
Equipment: None
Task: While sitting, pick buttocks off ground so that weight is supported on feet and hands. Maintaining this position walk forward (Crab Walk).
Variations:
  a. Walk backwards.
  b. Walk sideways.

Purpose: Arm and Shoulder Strength
Equipment: None
Task: Assume a push-up position. Walk forward on hands while dragging feet (Seal Crawl).
Variations:
  a. To make the task more difficult, gradually spread the arms farther apart.

Purpose: Arm and Shoulder Strength
Equipment: Horizontal Bar
Task: Grasp bar with palms facing outward. With the aid of a partner, place chin above the bar. Without support, maintain this position as long as possible.
Variations:
  a. For weaker children who cannot maintain the chin above the bar position for at least 10 seconds, allow partner to provide some support.

Playground Activities

Purpose: Arm and Shoulder Strength
Equipment: Horizontal Ladder
Task: Grasp bar so that palms of hands face outward. Child attempts to reach the other end of the ladder by alternately grasping each rung.
Variations:
  a. Grasp every other rung.
  b. For young child, a simple bar hang (no traveling) can be utilized.

Purpose: Arm and Shoulder Strength
Equipment: Horizontal Bar
Task: Grasp bar with palms facing outward. Attempt to pull up until chin touches bar. Slowly return to starting position, and repeat.
Variations:
  a. Grasp bar with palms facing backwards.

Purpose: Arm, Shoulder and Leg Strength
Equipment: Vertical Pole
Task: Attempt to climb pole utilizing a hand-over-hand motion. The legs are wrapped around pole to assist in the climb.

96   Fitness

Isometrics

Purpose: Shoulder, Arm, and Leg Strength
Equipment: Jump Rope
Task: Tie rope around securely anchored pole. Attempt to pull the pole to the ground.

An isometric tug-of-war

Purpose: Shoulder, Arm, Wrist Strength
Equipment: Jump Rope
Task: Grasp both ends of the jump rope. While standing on the middle of the rope, attempt to pull yourself off the ground.

Purpose: Shoulder and Chest Strength
Equipment: None
Task: Place palms of hands together at chest level and push against one another.

Attempt to lift yourself into the air.   *Pushing palms together*

Purpose: Shoulder and Chest Strength
Equipment: Playground Ball
Task: Place palms of hands on each side of ball. Attempt to squash ball while holding ball at chest level.

Purpose: Shoulder and Leg Strength
Equipment: Wall
Task: Place palms of hands against a wall. Attempt to push the wall down.

Attempt to pop the ball.   *Can you push down the wall?*

Purpose: Abdominal Strength
Equipment: None
Task: Lie on back with legs bent and arms folded across chest. While partner holds shoulders against floor, attempt to sit up.

Developing abdominal strength with isometrics

Fitness 97

Squeeze the ball between your knees to develop leg strength.

Purpose: Leg Strength
Equipment: Playground Ball
Task: While standing, squeeze ball between knees.

Developing leg strength with partner's assistance

Purpose: Leg Strength (Hamstrings)
Equipment: None
Task: Lie on stomach with legs straight. Attempt to touch heels to buttocks while a partner supplies a downward resistance to the heels.

Strengthening the quadriceps with isometrics

Purpose: Leg Strength (Quadriceps)
Equipment: Chairs or Table
Task: Assume a sitting position. Attempt to straighten one leg at a time while a partner applies downward resistance.

Developing back strength

Purpose: Back Strength
Equipment: None
Task: From a standing position, bend at the waist and attempt to touch toes. Attempt to once again stand erect while a partner applies downward resistance to your shoulders.

98   Fitness

A single rope swing aids developing muscles.

Building strength at home

Myths Associated with Strength Development

Myth: Strength development in females is accompanied by bulging muscles.

Fact: Due to differences in sex hormones and other physiological factors between males and females, the likelihood of the average female developing bulging muscles is remote.

Myth: When one stops training for strength, the added muscle tissue accumulated during training will turn to fat.

Fact: It is important to realize that muscle and fat are two different types of tissue. As such, there is no possible way for these tissues to reverse roles.

Body Composition — Percent of Body Fat

A major health problem facing today's society is the overweight and obese individual. A high percentage of weight problems can be found in children. Obese children tend to have a very high percent of body fat, compared to their lean muscle mass. The importance of maintaining an acceptable fat-to-lean muscle mass ratio is outlined below.

1. Overweight children tend to be excluded from many social groups. This is often due to their inability to perform motor skills as efficiently as their peers.

2. When participating in physical activities, overweight children tend to be more prone to injury than children in the normal weight ranges.

3. Excess adipose tissue (fat) is a leading cause of cardiovascular disease and other illnesses. For each pound of fat, one additional mile of blood vessels is required to supply nourishment, creating a heavier circulatory burden.

Determining the Body's Fat Content. A relatively simple procedure for determining the body's fat content is the use of a special instructment called a skinfold caliper. The caliper is used to measure the amount of fat (thickness) on various body sites. The most commonly assessed body site of elementary school children is the tricep. This location tends to be the best practical predictor of percent of body fat in children.

Changing the Body's Fat Content. Successful fat reduction is dependent primarily on an individual's caloric intake. Calories are the energy source taken in as part of the diet, and are burned off by bodily function including exercise. This balance between intake and body need determines the increase or decrease in body fat. Those calories not burned off are stored as fat. This balancing of calories is pri-

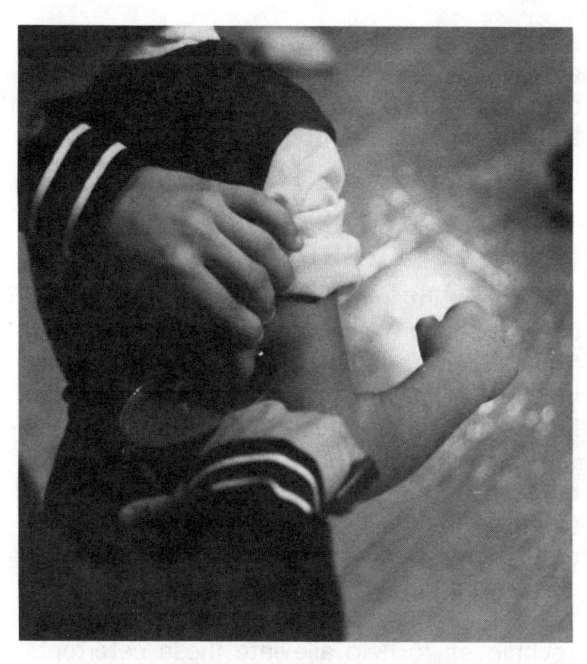

Using skinfold caliper to measure body fat

Figure 6-6. Caloric Content of Fast Foods

ARBY'S	
Junior Roast Beef	240
Super Roast Beef	750
BURGER KING	
Whopper	630
French Fries	220
McDONALD'S	
Big Mac	557
Filet-o-Fish	406
Quarter Pounder	414
PIZZA HUT	
Cheese Pizza:	
Individual	1030
One-half of 13-inch	900
BASKIN ROBBINS	
One scoop of ice cream on sugar cone:	
Chocolate Fudge	229
French Vanilla	217
DAIRY QUEEN	
Super Brazier	850
Small Malt	400
Banana Split	580

marily accomplished through diet. Dieting is a tricky business and should only be done under the guidance of a doctor. Diet books and crash diets should not be used. The recommended rate of weight loss is one to two pounds per week. Food intake during diets should include the basic food groups with an eye on a calorie chart to determine amounts. Junk foods (candy, French Fries, chips, etc.) and fast foods tend to be high in calories and fat. The caloric content of selected fast foods is presented in Figure 6-6.

Exercise is a complement to any diet program. Although it is secondary, it can make a significant contribution in the fight. Exercise for weight control has been criticized because of the amount required for reducing. It can be shown, however, that a regular exercise program over a year's time can keep as much as ten to twelve excess pounds of fat from accumulating. Over a period of years, such losses can make a significant contribution to health.

Motor Fitness Components

Power, agility, balance, coordination, reaction time, and speed are all motor fitness components. Since they play a major role in physical growth and development, a physical education program should include extensive work on these fitness components. In addition, a minimal degree of competency in these fitness components has been found to foster both social and emotional development. This is because children are more readily accepted in the peer group if they can perform well physically. Unlike academic shortcomings, physical performance cannot be hidden. Clumsy children, therefore, are easily identified by peers and frequently ostracized. The implication of such exclusion should be obvious. A major physical education goal should be the identification of and help for clumsy individuals. This is not to say that every child should be a super athlete — only an efficiently functioning human being who can achieve success through movement.

The specificity of motor development precludes a lengthy discussion of motor fitness development. This is to say, for example, that speed in basketball will have little carry-over to speed in badminton or that an individual who possesses speed of hand may not possess speed of foot. Training programs, therefore, must be specifically designed for each motor fitness component. In an early childhood physical education program, a wide variety of motor development activities should be provided as a foundation for more specific training later. An early childhood motor development program should provide extensive eye-hand coordination, speed, power, reaction time, agility and balance training.

100 Fitness

Coordination

The ability to combine two or more body parts to produce a skilled movement is termed coordination. Coordination is developed primarily through use of objects such as balls, beanbags, scoops, etc. Children should be able to explore throwing, catching, kicking, and striking a wide variety of objects.

Speed

The ability to get from one place to another quickly, such as in sprint racing is classified as speed. Although an individual's ultimate speed is determined by heredity, training can be used to realize potential. For the elementary child, running, and particularly short races requiring sprinting, will insure at least minimal speed development. The development of stronger legs and more flexible hips can also improve speed indirectly by increasing one's stride length.

Power

Power is a combination of speed and strength. An example would be the broad jump.

Reaction time

The time required to react to a stimulus and make an appropriate muscular response is known as reaction time. The teacher should provide such stimuli in a situation requiring quick student response. Yarn balls can be thrown at any speed and at any body part without fear of injury. This is just one example of how students can respond quickly.

Agility

Agility is the ability to change total body direction quickly while maintaining balance. Obstacle courses and verbal commands can be used to develop agility. The obstacle course should be designed to require frequent changes in direction. Verbal commands can be used to get children moving quickly in different directions. When doing agility-type activities, a safe surface must be used. Blacktop should never be used for agility training. Indoor areas should be cleared of all dangerous objects, and children should be kept away from walls. The best agility training area is a large grass area.

Balance

There are two types of balance: static and dynamic. Static balance would be required to do a handstand; walking a balance beam would be a dynamic balance activity. The balance development program should allow children to practice on many different types of apparatus, with eyes opened and closed.

MOTIVATING CHILDREN TO EXERCISE

To this point, information has been presented on methods of evaluating and developing each fitness component. Understanding training methods is only the first step in developing the fitness. If children refuse to participate, fitness will not be improved. One of the primary roles of the teacher, therefore, is to keep children motivated so they will not become exercise dropouts. Common deterrents to exercise tend to be discomfort during exercise performance and muscle soreness following exercise routines. Techniques to help alleviate these deterrents were presented earlier. Another major factor accounting for exercise dropouts is boredom. Children get tired of performing the same old calisthenics and exercises day after day. Just a little teacher creativity can change one's attitude toward exercise participation. The following motivational techniques have been successful:

1. **Music** played during the physical education period tends to take the children's mind off of the discomfort which is sometimes associated with selected tasks. This probably in part accounts for the recent popularity in aerobic dance.
2. **Change exercise environments;** try to avoid conducting the class in the same location every day.
3. **A fitness report card** should be sent home after each testing period. This will allow both child and parents to keep abreast of fitness changes and will hopefully create intrinsic motivation.
4. **Fitness clubs** tend to challenge children to see who can accumulate the most miles run in a given time period. Many schools even award T-shirts to individuals denoting their accomplishments such as "25-mile club," "50-mile club," etc.
5. **"Running for life"** is a special fitness program which has proven successful as a motivator for exercise participation. Refer to Appendix A for complete details about this program.

The key to motivating is variety.

POSTURE

Posture refers to the alignment of the body segments. Posture is closely related to physiological fitness since strength and health are common to both. Two aspects of strength are important to posture. One is the imbalance between muscles causing unnatural spinal column curves while the other is a lack of strength necessary to maintain good posture. Fortunately, such muscular deviations, if discovered in time, can usually be corrected through exercise.

If these *functional* (correctable) problems are ignored or not identified, they can lead to *structural* abnormalities and physiological problems which adversely affect health. Structural problems which can only be corrected through use of braces or surgery. Problems left unattended can sometimes cause severe crippling. Early diagnosis and treatment can usually prevent these problems.

Physiological problems are another possible outcome of postural deviations. Skeletal changes can cause pain as well as an unusual way of moving. Such movement changes can cause unequal body part stress in a "domino theory" breakdown. Since the human animal's bony structure was never designed for upright movement (on two feet), even slight changes can create abnormal force on body parts. Internal organic problems have also been associated with postural deviations which cause nerve involvement.

Lower back pain, a leading reason given for visits to doctors, is often related to posture. Imbalance between the back muscles and abdominal muscles causes an increase in the anterior/posterior lower back curvature (lumbar region) known as lordosis. This accentuation causes lower back pain and in severe cases may have nerve involvement as a result of disc herniation (commonly and incorrectly called a slipped disc).

There is no doubt about the importance of early identification and treatment of postural deviations. Such screening, if done systematically, can be efficient. Left undone, the consequences are far-reaching.

Screening

The teacher has a unique opportunity to evaluate which is usually not available to parents. By comparing numerous children, those with postural deviations are more likely to stand out. A properly prepared teacher should also have more postural knowledge than parents. Ideally, each preschool child should have been under a pediatrician's care as part of a comprehensive health program. Such care would include anthropometric examination and treatment of defects. In reality, only a small percentage of children (probably those who need it least) have good health care prior to entering school. The responsibility, therefore, falls on a qualified teacher to identify those needing further examination.

Systematic Observation. A screening device such as a checklist can be used to obtain information on children. This checklist can be used while children are in a guided movement activity. It is guided to allow for recording of information on each child. The arrangement can take the form of a circle or an obstacle course in which the children play follow the leader doing

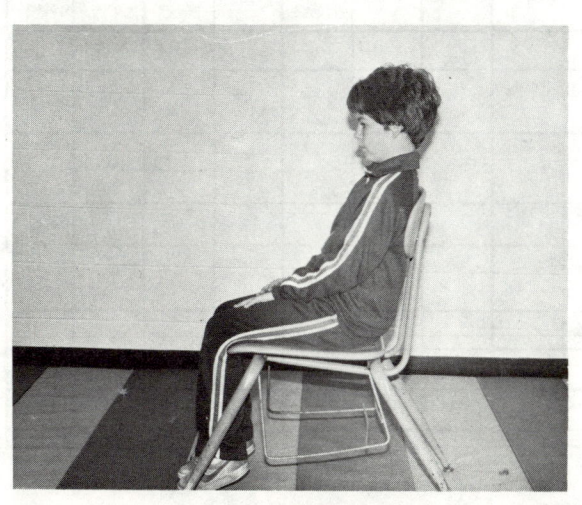

An example of good posture

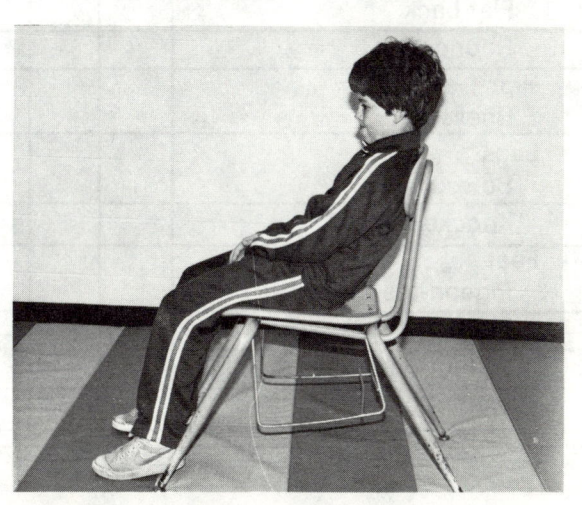

. . . and an example of poor posture.

activities directed by the teacher. These activities should include walking, running, skipping, and other movement activities during which posture can be observed. No matter which arrangement is used, however, the teacher must be sure that each child is systematically observed. Movement activities are more valuable than static observation since children will be more natural, will have more fun, and will be developing movement competencies rather than standing in a line waiting to be tested. To insure naturalness, children should not be told the purpose of the activity. For those working with many children, a numbering arrangement can be used for more accurate identification of children.

Observational Checklist. The checklist should be logically arranged to insure systematic observation. A sample checklist is shown in Figure 6-7. As can be seen, the focus goes from head to feet. For ease of scoring, a child's number or name is recorded in the appropriate box.

Figure 6.7. Postural Checklist

Group Observation

This form is designed for use while systematically observing children during dynamic movement activites. Systematic observation can be accomplished by having children move in a circle while using the checklist as a guide. Any abnormal deviation should be recorded below the child's name.

Name / Body Part									
Head Forward									
Shoulders Forward									
Uneven									
Rounded									
Back (back view) "S" Curve									
"C" Curve									
Back (side view) Lordosis									
Flat back									
Rounded									
Hips Uneven									
Legs Bowed									
Knocked-kneed									
Feet Pigeon-toed									
Duck feet									
Weight on inside									
Weight on outside									

Individual Testing. Certain deviations such as spinal cord lateral deviations (scoliosis) are most effectively identified during individual testing. There are basically two types of scoliosis, the S curve and C curve. The child, stripped from the waist up, is observed from the back while standing and also when bent ninety degrees at the waist. When viewing the child from the rear, one should look for uneven hips or shoulders as well as obvious spinal curvatures. When the child bends over, check for bumps or raised areas of the back which appear on only one side.

Team Approach

Diagnosis and correction should be a team approach. Diagnostic screening can be done by the classroom teacher or physical educator in conjunction with the school nurse. All suspected cases should be directed to a physician who can prescribe remedial work. Corrective exercises should be prescribed only by a medically qualified individual. By providing the doctor with a form such as that shown in Figure 6-8, communication will be facilitated.

Name of Student _____

Doctor's Name _____

Date _____

The above named child has been diagnosed as having a postural deviation which:

☐ Restricts his activities as noted below

☐ Can be aided by the exercises listed below

Restrictions:

Exercises:

Signed _____

Figure 6.8. Medical Feedback Sheet for Children with Postural Problems

104 Fitness

Exercises

Only those exercises designed for the normal postural development should be given unless a physician has prescribed corrective exercises. Teachers are not qualified to make final postural diagnosis nor do most have the training to determine corrective measures. Exercises such as sit-ups, leg raises, back exercises, and general strength development exercises, however, should be given to all children to aid normal development.

Strength. Overall postural is enhanced by a balanced strength development program. No one part of the body or body side should be neglected. Particular care must be given not to overstrengthen one body part thus causing unnatural skeletal curves. Children will favor the dominant side of the body in movement activities. They must be encouraged to use both sides for even development.

Flexibility. Although most people do not think of children having flexibility problems, many do, particularly some special education children. This poor movement range can cause postural problems. Flexibility exercises for all children are important.

REFERENCES

1. Allsen, P., J. Harrison and B. Vance. *Fitness for Life* (2nd Ed.). Dubuque: William C. Brown Company, 1980.
2. Beaulieu, J. "Stretch Your Potential. *Racquetball,* June 1981, pp. 27-29.
3. Corbin, C. "Relationships Between Physical Working Capacity and Running Performance of Young Boys." *Research Quarterly,* 43: 235-238.
4. Corbin, C. *A Textbook of Motor Development.* Dubuque: William C. Brown Company, 1973.
5. Dauer, V. and R. Pangrazi. *Dynamic Physical Education for Elementary School Children.* Minneapolis: Burgess Publishing Co., 1975.
6. Dintiman, G. and R. Davis. "A Complete, Practical Fitness Package for Your School." Unpublished paper, Virginia Commonwealth University, Richmond, Virginia, 1977.
7. Dintiman, G., R. Davis, and W. Miller. V.C.U. Fitness Test. Unpublished Test, Virginia Commonwealth University, Richmond, Virginia, 1977.
8. Foster, J. and G. Rochat. "Concepts on the Gym Floor." Presentation of AAHPER National Convention, Seattle, 1977.
9. Galton, L. "Does Your Child Have Hypertension?" *Parade.* March 27, 1977, pp. 12-13.
10. Hunsicker, P. and G. Reiff. "Youth Fitness Report: 1958-1965-1975." *JOHPER,* January 1977, pp. 31-33.
11. Isaacs, L. and G. Roswall. *Conditioning for Tennis: A Layman's Guide to Tennis Fitness.* College Park, Maryland: University of Maryland Printing, 1977.
12. Jackson, A. and A. Coleman. "Validation of Distance Run Tests for Elementary School Children." *Research Quarterly,* 47: 86-94.
13. Larson, L. (Ed.). *Knowledge and Understanding in Physical Education.* Washington: AAHPER, 1973.
14. *Physical Fitness Research Digest.* Series 7, Numbers 1 & 2, 1977.
15. Reiff, G. and P. Hunsicker. "Youth Fitness, 1975." *Update,* June, 1976, p. 5.
16. Schurr, E. *Movement Experiences for Children* (3rd Ed.). Englewood Cliffs: Prentice-Hall, 1980, p. 211.
17. Seltzer, C. and J. Mayer, "A Simple Criterion of Obesity." *Postgraduate Medicine,* 38: A-101, 1965. Cited in Corbin, C. *A Textbook of Motor Development.* Dubuque: William C. Brown Company, 1973, p. 98.
18. Shon, D. and L. Treadway, "Flexibility Testing and Development for Sport." *Physician and Sportsmedicine,* 6: 137-138, 1978.
19. "Skinfold Thickness of Children 6-11 Years." U.S. Dept. of Health, Education, and Welfare, HSM 73-106, Series 11, No. 120.
20. Stewart, K. and B. Gutin. "Effects of Physical Training on Cardiorespiratory Fitness in Children." *Research Quarterly,* 47: 110-120.
21. Vodak, P. and J. Wilmore. "Validity of the Six-Minute Jog-Walk and the 600-Yard Run-Walk in Estimating Endurance Capacity in Boys 12 Years of Age." *Research Quarterly,* 46: 230-234.

Fitness 107

3. Administer to a classmate or an elementary school age child the five evaluative tests of flexibility presented in this chapter.* Record the results below and circle any body region which should be subjected to further training.

    A. Shoulder flexibility
        Distance between mat and palms of hands: _____ inches.

    B Lower back flexibility
        Distance between nose and knee: _____ inches.

    C. Quadricep flexibility
        Distance from heels to buttock: _____ inches.
          or
        Angle formed by upper and lower leg: _____ degrees.

    D. Hamstring flexibility
        The trunk and raised leg should form a 90 degree angle. Check if desired angle is obtained. _____

    E. Calf muscle flexibility
        Angle between lower leg and foot: _____ degrees.

*Refer to page 90 for test item descriptions.

4. Describe three isometric exercises which can be utilized to strengthen the bicep muscles (anterior portion of upper arm). Do not describe examples presented in this text; be creative and design new ones of your own.

    Isometric Exercise One:

    Isometric Exercise Two:

108 *Fitness*

Isometric Exercise Three:

5. Draw a circuit training course designed to develop both shoulder girdle strength and cardiovascular endurance. The circuit is to be made up of eight different stations.

ELEMENTARY PHYSICAL EDUCATION

SECTION 2
CURRICULUM CONSIDERATIONS

DESCRIPTION OF SECTION II

After reading this section description, the student should be able to:

1. Design a lesson plan for each group in Chapter 7-10.
2. Design one integrated activity for each of the following subject areas: language arts, science, social studies, and math.
3. Analyze a game using the five-point scale discussed; the points assigned should not deviate more than ±1 from those values given in the curriculum Chapters 7-10.

Section II is a presentation of the elementary physical education curriculum. The five curriculum chapters (7-11) are designed for the normal child and focus on four age groupings: (except Chapter 11) kindergarten, first and second grade, third and fourth grade, and fifth and sixth grade. These divisions are based on research findings dealing with the characteristics of children.

Although a separate chapter is devoted to children with special needs, the information from every curriculum chapter can be used with handicapped children. By studying Chapter 12, the reader will learn how to aid handicapped children using information from Chapters 7-11.

Chapters 7-10 are each divided into the following sections:

    I.   Characteristics of the Age Group and Implications for Instruction
    II.   Curriculum Emphasis
    III. Teaching Approaches
    V.   Goals, Objectives, and Development Activities
    VI. Games
    VII. Example Lesson Plans

Chapter 11 is devoted exclusively to creative dance for children 6-12 years of age.

Goals, Objectives, and Developmental Activities

An outline in each curriculum chapter 7-10 deals with the goals, objectives, and developmental activities for the age group in question. This is a quick reference page to find any developmental activity included in the chapter. There are numerous activities in each chapter but they represent only a portion of those possible. Using the ones presented, the reader should be able to design others. Those activities included have all been field tested in several public school settings including both urban and suburban schools.

Designing Lesson Plans Curriculum Chapters 7-10

When designing a lesson plan (See Chapter 5), the first two activities should be drawn from the developmental activities area of the chapter. Integrated activities (see below) should be used whenever possible. Some games which have 100 percent participation can be utilized in the lesson's opening two activities, but they should be used sparingly. Games are more appropriate to end the lesson. In some instances, there may be no games at all in a lesson, particularly at the kindergarten level.

Goals and Objectives

Goals and objectives are to guide the teacher in selecting developmental activities. The list of goals in the curriculum chapters is fairly comprehensive for each age group in question, but no individual goal is an absolute for all the children in a particular age group. Most children, however, will be able to accomplish the objectives associated with a goal sometime during the year or two years they are in a particular age group.

One should be concerned when a child shows a pattern of failure involving several objectives. Most frequently, such children only need additional attention or time. Failure to accomplish objectives in motor performance, of course, is less critical than problems in health fitness objectives. All children, however, should make significant progress in accomplishing objectives in each educational domain.

INTEGRATED GAMES AND ACTIVITES

Several games and activities are designated as integrated. The main purpose of these activities is developing some physical education objective. A secondary objective is devoted to learning in some other subject area. Since children enjoy movement, using movement as a teaching medium can be valuable. With formal education at age five, movement is slowly reduced as a learning medium until most children, by age six, are expected to sit and learn using only the auditory and visual senses. This non-movement approach is unfortunate, since research supports the value of using movement activities and games to totally involve the child in the learning process. Asher (1) has found movement valuable for teaching a second language. Closely linked to Asher's work is that of Humphrey (3) which focuses on teaching children reading, math, and science concepts. Humphrey and others have done considerable research using the movement medium and have found it to be successful.

Work and writings by Humphrey, Cratty (2), Asher, and others have created a trend toward a multidisciplinary approach to curriculum planning. Attempts have been made to accomplish common goals in such areas as music, art, language arts, and math through cooperative planning. For purposes of clarification, activities which include information from other subjects will be termed integrated games or activites.

Some physical educators, in their enthusiasm to help children learn, have compromised physical education goals and objectives by teaching academic concepts during physical education. Some perceptual-motor specialists and others responsible for physical education instruction have been teaching academics during physical education time. The approach used by these individuals has been based on Humphrey's Cognitive Physical Education (3). The title is a misleading one since Humphrey has emphasized that teaching academic concepts using his approach has no place in physical education. In his approach, the movement is merely the medium while the objective clearly is academic learning, not physical education. Two examples presented during physical education class might help to emphasize why certain activities should not be in physical education.

Example 1: A physical education student teacher had a second grade class sitting on the floor with jump ropes. He was presenting such problems as, "Can you make an "A" with your rope?" and "Can you make an "M" inside a circle?" Nearly 15 minutes of a 25-minute physical education class were devoted to this activity involving only the ropes. Although not all physical education activities have to be vigorous in nature, such an activity clearly had no place in physical education. The child could have made shapes, letters, etc., and then walked on the rope (balance) or used some basic movements such as jumping in and out of the shape or going around the rope. (4)

Movement using rope shapes

Balance activities using rope shapes

112 Section II

Example 2: During physical education, a group of special education children (third grade, mentally retarded) were asked to form the equation, 11 + 2 = 13. They seemed confused; the physical educator and three assistants very firmly placed the children on the floor to form the different numbers and symbols. After class, the physical educator was asked what the activity had to do with physical education. She was unable to provide an answer. She did indicate, however, that the children seemed to learn the math concept better through the activity. It is hard to argue with successful learning, but this particular activity was more appropriate for a mathematics class. For most mentally retarded children, physical education provides some of their only successes during the day. The frustrations of academic learning should not interfere with the joy of physical education activities. Although a multidisciplinary approach is valuable, each subject in the curriculum makes a unique contribution to growth and development. The identity of physical education, therefore, should not be lost in the teacher's preoccupation with reading and mathematics.

Although subjects like reading and mathematics are a part of an integrated activity, the primary objective for the class must be physical education. Learning in the other subject area is merely a bonus, like getting two things for the price of one. As in any physical education program, the activities selected should provide for total physical involvement by the children. The best source of information on what academic concepts to present is the classroom teacher. This person knows where the children are in all subjects and can be a valuable aid in designing integrated activities.

Designing an Integrated Activity

Many physical education activities lend themselves to having other subjects integrated with them. The primary objective, however, must be appropriate to physical education. There should be 100 percent physical participation in an integrated activity, and in no way can the other subject area detract from full physical participation by every child.

Language Arts. Reading and spelling are relatively easy to integrate with physical education at every grade level. Flash cards can be used primarily with younger children while all children can benefit from written instructions at stations and learning centers. Older children can use learning packets (Chapter 5) which

Crows and Cranes

have written materials; all children can act out poems through movement. A game such as Crows and Cranes, p. 183 can be modified to help children learn vowels and consonants. One group is the vowels and the other consonants. If the word called out begins with a vowel, the vowel group runs toward the safe base while being chased by the consonants and vice versa.

Science. There are numerous opportunities to integrate science with physical education. Story plays can be used with younger children to learn about animals and their habits, places such as the ocean, jungle, outer space, and things like how plants grow and the weather. The older children can learn about the science of physiological responses to exercise, and the science of movement.

Social Studies. The primary way to integrate social studies is through rhythmic activities although children can also play games that are unique to a particular country or groups of people.

Math. Although math can be integrated with physical education, it is the least accepted by children. Perhaps the poor interest stems from frustration in the classroom. One must be careful, therefore, with integrated math activities so children will not experience frustration during physical education. The younger children can learn math shapes with their body by trying to form the shapes shown on flash cards. The shapes can also be targets. When doing stations, children can keep their score as they do various self-testing activities. In games like Old Mother Witch, p. 183, and The Three Bears, p.

Children form letter from flashcard.

Evaluating body image using Simon Says

183, the concepts of more than, less than and equal to can be learned. Suppose, for example, that Billy tagged a total of five children on his two turns. Mary then tagged two on her first turn. The teacher can then ask, "How many more does Mary need to have more than Billy?" or "How many does she need to be equal to Billy?" These questions and their answers only take a few moments, and can be done as children are preparing for the next turn. Since this is an integrated activity, the majority of time and emphasis should be on physical education objectives.

GAMES

Games are activities which have rules and involve winning and losing. Most games are enjoyed by children and can play an integral part in their growth and development both in and out of school. Carefully selected games can also be a valuable part of a physical education program.

Some possible negative effects have caused games to come under attack by some physical educators. Certain gains, such as many circle games, provide little participation; others, if not handled properly, can injure a child's self-concept. While these concerns are justified, games also have positive values, and a teacher should be aware of both the positive and negative effects. If carefully selected and conducted, games can have positive effect on the growth and development of children.

Developmental Value

Some games can be used to evaluate a child's ability or knowledge. Games like Simon Says (page 152), Brothers (page 152), or Busy Bee (page 152) can all be used to evaluate the child's body image. By having children close their eyes during Simon Says, for example, you can get a general idea of the body parts which are known to children — "Simon Says, touch your wrists" or "Simon Says, touch your waist." Children can also be observed during Busy Bee to see how freely they mix with each other; i.e., are some children rejected, others popular? How do they mix racially and according to sex? How reluctant are they to assume certain positions, such as cheek to cheek? If the games are carefully selected and conducted, valuable physical, emotional, social and intellectual data can be obtained through observation.

Psychomotor Value

Movement and fitness are two of the major psychomotor components which can be enhanced through games. To be of psychomotor value, nearly every child should be active. Such activites as circle games and relays usually fail to qualify in this respect. Activities do not necessarily have to be vigorous, since stretching, bending twisting, turning, and many motor fitness components do not require strenuous movement. To improve cardiovascular endurance, however, the activity not only has to be vigorous, it must be of sufficient duration. (See Chapter 6.)

To improve psychomotor ability, few games are as valuable as the developmental activities in Chapters 7-12. Some games get everybody moving, but many have periods of inactivity during which no psychomotor development is taking place.

Most circle games provide little participation.

Affective Value

Most games can benefit the child's social and emotional development. By their nature, games require interaction among children, and the winning and fun aspects make children experience many emotions. The particular game and how it is played will determine its value. Properly conducted, games can have a profound effect on affective development. Unfortunately, the converse is true since a child's self-concept may be harmed by high emotion stress.

Components of the effective domain, such as leadership, self-discipline, sportmanship, and honesty, can all be developed through games. To be effective in these areas, children should conduct their own games once they learn them. The teacher has an obligation to supervise but does not have to dominate as is frequently the case. As an example, ask the class what games they would like to play. If enough children express interest in a particular game, assign them an area of the playground which can be supervised and tell them to conduct their own game. The remaining children continue to suggest games and are assigned areas in turn. It is not unusual or impossible to have three or four child-controlled games going on at once. Sometimes one or two children do not want to play any of the games and elect to do nothing. Although they should be encouraged to participate, they should not be forced. The teacher, through discussion with the child, can find the reasons for nonparticipation. The other teacher functions are supervision and assistance with problems. If a group is having trouble, the teacher should go to the group and, through a problem-solving (questioning) technique, assist the children to self-evaluate. For example: "Why are you having a problem?", "In that case, what would be the best solution?", etc. The teacher should not solve the problem for the group. Only safety hazards should be dealt with promptly.

Sportsmanship. Unsportsmanlike behavior, such as booing, occurs even in very young children. Such behavior gives a teacher the opportunity to discuss sportsmanship. Although it is difficult to overcome behavior which is so prevalent in society, it should not be ignored. Whether good sportsmanship in games carries over to honesty in other situations is unknown, but it should be promoted in all areas.

Values. Other values, which can be developed through games include: (1) respect for the rights of others, (2) self-respect, (3) sharing, (4) patience, and (5) accepting others who are different. As mentioned earlier, the teacher can find many opportunities during games to discuss these values as they relate to some behavior which has been exhibited during a game. Problem-solving discussions are one way to help the class think through a situation and find a solution. A teacher-dominated lecture on values will probably have little effect.

Cognitive Value

Any aspect of an educational program should contribute to cognitive development. Physical education games make such a contribution in several ways: (1) the students must use cognitive ability to learn rules and to apply those rules in a dynamic situation; (2) children can, if given the opportunity, develop their own games; and (3) some games may teach or reinforce academic concepts (see Chapter 15).

Rules and Regulations. Any game, by definition, has rules which must be followed if the game is to be successful. The cognitive involvement is directly related to the games complexity (number of rules). Upper elementary children often become involved in sophisticated games such as basketball and soccer. Such games must be greatly modified, not only for physical success, but mental as well. By asking questions about rules and rule violations during play, a teacher can contribute to cognitive knowledge. Since children must think quickly because of the dynamic nature of the activity, even simple games make a contribution. Few classroom activities require such quick "thinking on the feet."

Student-Designed Games. Since creativity is one of the highest levels of cognitive ability, teachers should constantly strive to develop it. Children eight years and older should be given the opportunity to design their own games. Using a problem-solving approach children can be encouraged to create a game; i.e., what game can you make up using a ball and the rule that it may not touch the ground? Another approach is to put rules on cards. After selecting one card, a game is begun using only that rule. Then another rule is randomly drawn and the game must be modified to fit the new rule. This process continues until all the rules are included or the game has a logical conclusion. Children should also feel free to modify games presented by the teacher to make the games more interesting.

Rating a Game

Each game presented in Chapters 7-10 is rated on a five-point scale according to its contribution to psychomotor, affective, or cognitive development. A "5" rating indicates a high contribution and a "1" indicates a low contribution. These ratings are based on the written description of each game. Although the game titles are similar or identical to those in other books, the descriptions are frequently different, and must be played as described if the rating values indicated are to be realized.

Ratings have been assigned by determining how many people are actually involved in the developmental process. Although two people may be very active while running around a circle, the vast majority of children are totally inactive. A similiar inactivity exists in relays. Both of these activities would, therefore, receive a low psychomotor rating. For high ratings, nearly all the children should be actively involved in learning. A game like Fox and Hound (page 153) receives a "5" for physical development since everyone is chasing or running, and Busy Bee (page 152) gets a "5" for social development since every child is interacting with another child. The ratings given other games vary according to the children's active involvement. With a little practice, a game selected from any source can be evaluated and changed if necessary to increase its value in a particular domain. A humanistic teacher is sensitive to children's needs and selects activities according to their developmental value as well as their suitability for an age group.

Although some games in the chapters are rated fairly low, all are fun and children enjoy playing them. By using them prudently as suggested under affective development, each has value. Whether developmental or not, the fun aspect should not be overlooked since it is a good starting point in creating a positive attitude toward physical education, in general, and physical activity specifically.

The ratings charts preceding the game descriptions also include a suggested location for the game. The locations are listed in their order of desirability; some activities are completely unsuited for certain areas such as the classroom. Games receiving checks under more than one area indicate the activity's flexibility. When selecting a site, however, grass is usually preferred, followed by a gymnasium (multipurpose room), a hardtop, and lease desirable, the classroom or hallway. A final category is evaluation. A game receiving a check in this area can be used for evaluative purposes.

REFERENCES

1. Asher, J. "The Total Physical Response Approach to Second Language Learning." *The Modern Language Journal,* L111, 1 Jan 1969.
2. Cratty, B. *Intelligence in Action.* Englewood Cliffs: Prentice Hall, Inc., 1973.
3. Humphrey, J. *Child Learning Through Elementary School Physical Education.* Dubuque: Wm. C. Brown Co., 1974.
4. Mason, S. "Exploring with Ropes in the Lower Elementary Physical Education Program." *JOHPER,* May 1974, p. 45.

STUDENT ACTIVITIES

1. Using the form below, design a lesson plan (not one included in this book) for one of the four age groups in Chapters 7-10. (See Chapter 5 for additional information on lesson planning.)

    Goal:

    Objective:

    Activities: Formation:
    I.   I.

2. Design one integrated activity for each of the following areas: language arts and science.

Language Arts
Grade Level: 4
Physical Education Goal: Continued Development of Eye-hand coordination.
Language Arts Goal: Develop continued understanding of parts of speech.
Description of Activity:

Depending on the size of the class, divide it into two groups. At the head of the classroom place two trash cans which carry the labels "nouns" or "verbs". Have flashcards with examples of the two parts of speech written on them. As the teacher or student shows the cards to classmates, the students must determine the part of speech represented and throw the beanbag into the appropriate trash can. If the class desires points can be kept to determine team winners. (Classroom must be appropriately arranged before start of this activity.)

Science
Grade Level: 6
Physical Education Goal: To develop non-locomotor abilities

Science Goal: Develop an understanding of sound waves in the Doppler effect.
Description of Activity:

After discussion of the Doppler effect, what it is and how sound waves react, ask class to find space on the floor pretend that they are the sound waves responding to a town whistle (Have recording on hand.) Ask children to bend or stretch according to the pitch of the sound. When it is far away, children will only flex and contract slowly. As the sound comes nearer the children will show the reactions of the sound waves as they begin to bend and stretch more rapidly. As the sound goes away, the children will again bend and stretch their bodies in a slower more relaxed way.

CHAPTER 7
CURRICULUM FOR FIVE-YEAR-OLDS

After completing this chapter, the student should be able to:

1. Give the instructional implications for the growth and development characteristics of the five-year-old.

2. Explain the curriculum emphases for the kindergarten child.

3. Describe the most effective way to approach the teaching of this age group.

4. List and explain the reason for five safety precautions which should be taken.

5. For each objective, describe at least two activities which can be used to develop the particular objective in question.

Characteristics of Five-Year-Olds and Implications for Instruction

Although the emphasis of this chapter is on the five-year-old, many activities are applicable to younger children. The five-year-old child is usually experiencing his or her first public education in kindergarten. For many children it is the first time away from their parents — a difficult adjustment time which the teacher must consider in establishing the learning atmosphere. Most five-year-olds are used to a lot of freedom and much of their earlier learning has been through movement. They are not ready for long periods of sitting and listening, nor are they oriented toward large group activities. This adjustment period must be handled carefully if future education is to be successful.

Physical Characteristics

1. By five years of age, normal children have developed the basic movements of creeping, crawling, walking, running, jumping, hopping, galloping, and leaping, and have the ability to do all the basic nonlocomotor movements of bending, stretching, twisting, turning, pulling, and pushing. The more difficult tasks, such as skipping, catching, and striking can be developed during this period.

Implication — Children need to be taught to move more efficiently (quality of movement). Most children need to explore movement under trained individuals who can expose them to a variety of movements and aid them in their movement efficiency. The more difficult skills of catching, throwing, and striking require more

Crawling

Creeping

specific instruction, although most children can be guided toward efficient movement in all skills.

2. Girls are more advanced than boys in most areas.

Implication — Past experience may provide boys an edge in the physical skills of throwing, catching, kicking, and striking. Girls usually excel in the gymnastics and dance activities. Physical differences between the sexes, however, are minimal.

Kindergarten

Developing movement quality through creative activities.

Testing perceptual-motor ability

3. Most children have developed a dominant side of the body.
Implication — When exploring movement, children will favor the dominant side, and should therefore be encouraged to use both sides of the body.

4. Eye-hand and eye-foot coordination are usually poor.
Implication — These areas should be worked on continually with caution exercised in equipment selection. Small balls, such as tennis balls or softballs, should not be used since frequent misses could cause injury. Objects such as 8 ½-inch playground balls, yarn balls, or sponge rubber balls should be used. Children should experience at least one activity a day which requires catching, kicking, or striking an object.

5. Large muscles are more well-developed than fine muscles.
Implication — Activities using large muscles will give the child more success than those requiring fine motor coordination. The majority of activities in physical education should aid large muscle development.

6. Children are noisy and vigorous, but tire easily.
Implication — Activities should allow for noise and lots of activity, but should be interspersed with rest periods or less vigorous activity.

7. Bladder control is still a problem for some children, particularly under tense situations.
Implication — Avoid pressure situations for children and allow them use of the bathroom upon request or when the obvious signals are given. Boys tend to hold themselves, while girls cross their legs when urination is imminent. Recognizing these and other signs will avoid embarrassing moments.

8. Perceptual-motor skills are not fully developed.
Implication — Design a program which allows for screening of perceptual-motor ability, and have a special program for those children with problems. A good developmental physical education program will provide the normal child with opportunities to develop these skills.

Social and Emotional Characteristics

1. The kindergarten child likes to play with other children, but is self-centered.
Implication — Have activities which are individual rather than group oriented. Groups, when used, should be small to provide each child lots of activity.

2. Most children like to test their skill.
Implication — Have individual activities in which the child can evaluate his or her own success (self-testing activities). This requires one piece of equipment per child in most cases. Targets which fall when hit are particularly motivating.

3. Children enjoy imitating.
Implication — Have creative activities which give the child an opportunity to act out different characters or situations. Story plays are an excellent vehicle for role playing. Having children move like different people or animals is another way of satisfying this need.

4. The kindergarten child wants to please adults.

Implication — Children will seek adult attention and approval, and the teacher must be ready to praise positive behavior. Praise can be given either verbally or nonverbally with a smile, a wink, a clap of hands, or a pat on the back. Giving approval is important in developing rapport with the child.

5. A child will often argue and fight with peers.

Implication — When everyone in a group is self-centered fights are inevitable. A teacher must recognize this fact and deal with problems according to the age group. Knowing that arguing and fighting are typical of five-year-olds, a teacher should not become overly concerned about this behavior, unless a particular child seems abnormally aggressive and interferes with the learning process.

6. Emotions are not fully developed and behavior such as crying is common.

Implication — Most incidents which cause an emotional response — crying, screaming, or fighting — are soon forgotten and should not be blown out of proportion. A crying child can be disruptive, particularly since all the other children want to comfort him, so avoid remarks or behavior which trigger this response. Eye contact, for example, is good for behavior control, but looking at the child too long, when he obviously knows he has done something wrong, can cause crying. Another typical teacher behavior is to confront the child verbally in front of peers. This not only can result in crying, but can cause the loss of class rapport. To avoid calling too much attention to the misbehaving child, get the other children into activity and then talk to him or her.

Intellectual Characteristics

1. A kindergartener's attention span is short.

Implication — Kindergarten children are not ready for long explanations, so instructions should be minimized and activity maximized.

2. Children enjoy story plays and poems.

Implication — As indicated earlier, children in this age group like imitation, story plays, and acting out poems.

3. Even simple games are difficult since rules are not easy for the young child to follow.

Implication — By definition, a game has rules, and even simple games may meet with limited success. Activities should be individual in nature — self-testing, creative, or rhythmic. Rules must be greatly modified or extremely simple. Games should be a part of the curriculum for all age levels, but they must be selected carefully to insure success and fun.

4. Problem-solving ability is still being developed.

Implication — The development process can be enhanced by using a teaching style which requires the child to think cognitively. By asking open-ended questions such as "How many different body parts can you use to throw the beanbag?" children must use their problem-solving ability. The problem-solving style should play a major role at all grade levels to aid cognitive development and to get student input.

5. Children are capable of learning the basics of health, fitness, and safety.

Implication — Determine those concepts about health, fitness, and safety, which the children are capable of learning and seek opportunities to teach these concepts.

CURRICULUM EMPHASES

Movement

The curriculum should emphasize learning and development through movement. Time should be allotted for both free and guided exploration. Although most children have learned the basic movements, such as walking, running, hopping, and leaping, few have learned to move with varying force, at different speeds, in personal and common space, or at various levels. Children must learn what, where, and how to move. This requires knowledge of their body and the space around them, and various movement experiences.

Learning through movement

124   Kindergarten

Incorrect performance is common.

Manipulative Skills

Children should have the opportunity to manipulate a variety of objects during physical education. The learning environment should include balls of varying sizes (soft), beanbags, hoops, tires, ropes, sticks, and other objects. Manipulation should include the use of hands, feet, elbows, knees, and any body part which can maneuver or strike an object.

Self-Concept

How a child feels about himself probably has more to do with learning than most other factors. As was pointed out in the introduction, the major educational emphasis at the elementary level should be positive self-concept development.

Interdisciplinary Planning

Whenever possible, integrated activities should be in the curriculum. As was explained in the Section II description, integrated activities can be used to aid learning in such areas as language arts, science, math, social studies and music. This interdisciplinary planning is particularly easy to do at the kindergarten level. Activities such as story plays can be used to learn about the world in which we live. Flash cards help develop sight vocabulary. The list of ways to integrate is nearly endless.

To aid in planning and learning, a section of integrated activities and games is included beginning on page 127. Other ideas are also included throughout the chapter.

TEACHING APPROACHES

The teacher's main function is to establish a positive learning environment in which children want to participate actively. Such an environment is created when a teacher uses praise, a child-centered teaching approach, provides a variety of interesting objects, and provides a safe, attractive play area. Teaching styles such as guided and free exploration and problem solving should be used (Chapter 4). Little stress should be placed on skill perfection, although if bad habits develop, they should be corrected.

SAFETY

Five-year-old children are still learning movement efficiency and tend to fall more easily than older children. This tendency can also be attributed to a high center of gravity. To protect children from these inevitable falls, a safe play area must be provided and rules established. Since the opportunities for collision are multiplied, rules are particularly important when the play area must be shared with other children.

Play Area

Grass. The best play area is usually grass, assuming, of course, it is free of stones and glass. Nearly any activity can be conducted on grass without real concern for injuries due to falls. Brightly-colored marker cones should be used to identify play area boundaries.

Indoors. The indoor play space should be cleared of obstacles and unmovable items should be padded. Furniture should not be used for boundaries or markers because of sharp edges; marker cones or tape should be used instead. If forced to use a relatively unsafe area, the teacher should modify or eliminate activities according to the restrictions.

Rules

1. No sliding. Young children like to slide on grass and floors and may injure themselves or others, and may damage clothes.
2. Stop, look, and listen when they hear the whistle.
3. No pushing or shoving.
4. Stay inside designated area.

Playground Safety

If used safely, a properly designed playground can aid a child's growth and development. Unfortunately, few playgrounds have developmental equipment nor do children always use it properly. A playground safety discussion should be held before children are allowed on equipment.

Injuries. Injuries are most frequent on equipment which has the least developmental value — swings, seesaws, sliding boards, and turning apparatus. Although equipment usually included on nursery or elementary school playgrounds has recreational value, one must weigh the benefits against the injury factor. It is recommended that this recreational equipment be supplemental to more developmental equipment.

Developmental Equipment. Injury is a real possibility, even on developmental equipment. Whenever a child is high in the air, such as on the jungle gym or in an inverted position on a horizontal bar, there is a potential for serious injury. One particular area of concern is the horizontal ladder. Most ladders are too high for young children. Children who fall off high ladders when swinging forward will strike the ground on their backs, causing a whipping action of the head and neck. The head will almost always strike the ground forcefully. Broken arms, legs, shoulders, and hips have been common injuries associated with these elevated ladders. On a properly placed ladder, the child's feet should only be ten to twelve inches off the ground. Taller children can spread their legs or bend their knees. Lowering the ladder does not take away from its developmental value, only the injury potential.

Equipment which aids the child's development in such areas as upper body strength, balance, and creativity should be on the playground. Climbing and hanging equipment, such as jungle gym, horizontal ladder, climbing poles, and horizontal bars can all be used to assist in strength development. Stationary balance beams should also be part of the playground. Equipment which stimulates the imagination and allows for exploration will help develop creativity.

Equipment Placement. Although there is a temptation to place such equipment on hardtop where wet weather will not affect its use, playground equipment should be placed on grass. Even when the equipment is on grass, wood chips or sand should be placed around it to cushion falls. Some schools surround equipment with soft and expensive outdoor mats. Such mats provide probably the best protection against injury, but are too costly for most school systems.

Children's feet should only be 10-12 inches off ground when crossing the horizontal ladder.

Dangerous equipment on a dangerous surface

126 Kindergarten

GOALS, OBJECTIVES AND DEVELOPMENTAL ACTIVITIES
SECTION OUTLINE

PSYCHOMOTOR DOMAIN, p. 127

Locomotor Movement, p. 127
   Integrated Planning, p. 127
   Locomotor Activities, p. 127
   Quality of Locomotor Movement, p. 128

Non-Locomotor Movement, p. 129
   Integrated Planning, p. 129
   Non-Locomotor Movement Activities, p. 129

Manipulative Skills, p. 130
   Integrated Planning, p. 130
   Manipulative Activities, p. 130

Kinesthetic Awareness, p. 131
   Kinesthetic and Proprioceptive Activities, p. 131

Balance, p. 132
   Balance Activities, p. 132

Tumbling and Gymnastics, p. 132
   Tumbling Activities, p. 132
   Gymnastics Activities, p. 133

Fitness, p. 134
   Integrated Planning, p. 134
   Fitness Activities, p. 135

Rhythmics, p. 135
   Integrated Planning, p. 135
   Rhythmic Activities, p. 135

Creativity, p. 140
   Integrated Planning, p. 140
   Creative Activities, p. 140

Relaxation, p. 144
   Relaxation Activities, p. 144

AFFECTIVE DOMAIN, p. 144

Self-Concept, p. 144
   Self-Concept Activities, p. 144

Honesty, p. 144
   Honesty Activities, p. 144

Sharing, p. 144
   Sharing Activities, p. 144

Respect for Authority, p. 144

Patience, p. 145

Respect for Self and Others, p. 145

Leading & Following, p. 145
   Leading & Following Activities, p. 145

Positive Attitudes, p. 145

COGNITIVE DOMAIN, p. 145

Problem-Solving Ability, p. 145
   Problem-Solving Activities, p. 145

Directional and Movement Terms, p. 146
   Integrated Planning, p. 146
   Directional and Movement Term Activities, p. 146

Body Image, p. 146
   Integrated Planning, p. 146
   Body Image Activities, p. 147

Rules and Regulations, p. 147

Fitness, Health and Safety Knowledge, p. 147
   Fitness Information, p. 147

INTEGRATED ACTIVITIES, p. 147

   Language Arts, p. 147
     Math, p. 148
     Science, p. 149
     Social Studies, p. 150
     Music, p. 150

GAMES, p. 151

EXAMPLE LESSON PLANS, p. 155

PSYCHOMOTOR DOMAIN
Locomotor Movement

Goal: By the age of six, children will have developed all the locomotor and nonlocomotor skills.

Objectives:

1. Before leaving kindergarten, most children should be able to do the following: (1) Run in a figure eight pattern without falling, (2) hop in place on either foot three times without losing balance, (3) do a ten-inch standing broad jump, (4) skip, (5) slide, (6) walk backward heel to toe, and (7) hop six inches forward on either foot without losing balance.

Goal: Children will improve the quality of their locomotor ability — force, speed, space, level, and direction.

Objectives:

1. Children will vary their force according to the music played — light moves for soft music and heavy moves for loud music.
2. When mimicking animals, children will apply varying forces according to the animal they are imitating.

Mimicking animals

3. Children will respond correctly to varying rhythmic speeds, and will be able to change speed as the tempo changes.
4. Children will be able to demonstrate slow motion action while mimicking sports activities.
5. By age five, a child should be able to walk briskly in a 15 by 20 foot area with 15 other children and not touch anyone.
6. Children should be able to demonstrate the ability to move at many levels, high and low, while traveling at different speeds and in various directions.
7. By the age of six, children should be able to do basic locomotor movements in any direction, forward, backward, or sideward.

Integrated Planning

Use flashcards with the movement terms on p. 146. Set up simple stations, Chapter 5, Which have locomotor movements.

Locomotor Activities

By the time a child is five, researchers have found that he or she usually possesses all the basic locomotor skills of walking, running, hopping, jumping, leaping, as well as some combination skills such as galloping, sliding, and skipping. Unless a teacher is working with nonambulatory children, the focus of instruction should be on the quality of locomotor ability. Although most children are capable of performing the locomotor skills in a rudimentary way, many have not experienced movement in any way except forward. Few can move effectively at various levels, in different directions, or with varying force.

1. Running — To run, one must alternate the lead foot with a momentary suspension (both feet off the ground) in the air. Although running is only one of the basic movements, it is singled out because of its importance to physical education and safety. A great deal of running is done in physical education and collisions and falls are the most frequent causes of injury. Children should learn to run in the following sequence: (1) straight, (2) in a circle, (3) a figure eight, (4) random direction (alone), (5) random direction in a small group, and (6) random direction in a large group. By age five, children should be able to run in a small group without collision following 15 minutes of practice and discussion. Children should also be able to run slowly for-

128 Kindergarten

ward, backward, and sideward without falling down.

2. Walking — In walking, the heel should strike the ground first followed by a rocking motion toward the toe. The toes are usually pointed slightly outward. Arms and legs should work in opposition, right arm forward when left leg is forward and vice versa.

3. Hopping — Hopping is done by jumping up on one foot and landing on the same foot.

4. Leaping — To leap, one must jump up on one foot, have a long suspension in the air, and land on the other foot.

5. Jumping — Jumping is leaping on one foot or two feet, and landing on two feet.

6. Galloping — To gallop, one must keep the same foot in the lead at all times.

7. Skipping — Skipping is a combination of a step and a hop. The child steps forward on one foot and then hops on that foot. The other foot then repeats the action.

A good way to develop locomotor ability is to have children move in many directions and ways (light, heavy, slow motion) while participating in enjoyable activities which could include:

  a. Races:
    In a straight line
    Out and back, going around a marker
  b. Automobiles: p. 153
    Running in a circle with frequent reversals.
  c. Obstacle course running:
    Have frequent changes of direction. Can be done outside or inside but no solid objects such as poles or trees should be used as markers for turning. Marker cones should be used to mark the course.
  d. Red Light, Green Light, p. 182
  e. Busy Bee, p. 152
  f. Brothers, p. 152
  g. Moving to flash cards
    Use terms such as "run slowly," "run backward," "run lightly," "run heavy," "walk in slow motion," "leap like a deer," "jump like a rabbit" (two feet), and "hop on your left foot."

A problem-solving approach can also be used with flash cards. The word in quotation marks would appear on the flash card.

  How many ways can you "move"?
  Can you move like different "animals"?
  Show me some animals which "run."
  Show me some animals which move "slowly."
  What are some animals which move "heavy"?
  Are there some animals which can move "backward"?
  What would an animal look like if it moved in "slow motion"?

  h. Moving to tom-tom or music
    Tom-tom or music can be played at different volumes to signify heavy or light movement. The movement speed can also be controlled using the tom-tom or the music. Changing volume could also mean high or low movement.

Quality of locomotor movement. Many of the activities mentioned above deal with the quality of movement which is essential to all locomotor movement. The four factors most closely associated with movement quality are: force, speed, level, and space (direction).

1. Force
  a. Tom-tom — Can you move softly when the sound from the tom-tom is soft and heavy when it is loud? Can you show a heavy movement when you hear a loud sound from the tom-tom?
  b. Music — Can you move either heavily or softly depending upon the music you hear?
  c. Mimicking — Can you move like an elephant? (heavily) Like a mouse? (lightly)
  d. Creativity — Can you move as if you were in outer space? How would you be able to move on the moon? Can you move in slow motion? Can you move like a cloud? Can you move like a rock rolling down a hill? Can you move like a feather? A piece of dust?

2. Space — Ability to move in common space is an important skill if injuries are to be prevented. Young children are usually unaccustomed to moving in a space shared by a number of other children. This lack of experience can lead to collisions. The following activities are designed to minimize these accidents:
  a. Have children move slowly to the beat of a tom-tom in a relatively large area. Emphasize the need to use the entire space by looking for open spaces and having frequent changes of direction. Prior to increasing the speed and cut-

ting down the size of the area, children should be asked, "How can you avoid hitting someone else?" After this problem-solving activity, the speed should be gradually increased while the space is decreased. After avoidance ability is improved, children can be asked to skip or gallop, walk backward or sideward, and void collisions. This early training is important at the beginning of each school year at least during the primary years (up to seven years of age).

3. Speed — Children should learn to do all locomotor movements at various speeds from slow motion to as fast as possible in all directions. Since agility is not well-developed, quick changes in direction may result in falls. The high center of gravity and unusual direction of travel, particularly backward, can also cause falls. In all cases where children may fall, the play surface must be considered. Activities in early childhood should be conducted on a soft surface (usually grass) whenever possible. If forced to use blacktop, speeds and quick changes of direction must be controlled by the teacher to avoid falls.

4. Level — Most children are familiar only with movement in the standing position. Few have experienced moving high (leaping) or low.

    a. Animal mimicking — Can you move like a mouse? A snake? A giraffe? A bird?

    b. Moving to a tom-tom or music — Can you move low when I play the tom-tom softly (or music) and high when I play it loud? Listen to the tom-tom and see at what level you should be.

5. Direction — Children should experience locomotor movement in all directions, forward, backward, and sideward.

    a. Tom-tom — When you hear a loud note on the tom-tom, I want you to change the direction — forward, backward, or sideward — while you are moving.

    b. Creativity — Can you show me something which can move backward? Sideward?

Nonlocomotor Movement

Goal: Children will develop nonlocomotor ability.

Objectives:

1. Children will be able to bend, stretch, twist, turn, shake, swing, and bounce all the body parts capable of such movements.

Children should experience a variety of movement.

2. Children will be able to show recognition of each nonlocomotor movement term by demonstrating appropriate body movement without any visual cues from the teacher.

Integrated Planning

Use flashcards, p. 128 and 148.

Nonlocomotor Activities

Frequently the nonlocomotor ability of children is not well developed due mostly to a lack of experience. Although most children are capable of all forms of nonlocomotor movements, many do not understand the terms. Movement problems are particularly apparent when children are asked to perform nonlocomotor movements while in unusual positions, such as inverted.

1. Tom-tom — Can you bend and stretch one body part and keep time with the tom-tom? Two body parts? Three? Two upper body parts? Two lower?

2. Music — Can you shake one body part to the music? Two? Three? How about your whole body? Can you twist, turn, or swing a body part to the music? Other body parts?

3. Creativity — Growing like a tree or flower. Emphasize nonlocomotor movement. Can you be a machine with moving parts? How many different body parts can you use to imitate the machine's parts? Can you be a can opener? A mixing machine? A washing machine?

130 Kindergarten

4. Do This, Do That, p. 153 — Emphasize nonlocomotor movements.

5. Mirror Maze — One child is the mirror and the other is standing in front of the mirror. Children are instructed to make large, slow nonlocomotor movements. Roles are reversed after a period of time. To give children the idea of the activity, the teacher can pretend to be the person in front of the mirror and all the children try to imitate the teacher's movements.

6. Have children do nonlocomotor movements while sitting, lying, or when upside down.

7. Do nonlocomotor movements at various speeds including slow motion.

Manipulative Skills

Goal: Children will be able to manipulate a variety of objects alone and with a partner.

Objectives:

1. With experience, the child by age 5 ½ should be able to do the following: (1) catch a beanbag with hands while standing; (2) kick an 8 ½-inch rolling playground ball; (3) hit a rolling 5-inch rubber ball with a 36-inch dowel; (4) run and kick a rolling 8 ½-inch rubber ball; (5) catch with both hands a 2-inch rubber ball which has been thrown underhand; (6) catch with one hand a 4-inch beanbag which has been thrown underhand; and (7) catch with both hands a beanbag which has been thrown overhand.

2. Children will demonstrate the ability to manipulate objects using either the right or left side of their body.

3. Given an open area, a child should be able to keep a round balloon in the air almost indefinitely using both upper and lower body parts. Body parts should include hands, elbows, shoulders, head, knees, and feet.

Integrated Planning.

Use flashcards, p. 128 and 148, and stations, Chapter 5.

Manipulative Activities

1. Free Exploration — Establish an environment containing many different manipulative objects, such as balloons, beanbags, balls, and hoops, and targets. Then give children freedom to explore.

2. Guided Exploration and Problem Solving

   a. How many different body parts can you use to hit a balloon?

Hoops can be used to aid children in learning directional and movement concepts.

   b. How many ways can you throw the beanbag? Catch the beanbag?

   c. Can you use different body parts to throw? To catch?

3. Hand-Eye Coordination Progression

   a. Balloons
   Can you keep the balloon in the air?
   Can you catch the balloon with your hands?

   b. Target activities — targets can be waste baskets, boxes, pins, plastic bottles.
   How many different ways can you throw the beanbag or sponge ball and hit the target?
   Can you throw, (over, under, or sidearm) and hit the target?
   Can you roll the ball and knock over the pins? Use your left hand?

   c. Throwing and catching by self — Begin with yarn balls, then beanbags, followed by sponge rubber balls, and finally, playground balls.
   How many different ways can you throw and catch the ball? Beanbag?
   Can you throw and catch while low? High? Lying down? Sitting? Kneeling?
   Can you use either hand?
   Can you bounce and catch the ball?

   d. Partner activities

Can you sit down and roll the ball back and forth with a partner?

Can you bounce the ball to your partner and have him catch it without moving?

Can you throw the yarn ball underhand and have your partner catch it? (Then sponge rubber ball, beanbag, and finally playground ball)

Can you throw the yarn ball (beanbag, sponge rubber ball, playground ball) many different ways with different body parts and still have your partner catch it?

e. Implements

Can you move the yarn ball around the room using the hockey stick?

Can you hit the ball with the hockey stick and make it go into the goal?

Can you run and still keep hitting the ball with the stick?

Can you throw the beanbag with your hand and catch it with the scoop?

Can you catch the bean bag with the scoop when it is thrown by a partner?

Can you throw the beanbag up by using the scoop?

Can you throw the beanbag back and forth with a partner using only the scoops?

Can you hit the yarn ball with your racket? (Nylon and hanger, see Chapter 16).

4. Foot-Eye Progression

   a. Can you move the sponge rubber ball around the room using only your feet? Left or right foot only?

   b. Can you kick the playground ball and hit the target (pins or plastic bottles)?

   c. Can you kick the moving ball and hit the target? With either foot?

   d. Can you kick the ball back and forth with a partner and not have to move to get it?

5. Non-Dominant Side Development

   a. Can you throw and catch the beanbag with the hand you do not write with?

   b. Can you throw the beanbag back and forth from one hand to the other?

   c. Can you throw with one hand? Now use the other hand?

   d. Can you kick with your foot? Now can you use the other foot?

Kinesthetic Awareness

Kinesthesia is a knowledge of body parts in space. This awareness is dependent upon proprioception which is sensory feedback from muscles. This section will focus on kinesthetic awareness and proprioceptive development.

Goal: Following training the child will improve kinesthetic awareness through proprioceptive development activities.

Objectives: Following instruction and practice, the child should be able to:

1. Without looking, be able to throw a beanbag to a stationary partner one out of two times. The child can look to make a judgment but then must close his eyes or turn his back before throwing. He should be successful at three different distances, using each hand, and be able to throw the beanbag at least three different ways.

2. Do a forward roll from a squatting position and end up in a sitting position.

3. Jump in the air, making at least a half turn, and land without losing his balance.

4. With eyes closed, stand five seconds on one foot without losing his balance.

Kinesthetic and Proprioceptive Activities

1. Have the child turn his back and throw a beanbag to a partner without looking. The eyes can be used initially to make a distance judgment, but then the child closes his eyes, or turns his back and throws, using sensory feedback to determine distance. Keeping the same distance, a kindergarten child should be able to throw it to a partner with two tries.

The distance can be varied and the throwing method changed as children experience success. After a child has mastered one distance, it should be changed. By throwing in different ways and with different body parts, proprioceptive ability will be enhanced.

2. Throwing toward sound — A child is blindfolded and given a beanbag. A partner moves to a spot in the room and calls the blindfolded child's name. The blindfolded child turns toward the sound and tries to throw the beanbag to the partner.

3. Balance Activities, p. 132

4. Tumbling Activities, p. 132

5. Do This, Do That, p. 153

Balance

Balance is one of the more important aspects of development since most locomotor movement depends on it.

Goal: Children will demonstrate static and dynamic balance with a variety of activities.

Objectives: Following exploration, the child should be able to:

1. Jump and make a half turn without falling.
2. Walk forward, backward, and sideward without falling off an eight foot balance beam, four inches wide and seven inches off the ground.
3. Run a figure eight without falling down.
4. Stand on one foot for five seconds with eyes closed and not have to put the other foot down.
5. Swing either foot without losing balance.
6. Hop forward six inches on either foot and not lose balance.
7. Hop in place five times on either foot and not lose balance.

Balance Activities

1. Static balance — Static balance is done on a fixed base of support with no locomotor movement.

   a. Stork stand — Child stands with hands on hips and one foot against opposite knee. Try it with eyes closed.

      Can you stand on one foot with your eyes closed?
      Can you balance on one body part? Two? Three?

   b. Statues, p. 152.

   c. Balance boards.

2. Dynamic balance — Balance while moving.

   a. Low balance beam — no higher than eight inches off the floor. Young children should not be permitted on any balance beam higher than eight inches. Most balance beams are eight to twelve feet long.

      Can you walk forward (backward, sideward) on the balance beam?
      Can you walk to the center, turn around and walk backward off?
      Can you step over a bar held at knee level while walking on the beam?

   b. Obstacle course — The course should have many balance activities.

   c. Have children balance a beanbag on different body parts while moving in different directions.

Tumbling and Gymnastics

Tumbling and gymnastics activities help in the development of kinesthetic awareness, balance, and fitness.

Goal: Children will experience a variety of tumbling and gymnastics activities.

Objectives: Following instruction and experience, the children will be able to demonstrate at least 80 percent of the tumbling and gymnastics activities on the following list.

Tumbling Activities

1. Children should be given the opportunity to explore movement on mats. If possible, there should not be more than two or three children to an eight foot mat. They should be encouraged to see how many ways they can get from one end of the mat to the other. Children who discover interesting ways of moving can be pointed out to others.

2. Log roll — To do a log roll, the child lies across the mat with the body straight, feet together, and hands over the head.

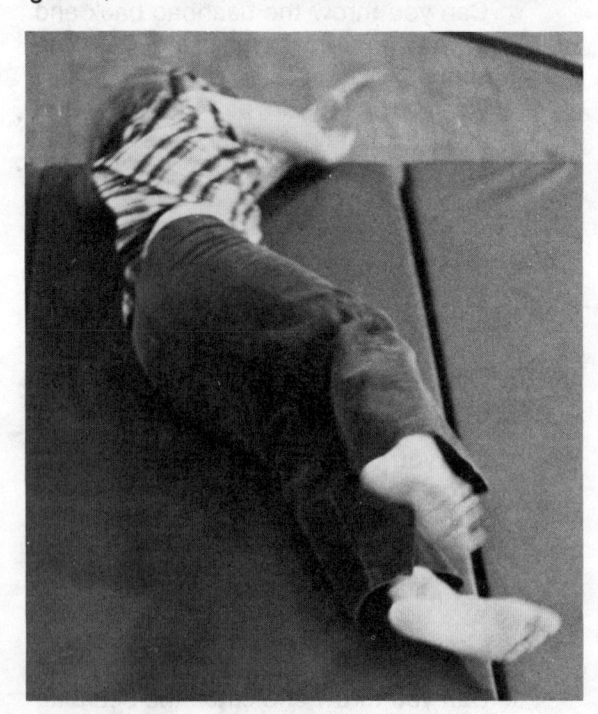

Log roll

Can you roll like a log down the mat and not go off to the sides?
How fast can you do a log roll? How slowly?

3. Egg roll — The egg roll is done by putting

the arms between the legs and grasping the ankles. The child then rolls sideways down the mat.

4. Human ball — The human ball is made by grasping the knees and pulling them up to the chest. The chin is tucked to the chest and the child rolls in all directions like a ball.

Human ball

5. Rolling forward — The child rolls forward similar to a forward roll done in later years, but no emphasis is placed on for. Children merely tuck their heads and roll ward to a sitting position.

6. Dog Walk — Place hands on floor and walk like a dog.

7. Duck Walk — Deep knee bend to squat position. Hands on hips and tucked under arm pits, walk without raising hips.

8. Elephant Walk — Bend forward keeping knees straight and place hands flat on floor. Walk forward and backward keeping knees and elbows straight.

9. Crab Walk — Sit on floor face up. Raise and support weight of body by keeping hands and feet on floor, keep back straight. Walk backward, forward, and sideward by using hand and feet.

10. Frog Hop — Squat position, place arms between legs and hands on floor. Take short hops by placing hands on floor ahead of feet and bringing feet up to hands.

11. Jump and slap heels — From standing position, jump up, extending heels to the side, and reach backward to slap heels.

Gymnastics Activities

1. Rings

    a. Inverted hang — Hang by hands in an inverted position while maintaining balance by placing feet against the support straps.

Inverted hang

   b. Flexed arm hang — Keep head between rings as long as possible in a flexed arm position.

Developing fitness on rings

   c. Spin on rings — Spin on rings by using feet on ground and then lift legs to un-spin.

134 Kindergarten

2. Climb rope ladder six feet high.

Climbing rope ladder

3. Go across horizontal ladder — The feet should not be higher than 12 — 18 inches off the ground when hanging from the ladder by the hands.

4. Climbing rope — Children should attempt to climb the rope using their hands and legs. No child should be permitted to go higher than his or her own height.

The trapeze

5. Trapeze
   a. Swing while holding on with hands.
   b. Pull up, hook knees, and hang by knees.

Hanging by knees

   c. Pull knees and legs between hands and reach feet down, finally letting go when feet are nearly on the mat.

6. Balance beam, p. 132.

7. Vaulting box — Run and jump; get over box in as many safe ways as possible.

Fitness

The emphasis is on health-related fitness components rather than motor fitness components (see Chapter 6).

Goal: Children will show improvement in all aspects of fitness each time a test is given.

Objectives:

1. To be able to jog continuously for a minimum of six minutes.

2. To be able to do five sit-ups, hands across chest while someone holds feet down and knees are bent.

3. To do ten modified (knee) push-ups.

4. To be able to touch toes without bending knees.

5. To be able to keep chin over a bar for a minimum of three seconds while doing a flexed arm hang.

Integrated Planning

While developing fitness, attempt to introduce information about fitness to the children. Concepts such as muscles get stronger with exercise, heart-rate increase when exercising, and why fitness is important are all ways to integrate physiology with physical education.

Flashcards with names of exercises on them can be used to help children learn new words.

Fitness Activities

1. Cardiovascular development
   a. Running
   b. Rope jumping
   c. Aerobic dance
2. Upper body strength
   a. Climbing activities
   b. Hanging
   c. Gymnastics and tumbling, p. 132
   d. Push-ups
   e. Rope climbing
3. Abdominal strength
   a. Tumbling and gymnastics, p. 132
   b. Sit-ups
4. Flexibility
   a. Tumbling and gymnastics, p. 132
   b. Stretching and exercises.
5. Posture (Chapter 6)

Rhythmics

Rhythmic development should be a major component of early childhood education. Although many think of rhythms being only in music, many basic locomotor movements such as walking and running are examples of rhythmic activity. (Also see Chapter 11.)

Goal: Children will exhibit rhythmic development in a variety of movement activities, including dance.

Objectives:

1. Children will demonstrate rhythmic ability in basic locomotor movements by moving to a tom-tom.
2. Children will keep time to music, using body parts or the entire body.
3. Children will recognize tempo changes, and make appropriate rhythmic adjustments with the body or body parts.
4. Children will keep time to music using lummi sticks.
5. Children will move creatively to different types of music.
6. Children will be able to do simple singing dances.

Integrated Planning

The obvious subject which can be integrated with rhythmics is music, but social studies can also be included. By participating in dances from other countries, children may learn about other people. In music, children can learn phrasing, accenting, and the classics.

Rhythmic Activities

1. Moving to music

   a. Classics — The wide variety of tempos and moods make classical music ideal for children's movement. Short selections recorded on tape and carefully arranged can help develop all the basic movement competencies, including rhythmic ability.

   b. Modern — Children enjoy moving to contemporary selections. Unfortunately, the variety of movement is limited and is usually imitative, rather than creative. Although rhythmic ability is enhanced, little creativity is developed.

   c. Musical Statues — When the music begins, the children begin moving around the room in a way in which the music makes them feel. When the music stops, everyone freezes. Children move only through empty spaces. Everyone begins moving again when the music plays.

   Before starting, this activity could be limited to animal statues or sport statues.

   d. Musical Accompaniment — Each child has a stick and a milk jug. They move around the room, walking, marching, skipping, etc., in time to the music and beat the jug in time to the music. Different types of music can be used for different tempos, etc.

   e. Child created — Children can create their own rhythm. Rhythm and movement can then be combined.

2. Tom-tom — The tom-tom can be used to aid rhythmic development. The teacher is free to change beats rapidly, accent notes at will, and generally guide development. A plastic container can be used as a tom-tom or tom-toms can be purchased.

3. Lummi Sticks — These sticks are sometimes called rhythm sticks and can provide a restful period between two more strenuous activities. Both rhythmic ability and hand-eye coordination can be enhanced through the use of

...dergartners can keep rhythm ...on the floor, or together while ...g around the room.
...ordination can be developed by ...cks or tossing and catching them ...ing rhythm. No partner activites ...nanging sticks, such as those done with older children, should be done at the kindergarten level.

A circle dance

4. Singing dances, sources, p. 395.

    a. Moving to Nursery Rhymes. Find a partner and act out these rhymes. Note: Children should say rhymes once they learn the words.

    1. Hickory, dickory, dock
       The mouse ran up the clock
       The clock struck one
       The mouse ran down
       Hickory, dickory, dock.

    2. Jack be nimble, Jack be quick,
       Jack jump over the candlestick.

    3. Humpty Dumpty sat on a wall,
       Humpty Dumpty had a great fall,
       All the kings horses and all the kings men,
       Couldn't put Humpty Dumpty together again.

    4. I'm a little teapot, short and stout,
       Here is my handle, and here is my spout.
       When I get all steamed up, hear me shout
       Just tip me over and pour me out.

       I'm a very clever pot it's true,
       Here's an example of what I can do.
       I can change my handle and my spout,
       Just tip me over and pour me out.

    b. Touch Your Shoulders. Sing and act out.

    1. Touch your shoulders and your knees,
       Touch your shoulders and your knees.
       Touch your shoulders and your knees,
       Make your feet go stamp, stamp, stamp.

    2. Touch your elbows and your toes,
       Touch your elbows and your toes.
       Touch your elbows and your toes,
       Make your hands go clap, clap, clap.

    3. Touch your ankles, reach up high,
       Touch your ankles, reach up high.
       Touch your ankles, reach up high,
       Shake yourself up in the sky.

    c. I Can Move.

       Children are scattered around the room. You could start by sitting or standing. Using the following song, each child should get a turn to show what they can move. Once they show what they can move, everyone joins in moving and singing.

       I can move my elbows.
       So can you.
       I can move my elbows.
       So can you.

       I can move my elbows.
       So can you.
       Show us another part we can move.

I Can Move

I can move my el-bows, So can you. I can move my el-bows, So can you.

I can move my el-bows, So can you. Show us an-other part We can move.

Kindergarten 137

d. Ring Around The Rosey

Children sing and act out the song.

Ring-a-Round a Rosey,
A pocketfull of posies.
Ashes, ashes,
All fall down.

-or-

Ring around the Rosy,
A pocketfull of posies,
One, two, three,
And squat where you be.

The children join hands, walk, skip, or slide around the circle.

e. My Feet Went Walking

Children are scattered around the room. Using the following song, the children will have a chance to think up something or somehow they can move with their feet.

1. My feet went walking down the street,
   Down the street
   Down the street,
   My feet went walking down the street,
   Then they stopped.

2. My roller skates went rolling on the sidewalk,
   on the sidewalk,
   on the sidewalk,
   My roller skates went rolling on the sidewalk,
   and then they stopped.

f. Up, Down, and Around

The children are scattered around the room either sitting or standing. Using the following song, the children will learn concepts such as up, down, around, right, left, high, and low.

We can go up (high),
We can go down (low).

g. Look at Me

The children are scattered around the room sitting Indian style or sitting in their desks. Using the song that follows, each child gets a turn to name and point at a body part. Once they point to and name a body part, everyone joins in pointing to their same body part and sings.

Look at me _____,
Look at me_____.

Here's my _____,
Here's my _____.

Look at me _____,
Look at me _____.

See my _____.

138 Kindergarten

h. I'm Tall, I'm Small

One child stands in the center of the circle with his eyes closed. Circle players walk slowly around, singing:

I'm tall, I'm small,
I'm small, I'm very tall.
Sometimes I'm tall,
Sometimes I'm small,
Guess what I am now?

As children walk and sing "tall" or "very tall," or "small" or "very small," they stretch up or stoop down depending on the words. At the end of the singing, the leader signals circle players to assume a stretching or stooping position. The center player then guesses which position they have taken. If the center player guesses correctly, he remains; if unsuccessful, a new player is selected. This game may be played using concepts such as high, low, big, little, etc.

5. Simple dances, sources, p. 135.

6. Long rope (13 feet) jumping progression

   a. Snakes (class of 25) — Four long ropes are held between eight children, four on each side, who wiggle ropes to create snakes. The remaining children run the guantlet trying not to touch the ropes. Many children can go at a time if they travel only one way and return to the starting point by going behind rope shakers.

Snakes

b. Waves — Same arrangement as snakes, except children create waves with ropes. Children go through ropes the same as in snakes.

c. Rocker — Two enders rock rope back and forth while child in middle jumps it each time it goes under his feet. Most children will use a two beat jump in which a small jump is taken between each actual rope jump.

d. Turn and Jump — The rope is turned while the child stands in the center, jumping at the appropriate time. Children must be taught to turn the rope properly, which requires a full arm circle for success.

e. Frontdoor and backdoor — Getting in and jumping after the children begin turning the rope is called frontdoor or backdoor depending upon the rope's direction. If the rope is coming down toward the waiting jumper's head, it is called frontdoor, while a rope coming up toward the chin is the harder backdoor. Front door is easier since there is more time to get in before one has to jump. Both entrances are advanced for some kindergarten children (particularly boys).

f. Getting started — "Let me see how many of you can do long rope jumping." Based upon the children's performance, the teacher can individualize instruction by giving poor jumpers added attention while letting more advanced students (usually the girls), try more difficult skills such as front and backdoor.

Rope jumping can be done to music, a tom-tom, chants, or with no accompaniment. Rhythmic ability, coordination, and (if done long enough), cardiovascular fitness are all developed through rope jumping.

7. Short Rope Jumping — Some five-year-olds may be ready for short rope jumping. Since the child must coordinate the rope as well as the jump, this is more difficult than long rope jumping. Children who have accomplished both front and backdoor should be allowed to do single rope jumping.

The parachute can be used for developing rhythmic ability.

8. Parachute — Although the parachute has frequently been promoted as the developer of every aspect of physical education, its main value (and probably its only real value), is rhythmic development. The tom-tom or records can be used along with the parachute.

   a. The mushroom — Children take three steps in, while raising the parachute up to form what looks like the top of a mushroom.

   b. The clam — Children form mushroom taking a half turn as they do so. Children drop to knees and snap parachute to ground in front of them disappearing inside chute.

   c. The mountain — Is the clam with the children on the outside. The children like to crawl on the chute and knock the air out.

   d. The cloud — The parachute is raised as in the mushroom and then released by everyone at the same time. A good release will cause the chute to float like a cloud before falling.

   e. Circle dances — Many folk dances and novelty rhythmics lend themselves to parachuting usage. Several records focusing on the parachute and rhythmic development have been produced (see page 395).

9. Cooperative Musical Hugs — The children skip around the room to the accompaniment of live music. When there is a pause in the music, each child gives someone else a big hug. The music begins again and the skipping continues. A pause in the music and 3 children hug together. This continues until all the children huddle together in one big hug. The locomotor movement can and should be changed frequently.

10. Streamers — Each child is given a plastic wand with a colorful paper streamer attached. While the music plays (use various selections of classical music) the children move on the floor using various locomotor or nonlocomotor movements and wave their streamers in time to the music.

11. Indian in the Forest — The teacher will lead the class in this to assist with the rhythm. The activity begins with the chant:

    Softly on his tip tip toes,
    the Indian through the forest goes
    Sh, Sh, Sh, Sh.

   Other chants ideas are:

   The Indian can run fast, skip softly, hop or creep through the forest.

   The Indian will meet a friend in the forest and run while holding hands.

   The Indians will form groups of 3 or 4, build a campfire and then dance around it.

Creativity

Probably the most difficult developmental aspect to measure is creativity. Measurability, however, is not critical since there is general agreement on the importance of creativity and its need at all levels. Activities which aid the child's creative development should be a part of nearly every lesson.

Goal: Children will exhibit creativity in a variety of activities.

Objectives:

1. Each child will be able to create one original move to music if asked.
2. Children will move creatively to music.
3. Children will create original solutions to situations in a story play.
4. Five-year-olds will be able to create a lummi stick routine with three different moves.

Integrated Planning

Many things can be learned through creative activities. Science and historical information lend themselves well to story plays (see below).

Creative Activities

1. Story Plays — One of the more popular activities is a story play. Children can travel anywhere and do anything through imagination. The teacher's role in a story play is to: (1) set the theme (going to the circus, moon, jungle), (2) create problem-solving situations for the students which aid development of movement qualities, such as force, time, space, level, and (3) allow for student design of the story (creativity) and the movements. The teacher should not join in too much since the children will tend to imitate the teacher's movement.

   a. Trip to the Jungle.
   Today we are going to the jungle. How can we get to the jungle? (Plane, boat, car, train.) You go the way you want to. Ready, go. (Children race around the room imitating their transportation mode.) Has anyone found the jungle? What does it look like? (Dark.) Is it hot or cold? How should we travel through the jungle? (Truck, walk.) Children begin moving through the jungle. These trees and vines are getting very low. How will we have to move? Did anyone bring a big knife to cut through this? (Children chop away). What do we see in a jungle? (Snakes, spiders, etc.) Can you move like a spider? I see some squicksand and some of you are sinking in it. How can we rescue them, boys and girls? (Throw a rope, reach a hand.) Let's pull them out. Boy, is that hard! How can we get over this quicksand? (Jump, leap, swing on vine.)

   b. Blizzard
   Two children are lost in a snowstorm and are trying to get back home. One of the children is "snow-blind" and the other can see. The objective is to lead the snow-blind friend (who has his eyes shut or blindfolded) through the blizzard (obstacle course) to safety. In pairs, the children go through a snow tunnel (hoop), under an ice log (bench), over a partially frozen river (small mat), and across a snow bridge (bench). Partners hold hands or link arms and try not to let go so no one gets lost alone in the storm. Once they reach "safety," the partners can switch roles.

   Older children can attempt to direct their partner through the course safely by talking to him, by singing to him, or by a special code other than talking or holding hands. (Example: Clasp hands to move one way; tap on shoulder to step up; or snap fingers.) The blizzard story could also be changed to something like "control tower to pilot." The pilot cannot see because of heavy fog. The objective is for the controller to direct the pilot safely through various obstacles and onto the runway.

   c. Red Riding Hood
   The order of the story will be as follows and the students will act accordingly. When the story begins, Red Riding Hood is picking flowers, Grandma is at home in bed sick, and the wolf is at the house looking out the window. Afterwards —
   1. Red Riding Hood skips in the direction of Grandma's house with a basket on her arm.
   2. She picks flowers every few skips.
   3. The wolf sees Red Riding Hood.
   4. He runs to her and asks where she's going.
   5. She replies "to Grandma's house."
   6. Red Riding Hood continues to skip to Grandma's house.
   7. The wolf arrives at Grandma's house before Red Riding Hood does.
   8. He hides Grandma in the house.

Kindergarten 141

9. Then he dresses up in her nightclothes and glasses and lies in the bed awaiting Red Riding Hood.
10. Red Riding Hood knocks on Grandma's door.
11. The wolf (Grandma) says "come in." So Red Riding Hood goes in.
12. She is surprised to see how much Grandma has changed: "Grandma, what big eyes you have!" "Grandma, what a big nose you have!" "Grandma, what a big mouth you have!"
13. The wolf answers, "The better to eat you with."
14. Red Riding Hood realizes that that is the wolf in Grandma's bed.
15. She tries to get out of the house — and finally does.
16. The wolf chases her and is finally captured by a hunter.
17. Red Riding Hood and Grandma are reunited.

d. Alice's Looking Glass

(1) Everyone spread out — find your place. (2) You see a tunnel — you drop down and crawl through to find out where it is going. Crawl gently and look to one side and to the other (with lead hand then opposite) to check things out. (3) Oops! Suddenly you are stopped by a tree growing in the tunnel path so you crawl backward and creep backward and go around it. (4) Now you're at the end of the dark tunnel and you step out to the warm light. You feel relaxed and warm and you start to walk (to beat of tom-tom). (5) Change pace and quality of steps to tom-tom. (6) Oh! You stop! You see a beautiful stream. How does water move? There are flowers — how do they feel? What do you do with the flowers? Oh! There's a butterfly! How does it move? (7) You want to cross over the stream and you have to walk very carefully from one rock to the other, putting one foot in front of the other and balancing yourself. (8) In the stream you see a frog and he's leaping from one lily pad to another. Find a partner who is wearing a color you have on and leap over each other as the frog does. (9) You cross now to the other side of the bridge where you see a nest of birds in a tree. Find a partner to be your brother or sister bird. Now pick a mother to feed you. Now pick a father to get food. (All children will be involved as roles change. They do not wait to be picked.) (10) Wow! Now you see a horse and decide to follow him. He's moving fast so you gallop to keep up with him. (11) Now he brings you to a pond where a family of flamingos are resting. (Brief explanation.) Can you rest on one foot like the flamingo? Can you change feet? (12) Passing you comes a rabbit singing, "I'm late." Let's sing the poem, "I'm late, I'm late, for a very important date," as we hop through wonderland to the rhythm of the poem. (13) You stop. You see a mirror. Find a partner and do what he does each take a turn. Point to body parts and name them. (14) Now you found the magic mirror and it's time to return home, so count to ten, close your eyes, find a friend's hand and say "Abra cadabra, we're home!" Hurray!

e. The Toy Shop

1. Reach and take toys from the high shelf.
2. Tin soldiers: walk forward and backward with stiff knees and arms bent at elbows.
3. Jack-in-the-box: squat with hands at sides. When teacher raises hands as if opening a box, children jump up, hands high overhead.
4. Train: run in circle with both hands on shoulders of the pupil in front, the leader guiding the line to the left and to the right.
5. Wind-up car: have partners, one to be car and one to wind up car; them change positions.

f. In the Country

The teacher formulates the setting and selects the structure for the children. Examples: picking berries, climbing to hayloft, planting crops, picking flowers, chasing butterflies, imitating farm animals.

g. Pioneer Days

This activity can incorporate the knowledge the children have received from study in the classroom. The object is for one group to act out and move to the different activities the pioneer families were involved in. The other group will act out similar activities, only they will be in the present day.

h. Other themes — holidays, seasons of the year, circus, outer space, into the future, and into the past.

i. Integrated themes — Science can easily be integrated into the story play. Trips to the moon can bring in terms like weightlessness, gravity, orbit, and retrofire; a scuba diving trip can introduce children to the names of saltwater fish; and a trip to the forest provides opportunities to talk about flowers, trees, and animals; and history can be integrated by doing story plays about past events and people.

2. Pantomimes — Children can move around the room pantomiming. Have several children trying to guess what they are or what they're doing. Children could be such things as soldiers, giants, Raggedy Ann, etc.

3. Raggedy Ann — All of the children will pretend to be rag dolls, loose and free with no definite form. They would be asked to perform several movements in the way they think Raggedy Ann would. First, they would be asked to walk, hop, skip, run and jump (basics) the way Raggedy Ann would. Afterwards the children would be asked to do more complex things, like sit in a chair, cheer at a game, turn around, bend over to touch her toes, or to act like Raggedy Ann caught outside in a strong wind. This activity is inexhaustible. The children could be asked to do any number of things in the fashion that they think Raggedy Ann would do them — right foot or left foot.

4. Body Dancing — Have children dance with different parts of the body. For example: "Boys and girls, let's dance only using your heads. How many different ways can you move your head to the music?" Then use another part of the body alone. Then you combine two or more parts together. This is an excellent activity for handicapped children or children who need work on body awareness.

5. Body Talk — After a thorough discussion of the emotions we feel, such as fear, excitement, sadness, joy, anger, love, etc., have the children feel comfortable with this activity, have them get in free formation. Have them communicate to you through bodily movement the action and emotional response of walking in rain, snow, on icy pavement, through sticky mud. The possibilities are endless.

6. Automobiles — The students will act as cars. A few students will be designated as service vehicles such as a police car, fire truck, and an ambulance. The teacher will signal the cars with three flash cards — *green* meaning to go, *red* meaning to stop, and *yellow* meaning to slow down in caution. When the cars are moving they would be required to give simple hand signals when turning — extending arm straight out in the right or left direction. The teacher will also call "emergency" on a service vehicle. For example, teacher may call "police emergency." The police car to pass; police car sound the siren and move fast, running stop lights cautiously. (The service vehicles will be traveling at a normal speed until the teacher calls out that vehicle as an emergency.)

7. Making a Snowman — The teacher says: (1) pull on your boots, (2) put on coat, cap and mittens, (3) walk through deep snow, (4) make a snowman, (5) run back and roll another snowball to make a head. Then ask what happens to the snowman when the sun comes out and it gets warm? Show me.

8. Weather — The teacher reads the poem and the children react.

> Swish goes the wind.
> It makes the leaves fly.
> Whoops, there's thunder
> And lightning up high.
> Down comes the rain
> In buckets so big
> In a near farm, it's just cleaned a pig.
> Out comes the sun, so yellow and bright
> It's drying the wetness with all of its might.
> Now, all the leaves get together and
> Make a beautiful sight.

9. Circus Parade — Children move freely around forming a large circle. They pretend to be in a circus parade. One group leads and others imitate horses, tigers, bears, etc.

10. Over, Under and Around — Students are instructed to move about; when they hear the command to freeze, they make some type of shape with their body. Then the teacher goes around and unfreezes 3 or 4 children who then proceed to go over, under and around all the other body shapes without touching anyone. Children should move quickly through the shapes. The activity is repeated until nearly every child has had a chance to go through the shapes.

11. If I Were . . . — The children move randomly around the play area until the teacher calls out, "If I were a (an) ____, I would move like this." The children then imitate whatever has been named.

12. Ringmaster — One child is selected as the ringmaster and stands in the center of the play area. He moves about the center and pretends to crack a whip as he calls out the names of animals. The children then imitate the circus animals. If he calls "all join the parade," they may imitate any animal they want in the parade.

13. Growing Like a Flower or Tree — Children can develop non-locomotor skills and creativity while learning about how things grow. Let's pretend you are a flower seed. What does a flower seed need to grow? (water, soil, sun) Do flowers grow slow or fast? (slow) Can you grow like a flower to the music? Decide what type of flower you are and try to form different flowers using your hands and arms. What happens when the wind blows? Somebody is coming by to pick you.

14. Moving to environmental sounds
    a. Wind
    b. Rain
    c. Train
    d. Jack hammer

15. Acting out poems — Be sure poem provides extensive opportunity for large muscle movement. As poem is read, each child interprets the words through movement. Originality of movement should be encouraged.

16. Being a machine — Children can act alone, with a partner to create a machine that moves or has moving parts. Possibilities include: car, washing mashine, typewriter, train, and tractor.

17. Other Ideas
    a. Moving to Music
    b. Moving like People
        Police officer
        Fire fighter
        Teacher
        Sports figures
        Dancers
    c. Moving like Animals
    d. Acting out Sports Activities
        Skiing
        Ice skating
        Bowling
        Baseball
    e. Statues — There are a variety of ways to play statues.
        Animal statues
        People statues
        Group statues — The teacher holds up a number on his or her fingers or on a card. Children who have been moving freely around the floor seek others to form groups corresponding to the number. When the whistle blows, the children must freeze in a group statue. Themes, such as sports, places, and people can be used to guide the statue's design. Through these activities children learn to think quickly.

A group statue

Playground equipment can be used to develop creativity.

Relaxation

In our pressurized world, many children have never experienced complete relaxation.

Goal: Children will exhibit relaxation in most activities.

Objective: A totally relaxed child who is lying down, should be very supple with no tension, particularly in the arms. If a limb is dropped (only do on mat), it should drop freely to the mat with no resistance from muscles.

Relaxation Activities

1. Raggedy Ann — Children are asked to be as loose as Raggedy Ann (teacher uses doll to demonstrate). Children follow with loose arm and leg movements. Children then lie on tumbling mats and are told to be as loose as possible. Raggedy Ann is placed on floor and used to demonstrate looseness. The teacher then moves around floor checking children for relaxation by moving limbs.

2. Talk through — Children are talked through relaxation by the teacher who alternates tension and relaxation to show comparisons. The teacher begins at the feet and works up.

"Think about your feet and toes. Tighten them as tight as you can. Now loosen them. Tight again and loose again." The teacher continues until all major body sections are done. Then the process begins again using only relaxation without first tightening.

"Relax your feet and toes, legs, stomach, chest, arms, fingers, neck, face. Feel yourself sinking into the floor; you are very heavy." Soft music adds to the atmosphere.

3. Melting like snowman — Children melt becoming water (loose).

4. Rubber man — Children pretend they are made of rubber (loose), and the teacher checks them as in Raggedy Ann activity above.

AFFECTIVE DOMAIN

Many of the affective domain objectives are idealistic and are meant only as guides for the teacher. Affective objectives are difficult to accomplish because attitudes are hard to develop and change. Many outside influences also counter much of the learning in school. Constant teacher effort and example, however, should pay off in the long run. (Also read the introduction to this book for additional thoughts about self-concept.)

Self-Concept

How a child feels about himself is termed self-concept.

Goal: Children will improve their self-concept.

Objective: Given an attitude questionnaire, nearly all the children will indicate a positive feeling about themselves.

Self-Concept Activities

1. Offer activities at the appropriate developmental level so children will experience success.

2. Discuss interpersonal relations with children (name calling, helping others, and being kind to each other).

3. Praise each student frequently.

4. Also see body image activities, p. 147.

5. Call children by name.

6. Give children various responsibilities for reward, such as door holder or line leader.

7. Show love for children.

Honesty

Goal: Children will exhibit honest behavior in most situations.

Objectives:

Children will admit to being caught in a tag game.

2. Children will admit guilt when they have done something wrong.

Honesty Activities

The teacher must constantly be alert to opportunities for discussion of honesty. Game situations provide opportunities for discussion of honesty.

Sharing

Goal: To have children share materials when there are not enough for each of them.

Objective:

Given a situation requiring sharing, children will voluntarily share with others.

Sharing Activities

1. Set up stations in which there is not enough equipment for everyone and then emphasize the need to share. After a couple of sharing discussions, set up a sharing situation and see if children voluntarily share.

2. Look for opportunities in all teaching situations to mention sharing.

Respect for Authority

Goal: Children will develop respect for those teachers who earn it.

Objectives:

1. No child will talk while the teacher is talking.

2. Children will stop, look, and listen on a pre-arranged signal.

3. Children will follow school and class rules.

Patience
Goal: Children will improve patience.
Objective:
Children will wait their turn without complaining.

Respect for Self and Others
Goal: Children will develop self-respect and respect for others.
Objectives:
1. Children will not make fun of others who are different.
2. Children will not gang up on another child.
3. A child will accept an assigned partner without verbal or non-verbal complaint.
4. Children will not endanger themselves or others by violating safety rules.
5. Children will say "please" and "thank you" when dealing with peers or adults.
6. Children will give verbal encouragement to others during physical performance.

Leading and Following
Goal: Children will be good leaders & followers where appropriate.
Objectives:
1. Children will follow and do what the leader does during a game of "Follow the Leader."
2. Children will do what the teacher asks.
3. When called upon, children will be willing leaders in small group situations (eight to ten children).

Leading and Following Activities

1. Play Follow the Leader.
2. Give children a "choice day" on which children can choose and conduct their own activities.
3. Give children various class responsibilities such as line leader, equipment carrier, or door holder. Rotate responsibilities frequently.

Positive Attitudes
Goal: Children will develop positive attitudes toward health and physical education.
Objectives: 1. Child will give a high rating to physical education on an attitude questionnaire.
2. Children will willingly participate in all activities.
3. Children will indicate positive attitudes toward health practices, including fitness, by their response to statements on an attitude questionnaire.

A happy child is the goal.

4. Children will indicate a positive attitude toward the teacher and peers by their response to statements on an attitude questionaire.

COGNITIVE DOMAIN

Many kindergarten activities provide opportunities to involve children cognitively. Flash cards with movement terms and letters, and problem-solving and creative activities all enhance cognitive knowledge and ability. One must not lose sight, however, of the main physical education objectives, which are primarily in the psychomotor domain.

Problem-Solving Ability
Goal: Children will improve problem-solving ability in a variety of situations.
Objective: Children will be able to solve movement problems at their own level in all psychomotor activities.

Problem-Solving Activities

1. Any activity can be problem-solving depending upon the approach used by the teacher. The best way to make children think is to ask open-ended questions (those with a multitude of possible answers), which the children solve through movement.

How many ways can you throw and catch the ball?

How many ways can you move across the

146 Kindergarten

room using two body parts? Three body parts?

How many ways can you go in and out of your hoop?

Can you use two pieces of equipment at one time?

Can you bounce the ball with two different body parts?

Can you move like a big animal? A tiny animal?

2. Children should be given the opportunity to think through class rules and have input, regarding the consequences of behavior good and bad.

3. Story plays are good for the developing problem-solving ability (See p. 140).

Directional and Movement Terms

Goal: Children will learn a number of directional and movement terms.

Objectives:

1. Children will demonstrate knowledge of the following directionality terms through pointing or appropriate movements: up, down, right, left, near, far, farther, nearer, over, under, on top of, beside, between, through, inside, next to, around, above, below, in front of, behind, upper, lower, and middle.

2. Children will demonstrate through movement an understanding of the following locomotor and non-locomotor terms: walk, run, hop, jump, leap, gallop, slide, skip, twist, turn, stretch, bend, shake, swing, and bounce.

Integrated Planning

Use flash cards with movement and directional terms.

Directional and Movement Term Activities

1. Use flashcards or an overhead projector to present terms to children who then show understanding through movement. Children can also be asked to say the word as they move.

2. Movement terms can also be used at learning centers.

3. Play activities in which movement terms are emphasized.

4. Use hoops to teach and reinforce terminology.

Can you go "around" your hoop? "Inside?" "Over?" "Through?" "Away from?" "Closer?" "In and out?"

Can you make a bridge "over" your hoop using two body parts? "Three?" "Four?"

Can you put two body parts "inside" the hoop? "Three?"

Children manipulate hoops

Can you move around and "between" two hoops?

Can you stand so the hoop is "in front of" you? "Behind?" "Beside?"

A beanbag or piece of paper can be substituted for the hoop although you do lose some movement opportunities, i.e., "Inside," "Through."

Body Image

Body image is a knowledge of body parts.

Goal: Children will learn a number of body parts.

Objectives:

1. A four-year-old should be able to touch each of the following parts when asked: head, eyes, ears, nose, mouth, hands, fingers, knees, feet, back and front.

2. The five-year-old should be able to touch each of the following parts when asked: all those the four-year-old identified, plus shoulders, elbows, wrists, waist, neck, chin, and side.

3. Upon request, children will be able to move various parts mentioned in one and two above.

4. By age five, a child will be able to draw a self-portrait including each of the following parts: head, eyes, nose, mouth, arms, fingers and legs.

Integrated Planning

Use flashcards with body parts on them, p. 148.

Busy Bee

Body Image Activities

1. Busy Bee, p. 152
2. Brothers, p. 152
3. Simon Says, p. 152
4. Touch Across — In this activity, two children sit across from each other. The teacher calls out body parts and children touch their partner's body part named.

Can you touch your partner's shoulders, elbows, knees, right hand, left shoulder with your right hand, etc.?

5. Beanbag Activities

Can you throw the beanbag with some right part of your body? Back part? Lower part? Right elbow? Left wrist?

6. Angels in the Snow

Child lies flat on his back on the mat with arms at his sides and feet together. First ask him to move feet apart as far as he can, keeping knees stiff. Then ask him to move arms along mat until hands meet above head. Next, slide legs back together until heels click and then arms down until hands slap sides. When child has mastered these movements, ask him to move his legs apart and at the same time move arms over his head. Next ask him to slide his legs apart and return his arms to sides at the same time. The next step would be to ask the child to move one body part only. Example: Move your left leg up, left leg down, etc. The next step would be to ask the child to move his right arm and right leg together. Then left arm and left leg. The next step would be to ask the child to move left leg and right arm together and vice versa. Variations: (1) change time from slow to fast or to music; (2) have child turn over on stomach and do each step; (3) have child put pillow under abdomen and repeat steps keeping arms and legs in air.

Rules and Regulations

Goal: Children will be able to follow simple rules for class activities and games.

Objectives:

1. Children will be able to play and follow the rules of at least five games without assistance from the teacher.
2. If asked, children will be able to give at least three class rules.
3. If asked children will be able to give at least two safety rules for tumbling and gymnastics.
4. If asked, children will be able to give the reason for a rule.

Fitness, Health, and Safety Knowledge

Goal: Children will learn fitness, health, and safety facts and concepts.

Objectives:

1. Children should be able to give at least two reasons for being physically fit.
2. Children should be able to give at least two reasons for doing each of the following: brushing teeth, keeping clean, exercising, wearing proper footwear for activity, following safety rules.
3. Children should be able to give at least one reason for each of the following safety rules: no pushing, no sliding on floor, staying inside boundaries, staying away from animals on playground, stopping on a given signal, staying away from strangers, no horseplay during gymnastics and tumbling, and no running when in line.

Fitness Information

1. Improved fitness will make you feel better and look better.
2. Being fit will help you to run faster, throw and kick farther, and jump higher.
3. Being fit will make your insides work better, particularly heart and lungs.
4. See Chapter 6 for more information.

INTEGRATED ACTIVITIES AND GAMES

Integrated activities and games incorporate some academic subject into the physical education curriculum without diluting the physical education objective. A more detailed description of integrated activities and games is given on p. 111.

Language Arts

Flash Cards. Traditionally, most instructions in physcial education are given verbally. By using words and instructions on flashcards, children can increase their sight vocabulary.

Children should say the word and then move to the word, i.e., WALK, RUN, SKIP, HOP, GALLOP, JOG, WALK BACKWARD, WALK TO THE LEFT, SKIP BACKWARDS. Flash cards can be held up or put on a transparency and flashed on the wall using an overhead projector. Children can also be asked to spell the words as they begin moving.

Letters can also be used on flash cards for reinforcement of letters. Children can be asked to make the letter with their body or find a friend or friends to form the letter with. They can also be asked to move and form the letters, i.e. walk backward and form this letter — A.

Example Activity:

Name: Body Parts

Value: Learning body parts and ability to distinguished right from left.

Hold up a flashcard with the name of a body part and in some cases the word "right" or "left."

Do an exercise that make your "left leg" move.

Do an exercise that moves your "head."

Acting Out Poems. Many poems have a great deal of movement associated with them, and children can be asked to act out the movement as the poem is being read. Emphasis should be placed on originality of movement.

Math

Flash Cards. Flash cards can also aid in mathematics development. Children can be asked to form numbers with their bodies or combine with a friend or friends to make the numbers. Children can also be asked to form shapes.

As different shapes or numbers are held up, the children can be asked to call out the shape or number. The word corresponding to the shape or number can also be held simultaneously to help children make associations. Children who are slow should be helped by seeing the number and word, and hearing the other children say it. Shapes can be used as targets in hand-eye coordination activities.

Example Activity:

Name: Bean Bag Shuffleboard

Value: Manipulative development and number recognition.

A large piece of cardboard is placed on the floor. Numbers are placed on the card similar to shuffleboard. The children stand behind a re-

Figure 7-1. Flash Card Words, Numbers, and Shapes

Walk	Neck	1 - 20
Run	Nose	20 Twenty
Jump	Ears	30 Thirty
Leap	Mouth	40 Forty
Skip	Chin	Etc.
Right	Wrist	
Left	Waist	
Slow	Elbow	
Fast	Knee	Rectangle
Forward	Hips	
Sideward	Gallop	
Backward	Slide	Triangle
Hand	Twist	
Foot	Turn	
Arm	Bend	Square
Leg	Stretch	
Shoulders	Spin	Circle
Head		

straining line about four feet from the target. Children then try to toss the beanbag so it lands on certain numbers designated by the teacher. Each child can have his or her own board, or numbers can be placed on old sheets which then can be folded and easily stored. Children can also play with someone else and see who can land on the highest number, lowest number, an even number on an odd number.

Example Games:

Old Mother Witch. See page 183.
Dog Catcher. See page 182.
Three Bears. See page 182.

All three of these activities can help young children understand the concepts of "more than," "less than," and "equal to." Suppose, for example, that Billy tagged a total of five children on his two turns. Mary then tagged two on her first turn. The teacher can then ask, "How many more does Mary need to have more than Billy?" or "How many does she need to be equal to Billy?" These questions and their answers only take a few moments, and can be done as children are preparing for the next turn. Since this is an integrated activity, the majority of time and emphasis should be on physical education objectives.

Science

Physical education offers numerous opportunities to integrate science.

Story Plays. Designed for children four to seven years of age, story plays open up numerous opportunities for developing movements competencies, creativity, and integration of other subject areas with physical education.

SCUBA Diving is a story play which usually follows some classroom discussion of the sport. Children can then be asked, "What are some ways to get to the beach?" Children then move rapidly around the play area until someone finds the "beach." Then ask, "How can we get out into the ocean?" These questions can be followed by "What is the first thing we must do?", "What must we do for safety?", and "What are some things that you see under the water?" As in all story plays, the emphasis is on movement. The teacher acts as a guide with most of the ideas coming from the students. Creativity is emphasized.

Firemen, like SCUBA diving, usually follows a classroom discussion or perhaps a demonstration by the fire department. Play can begin with the firemen asleep followed by getting to the fire, setting up, rescuing people, fighting the fire, cleaning up, and returning to the firehouse. Movements such as running, climbing, crawling, creeping, jumping, and leaping can be emphasized. Children also can learn about firemen, water pressure, water freezing during cold weather, surface friction when using foam and air masks.

A Trip to the Moon offers opportunities to talk about gravity, weightlessness, blast-off, retrofire, and docking. The weightless state gives children a chance to show creative movement.

A Trip to the Jungle includes swinging on vines, leaping, jumping, quicksand, all the different animals, the type of climate, the location of jungles, the dangers, and the plant growth.

Creative Activities. A number of creative activities lend themselves to integration with science:

Growing like a flower or tree can include: the basic needs for flower or tree growth such as soil, sun, and water; the many different kinds of flowers and trees; the effects of wind and pollution, and life cycles. Movements can include bending, twisting, turning, and stretching.

Moving like different animals can help children understand more about the animals as well as their eating and sleeping habits, relationship between different types of animals, and the dangers when encountering certain animals.

Example Activities:

Name: Caterpillars

Value: Creativity, and science knowledge.

Have all the children imagine they are caterpillars. Ask all the children if they know what a caterpillar is and show flashcards. Then ask if they can move like a caterpillar. Then does anyone know anything else about a caterpillar. Well, they have a dream. And that dream is to be a what? A butterfly. Show flashcards. Can anyone move like a butterfly? What colors can a butterfly be? Well now, how does a caterpillar become a butterfly? The caterpillar finds a branch on a tree. Let's all find our own branch. Can you be a caterpillar hanging on a tree? Then the caterpillar make a what? A cocoon. Show flashcard. What is a cocoon? Silky threads wrapped around themselves. Now let's see you wrap yourself in a cocoon. Now let's see what happens to your little caterpillars. It takes time for a caterpillar to turn into a butterfly.

150 Kindergarten

Now's the time. Let's see the new butterflies. Let's show off our new lovely wings!

Variation: Any animal that undergoes a change — polliwog to a frog — or a summer leaf changing to a fall leaf.

Name: Animal Movement

Value: Creativity and science knowledge

The class has completed a unit on pets covering the rules of healthful living for animals. One way to correlate this unit with physical eduation is through creative movement.

Let the class become a bowl of goldfish, swimming toward each other using cupped hands and an elbow movement. Let them raise their heads upward the surface of the water and blow for air. When something frightens them, the formation scurries away using finning movement. Ask the class to become a snake, using turning movement to go downward into a coil and then striking with a sudden sharp leap. Now ask the children to portray the movements of a hunting dog — long lanky movements across space. Exaggerate the pointing activity, and just as the movement of pointing, each dog freezes with one leg up and the opposite arm extended. With a little help in the beginning and encouragement for the development of each child's ideas, the class can devise many wonderful things.

Social Studies

The main way to integrate social studies with physical education is through dance, although playing games unique to other countries is also valuable. Doing dances from other countries is a way to understand the culture and people of other lands. *The Methodist World of Fun* record series provides music and instructions for dances from a number of countries. Certain games are played primarily by children in a particular country, and playing these games can given insight into the characteristics of these children.

Music

Music has always been a part of elementary physical education. The full value of its use, however, is seldom realized. As mentioned above, music is a part of social studies integration. Other aspects of music such as phrasing, accents, tempo, and style can be emphasized during creative movement to music, simple and complex dances, and routines to music using ropes, lummi sticks, tinikling, or wands.

Moving to Classical Music. Listening and moving to classical selections can help overcome the rather poor quality music to which most children are exposed. The *50 Great Moments of Music* has a variety of classical selections which can bring out a number of emotional and movement responses by children. However, any classical music, if carefully selected, will do.

KINDERGARTEN GAMES

As was mentioned earlier, games should not be a major part of the kindergarten curriculum. Games, however, do provide opportunities for development in both the affective and cognitive domains and, if carefully selected, can aid psychomotor development. A developmental game should have nearly 100% of the children moving most of the time.

The games listed below have been rated using the criteria established in discussion of games, p. 113. The description can be found on the page listed to the right of the game.

KINDERGARTEN GAMES

NAME	Page	Psychomotor	Affective	Cognitive	Grass	Multipurpose Room	Hardtop	Classroom	Can be Adapted for Any Area	Can be Used for Evaluation
Busy Bee	152	4	5	2					x	x
Brothers	152	4	4	2					x	x
Simon Says—Body Image	152	1	3	4					x	x
Simon Says—Exercise	152	4	1	1					x	
Statues	152	4	3	1					x	
Whistle Stop	152	4	3	1					x	
Do This, Do That	153	4	1	1					x	x
Fox and Hound	153	5	1	1	x					
Tag Games	153	4	2	1	x					
Red Rover	183	3	2	2	x	x				
Squirrels in Trees	153	4	4	1					x	
Where's a Partner	153	5	5	1					x	
Scat	154	5	2	1	x	x				
Red and White	154	4	2	1	x	x				
Jump the Creek	154	4	1	1					x	
Beanbag Throw	154	5	1	1					x	
Bowling	154	3	1	1					x	
Hit the Bucket	155	5	1	1					x	
Ring Toss	155	5	1	2					x	
Tire or Hoop Targets	155	5	1	1	x	x	x			

Game Code:
- N= Name of game
- DA= Developmental age for which game was designed
- DV= What the child should get from the game (developmental value)
- F= Formation
- E= Equipment required
- D= Description of the game

Game Descriptions

Code: N: = Name
DV: = Developmental Value
DA: = Developmental Age
F: = Formation
E: = Equipment
D: = Description of Activity

N: Busy Bee
DA: 5 - 7
DV: Body Image and Social Development
F: Free
E: None
D: Children move freely around the play area until the teacher calls out, "back to back," "right knee to right knee," or some other body image concept. Upon hearing the instructions, children immediately find any partner and take the position called for. There must be an uneven number of children at the beginning of the game. If there is an even number of children at the start, the teacher can join the game to make an uneven number. The person without a partner during the game is the Busy Bee and receives one point each time he or she is left without a partner. Those at the end of the game with the least number of points are the winners. Since the "Busy Bee" receives a lot of attention, some children will deliberately avoid getting a partner, and thus ruin the game. The "point" idea will usually get the game moving well, and a reminder about the rules to those trying to become the Busy Bee will usually suffice. The teacher can evaluate the child's knowledge of body parts, right and left, and the social interaction of the class during this game.

N: Brothers
DA: 5 - 7
DV: Body Image and Visual Discrimination
F: Partners
E: None
D: Partners are in free formation around the play area. On the signal to go, children move away from their partners. Basic movements such as walking, running, etc., can be used. When the leader calls out, "back to back," or "right knee to right knee," partners must get back together solving the task established. The last two to come together get one point with a rule that any set getting more than three points has to sit out one turn. At the end, those with no points can be given special attention. Emphasis should be given to avoid collisions with others and a rule of no collisions could be added to the game to help develop better visual discrimination. This game, like Busy Bee, can be used to evaluate body image.

N: Simon Says — Body Image
   Simon Says — Exercises
DA: 6 - 8
DV: Body Image and Auditory Discrimination, or Fitness
F: Free
E: None
D: One of the most versatile games, which is too frequently misused, is Simon Says. The game can be played in many ways depending on the objective. Basically, however, the children must do any command preceded by the phrase, "Simon Says . . ." Anyone doing the activity not preceded by the phrase is given one point. At the end, those with the least number of points are the winners. Asking the children to touch body parts can aid the development of body image. Exercises can be called for, as well as basic locomotor and nonlocomotor moves. For purposes of evaluation, children can be asked to lie down and close their eyes as body parts are touched. This arrangement reduces the possibility of children watching each other, and gives a truer picture of each child's knowledge of his body parts.

N: Statues or Whistle Stop
DA: 4 - 7
DV: Creativity and Social Interaction
F: Free
E: Whistle
D: Statues or Whistle Stop, as it is sometimes called, is easy to organize and play since it can be done most anywhere in a free formation. Children are asked to move freely around the play area until a given signal, "freeze" or a whistle is blown, at which time they freeze like statues. Specific criteria for the statues adds to the value, i.e., freeze like animals, people, sports figures, etc. Socialization is added by asking children to make group statues. The leader can hold up fingers to indicate how many

people are to be in the statue just prior to giving the stop signal. Groups with the proper number are praised. Children can learn the math concept of grouping and remainders using this approach.

N: Do This, Do That
DA: 6 - 8
DV: Fitness and Auditory Discrimination
F: Free
E: None
D: When the leader makes some physical move such as raising the arm and says, "do this," everyone should do it. But if the action is followed by "do that" anyone doing it receives a point. After a period of time, those with the fewest points are declared the best listeners. Exercise moves can be used in this game for fitness development.

N: Fox and Hound
DA: 6 - 8
DV: Running, Agility
F: Free
E: None
D: This game requires a large grassy area. One child is the fox and all others are the hounds. The fox is given a head start, but must stay in a designated safe area. The hounds chase the fox until one hound tags the fox. The tagger then becomes the fox, and the game begins again. If done long enough, this activity could aid in the development of cardiovascular efficiency. See Chapter 6 for a discussion of fitness.

N: Tag Games
DA: 5 - 8
DV: Running, Chasing, Tagging
F: Free
E: Varies with tag game played
D: Tag games are fun for children, but must be handled carefully if they are to be successful at all. The "it" position must be made unattractive since "it" receives so much attention. Saying, "All those who have not been tagged during the game will be the winners," will help. Otherwise, children who are not "it" will attempt to be tagged in order to be the center of attention, and the game will be destroyed. It might also be necessary to set a time limit on the person who is supposed to tag. Often this person will not try very hard since tagging someone else will take him away from center stage. For safety, tagging must be done by touching, not pushing on the back. Also, no solid object such as a tree or pole should be used as a safe base. Over-anxious children can trip or be pushed into the object and serious injuries can result.

Shadow Tag — Can only be played on a sunny day. "It" must step on someone's shadow to tag him.

T.V. Tag — The child is safe when he squats down and names a T.V. show (shows cannot be repeated). The child must get out of the squat position after "it" moves away.

Line Tag — For this game, there must be a number of lines in the gymnasium or multipurpose room. Children must stay on lines and may only switch where lines cross. The tagger must be on the same line with the child being tagged (no reaching across to tag a child on an adjacent line).

N: Squirrels in Trees
DA: 5 - 7
DV: Social Interaction and Movement Competencies
F: Groups of threes
E: Hoops if playing variation
D: Two children make a tree by holding hands. The squirrel gets in the tree. There can be one or two squirrels without a tree. When the leader calls, "change," squirrels must find a new tree. As soon as "change" is called, the trees begin to turn and keep turning until a new squirrel gets in the tree. A variation to increase social interaction is to have everyone change on the signal. A tree finds a new partner to make a tree (trees must seek out other trees, not pair up with a squirrel), and begins turning as soon as the tree is made. Squirrels must seek out a tree as soon as one is made. Each time a squirrel is left without a tree, he gets one point. At the end, the squirrels with the least number of points are declared the best squirrels. Everyone should get a chance to be a squirrel. Hoops can be used as trees to increase the movement value.

N: Where's A Partner?
DA: 5 - 7
DV: Locomotor Movement, Social Interaction
F: Double Circle — partners facing
E: None

D: Children are arranged in a double circle with partners facing. The inside circle has one more player than the outside. When the signal is given, the circles skip (or another locomotor movement) to the player's right. This means they are skipping in opposite directions. When the command "Halt" is given, the circles face each other to find partners. The player left without a partner is in the "Mush Pot" attempting to get a partner when the command "Halt" is given. The game can also be played using a record and record player. When the music stops, the players seek partners.

N: Scat
DA: 5 - 7
DV: Running, Agility, Fitness
F: Single line facing leader.
E: None
D: Players form a line facing the leader. The leader leads the players in exercises. Suddenly he calls "scat" and pursues the runners, who are trying to run to the other goal line. A runner who is caught assists the leader in catching the other players. The last person caught is the new leader.

N: Red and White
DA: 6 - 8
DV: Visual Discrimination, Running, Agility, Catching
F: Two teams on parallel lines about 40 feet apart
E: Round disc painted red on three sides and white on three sides.
D: Each team advances toward the center. When they are about five feet apart, the teacher rolls the cube or tosses the disc. If, when it falls, the red side is up, the teacher calls, "Red." The reds chase the whites back to their base, trying to tag as many as possible. If the white side is up, the whites chase the reds. The players who are tagged must join the other team. After a given length of time, the team with the greater number of players wins.

N: Jump the Creek
DA: 6 - 7
DV: Jumping, Auditory Discrimination
F: 2 parallel lines 2 to 3 feet apart, players behind one line
E: None
D: A creek is formed by drawing 2 parallel lines 2 to 3 feet apart, depending upon the ability of the children. The lines should be long enough to accommodate the children comfortably with enough room for each to jump. If necessary, two or three sets of lines can be drawn. The children line up on one of the banks all facing the creek and facing the same direction. The teacher or leader gives one of two directions: "In the creek" or "on the bank." Children now on the bank, jump into the creek or over to the other bank depending upon the command. When they jump on the bank, they immediately turn around and get ready for the next command. If the command "In the creek" is given, they must not move. Errors are committed when a child steps on a line, makes a wrong jump, or moves when he should remain still. Children who make a mistake could be sent "home" to change shoes. After pretending to change to dry shoes, the player may join in again.

N: Bean Bag Throw
DA: 5 - 8
DV: Eye-Hand Coordination
F: Partners
E: Chalk drawn circles, bean bags
D: A circle 12 inches in diameter is drawn for every two people (Partners). Each child is given two bean bags and stands on opposite sides of the circle from his partner. Taking turns, they begin tossing each bean bag into the circle from a distance close to the circle. With each successful toss, the child takes a step back and tries tossing from a distance farther away from the circle. The one who gets furthest away and can still get it in the circle is the winner.

N: Bowling
DA: 5 - 8
DV: Eye-Hand Coordination
F: Partners
E: Bowling pins, balls
D: Partners get 3 pins between them and a ball each. Stand pins up close to each other side by side or in a triangle. One child stands behind a line 15 feet away and rolls the ball at the pins trying to knock the pins down. The partner stands near the pins, retrieves the ball and goes to the restraining line. The one who knocked down the pins sets them up for his partner.

Good indoor games ↓

N: Hit the Bucket
DA: 5 - 8
DV: Eye-Hand Coordination
F: Partners
E: Baskets (trashcans) and small rubber ball or yarn balls
D: There is one basket for each 2 partners and one ball for each student. Partners stand on opposite sides of the trash cans and take turns tossing the ball into the basket. Students begin tossing the ball into the basket from a distance close to the basket and take a step back with each successful throw.

N: Ring Toss
DA: 5 - 8
DV: Eye-Hand Coordination
F: Scattered
E: Deck tennis rings, stands
D: A stand and 2 rings are given to each student. The student attempts to toss the rings over the stand, moving farther away with each successful try. A point system could be set up with older children and scores could be kept by each child.

N: Tire or Hoops Targets
DA: 5 - 8
DV: Eye-Hand Coordination
F: Partners
E: Yarnballs, rope or cord fastened between two posts about shoulder high, several bike tires hung on the rope.
D: Partners stand on opposite sides of hanging tires behind restraining lines 5, 10, 15, and 20 feet from the tires. Practice tossing back and forth through tires from 5 foot line. If successful, move on to the next line. How many times can you get the ball through the tire at each line?

EXAMPLE LESSON PLANS FOR KINDERGARTEN

1. Kindergarten

   Multipurpose Room

   Objectives:

   1. The students will be able to execute basic locomotor skills to a record by listening and following directions.
   2. When given a hoop, the students will be able to create some type of body or hoop movement to the music.

Activities	Formation
I. Exercises to music. Students do exercises keeping the beat of the music.	I. Free
II. Activity Songs Birds in a circle — Each child has a hula hoop and follows the words to the song, jumping, hopping, leaps, gallop and balance in and out of the hoop. Move around the color — Using the same hoops, students follow the song moving around the colors using different locomotor skills. Hoop Activity — Students show different ways to move in, out and around their hoop while the music plays.	II. Free
III. Hokey Pokey Dance	III. Circle

   Safety: No running, sliding or throwing hoops.

2. Kindergarten

   Multipurpose Room

   Objectives:

   1. The students will be able to execute the locomotor skills of walking forward and backwards, and marching while keeping a beat with their lummi sticks.

2. While listening to a record, the students will be able to create body movements to the story that will be told.

Activities	Formation
I. Dance to Music	I. Free

A popular song will be played for the students to dance to any way they wish.

II. Lummi Sticks | II. Free

Students will follow a structured pattern following the teacher. Then they will create their own pattern to the music. The teacher then asks: Can you walk forward while hitting your sticks? Backwards? March?

III. Dance a Story | III. Free

Students listen to a story and act out what is being said.

Safety: No throwing sticks.

3. Kindergarten

Multipurpose Room

Objectives:

1. The students will be able to throw the ball and catch it 5 times without the ball hitting the floor.
2. 80% of the students will be able to bounce the ball while executing the locomotor skills of walking slow, fast, backwards and in a circle.

Activities	Formation
I. Animal Exercises

Can you? Walk like a crab? Jump like a frog? Walk like a bear? Etc.

II. Hand-eye coordination | II. Free

Using large plastic balls, students will do movement exploration. Then the teacher can ask: Can you bounce and catch the ball with one hand? Throw and catch the ball five times? Throw and clap your hands as many times as possible before catching the ball. Bounce the ball while walking fast, slow, backward, in a circle, etc.

III. Ball Handling with Partner | III. Partners

Students get a partner and throw and catch the ball as many ways as possible.

Safety: No kicking the ball and no sliding on the floor.

4. Kindergarten

Multipurpose Room

Objective:

The students will be able to throw and catch the different balls at each station at least two times without the ball hitting the floor.

Activities	Formation
I. Statue Freeze Game (Whistle Stop)	I. Free
II. Station Arrangement for Developing Hand-Eye Coordination	II. Four Stations

Students will show everything they can do with the ball at the station.

1. Big plastic balls	3. Scoops and balls
2. Sponge rubber balls	4. Hula Hoops and balls

   III. Children choose a game to play

Safety: No kicking the balls, and no throwing at someone else.

5. Kindergarten

    Multipurpose Room

    Objective:

    > When given a short jump rope, the students will be able to jump rope one time using both feet.

Activities	Formation
I. Movement Exploration with Ropes	I. Free
Teacher gives free time for students to show everything they can do with their ropes.	
II. Rope activities	II. Free — one rope per child
Make forms with ropes and then do locomotor movements in and out, around, etc., using the forms.	
How many ways and how many times can you jump your rope?	
III. Moving creatively to music	III. Free

Safety: No swinging the ropes at anyone.

6. Kindergarten

    Outside

    Objective:

    > The students will be able to throw a 6-inch sponge rubber ball and hit a target 5 feet away.

Activities	Formation
I. Follow the Leader	I. One line behind the teacher and then 5 lines with student leaders.
II. Target Activities	II. Free
How many different ways can you throw the ball and hit the target?	
Can you throw underhand, overhand, or sidearm and hit the target?	
Can you roll the ball and hit the target?	
III. Squirrels in Trees	III. Groups of threes

Safety: No throwing balls at anyone.

158 Kindergarten

7. Kindergarten

   Outside

   Objective:

   > The students will be able to change their locomotor movements to varying speeds and tempos of a tom-tom.

Activities	Formation
I. Busy Bee	I. Free
II. Quality of locomotor movement to tom-tom	II. Free

   Can you listen to the tom-tom and do what it tells you to do?

   Fast and slow   Heavy and soft
   High and low   Loud and soft

   III. Fox and Hound   III. Free

   Safety: No bumping others

8. Kindergarten

   Outside

   Objective:

   > The students will be able to catch the beanbag with their hands while standing, and will be able to catch a beanbag thrown underhand from a partner 15 feet away.

Activities	Formation
I. Moving to Music	I. Free
II. Beanbag Activities	II. One beanbag per child in a free position

   How many ways can you throw the beanbag? Catch it?

   How many body parts can you use to throw the beanbag? Catch it?

   Can you throw and catch with a partner?

   Can you throw underhand and catch it with a partner?

   III. Red Rover

   Safety: No hard throwing at your partners.

REFERENCES

1. Arnheim, D. and R. Pestolesi. *Elementary Physical Education*. St. Louis: The C. V. Mosby Company, 1978.
2. Burton, E. *The New Physical Education for Elementary School Children*. Boston: Houghton Mifflin Co., 1977.
3. Cochran, N., et. al. *A Teacher's Guide to Elementary School Physical Education*. Dubuque: Kendall/Hunt, 1971.
4. Cochran, N., et. al. *Learning on the Move*. Dubuque: Kendall/Hunt Publishing Co., 1975.
5. Dauer, V. *Essential Movement Experiences for Preschool and Primary Children*. Minneapolis: Burgess Publishing Co., 1972.
6. Dauer, V. and R. Pangrazi. *Dynamic Physical Education for Elementary School Children*. Minneapolis: Burgess Publishing Co., 1975.
7. Fait, H. *Physical Education for the Elementary School Child*. Philadelphia: W. B. Saunders Co., 1976.
8. Kirchner, G. *Physical Education for Elementary School Children*. Dubuque: Wm. C. Brown Co., 1974.
9. Seagraves, M. *Move to Learn*. Winston-Salem: Hunter Publishing Co., 1979.

STUDENT ACTIVITIES

1. Write an original lesson plan for kindergarten children.

   Goal:

   Objective:

   Activity   Formation

160 Kindergarten

2. Observe a kindergarten class and record your observations of one child on the form below.

   Length of Class _____ Sex of observed child _____

   Activities presented:

   Number of interactions with other children _____

   Amount of time child spent in activity _____

   Behavior of child: Record behavior being exhibited every 3 minutes or record all unique episodes of behavior.

CHAPTER 8
CURRICULUM FOR SIX- AND SEVEN-YEAR-OLDS

After completing this chapter, the student should be able to:

1. Give the instructional implications for the growth and development characteristics in the chapter.
2. List and explain the curriculum emphases for this age group.
3. Describe the most effective approach to teaching the six and seven-year-old child.
4. For each objective, describe at least two activities which can be used to develop the particular objective in question.

For many children, first grade is their initial public school experience. The six-year-old without kindergarten experience or a good physical education background will benefit most by using many of the activities from Chapter 7 when designing the curriculum. These kindergarten activities can actually be used by both first and second graders. In fact, there is nearly no difference between kindergarten and first and second graders when dealing with the affective domain. No new information from the affective domain, therefore, has been added in this chapter. The reader is referred to Chapter 7 for affective information. Other areas with great similarity between the two age groupings are creativity and rhythmics. In these latter two areas, however, new information is presented in this chapter and the reader is referred to Chapter 7 for additional ideas. Although these activities are appropriate for both age groupings, care must be taken not to repeat activities too frequently over a three-year period. Children enjoy demonstrating their knowledge by doing activities from the previous year, but boredom can occur when children are not challenged enough with new activities.

Frequent cross-references are made to Chapter 7 activities. The teacher must judge which ones are appropriate for a particular group of children. So before using information from this chapter in designing a curriculum, study Chapter 7.

Characteristics of Six- and Seven-Year-Olds and Implications for Instruction

First grade is the initial experience with public school for many children. Since kindergarten is neither required nor available in some places, first grade is a big adjustment period. The year is even more difficult than kindergarten since most first graders attend a full day rather than a half-day as many kindergarteners do. The range of sophistication of the children in this age group is wide. The six-year-old with kindergarten experience will usually show more maturity than those without such training.

Physical Characteristics

1. Poor posture will be evident.
Implication — A teacher has the opportunity to compare a child against many others, and should therefore be able to identify posture deviations. Most problems at this age are functional (correctible with exercise) rather than structural (non-correctible or changed only by drastic means such as surgery). The child is still growing, bones have not hardened completely, and muscle development is ongoing. Corrections are much easier at this time, but no corrections will be possible unless identification of a problem is made (see Chapter 6).

2. Eye-hand coordination along with other motor skills still needs work.
Implication — A variety of activities should be used to identify as well as to correct motor deficiencies. Most perceptual skills are not fully refined until age seven.

3. Full of energy but fatigue easily.
Implication — Vigorous activities should play a major role in the curriculum, but should be interspersed with more restful activity. Children tend to give up during vigorous activities requiring cardiovascular endurance. If any real development is to take place, they must be pushed a little. Caution must be exercised, however, par-

Scoops and balls for developing hand-eye coordination

ticularly under hot humid weather conditions.

4. Endurance is low.

Implication — Although a child's ability to persist in vigorous activity is low, cardiovascular endurance should be developed through a systematic, progressive program.

5. Abdominal strength and fitness in general is low in early childhood.

Implication — This country's sedentary lifestyle is quickly creating generations of weak, overweight children. Children need a vigorous daily physical fitness program (see Chapter 6).

Sit-ups will aid abdominal development.

6. Significant gains can be made by these children in all areas.

Implication — This age group is pleasing to work with since real progress can be seen and measured. It can be a fertile period with the seeds of development bearing fruit for years to come.

7. Sex differences are apparent.

Implication — The varying background experience of boys and girls is apparent at this age level with boys excelling in most sports skills while girls are superior in gymnastics and dance. Instruction should be individualized to account for these differences (see Chapter 5).

Social and Emotional Characteristics

1. Likes to be first and win (self-centered behavior).

Implication — Competition should be kept to a minimum although children in American society are competitive from early childhood. When winning is an inherent part of an activity, the activity should be designed to allow for individual rather than group winners. This age child is not team-oriented, although the influence of professional athletics is making him somewhat more team conscious. Since they are still self-centered, however, they do prefer individual attention. Activities also should be selected or designed to make every child a winner. Children should compete against themselves with each child being a winner when he has done his best (see Chapter 14).

2. Children are more aware of opposite sex.

Implication — The changing morality has had its effect even on young children. Girls are more embarrassed and may not perform if their underpants show. Boys tend to be giddy and disruptive when girls' pants show during tumbling activities or activities requiring getting on the floor. Although uniforms are inappropriate for this age level, all children should be encouraged to wear clothes which allow for all types of activity, including tumbling. An easy-to-slip-on pair of shorts or slacks can solve the problem.

3. Emotions are more intense but do not last as long as adults.

Implication — Short outbursts of negative emotions should be ignored whenever possible. Many words directed at the teacher during these outbursts do not indicate a child's true feelings and should, therefore, be taken lightly. Blowing these incidents out of proportion could harm the child's development.

4. Like new things and variety.

Implication — The teacher should design the curriculum to provide a variety of activities, including both new and old activities. Although children like new things, they also like to show how they remember the old activities.

5. Desire affection and praise from adults.
Implication — Since adults are very important in a child's life, their affection and praise go a long way toward insuring healthy development. Each child should be given encouragement, praise, and affection each class period. This can be done both verbally and non-verbally. The learning atmosphere and discipline procedures should be positive.

6. Like to play together but not in teams.
Implication — Team activities have little place in the curriculum for these children. Small groups, partners, and individual activities should be the most common arrangement.

Group play

7. Friendships change frequently.
Implication — Some children will experience strong emotions as a result of changing alliances among the children. This is not unusual and should be dealt with as mildly as possible unless a child seems unable to cope with the situation. It can also cause problems when selecting partners for activities. Often one child is fought over by others. The teacher must be ready to move in and pair children to avoid a delay in the activity. For the most part, children take these changing friendships in stride.

8. Will tell on peers.
Implication — It is considered normal behavior to have them "squeal" on each other when one does something wrong. A teacher must not encourage such behavior, but should work toward helping the children accept responsibility for their own actions. This approach will help develop self-discipline.

Intellectual Characteristics

1. Attention span is short.
Implication — Get children into activity quickly. Do not have activities which require long explanations.

2. Like to have fun and fantasize.
Implication — Although all activities should be fun, the last activity in the lesson should be one which guarantees fun for everyone. Not only will such an arrangement help to satisfy children's needs, it will also help to build a positive attitude toward physical education.
Fantasy is a part of a child's world at this age, and creative activities and story plays will be developmentally useful. Students should participate actively in designing the story plays.

3. Have a good imagination.
Implication — Make use of the children's ideas, since their imagination may be better than the teacher's.

Developing creativity by exploring movement

4. Can be reasoned with.
Implication — Although these children are not highly sophisticated nor do they have a large bank of knowledge, they can be reasoned with. Discussing reasons for rules, actions, and ac-

tivities is important for understanding and for developing rapport. Although children are not miniature adults, they should not be treated like babies. By involving them in decision-making, a teacher will aid their intellectual growth.

5. Have good listening vocabulary.

Implication — This supports the discussion in 4 above.

6. Can develop sight vocabulary.

Implication — The reading process begins with listening (auditory) and moves to word recognition (reading). Traditionally, physical education instruction has been done verbally. By using flash cards with movement terms, children can increase their reading vocabulary. Words such as walk, run, skip, gallop, right, left, forward, backward, up and down can be placed on cards and used to give the children movement instructions. Instructions can also be placed on cards and used in a stations arrangement.

CURRICULUM EMPHASES

The curriculum emphasis for the six and seven-year-old should be general movement and the development of some specific skills. The teacher should focus on the quality of movement and creativity. Skills include throwing, catching, and kicking as well as gymnastics and tumbling skills like headstand, forward roll, and backward roll.

The primary psychomotor goal is the development of a movement foundation upon which the child can build. This movement foundation includes creativity and perceptual-motor skills. Without such a base upon which to build, children will experience frustration in later movement endeavors. Such frustration could lead to a poor self-concept.

A second major goal for physical education is the development of affective qualities including self-concept. Areas such as interpersonal relationships, fair play, self respect, and leadership should all receive considerable attention when working with six and seven-year-olds.

In attempts to accomplish curriculum goals, it must be remembered that many six-year-olds are experiencing their first formal schooling, and may not, therefore, bring with them a very good movement background. An evaluation must be made of all six-year-olds to determine their incoming abilities. The curriculum for the inexperienced child will be very similar to that for kindergarten children. Many curriculum objectives and activities listen in this chapter therefore are cross referenced to the previous chapter.

Interdisciplinary Planning

Whenever possible, integrated activities should be in the curriculum. As was explained in the Section II description, integrated activities can be used to aid learning in such areas as language arts, science, math, social studies and music. This interdisciplinary planning is particularly easy to do at this level. Activities such as story plays can be used to learn about the world in which we live. Flash cards help develop sight vocabulary. The list of ways to integrate is nearly endless.

To aid in planning and learning, a section of integrated activities and games is included beginning on page 177. Other ideas are also included throughout the chapter.

TEACHING APPROACHES

The teaching of six and seven-year-old children should combine exploration, problem-solving, and guided discovery. It may also be helpful to use the task approach at times. In some cases even command teaching may be necessary. Exploration is most useful with the six-year-olds when teaching creative movement. The other teaching styles can be used to help develop the more specific skills. The command style should be avoided and the student-centered approaches such as problem-solving and guided exploration utilized.

Although skilled movement is the desired outcome, there are many ways a child can reach the objective if given the opportunity. Participation is fostered through student-centered approaches. High levels of skilled performance are not necessary at this age level, so perfection should not be sought at the expense of self-concept. Children who do their best should receive the same praise as the more skillful performers. Pressure to perform at a specified level may produce anxiety resulting in poor skill development and a weakened self-concept.

Learning centers and other individual techniques can be used with six and seven-year-olds. Since most young children have limited reading ability, audio-visual aids will be necessary for message transmission. Loop films, slide-tapes, audio-tapes, and video-tapes are very effective for teaching and learning (see Chapter 5).

Integrated activities and particularly the use of flash cards with movement terms are successful at this age level. Movement terms, shapes, and letters can be learned by young children through physical education activities.

SAFETY

This age group tends to be very physical. Children are constantly pushing, pulling, and shoving, sometimes in fun and at other times while fighting. Tagging often takes the form of a shove or tackle. Lines and circles are often disrupted by pushing and pulling matches, and arguments develop over who was in front of whom when lining up. This physical nature invariably leads to injury. The number one safety consideration, therefore, is to teach children how to tag properly and play together without causing injuries to others. Rules and discussions are an effective approach to use in reducing injurious behavior.

Playground Safety

This age group is very adventurous and has little fear. Playground equipment, therefore, is often misused, while trees and other climbable objects present dangerous challenges to the children. School personnel have the responsibility to protect children and must insist upon the proper use of equipment while stopping other dangerous behavior.

Rules must be established and upheld by all personnel responsible for student safety and welfare. These rules should be covered at the beginning of the year and periodically throughout the year as needed. Deviations from the rules must be dealt with quickly to protect all the children.

GOALS, OBJECTIVES, AND DEVELOPMENTAL ACTIVITIES
SECTION OUTLINE

PSYCHOMOTOR DOMAIN, p. 166

Movement Quality, p. 166
   Integrated Planning, p. 166
   Movement Quality Activities, p. 166
   Visual Discrimination and Manipulative Skills, p.167
   Integrated Planning, p. 167
   Visual Discrimination and Manipulative Skills Activities, p. 167
     Hand-Eye Coordination, p. 167
     Eye-Foot Coordination, p. 168
     Non-Dominant Side Development, p. 169
Kinesthetic Development, p. 169
   Kinesthetic Development Activities, p. 169
Rhythmics, p. 170
   Integrated Planning, p. 170
   Rhythmic Activities, p. 170
Creativity, p. 172
   Integrated Planning, p. 172
   Creative Activities, p. 172
Tumbling and Gymnastics, p. 173
   Tumbling Activities, p. 173
   Gymnastics Activities, p. 175
Fitness, p. 175
   Integrated Planning, p. 176
   Fitness Activities, p. 176
Relaxation, p. 176
   Relaxation Activities, p. 144
Body Image, p. 176

AFFECTIVE DOMAIN, p. 176

Self-Concept, p. 144
   Self-Concept Activities, p. 144
Honesty, p. 144
   Honesty Activities, p. 144
Sharing, p. 144
   Sharing Activities, p. 144
Respect for Authority, p. 144
Patience, p. 145
Leadership, p. 145
   Leadership Activities, p. 145
Positive Attitudes, p. 145

COGNITIVE DOMAIN, p. 176

Problem-Solving Ability, p. 176
   Problem-Solving Activities, p. 176
Creativity, p. 176
   Creative Activities, p. 176
Body Image, p. 177
   Integrated Planning, p. 177
   Body Image Activities, p. 177
Directional and Movement Terms p. 177
   Directional and Movement Activities, p. 177
Rules and Regulations, p. 177
   Rules and Regulations Activities, p. 177
Fitness, Heatlh and Safety Knowledge, p. 177
   Fitness Knowledge, p. 177
   Health Knowledge, p. 177
   Safety Knowledge, p. 177

INTEGRATED ACTIVITIES, p. 177
   Language Arts, p. 177
   Math, p. 179
   Science, p. 179

GAMES, p. 181

EXAMPLE LESSON PLANS, p. 187

PSYCHOMOTOR DOMAIN

Movement Quality

The movement qualities are force, time, space, and level, all of which play a vital role in movement efficiency. These qualities are important to efficient locomotor and non-locomotor movement.

Goal: The students will be able to demonstrate the qualities of movement, force, time, space, and level, in a variety of situations.

Objectives:
1. Students will demonstrate force with body actions in response to loud and soft beats of a tom-tom.
2. The children's movements will be either slow, medium, or fast depending upon the rhythmic tempo.
3. Children will be able to move in a limited space with a number of children without bumping into one another.
4. Children will be able to bend, stretch, twist, turn, shake, bounce, rotate, and spin, demonstrating various forces and speeds appropriate (heavy to hard and slow to fast) to various stimuli (tom-tom, music, or chant).
5. Students will be able to do all the locomotor movements at both high, medium, and low levels and in all directions.
6. Children will demonstrate proper use of arm, legs, and head while running, walking, skipping, leaping, and galloping.

Integrated Planning

Use flashcards (p. 148) with movement terms. Also, story plays can be used to integrate science while also emphasizing movement (p. 140).

Movement Quality Activities

1. Personal Space
   How low can you get in your space?
   How high?
   How much room can you take up in your personal space?
   How small can you be?
   What are some different ways you can balance in your space?
   a. Moving to Music
      Can you swing one body part to this music? Two? Three?
      Can you shake a body part? Two? Three?
      Can you twist, turn, bend, and stretch body parts to the music?

Movement quality development through animal mimetics

   How can you move to the music in your personal space?
   b. Have child explore space creatively; emphasize unusual body positions.
2. Common Space
   a. Moving to tom-tom in limited space with others. Also can use music. Emphasize ways to avoid collisions. Begin slowly and increase speed.
   b. Use different basic locomotor movement both forward, backward, and sideward while moving in common space.
   c. Do creative movements.
3. Force
   How lightly can you move around the room?
   How heavily?
   Can you move like a mouse? An elephant?
   a. Have them move from lightly to heavily, back to lightly by varying a drum beat or music volume.
   b. Can you show force with a body part (use tom-tom)?
4. Time (Speed)
   Can you move in slow motion?
   How quickly can you move one body part? Two body parts?
   Can you move one body part quickly while moving another slowly?
   a. Have children move to varying music tempos and tom-tom beats.
   b. Move alone, with partner, and in a small group in different ways (circle, around area, one slow and others fast or some slow and some fast).

Hand-eye coordination and balance activity

5. Level
 Can you move like a tiny little animal? A giant?
 Can you move while changing your level to the music volume?
 a. Use story plays which require children to creep, crawl, slither, leap, and jump.
6. Also see Movement Quality, p. 128.

Visual Discrimination and Manipulative Skills

Goal: The student will develop hand-eye coordination.
Objectives:
 1. A child will be able to throw (stepping forward with the opposite foot), and catch a six inch beanbag four out of five times with a partner 15 feet away.
 2. Playing alone, a child can throw and catch (using hands only) an 8½ inch playground ball four out of five times when thrown above the head.
 3. Child can throw and catch a seven inch sponge rubber ball with a partner and catch it four out of five times from a distance of ten feet.
 4. Child can throw and hit a marker ten feet away with an 8½ inch playground ball three out of four times.
 5. Child will be able to bounce and catch an 8½ inch playground ball four out of five times with a partner fifteen feet away.
 6. Child will be able to dribble an 8½ inch playground ball while walking forward, backward, or sideward.

Goal: Student will develop eye-foot coordination.
 1. Child will be able to kick a stationary, 8½ inch playground ball 20 feet.
 2. Child will be able to kick a stationary, 8½ inch playground ball and hit a bowling pin ten feet away one out of three times.
 3. The child will be able to do long rope jumping, including getting in front door.
 4. Child will be able to do single rope jumping, forward and backward four times in a row.
 5. The child will be able to run forward for five steps while jumping a short rope.
Goal: The child will develop the non-dominant side of the body.
 1. Students will be able to accomplish at least 60 percent of the hand-eye and foot-eye coordination activities using the non-dominant side of the body.

Integrated Planning

Use stations, Chapter 5, which have various visual discrimination tasks and manipulative activities. Math can also be used in a stations approach by having children keep their scores on various self-testing activities.

Visual Discrimination and Manipulative Skills Activities

Unlike the kindergarten child, the first and second grader should be more attentive to the correct techniques for catching, throwing, kicking, and striking. This is not to suggest a command style approach, but rather a guided discovery technique to lead the child toward skilled movement patterns. Many activities including the progressions for hand-eye and foot-eye coordination outlined in the previous chapter can be used with first and second graders.

Eye-hand Coordination

1. Throwing
 a. Step with opposite foot forward.
 b. Practice throwing with each hand.
 c. Throw side arm, overhead, and underhand at targets or to partners.
 d. Use a variety of challenging activities:
  1. Vary size and distance of targets.
  2. Use a variety of targets, particularly ones that fall when hit.
 Ask students to see how many times they can hit the target or how many ways they can throw (with opposite foot forward and still hit the target).

168 *Grades One and Two*

   e. Play games using beanbags or yarn balls or modify games so beanbags or yarn balls are used. Cowboys and Indians (p. 172) can be modified to use beanbags to tag (throw and hit) instead of hands. Beanbags can be used to tag in any tagging game.
   f. Play Progressive Tag (p. 185).
2. Catching
   a. Use beanbags, yarn balls, and sponge rubber balls during initial stages of learning.
   b. Emphasize the use of hands to catch. Thumbs together for high throws and little fingers together for low throws.
   c. Objects should be thrown up by child and caught; then another child can throw underhand to a partner; and finally, object can be thrown overhand.
   d. Vary the distance: Challenge them by saying, "Every time you catch it take one step back and with each miss, two steps forward. Let us see who can get the farthest away from his partner. Children should not get into a spread pattern where the object being thrown could hit others.
   e. Vary the way the object is thrown so it is coming at the catcher from many different angles.
   f. When using 8½ inch playground balls, be sure ball is initially bounced until children get used to size and weight.
      1. Rolling
      2. Bounced
      3. Throw underhand
      4. Throw overhand
   g. Have children catch while at different level — squatting, on knees, lying on back, and jumping in air.
3. Dribbling — one-hand bouncing.
   a. Have a child dribble 8½ inch playground ball by pushing (not slapping it).
   Can you move forward and dribble? Sideward right or left? Backward?
   Can you dribble to the music?

Eye-Foot Coordination

1. Kicking
   a. Have children explore movement of the ball with their feet.
   Can you control the ball while moving it with your feet?
   Can you stop the ball with your feet when the whistle blows?
   Can you move the ball using only the outside of your feet?
   b. Kick stationary 8½ inch playground balls for distance.
   c. Kick stationary ball at targets ten to 20 feet away.
2. Long rope jumping
   a. Stand in and jump.
   b. Front door.
   c. Back door.
3. Short rope jumping
   How many different ways can you jump the rope?
   Can you jump forward five times without a miss?
   a. Children will usually do double-beat jumping at first — two jumps for each turn of the rope.
   b. They should be able to do single beat by the end of the first grade.
   c. Do basic movements while jumping. Can you walk and jump rope? Run? Skip? Gallop?
   d. Partner jumping
   How many different ways can you jump rope with a partner?

Rope jumping is an excellent developmental activity.

Grades One and Two   169

Non-Dominant Side Development

1. Encourage use of both sides of the body.
2. Set up situations which require the use of each side of the body as well as using them together.

How far can you throw the ball with one hand? The other hand? Both hands?

How far can you kick the ball using the right foot? Left foot?

Kinesthetic Development

Kinesthesis is a knowledge of body parts in space, and is dependent upon sensory feedback from muscles (proprioception). This ability is important to movement quality particularly in the areas of dance and gymnastics or any other activity which may place individuals in unusual positions.

Goals: The child will improve kinesthetic awareness through proprioceptive development activities.

Objectives:

1. Given a beanbag, the child will be able to throw it to a partner one out of two times without looking. The child can make a visual judgment prior to throwing, but must turn his back or close his eyes just before the actual throw. This should be accomplished using either hand in a variety of ways up to a distance of 20 feet.
2. The child should be able to jump in the air, make a three-quarter turn, and land on his feet without losing his balance.
3. The child should be able to do 80 percent of the tumbling and gymnastics activities beginning on page 173.

Kinesthetic Development Activities

1. Have children do jump and turns to see how far they can go while maintaining balance. Emphasize head and arm usage.

Hopscotch for kinesthetic awareness

Can you jump and make a one-half turn without falling? A three-quarter turn? A full turn?

How high can you jump and still turn?

2. Have children explore how many ways they can move on a mat.
3. Play Statues, page 152, and encourage multiple statues (two or more children) and balance.
4. Also see the following activities which can be used to develop proprioception:
   a. Movement Quality, Force, p. 164
   b. Tumbling and Gymnastics, p. 173
   c. Visual Discrimination and Manipulative Skills, p. 167
   d. Rhythmics, p. 170
   e. Kinesthetic and Proprioceptive Activities for kindergarten children, Chapter 7, can also be used with first graders.

Developing kinesthetic awareness

170 Grades One and Two

Rhythmics

Goal: Children will develop rhythmic ability
1. Child will be able to walk, run, slide, gallop, hop, jump, and clap in rhythm.
2. Child will be able to keep time with music using lummi sticks.
3. Children will recognize phrases in music by changing direction with each new phrase.
4. Child will be able to bounce a ball rhythmically to music.
5. Children will be able to do five simple folk dances without assistance from the teacher.
6. Child will move appropriately to different rhythms, i.e., fast to fast and slow to slow.
7. Children will move creatively to music.
8. Children will be able to demonstrate originality in movement to various musical selections.

Integrated Planning

Music is the obvious subject which can be integrated, but social studies also can be a part of rhythmics. By doing dances from other countries, children can learn about far away people and places. In music children can learn phrasing and accents, and by using classical music, they may learn more about the classics.

Rhythmic Activities

(Record Sources, p. 395)

1. Do basic movements to tom-tom or music.
2. Lummi sticks:
    a. Keep rhythm by mimicking teacher — hit on floor or two sticks together.
    b. Keep rhythm to various tempos.
    c. Move in rhythm around room while hitting sticks together.
    d. Sit on floor and work with partner.
    e. Hold sticks on one end and hit other end or hold sticks in middle and hit vertically.
    f. Flip sticks and keep time to music. What ways can you move while on your feet and keep time to the music with your body and sticks?
    How can you sit and move your body and sticks to the music?
    What can you do with a partner and still keep time to the music?
3. Phrasing:
    a. Children will change the direction of movement at the end of each musical phrase.
    b. Children will accent the beginning of each musical phrase with their body or a body part.
4. Bouncing ball to music:
    a. Bounce and catch alone; with partner.
    b. Design small routine to music.
    c. Dribble and keep time to music in which the tempo is varied.

Keep folk dances simple

5. Folk Dances:
   a. Loobie Loo

   Children sing the song and move as follows:

Here we go Loobie Loo,	Circle left using walk, skip, or slide
Here we go Loobie Light,	Sing chorus at start, between
Here we go Loobie Loo,	stanzas, and at end of game.
All on a Saturday night.	Every one drops hands — faces Center.

   Verse 1

I put my right hand in,	Place right hand to center
I put my right hand out,	Place right hand out
I give my hand a shake, shake, shake	Shake hand
And turn myself about	Turn in place.

   Other Verses (Repeat chorus after each verse)

   2. I put my left hand in . . .
   3. I put my two hands in . . .
   4. I put my right foot in . . .
   5. I put my left foot in . . .
   6. I put my elbows in . . .
   7. I put my shoulders in . . .
   8. I put my big head in . . .
   9. I put my whole self in . . .

   b. Chicken Fat

   "Chicken Fat" is a different way for children to learn to exercise all parts of the body and develop Rhythm as the music plays. The types of exercises the child will get exposed to are: toe touch, push-ups, march in place (left foot first), sit-ups, torso twist, pogo spring, jumping jacks, march in place, arm circles, bicycle ride, deep breathing, and tortoise and hare.

   Variations: Let child stand in front of the class to lead the exercises and keep count.

   c. Did you Ever See a Lassie

   Children sing song and move as follows:

Did you ever see a lassie (laddie)?	All join hands and skip to left
A lassie, a lassie,	swinging joined hands.
Did you ever see a lassie,	
Go this way and that?	

   Chorus

Go this way and that way.	All stop, release hands, face child
Go this way and that way.	in center and imitate his movements.
Did you ever see a lassie	Repeat singing games with new leader.
Go this way and that?	

   d. Baa, Baa, Black Sheep

   Children sing the song and act out the words.

Baa, Baa, Black sheep,	Eight walking steps right. Place
Have you any wool?	hands on hips and not on word "yes"
Yes sir, yes sir,	hold 3 fingers up on word "three" and
Three bags full.	arms out to show a large bag.

One for my master,	Turn right and bow or curtsey.
One for my dame,	Turn left and bow or curtsey.
And one for the little boy,	Face center and bow or curtsey.
Who lives in the lane.	

172 Grades One and Two

e. Farmer in the Dell

The children sing the song. The "farmer" picks a "wife" as the song says. When he picks another child that child joins hands on the farmer's waist facing his back. They walk in one direction outside the circle while the circle players walk, skip, or slide in another direction. Each child that is picked puts their hands on the waist of the one that picked them and moves with them.

The farmer in the dell,	The wife takes a child, etc.
The farmer in the dell,	The child takes a nurse, etc.
Heigh-ho! the cherry-o	
The farmer in the dell.	The nurse takes a dog, etc.
The farmer takes a wife,	The dog takes a cat, etc.
The farmer takes a wife,	
Heigh-ho! the cherry-o,	The cat takes a rat, etc.
The farmer takes a wife.	The rat takes the cheese, etc.
	The cheese stands alone,
	The farmer runs away, etc.

(Repeat for each player as he leaves the circle.)

f. Others

- Hokey Pokey
- Klapptanz
- Chimes of Dunkirk
- Go Round and Round the Village
- Did you Ever See a Lassie
- Paw Paw Patch
- Galaway Piper

6. Creative rhythmics:
   a. Move to classical music.
   b. Move to modern music.
   c. Have children create a routine with one high move, one low move, and one middle level move.
   d. Emphasize force, time, space, and level.

Creativity

Goal: Children will exhibit creativity in a variety of activities.

Objectives:

1. Children will be able to design original activities as part of story plays.

2. Children will create an original dance to music. This dance will include the following: force, time, space, and level.

3. Children working in groups will create original routines using lummi sticks.

Integrated Planning

The subject which can best be integrated with creativity is science. By using story plays, (p. 179) numerous science terms and concepts can be learned.

Creative Activities

1. Chaining

   First child begins chain by freezing in a position. Each child then joins the chain by running and freezing in a position while touching the first child. This continues until all children are chained together. Emphasis should be placed on fitting pieces together creatively.

Chaining — a creative activity

2. Dissolving
    Children form a group statue of eight to ten people, which then dissolves into another statue by children changing positions and levels.
3. Quickies
    Children form group statues which change quickly on the teacher's command. Series of approximately ten changes should be made followed by a change in the statues' sizes (number of people).
4. Moving creatively to music, p. 170.
5. Sticky Popcorn
    The children begin this game by "popping" — jumping or hopping — about the gym as individual pieces of sticky popcorn, searching for other pieces of popcorn. When one piece of popcorn comes into contact with another piece, they stick together. Once stuck, they continue to pop around together, sticking to other pieces, until they all end up in a big popcorn ball.
6. Puppet Movement
    Have the children observe the way a puppet moves. While you work the puppet ask, "Does a puppet move just like a person or are there differences?" "What are the differences?" Have the children imagine how it feels for a puppet master to slowly bring a puppet to life. Remind the children to feel like a puppet and to focus their attention on what the real puppet is doing. From here it is up to the teacher. Have the puppet do exercises: move fast or slowly in their own spaces; work on left, right discrimination, etc.
7. For additional creative activities, which can be used with six and seven year olds, see p. 140.

Tumbling and Gymnastics

Goal. Children will develop tumbling and gymnastics ability.

Objectives:

1. Each child will be able to do at least 80 percent of the skills listed on p. 173-174.

2. Each child will be able to do 95 percent of the kindergarten tumbling and gymnastics activities, p. 132-133.

3. Each child will be able to do 80 percent of the tumbling and gymnastic activities listed below.

Tumbling and Gymnastics Activities

Extreme caution must be exercised with weak or overweight children. Additional tumbling and gymnastics activities can be found in Chapter 7.

Tumbling (See illustrations on p. 174.)

1. Forward roll
    a. Explore rolling on mats.
    b. Egg roll — hold knees with arms and roll sideways.
    c. Start from a squat, put chin on chest, place hands outside knees, roll forward, do not let head touch mat; stay in a tucked position, reach out with hands and come up on feet. To keep the chin on the chest, have the child hold a beanbag between their chin and chest.
    d. Start from standing position.
    e. Do forward roll from walk.
    f. Spread leg — start with legs spread, keep legs straight and end in sitting position, legs spread.
2. Backward roll
    a. Roll backward and touch feet above head.
    b. Start from squat, place hands beside ears with thumbs against ears, keep knees against chest entire time; tuck chin to chest, roll backward, and push evenly with both hands landing on feet (no knees).
    c. Start backward roll from stand.
    d. Straddle backward roll.
3. Tripod
    Squat down, place hands on floor so elbows are on inside of knee; tip forward so head is on mat and weight is being held up by hands and head.
4. Tip-up. Do tripod, but do not allow head to touch mat (balance on hands).
5. Headstand with assistance
    a. Place hands and head on mat to form triangle.
    b. Forehead (at hairline) should be placed on mat and fingers should be pointed up past head.
    c. Take a tripod position.
    d. Feet should go straight up and the assistant should only help in maintaining balance.
    e. Child should come down same way he went up, and not do a forward roll.

174 *Grades One and Two*

Egg roll

Backward roll

Tripod

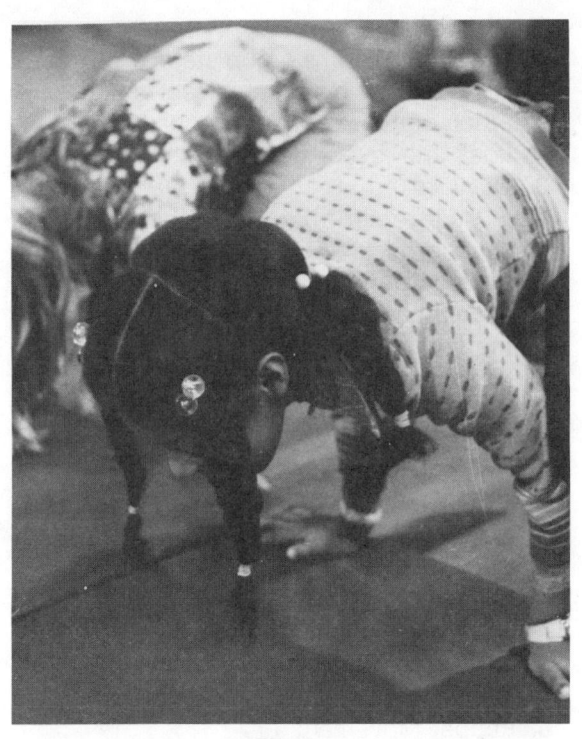

Tip-up

Headstand with spotter

Gymnastics

1. Low vaulting box and Reuther board
   a. Spring off Reuther board to knees on top of box and spring off knees and onto feet on far side.
   b. Spring to feet, stand up and jump off.
   c. Spring over box using hands only.
2. Rings or use two ropes next to each other
   a. Inverted hang placing feet against ropes for balance.
   b. Bird's nest. Hook feet in rings with hands and push stomach out.
   c. Skin the cat. Bring feet between hands and go into an inverted position, feet pointing toward ground.
3. Climbing ropes
   a. If two ropes are close together, child can do skills under "Rings," above.
   b. Climb the rope so feet are at the level of the child's height.
4. Horizontal ladder
   Travel eight feet across ladder using hands only.
5. Balance
   a. Explore different ways to balance. How many different ways can you balance? Can you balance on two body parts? Three? Four?
   b. Play Statues, and Whistle Stop, page 152.
      1. Encourage balancing high and low.
      2. Reward unusual ways of balancing.
   c. Low balance beam activities.
      1. Walk beam forward, backward, sideward right and sideward left.
      2. Walk to the center, make a half turn and walk off backward.
      3. Step over a stick held at knee height.
         a. Jump up and come down on beam, maintaining balance.
         b. Cross beam using hands and feet.
         c. Jump and touch heels.
         d. Squat and make half-turn.
      What are other things you can do on the beam?

Getting over the vaulting box

Springing to feet and jumping off

Fitness

Goal. Children will improve on all physiological and motor fitness items each time the test is given.

Objectives:
1. Child will be able to touch his toes without bending his knees.
2. Run a minimum of 450 meters in six minutes.
3. Do a flexed-arm hang for a minimum of five seconds.
4. Do a standing broad jump the distance of his height.
5. Do ten push-ups.
6. Do ten bent-knee sit-ups with someone holding his feet.
7. Run, change direction on a given signal, and not fall down.
8. Run 30 yards in eight seconds.

Integrated Planning

Teach as much of the physiology listed under fitness activities and the Cognitive Domain, (below) as possible while the children are actually doing the fitness activities.

Fitness Activities and Information
(Also see Chapter 6)

1. Muscle building activities
   a. Push-ups (triceps) — Lie on stomach, place hands under shoulders, keep back straight, stay on toes, keep head up, push up until arms are straight, lower till chest touches ground (do not put weight down), and then repeat action.
   b. Modified pull-ups (biceps).
   c. Sit-up progression (abdominals) — Legs straight and use arms to assist. Spread legs, place hands across chest. Bend knees, hands across chest. Place hands behind head with knees bent.
2. Cardiovascular
   a. Teach children how to take pulse at brachial artery (wrist).
   b. Do activities (running and rope jumping) to increase pulse rate.
   c. Emphasize that the heart is a muscle which must be exercised and gets better when it has to beat faster.
   d. Gradually increase running time till children can run for six to ten minutes without stopping.
3. Flexibility
   a. Explain what flexibility is.
   b. Do toe touches.
   c. Do hurdlers stretch.
   d. Do back bends.
4. Body fat
   a. Explain the problems of being overweight.
   b. Tell them how they can help.
      1. Less junk food.
      2. Fewer desserts.
      3. Have bulletin boards emphasizing food groups and balanced diet.
   c. Emphasize regular exercise program at home.
5. Motor fitness
   a. Have races.
   b. Use obstacle courses to develop agility and balance.
   c. Set up challenging activities in which children can measure how far and high they can jump; how far they can throw; and how fast they can run.
6. Set up home fitness packets for all children.
7. Have regular fitness testing (Appendix A).

Relaxation

Relaxation goals, objectives, and activities do not differ from those for kindergarten children. The section on relaxation, Chapter 7, can be used with six and seven-year-olds.

Body Image (See Cognitive Domain, below)

AFFECTIVE DOMAIN

The goals, objectives, and developmental activities for six and seven-year-old children differ only slightly from those for kindergarten youngsters. Rather than repeating material presented in Chapter 7, reference is made to the pages where the information can be found:

Self Concept, p. 144
Honesty, p. 144
Sharing, p. 144
Respect for Authority, p. 144
Patience, p. 145
Respect for Self and Others, p. 145
Leading and Following, p. 145
Positive Attitudes, p. 145

COGNITIVE DOMAIN
Problem-Solving Ability

Goal. Children will develop some problem-solving ability.
Objective:
During a problem-solving activity, each child will be able to think of one solution on his own for most of the problems presented.

Problem-Solving Activities

1. Story plays, p. 179
2. Creative activities, p. 172
3. Statues, p. 152

Creativity

Goal: Children will develop creativity.
Objective:
Given a creative movement situation, the child will be able to come up with one unique way of moving.

Creative Activities (See page 140)

Body Image

Goal: The children will learn various body parts and how they move.

Objectives:

1. Children will be able to identify each of the following body parts by touching them if asked: wrist, waist, shoulders, elbows, ankles, cheeks, and forehead, plus all those identified by the five year olds, p. 146

2. Children will be able to keep time with music using various body parts.

3. A child will draw a self-portrait and include each of the following: head, eyes, ears, nose, mouth, body, arms, fingers, legs, and feet.

Integrated Planning

Use flashcards (p. 148) with names of body parts on them.

Body Image Activities

1. Simon Says, p. 152
2. Busy Bee, p. 152
3. Brothers, p. 152
4. Rhythmic Activities, p. 170
5. Creative Activities, p. 172
6. Non-Locomotor Movement, p. 129

Directional and Movement Terms

(See page 146)

Directional and Movement Activities

(See page 146)

Rules and Regulations

Goal: Children will learn new games and dances each year. Children will know the rules of the class.

Objectives:

1. If asked, at least 80 percent of the students will be able to give three class rules.
2. If asked, children will be able to give the reason for a rule.
3. Children will be able to play five new games and do five new dances a year from memory.

Rules and Regulations Activities

1. After teaching games, give children a chance to conduct games on their own to see if they remember the rules.
2. The last phase of teaching a folk dance is to allow children the opportunity to dance without the teacher's aid.

Fitness, Health, and Safety Knowledge

Goal: Children will gain safety, fitness, and health knowledge.

Objectives:

1. If asked, children will be able to give one reason for each safety rule established.
2. If asked, children should be able to give five class safety rules.
3. Children will be able to give one reason for each of the following: cleanliness, brushing the teeth after meals, cooling down slowly after a workout, being physically fit, running, and exercises.

Fitness Knowledge

1. How to take pulse at wrist.
2. Why heart beats faster during exercise.
3. Exercises to develop fitness.
4. The necessity to cool down after an exercise bout.
5. Dangers of over-exercising in extreme heat.
6. The need for liquids during and after exercise which produces extensive sweating.

Safety Knowledge

1. Proper footwear.
2. Following game rules.
3. Tagging.
4. No sliding on floor or grass.
5. Staying inside designated areas.
6. No horseplay during gymnastics.
7. Protecting head and neck during gymnastics.
8. Wearing safety goggles over glasses.

Health Knowledge

1. Proper diet.
2. Rest needs.
3. Exercise needs.
4. Cleanliness.

INTEGRATED ACTIVITIES

For an explanation of integrated activities, see Section II, p. 111.

Language Arts

1. Moving to Poetry

Begin by telling the children that they are going to let their bodies be trains. They will move on the floor to "Song of the Train" by David McCord.

(1) Clickety-clack
   Wheels on the track,
   This is the way
   They begin the attack:
   Click-ety-clack,
   Click-ety-clack,
   Clickety, clackety,
   Click-ety clack
(2) Clickety-clack
   Over the crack
   Faster and faster
   The song of the track:
   Clickety-clack
   Clickety-clack,
   Clickety-clackety
   Clackety Clack.
(3) Riding in front,
   Riding in back,
   Everyone hears
   The song of the track
   Clickety-clack,
   Clickety-clack,
   Clickety, clickety,
   Clackety, clack.

Do this from slow to fast to faster.

"Trucks" by James S. Tippett

Big trucks for steal beams,
Big trucks for coal,
Rumbling down the broad streets,
Heavily they roll.

Little trucks for groceries,
Little trucks for bread,
Turning into every street,
Rushing on ahead.

Big trucks, little trucks,
In never-ending lines,
Rumble on and rush ahead
While I read their signs.

"Feet" by Myra Cohn Livingston

Feet are very special things
For special kinds of fun.

On weekdays they walk off to school
Or skip — or hop — or run —

On Saturdays they roller skate
Or bicycle or hike

On Sundays they just do the things
That other people like.

2. Ten Little Indians
1. Each child acts out each verse (game was designed to be an elimination game. However, this is an example of how a negative idea can be transformed) using their fingers to signify the number of Indians in the verse. 2. Leader says verse and children repeat while acting it out as they wish, allowing for some level of creativity in terms of "how they play in the sun" or how they "play pretty tricks." 3. Encourage movement in different directions. Suggestions for verses follow:

Verse 1 — hands up, fingers out — one down for nine children can walk as if going home; 2. move as swinging on a gate — jump off suggest children close eyes and jump; 3. Staying at tavern — sitting and getting up to leave; 4. Playing tricks — each child makes up her own and rides according to bicycle, car, train, etc; 5. Dive "gently" and swim movement; 6. Following words in verse to guide movement for remaining verses.

4. Allow children to make up a tune to the verses and tape them. This recording could be used as the lead or a fun way to end the activity time. 5. A child may enjoy being his own human tom-tom to intensify rhythm; other children may wish to take a turn at this. Selections for this role by the teacher. One child per verse.

Ten Little Indians

Ten little Indians
Standing in a line
One went home
and then there were nine

Nine little Indians
swinging on a gate
one jumped off
And then there were eight

Eight little Indians
staying at a tavern
one went away
and then there were seven

Seven little Indians
playing pretty tricks
one went to ride
and then there were six

Six little Indians
learning how to dive
One swam away
and then there were five

Five little Indians
peeped through the door
One ran behind
and then there were four

Four little Indians
Climbed up a tree
one slid down
and then there were three.

Three little Indians
Out in a canoe
One hopped to land
And then there were two

Two little Indians
playing in the sun
One fell asleep
and then there was one

One little Indian
playing all alone
he went in the house
and then there were none.

Math

1. Target Numbers
   Use targets with numbers on them and beanbags. Have children throw at the numbers, i.e., "Can you hit the six, three, etc.?" Increase the distance from the target and have the children use the non-dominant hand.

2. Stations
   A number of stations can be set up in which points are awarded for accomplishing certain tasks. The children can use a pencil and paper to keep score as they move from one station to the other.

3. Crows and Cranes Math
   See page 183 for a complete description of the game. Math problems, which have either an even number or an odd number answer, are called out. The two groups are designated as "Even" or "Odd." If the answer is even, the "Even" group runs and vice versa. The degree of difficulty of the problem will determine the grade level suitability. Children can be turned off by integrated math activities, so care must be exercised to make the game exciting. Perhaps many children experience so much frustration with math in the classroom, they want nothing to do with math during physical education.

4. Spud Math
   A simple math problem which has an answer equal to a number given a child is called out. The child must then try to catch or retrieve the ball. See page 183.

5. A-B-C Animals
   This activity would be used after a classroom discussion about animals. Hold up a letter and ask the children to think of an animal whose name begins with that letter. Then ask, "Does this animal move fast or slow? How does it hunt food? How does it eat? Can you pretend your animal is moving backwards? Sideways? In slow motion?"

6. Alphabet Tag
   One child is designated as "it." The game is played like regular tag. The teacher will hold up a letter of the alphabet. If a child is tagged, he must give a word beginning with that letter. If he cannot, he is "it." Letters should be changed frequently.

Science

1. Story Plays
   a. Under the Sea
      The class is going on a pioneer journey underneath the sea. Since you need a vessel to get there, have the class line up to form a submarine: the first two children raise their arms as the periscope; it may help to explain that the periscope is the "eye" of the ship. First the submarine must submerge (get lower and lower as it travels around the room). The periscope people lead the group, wave their hands slowly when it isn't safe to go, and hold the group back when the danger is past. When the submarine is totally submerged (the group crouched as low as possible), let the group slowly disperse. Explain that they are in water and their bodies are lighter. They must move slowly because of the resistance of the water. They must move slowly with no sudden actions. Sometimes they can float. Let them move as you talk. On the next step of the journey they will become seaweed. Since seaweed is very light, and has no weight of its own, the waves may push seaweed into all sorts of strange entangled twistings. You could use music at this point to encourage the children to roll on the floor, against a wall, and to tangle their bodies in interesting and unusual shapes. Two pieces of seaweed could become entangled with each other and change their shapes as the water pushed them in different directions and toward and away from each other. To accelerate the movement, you can make the movement louder. When the seaweed untangles, the group become sea turtles. They go onto their knees and lean on their forearms. Once they are crouched in this position, explain that a sea turtle moves by advancing its right arm and foot at the same time, then its left arm and foot. This produces a waddling effect. Once in a while, the turtle reaches its long neck out, searching for food — or has it heard something? Let the children experiment with reaching their necks out as far as they will go. Add to the story

by giving a loud bang on the drum, even yell aloud sound from time to time. That frightens the turtles, so they hurriedly draw their necks and heads in and hide them deep within themselves. One of the children can become the leader for the Portuguese man o'war. The other children will also follow him. You could show the class a picture of a real man o'war jellyfish, explain how dangerous they are and that they have never been touched. These creatures are soft and slinky; they slowly undulate their arms and legs, hoping to engulf anything that comes their way. Other children can be tiny fish that float on their bellies, trying to escape the clutches of the men o'war. If a fish is caught, he must roll over wounded (to the side of the room), for the soft blobs are powerful and poisonous. When most of the fish have been caught, tell the class to relax on the floor with their arms stretched over their heads. They are now ordinary jellyfish. This is one of the best parts of the game. The teacher walks over to each child and says, "Are you as relaxed as a jellyfish would be?" Lift his or her arm or leg up to see if it feels heavy, then explain that when someone is relaxed, the arm will feel extremely heavy and go down with a thud when you release it. If the children are relaxed, give them each a "ride," pulling each one around in circles by that arm or leg, turning, spinning, or spiraling them across the floor. When you finish with the "rides," throw their leg or arm over them in any position and explain.

b. See other story plays, p. 140.

2. Learning about animals
   a. Moving Like Animals
   How would you move if you were a small elephant, if you were a great big elephant? (children move) "If you were a small horse, how would you move? Could you move fast or slow? Why couldn't you move fast? Pretend that you were a baby horse and you were just learning to stand up. How do your legs feel? Do they feel wobbly? Let's move like we were a small horse (colt). The colt is getting larger now. How do you think he would move now? What about his legs? Are they still wobbly now? Let's gallop like we were a big horse. Can he gallop fast or slow? (both). First let's gallop slow. Now let's gallop fast." Continue with the other pictures of animals and ask motivating questions, and let the children act out the movements, creatively. (1) elephant (2) horse (3) rabbit (4) bird (5) fish (6) frog. The children could also spell the animal's name and the different ways of movement they make.

   b. Animal Flashcards
   The teacher holds up a card with an animal's name on it. Students say the name and then move like the animal. The teacher can add variety by asking the children to move in different ways, i.e., forward, backward, in slow motion, etc.

   c. Getting Ready for Winter
   The teacher tells the children to pretend they are animals getting ready for winter. Pretend you are a squirrel gathering nuts and burying them. A bird flying south. A bear looking for a den.

3. Signs of the Season
   After having a class discussion about what the four seasons of the year are called and when they occur, the children are asked, "What do you notice happening when fall comes? Winter? Spring? Summer?" Children act different things such as falling leaves, ice skating, swimming, or anything which is appropriate for the season mentioned.

GAMES

See Section II for a detailed explanation of games

FIRST AND SECOND GRADE GAMES

Name	Page	Psychomotor	Affective	Cognitive	Grass	Multipurpose Room	Hardtop	Classroom	Can be Adapted to Any Area	Can be used for Evaluation
Whistle Stop	152	4	3	1					x	
Simon Says	152	4	1	1					x	
Brothers	152	3	5	2					x	x
Busy Bee	152	3	5	2					x	x
Automobiles	182	5	1	1	x	x				
Tag Games	153	4	2	1	x	x				
Do This, Do That	153	3	1	1					x	x
Dog Catcher	182	4	2	1	x	x				
Jump the Shot	182	4	1	1	x	x	x			
Fox and Hound	153	5	1	1	x					
Red Light	182	4	2	1					x	
Cowboys and Indians	182	3	2	1	x	x				
Three Bears	183	3	2	1	x	x				
Red Rover	183	3	2	2	x	x				
Squirrels in Trees	153	4	4	1					x	
Old Mother Witch	183	3	1	1	x	x				
Crows and Cranes	183	4	2	1	x	x				
Spud	183	3	1	1	x	x	x			
Trades	184	3	2	2	x	x				
Dodgeball	184	2	1	1	x	x	x			
Guard the Pin	184	2	1	1	x	x	x			
Tug of War	184	5	1	1	x	x				
Old Plug	184	5	2	1	x	x				
Hill Dill	185	3	2	1	x					
Bull in the Ring	185	2	1	1	x					
Hit the Mat	185	3	1	1	x	x	x			
Electric Shock	185	3	2	1	x					
Guess the Leader	185	4	2	1					x	
Progressive Tag	186	5	3	1	x	x				
Mousetrap	186	3	2	1					x	
Guess Who	186	3	3	2					x	
Clean Out the Backyard	186	5	1	1	x					
Heads, Bodies, and Legs	186	5	5	2					x	
Balloon Volleyball	186	4	1	1					x	
Octopus	187	3	2	1	x	x				
Four Corners	187	4	1	1					x	

Game Code:
- N = Name of game
- DA = Developmental age for which game was designed
- DV = What the child should get from the game (developmental value)
- F = Formation
- E = Equipment required
- D = Description of the game

182 *Grades One and Two*

N: Automobiles
DA: 6-7
DV: Running & Agility
 F: Large Circle
 E: None
 D: Each child has an imaginary racing car, and each is on the circle facing in the same direction. On the signal to go, children begin running and are allowed to pass but not touch anyone else. The only real object of the activity is running, but children enjoy pretending they are at an auto race and making appropriate motor sounds. Children can go to the center of the circle for gas and repairs. To improve agility, the leader can call for a change of direction, which means turning around and going the other way. This activity is good for the beginning of a class, since it is easy to organize and provides maximum participation. It is best suited for a grassy area or possibly a large, clear indoor area. Winners are all those who do not run into anyone else.

N: Dog Catcher
DA: 6 - 8
DV: Running, Fitness
 F: Single line (Follow the leader)
 E: None
 D: The dog catcher leads the class away from a safe base area. The followers must do anything the leader does; run, walk, crawl, etc. When the dog catcher turns to say "run," everyone must try to make it to the safe base without being tagged by the catcher. Anyone tagged has to help the catcher during his second turn. After two turns, a new leader is chosen from those not caught. Those not tagged at the end are the winners.

N: Jump the Shot
DA: 6 - 12
DV: Eye, Foot Coordination, and Fitness
 F: Circle of six or seven children with one child in the middle
 E: Ten foot long ropes with beanbag tied to end
 D: The center person turns a rope with a beanbag tied on the end in a circle. Children stay outside the arch of the beanbag until the rope is going (beanbag is kept close to floor), and then try to "jump in" as soon as possible. Anyone hit by the rope gets a point. Each person should take a turn in the center. At the end, those with the least number of points are the winners. To avoid dizziness, the center person should try to take the rope behind his back rather than turning in a circle. Older children should have no difficulty with the behind the back move.

N: Red Light
DA: 6 - 7
DV: Stopping and Starting
 F: One straight line, children side by side, facing the leader on the other side of the play area.
 E: None
 D: Leader calls out, "green light," as he turns his back to the group, which begins moving toward the goal line. He counts to three or five depending upon the size of the area, and then turns to face the approaching group as he calls out "red light." Anyone caught moving *after* red light is called is sent back to the starting line to begin again. Game continues until one person crosses the goal line. This person becomes the new leader and the game starts again from the beginning. Children should call others by name which can aid the teacher and the children in learning names, particularly at the beginning of the year.

N: Cowboys and Indians
DA: 6 - 8
DV: Running, Chasing, and Tagging
 F: Two lines at opposite ends of play area
 E: Beanbags if playing variation described
 D: Class is divided in half. One half of class, the cowboys, turn their backs to other half, the Indians, who are standing at the opposite end of the play area. The Indians then quietly come up behind the group with their backs turned — no closer than four feet — and turn sideways to get ready to run back to their safe base. It is important for safety to have children turn sideways to avoid tangling feet and falling, which may cause others to trip. When the leader calls, "Here come the Indians," the cowboys turn and chase the Indians, trying to tag them. Anyone tagged joins the other team and roles are reversed with the cowboys coming up behind the Indians. Auditory discrimination can be developed by saying something like, "Here come the elephants," to see if children are really listening. Anyone running on the wrong signal must change

teams. Hand-eye coordination can be added by giving each child a beanbag. The chasing team then tries to hit the fleeing group with the beanbag rather than tagging with the hand.

N: The Three Bears
DA: 6 - 7
DV: Chasing and Tagging
F: One straight line side by side facing the four leaders
E: None
D: Four children are chosen to be Goldilocks, Momma Bear, Poppa Bear, and Baby Bear. They face the rest of the children. Children call out, "Who's home?" Each leader takes a turn answering, and may answer any one of the four names — Momma Bear, Poppa Bear, Baby Bear, or Goldilocks. Children continue to ask "Who's home?" until one of the leaders answers "Poppa Bear". This is the signal for the children to run to a predetermined safe base while being chased by the four leaders. Those tagged join the leaders for one more turn. After two turns, four new leaders are chosen from those not tagged.

N: Red Rover
DA: 6 - 7
DV: Running, Chasing, Learning Colors
F: One line side by side and one "it"
E: None
D: "It" calls out "red rover, red rover, I dare anyone with (some color is called) to come over." With that anyone who has that color on must try to make it across the tagging area to safe base on the opposite side. Anyone tagged must stay in center and help "it" catch others. Once on the far safe-base, children stay there until everyone has crossed over — this is to avoid collisions. "It" continues to call colors until everyone has had a chance to cross over. A new "it" is chosen from those not tagged.

N: Old Mother Witch or Midnight
DA: 6 - 7
DV: Running, Chasing, and Tagging
F: Free formation with one leader
E: None
D: The "Old Mother Witch" leads the rest of the class off safe base. All children chant, "Old Mother Witch, fell in a ditch, picked up a penny and thought she was rich." Children act out chant as they move behind the witch. The children then say, "What time is it?" Old Mother Witch can say any time she wants. After each time is called out, children again ask, "What time is it?" If she says "midnight" they all run back to safe base while she tries to tag as many as possible. All those tagged help her during her second chance. After two turns, a new witch is picked from the group not caught.

N: Crows and Cranes
DA: 6 - 8
DV: Auditory Discrimination, Running, Chasing, and Tagging
F: Two lines side by side — separated by about four feet
E: None
D: One group is the Crows and the other Cranes. If the leader calls out "Crows", they run to a predetermined safe base (goal line) while the Cranes chase and try to tag them. If "Cranes" is called, they run and the Crows chase. Anyone tagged must go with the tagging group. By adding confusing visual cues along with the verbal, the leader can increase the need to listen carefully, i.e., call Cranes, but point with hand toward direction Crows would run. Leader can also call things like elephants or tigers to keep children on their toes.

N: Spud
DA: 6 - 8
DV: Fun
F: Free
E: One 8½ Playground Ball
D: Each person is assigned a number. A player is chosen to throw up the ball and call a number. The person whose number is called attempts to catch the ball before it hits the ground. If he is successful, he immediately throws it up and calls someone else's number. As soon as the ball hits the ground, the person attempting to catch it must retrieve it and call "spud." The rest of the players whose numbers are not called run as far as possible (within a designated area) away from the player trying to retrieve the ball. When "spud" is called out, all players must stop and not move. The player with the ball then rolls it at any player. If he hits one (they cannot move their feet), they get an "S". If he misses, he gets an "S". Anyone who gets S-P-U-D is out of the game. The winners at the end are those with the least number of letters. The game should end before anyone is eliminated.

184 *Grades One and Two*

N: Trades
DA: 6 - 8
DV: Creativity, Learning about Jobs in the Community, Chasing, and Tagging
 F: Class divided in half
 E: None
 D: One half the class decides in secret what trade (occupation) they would like to imitate. All players must imitate the same occupation. After deciding, they walk in a line side by side across the play area saying, "Here we come." The other half of the class whom they are walking toward ask, "Where from?" While still advancing forward, the first group responds, "New York" (or the children's home town). The other group then asks, "What is your trade?", which is answered by "Lemonade." By this time the moving group should be within about five to six feet of the other group, which says finally, "Show us." With that, each person begins imitating (no sound) the trade. Children from the other group raise their hand and when called upon, guess. If they guess the correct occupation the imitation group turns and runs toward safe base while being chased by the other group. Anyone caught joins the chasing group, which then gets the chance to do the imitating. The game continues for a set period of time with winners being the biggest group and those not tagged at all during the game.

N: Dodgeball
DA: 6 - 12
DV: Agility
 F: Usually a circle
 E: Playground balls or spongeballs
 D: There are a number of variations of dodgeball, most of which are fun, but have little developmental value. The value can be increased by dividing the class into small groups of six or seven people with only one person in the circle at a time. The group then tries to see how many times they can hit the person in the center in a given time period. Each person takes a turn in the circle with the winner being the person hit the least.

 Another variation is a team game in which the class is divided into two teams with one team trying to stay in the center the longest time. Every person must be hit below the waist, and balls (usually two balls are used) must be rolled. After one team is eliminated, the teams switch places. Whenever a game uses more than one playground ball, the balls must be rolled instead of thrown. If sponge balls are used, they can be thrown.

N: Guard the Pin
DA: 6 - 9
DV: Fun and Hand-Eye Coordination
 F: Circle with four people in center
 E: 8½" Playground balls & plastic containers
 D: To increase the activity, the class should be divided in half with two games going at once. Four children are in the center of the circle with each one guarding a plastic milk container. Children on the circle use several balls to try and knock over a container. If a child knocks over a container, he switches places with the child in the center. Balls must be rolled.

N: Tug of War
DA: 6 - 12
DV: Strength Development
 F: Class evenly divided — straight lines facing other team
 E: Tug of war rope
 D: Children on the same team should alternate sides of the rope to avoid getting their feet tangled. No child should be permitted to get inside the loop which is frequently at the end of a tug of war rope. On the signal to go, children try to pull the other team for a specified distance. All children must stop on a given signal (a whistle).

N: Old Plug
DA: 6 - 8
DV: Agility, Group Cooperation
 F: Groups of four
 E: Beanbags — one per group.
 D: Three persons make a horse, "Old Plug." One person is the head, one the body, and another the tail, all of which are joined by holding onto each other's waist. One person is the farmer who wants to give Old Plug a shot (with a beanbag) in the tail. The head tries to protect the tail by keeping the farmer in front at all times. The farmer is allowed to do anything short of touching Old Plug to get to the tail and administer the shot (hit the tail with the beanbag). If the farmer is successful by hitting the tail or by causing the horse to come apart he becomes the new head, and the tail becomes the farmer. The idea is to be the head as long as possible. For safety, chil-

dren must be instructed to stay in a designated area and not try to move, usually backward, all over the play area.

N: Hill Dill
DA: 6 - 8
DV: Running, Chasing, and Tagging
 F: One long line and one chaser
 E: None
 D: Chaser says, "Hill Dill come over the hill before I catch you standing —." If the caller says "still," children must run to a safe base area. Anyone tagged must help the original chaser. Each time the children who are chasers say the rhyme with the decision on the last word being made by the original tagger. If he says anything other than "still," anyone who runs is automatically tagged, and must immediately join the tagging group. Game continues until nearly everyone is caught. The new chaser is chosen from those not caught.

N: Bull in the Ring
DA: 6 - 9
DV: Running
 F: Circle with one child in center
 E: None
 D: Child in center tries to get out of the circle by ducking under the hands being held by the children or by breaking through the hands (child may not try to jump over hands). If he successfully gets out, everyone except the two people who let him get out chase him, with the first person to tag him being the next bull in the ring. Children in the circle may only bend at the waist to prevent bull from getting out and may not bend their legs.

N: Hit the Mat (or Ball)
DA: 6 - 8
DV: Hand-Eye Coordination
 F: Two groups facing each other
 E: One beanbag per child and mat or 16" playground balls (2 or 3)
 D: One team is on each side of a mat standing on its end (only certain mats will work). Each child is given a beanbag. Upon the signal to throw by the leader, everyone must throw at the same time — late throws will not count. The object is to make the mat fall toward the other team. If successful, a team gets one point. Children retrieve any beanbag and get back into place quickly, but may not throw until the signal is given.

A large ball can be used in place of the mat with a team receiving a point if the ball ends up closer to the other team. If the class is large, two or three balls can be placed in the center. Balls can be placed on deck tennis rings to keep them in place until hit.

N: Electric Shock
DA: 6 - 7
DV: Running, Chasing, and Tagging
 F: One line and one "It"
 E: None
 D: A long line of children hold hands while facing a chaser. An electric shock, squeeze of hands, is sent from each end toward the middle where a prearranged person will yell, "Ouch," upon receiving the signal from either side. The "Ouch" is the signal for those holding hands to release, turn and run, while being chased to a prearranged safe base. Anyone being tagged before making base must aid the tagger. This progresses until nearly everyone is caught with those not tagged being declared the fastest runners.

N: Guess the Leader
DA: 6 - 9
DV: Fitness
 F: Circle
 E: None
 D: Children stand in a circle while one child turns his back. A leader is chosen and all children must do what he or she does while remaining on the circle. Children should be instructed not to stare at the leader. The leader can do exercises or movements of any kind as long as he remains in place. The person who will try to guess the leader then turns around and watches the children while attempting to determine the leader. The leader should make frequent changes of his activity to give the guesser a chance. If after two or three guesses, the leader is not recognized, a new guesser is selected. If the guesser picks the leader, he gets one more turn. If successful a second time, he can choose a new guesser. Try to give everyone a chance before allowing one person two turns as leader or guesser or a combination of the two. Set a time limit for making the guess.

N: Progressive Tag
DA: 6 - 9
DV: Hand-Eye Coordination and Agility
F: Free
E: None
D: The child who is "it" attempts to tag another person by hitting them below the waist with a beanbag. Once a person is hit, he stays "it" till the end of the game, and continues to hit others who then must help tag the rest of the children. All children not hit at the end of a time period are the winners. Since a number of beanbags will be going at once, the teacher must insist they be thrown low. The original tagger can have a chance to win since he must also be hit below the waist. However, he is the only one who is no longer "it" after hitting someone.

N: Mousetraps
DA: 6 - 7
DV: Basic locomotor movements
F: Players stand in two concentric circles
E: None
D: Players stand in two circles, the inside circle is made up of three to six players who take hold of hands; this is the mousetrap. The other players stand at some distance outside of the trap in another circle and do not hold hands. On a signal from the leader, the two circles start moving in opposite directions until the leader says "stop." At this the trap players lift their hands and the mice walk, skip, gallop, etc., in, around, and out of the trap. Suddenly the leader says "snap;" when the trap is shut quickly, by dropping hands, some of the mice will be caught. These mice then join the trap, making it larger.

N: Guess Who
DA: 6 - 7
DV: Basic Locomotor Movements
F: Children in line side by side, leader in the middle, "It" in front
E: None
D: Small groups are best. Each group has a leader and lines up side by side, with the leader in the middle. One odd player stands in front of the line facing it. The odd player asks: "Have you seen my friend?" The line answers: "No." Odd player: "Will you go and find him?" Line: "Yes." Odd player: "Put your finger on your lips and follow me." The player in front then turns around and with finger to his lips, runs (skips, gallops, etc.) to another part of the play area, all the row falling in behind and following him. When they have reached the new area the odd player stops with his back to the group, which reforms in a new order under the direction of the leader. One player from the row, selected by the leader, now steps forward behind the odd player and says, trying to disguise his voice: "Guess who stands behind you?" If the odd player guesses correctly, he retains his position, turns around, and the dialogue begins again. If the guess is wrong, then the two change places.

N: Clean Out the Backyard
DA: 6 - 7
DV: Throwing, catching, stopping ball with feet or hands, rolling ball
F: Class divided into two groups
E: *Foam balls,* one for each student, or as many as possible
D: Play area is divided into two courts, half of the class on each side. On signal, each person throws his ball across the center line. The object is to keep the balls in the opposite court. On signal all activity stops and balls are counted — the side with the least number of balls in its court wins.
Modification: 1. Balls may be rolled instead of thrown, especially for kindergarten.
2. Balls may be stopped with feet, dribbled to the center line and kicked over center line (without using hands).

N: Heads, Bodies, Legs
DA: 6 - 7
DV: Creativity and social interaction
F: Free
E: None
D: Children are divided into three equal groups, heads, bodies, and legs. They walk around at random imitating their body part so others will know what they are. The teacher calls out, "Make a person." Children then move quickly into groups to form a complete body — one head, one body and legs. Body parts left over have one point against them. Winners are those with least number of points.

N: Balloon Volleyball
DA: 6 - 7
DV: Eye-Hand Coordination
F: Seated on floor

E: Piece of rope, standards and balloons
D: A rope is suspended in air above the childrens' head level between two groups of equal numbers of children. Many balloons are batted back and forth over the rope. Children must remain seated. A point is scored for the opposing team if a child stands up or a balloon hits the floor.

N: Octopus
DA: Running, agility
DV: 6 - 7
F: All players begin behind a line on one side of the play area. One person is in the middle of the play area and is the tagger.
E: None or may use a ball to tag.
D: The "it" player calls, "Come fish, come." Everyone must run to the other safe base on the opposite side of the floor while "it" tries to take as many people as possible. If tagged, the child must freeze on the spot. When the game is begun again, the tagged players can pivot on one foot to help "it" tag others as they go by. After seven people have been tagged, a new "it" is selected from those who have not been tagged.

N: Four Corners
DA: 6 - 7
DV: Quality of Movement
F: All children in one of four corners
E: Blindfold
D: One child stands in the middle of the play area with eyes closed or blindfolded. On a signal, the other children run to one (their choice) of the four corners. The center child then points to one corner. If he selects the corner with the most number of people, they each get one point. The center child can have a couple turns, and then another child who has no points is selected to take his place. When going from one corner to the next, the children will be instructed to "run backward, run softly, move lightly, etc." The emphasis should be on the quality of locomotor movement.

EXAMPLE LESSON PLANS

1. 1st and 2nd

    Multipurpose Room

    Objectives:

    1. The students will be able to execute a forward, log, egg, and backward roll as discussed in class.
    2. The students will be able to identify body parts and be aware of body space and direction by listening and following directions in a song.

Activities	Formation
I. Students will practice listening and following directions by doing exercises to a record.	I. Free
II. Gymnastics — self testing Students will practice the activities mentioned in objective 1 above.	II. Small groups of 4 or 5 children
III. Body awareness and listening to directions Students follow record lifting and relaxing body parts. Record: Smoke Drifts to the Sky.	III. Lying on backs on mats

Safety: No shoes or socks on and no horseplay.

188 *Grades One and Two*

2. 1st and 2nd

    Outside or Multipurpose Room

    Objectives:

    1. The students will be able to bounce the ball with their dominant hand while moving in different ways.
    2. The students will be able to throw and catch the ball 5 times without it hitting the floor.

Activities	Formation
I. Rockets — students run in place and when the teacher yells "blast off," they must jump and reach for the sky	I. Free

II. Eye-hand coordination
 	
Students have free time to do exploration with the balls.
Teacher then asks, "Can you . . . ?"
  Bounce the ball with one hand
  Bounce while walking forward, backward, running, etc.?
Can you catch the ball in different ways?
How many times can you catch it in a row?
	II. Free — one ball per child

III. Outside — Ball tossing with a partner Inside — ball handling and bouncing to music	III. Free

    Safety: No kicking the ball

3. 1st and 2nd

    Outside or Multipurpose Room

    Objectives:

    1. When given a short jump rope, the students will be able to jump rope with both feet and on the left and right foot three consecutive times.
    2. After instruction, the students will be able to run 5 steps while jumping with a short rope.

Activities	Formation
1. Frozen Statues (Whistle Stop)	I. Free
II. Jump rope activities Have children make shapes with ropes and then do locomotor movements using the rope shapes. Also emphasize body parts by having them place body parts inside shapes	II. One rope per child
III. Bunny Hop Race Students get in a straight line and all hop at the same time to the finish line.	III. Straight Line

    Safety: No swinging ropes at anyone

4. 1st and 2nd

   Outside or Multipurpose Room

   Objectives:

   1. The students will be able to throw and catch the different balls 3 times without them hitting the ground.
   2. The students will develop eye-foot coordination by kicking the ball between the cones at least once before leaving the station.

Activities	Formation
I. Simon Says — Exercises	I. Free
II. Stations — To explore with equipment and work on eye-foot and eye-hand coordination	II. 5 Stations

   Station 1. Scoops

   Station 2. Big plastic balls with cones

   Station 3. Sponge rubber balls

   Station 4. Hula hoops

   Station 5. Small balls

   III. After having rotated all the stations, the children can go to any station of their choice and play.

   Safety: No throwing balls at anyone.

5. 1st and 2nd

   Multipurpose Room

   Objectives:

   1. When given a hula hoop, the students will be able to move in, out and around their hoops while developing the quality of their locomotor movement.
   2. The students will know body parts and directions by being able to play hula hoop twister.

Activities	Formation
I. Busy Bee	I. Free
II. Exploration with hoops	II. One hoop per child

   Can you? Skip backward around your hoop?
   Slide right and left around? Walk fast?
   In slow motion?
   What else can you do with your hoop?

   III. Hoop Twister   III. Groups of three

   3 hoops are placed in a circle, all different colors. The teacher calls right hand red, left foot blue, and students do what is called for while maintaining balance. If the child falls, he gets one point.

   Safety: No pushing during twister.

190 *Grades One and Two*

6. 1st and 2nd

   Multipurpose Room

   Objectives:

   1. The students will be able to perform locomotor skills while keeping rhythm with the lummi sticks.
   2. The students will be able to perform a structured pattern and create their own pattern with lummi sticks while keeping time to music.

Activities	Formation
I. Musical movement — students move around the room to music. When the music stops, they must freeze.	I. Free
II. Lummi sticks — students keep time to the music while following the teacher. Can you? Move in different ways while keeping time to the music. Can you? Skip, gallop, hop, etc., while beating your sticks.	II. Free
III. Creative Groups — Students (no larger than 3 to a group) develop a little routine to music.	

   Safety: No throwing sticks.

7. 1st and 2nd

   Multipurpose Room

   Objectives:

   1. The students will be able to throw and catch the beanbag while listening and keeping time to a record.
   2. When given a bean bag and a partner, the students will be able to show creativity by creating a beanbag routine to the music.

Activities	Formation
I. Exercises to music. Follow the teacher.	I. Free
II. Hand-eye coordination using bean bags. Free exploration, then throw and catch to music. "Throw the beanbag and catch." First time throw by themselves. Repeat record, this time with partners.	II. Free
III. Movement exploration with beanbags to music. Make up beanbag routine with a partner.	III. Partners

   Safety: No throwing beanbags at people, no running, no sliding.

8. 1st and 2nd

Multipurpose Room

Objectives:

1. The students will be able to do 5 different exercises by being able to complete the station arrangement on physical fitness.
2. If asked, 80% of the students will be able to demonstrate a flexibility exercise and an arm strength exercise.

Activities | Formation

   I. Exercises and discussion about heart beat and strength/flexibility.   I. Free

  II. Station 1   II. Stations

Can you sit in a straddle and touch your nose on the floor?

Can you do a split? Can you touch your head to your feet? Can you touch your toes with straight legs?

Station 2

Agility — Can you run through the hoops? Can you hop through the hoops? How else can you get through the hoops?

Station 3

Leg Strength — Can you jump rope 10 times? Can you jump backwards? Can you jump on right foot/left foot? How else can you jump?

Station 4

Can you do a push-up? Can you get a partner and wheelbarrow down the mat? Can you crab walk?

Station 5

Standing Broad Jump. How far can you jump on two feet?

  III. Free Practice at last station working on what the poster says.

Safety: Follow signs only, no horse play on mats.

9. 1st and 2nd

Multipurpose Room

Objectives:

1. The students will be able to execute a forward and backward roll, log roll, front support, rear support cartwheel and push-up back bend as discussed in class.
2. If asked, 80% of the students will be able to demonstrate 3 different exercises used for flexibility.

192 *Grades One and Two*

    Activities

       I. Exercises working on flexibility and discussing flexibility while exercising.

      II. Tumbling: forward and backward roll
           log roll
           rear support
           front support
           push-up back bend
           cartwheel, with dominant hand

      III. Leap Frog on mats. Team that gets to end of mat first wins.

    Formation

       I. Free

      II. No more than four to a mat

      III. 5 or 6 teams

    Safety: no shoes, no horseplay, no falling on others.

10. 1st and 2nd

    Outside

    Objective:

      1. When given a sponge rubber ball, the students will be able to move the ball with their feet while going forward and changing directions.

    Activities

       I. Student-led exercises.

      II. Eye-foot coordination: Teacher asks can you? Move the ball forward; move the ball backwards; move the ball with just the right foot; move the ball with just the left foot; move the ball with the inside of the foot; move the ball while running forward; move the ball around the cones. Can you drop the ball and kick it before it hits the ground? Can you run up behind the ball and kick it.

      III. Dribble Race

    Students line up and dribble with their feet to the finish line, no long kicks allowed.

    Formation

       I. Free

      II. Free, 1 sponge ball per child

      III. Straight line.

    Safety: no kicking near anyone.

11. 1st and 2nd

    Multipurpose Room

    Objectives:

      1. The students will be able to complete each station by being able to execute the skills listed on the posters.
      2. When given a piece of equipment, 80% of the students will be able to create their own activity at each station.

Activities	Formation
I. Show me exercises.	I. Free

Student show the teacher exercises they know. Different students lead exercises.

II. Station I (Exploratory Stations)	II. Stations

Jump ropes — Can you jump *10* times?
What else can you do with your ropes.

Station II

Hula Hoop — Can you hula hoop *5* times around your waist? What else can you do?

Station III

Scoops — Can you scoop with a partner?
What else can you do?

Station IV

Sponge rubber balls — Can you throw and catch the ball with (1) hand? What else can you do?

Station V

Plastic Balls — Can you bounce the ball with (1) hand? What else can you do?

Safety: Stay in your own station, no kicking the ball, running or sliding.

12. 1st and 2nd

    Outside

    Objective:

    1. The students will be able to throw (stepping forward with the opposite foot), and catch a six inch beanbag four out of five times with a partner *15* feet away.

Activities	Formation
I. Brothers	I. Partners
II. Guided Discovery (Hand-eye Coordination)	
a. How many ways can you throw the beanbag and catch it?	a. Free
b. Can you throw the beanbag with a friend and catch it?	b. Partners
c. Can you throw and catch with your partner when you are *15* feet apart?	c. Partners

194 *Grades One and Two*

    d. Can you throw and catch with your partner when you are *15* feet apart 4 out of 5 times?

III. Hit the Mat	III. Two groups (lines) facing each other.

REFERENCES

1. Arnheim, D. and R. Pestolesi. *Elementary Physical Education*. St. Louis: The C. V. Mosby Company, 1978.
2. Burton, E. *The New Physical Education for Elementary School Children*. Boston: Houghton Mifflin Co., 1977.
3. Cochran, N., et. al. *A Teacher's Guide to Elementary School Physical Education*. Dubuque: Kendall/Hunt, 1971.
4. Cochran, N., et. al. *Learning on the Move*. Dubuque: Kendall/Hunt Publishing Co., 1975.
5. Dauer, V. *Essential Movement Experiences for Preschool and Primary Children*. Minneapolis: Burgess Publishing Co., 1972.
6. Dauer, V. and R. Pangrazi. *Dynamic Physical Education for Elementary School Children*. Minneapolis: Burgess Publishing Co., 1975.
7. Fait, H. *Physical Education for the Elementary School Child*. Philadelphia: W. B. Saunders Co., 1976.
8. Kirchner, G. *Physical Education for Elementary School Children*. Dubuque: Wm. C. Brown Co., 1974.
9. Seagraves, M. *Move to Learn*. Winston-Salem: Hunter Publishing Co., 1979.

STUDENT ACTIVITIES

1. Write an original lesson plan for first or second grade children.

    Goal:

    Objective:

    Activity   Formation

Grades One and Two

2. Observe a first or second grade class and record your observations of one child on the form below.

   Length of Class _____ Sex of observed child _____

   Activities presented:

   Number of interactions with other children _____

   Amount of time child spent in activity _____

   Behavior of child — record behavior being exhibited every 3 minutes or record all unique episodes of behavior.

CHAPTER 9
CURRICULUM FOR EIGHT- AND NINE-YEAR-OLDS

After completing this chapter, the student should be able to:
1. Give the instructional implications for the growth and development characteristics in the chapter.
2. List and explain the curriculum emphases for this age group.
3. Describe the most effective teaching approach to use with this age group.
4. Describe at least two activities which can be used to develop each of the curriculum objectives in this chapter.
5. Describe two integrated activities for each of the following subject areas: language arts, math, science, social studies, art and music.
6. Design one original integrated activity for this age group in each of the areas in "5" above.

The curriculum presented in this chapter is designed for normal eight and nine-year-old children. Since children have varying background experiences, many in this age group will be incapable of achieving at least 80% of the objectives listed. It may be necessary, therefore, to use objectives and activities from Chapter 8 with certain children or classes. The objectives and activities are merely teacher guides which can be modified if the situation dictates. Children should be able to accomplish at least 80% of the six and seven-year-old objectives (Chapter 8) if they are to be successful with the objectives in this chapter.

By the end of fourth grade, children should be able to accomplish at least 80% of the objectives for eight and nine-year-old children. The objectives, therefore, are long term which may necessitate the writing of interim objectives for the younger children in this age group.

Characteristics of the Eight and Nine-Year-Old and Implications for Instruction

Since there is an enthusiasm for learning, this is a rewarding age to teach. Most eight and nine-year-old children can read and have developed good physical skills as a result of a developmental physical education program in the lower grades; they will try most anything; they are anxious to please adults; and they have not yet formed cliques which can be difficult to deal with at the upper elementary level.

Physical Characteristics

1. Marked differences in skill ability are apparent among children.

Implication — The teacher must be aware of these differences and set up ways to help children begin at their own level and progress at their own rate. Girls tend to do better than boys in gymnastics and dance and boys are better at most sports skills. This is due primarily to differing interests and experiences outside of school. Dance and gymnastics schools and outside sports activities have a marked influence on the abilities of children, particularly in the middle to upper income areas. Differences are not as apparent in urban schools where children do not have as many outside opportunities.

2. The cardiovascular system is sufficiently developed to handle endurance activities.

Implication — Endurance, activities should be stressed to insure maximum cardiovascular system development. It was once believed that strenuous activities should be curtailed at this age level. On the contrary, children need vigorous physical activity.

3. Children are noisy and active.

Implication — Provide a space and activities which allow for noise and lots of activity. Explanations and demonstrations, if given at all, should be kept to a minimum allowing for maximum use of the time for physical activity.

4. Children like to do things correctly.

Implication — Give proper instruction and guidance to develop skills correctly. Incorrect skill development at this early age makes later skill learning much more difficult. Not only does one skill build on another in most cases, but correcting improperly learned skills is harder than teaching a new skill.

5. Eye-hand coordination is better developed than with six and seven year olds.

Implication — Smaller objects can be used for

Small objects can be caught.

throwing and catching, and games requiring well developed hand-eye coordination can be played. Many children, however, will not be as skilled as others, and some ability grouping may be required.

6. Small muscles are better developed than with six and seven year olds.

Implication — Although there are not a lot of fine motor skills required in physical education, activities such as lummi sticks and small ball handling require small muscle coordination. Children at this age level, therefore, will have more success with these activities than they would have in earlier years.

Social and Emotional Characteristics

1. Children are more concerned about clothes.

Implication — Children should be asked to change clothes for those activities which might ruin good pants, shoes or dresses. A way to hurt public relations with parents is by ruining expensive clothes.

2. Children have special friends.

Implication — Allow children to select their own partners although activities in which children change partners should be offered. Since friendships are stronger at this age level, a loss of a friend or argument between friends can cause an emotional strain on the child resulting in negative behavior in the classroom. It is important to find out the reason for behavior before taking action.

3. Children like group activities and have a sense of team loyalty.

Implication — Team games should play a part in the curriculum.

4. Children like school.

Implication — As indicated earlier, this age is conducive to learning and the teacher should take advantage of this opportunity.

5. Children can handle responsibility.

Implication — Children should be given the opportunity to assume responsibility, particularly as it relates to self-control. By backing off center stage, a teacher can help children to assume responsibility for their own actions. This can be done by allowing children to set up and run their own games and activities wherever it seems appropriate. An overly dominant teacher misses unique opportunities to help the social development of children.

6. The children have the capacity to develop good leadership ability.

Implication — As in 5 above, the teacher must

give children responsibility in these two areas. Activities such as follow the leader, and ones which are controlled by the students, will help develop good leaders.

7. Children like adult supervision.

Implication — Supervision means to see and control, not to dominate. For liability purposes, a teacher must supervise the children but can allow the children to run their own activities where appropriate.

8. Children are sensitive to criticism and are easily discouraged.

Implication — Criticism usually leads to discouragement. Teachers should and must correct performance if proper skill development is to take place. It is possible, however, to "sandwich" the criticism between two slices of praise. For example, a child does a forward roll but does not get his chin all the way to his chest, resulting in faulty performance. The first thing from the teacher should be praise for the correct part of the performance. This can be followed by asking the child, "What do you think would happen if you kept your chin all the way down on your chest?" Then some additional praise can be offered to encourage the child to try again. Critical analysis is an important part of skill development, but how it is done affects learning is to be encouraged.

Intellectual Characteristics

1. Attention span is increasing.

Implication — Children are capable of sitting and listening to explanations which should be kept to a minimum in physical education since children learn best by doing. Discussions focusing on physical fitness and health, can make a significant contribution to learning.

2. Children are learning their place in the world.

Implication — Children are becoming capable of conceptual thought and are more able to handle discussions regarding their actions and actions of others as they relate to the overall scheme of things.

3. There are marked individual differences among the children.

Implication — Some children will grasp ideas much quicker than others; some individualization of instruction, therefore, is essential.

4. Children like far off places.

Implication — The teacher can use interest to involve students in rhythms and activities common to distant countries. This is a means of integrating social studies with physical education.

5. The children can evaluate themselves.

Implication — Use a questioning technique to get students to do self-evaluation. The videotape can also be used to allow a child to evaluate his performance.

6. Children are creative.

Implication — With an extensive knowledge background, the child is able to be more creative than in the past. Unfortunately many teachers feel creative activities stop after six or seven years of age. Creative activities should be a part of every grade level.

Curriculum Emphases

In terms of physical skills, the eight and nine-year-old is in a transitional period. While still functioning at the basic skill level, these children are capable of many activities not possible in earlier years. Many simple lead-up games to individual and team sports can be introduced. Since movement efficiency is also an objective for this age level, skill development is not limited only to sports activities.

Other areas to emphasize include (1) fitness, (2) creativity, (3) rhythmics and dance, (4) games, (5) social/emotional development, and (6) cognitive development. The overall goal is the development of a child with a broad movement base upon which to build. This base includes skills, movement efficiency, creativity, a positive self-concept and conceptual knowledge about movement, fitness and health.

Integrated Activities

Integrated activities should be included in the curriculum for eight- and nine-year-olds wherever possible. Subjects which can be included are: science, language arts, social studies, math, art and music. Ideas for integrated activities are included throughout this chapter, and can be found by checking the section outline. For a better understanding of integrated activities, see the Section II explanation, p. 111.

Safety

The eight and nine-year-old child is extremely ambitious and willing to try most anything even when dangerous. Their ability often does not match their courage, which can lead to injury. Dares from the peer group and the desire to be accepted by others also affect children's behavior.

This age group is also very active thus creating more opportunities for injury. Fortunately, most injuries are minor. Since the activities are group rather than individual, collisions tend to be a common occurrence.

Most injuries occur during organized games and during recess, safety rules, therefore, must be enforced. Too frequently teachers set up dangerous situations, such as having large groups of students running at each other or using a number of balls in a game. The latter of these two can be found in the description of numerous games. The game Bombardment (page 219) appears in other books with descriptions allowing for the throwing rather than rolling of the balls.

In any activity where children may be accidently hit in the face by a ball, glasses should be removed or eyeglass protectors provided. Frequently children will opt to remove their glasses rather than use the protectors. The vision loss with glasses removed can also be a danger to the child or others.

The responsibility to protect children even from themselves is the teacher's responsibility. See Legal Liability, Chapter 13.

Teaching Approaches

The appropriate teaching strategy is dependent upon the desired outcome. If skill development is desired, a guided discovery approach or task approach would seem most appropriate while creativity, problem solving and movement efficiency might best be fostered through problem solving, guided exploration or free exploration. When first presenting a skill such as ball handling, questions can be used for evaluation:

"How many of you can throw and catch the ball?" Children respond by showing how they can throw and catch. The teacher observes and based upon the feedback can move children to the next step. If children seem to have good fundamental skills, the teacher can continue presenting questions as the children are guided to higher ability levels (guided discovery). "Can you dribble the ball?" "Can you move and dribble the ball?" "Can you move in many directions while dribbling the ball?" As the teacher sees children who are doing well, he may stop the class and have others watch. It may even be necessary for the teacher to do some explanation and demonstration although it should be a last resort used only with those children who really need it. As children observe another child perform, they can be cognitively involved by asking:

"Where does she keep her eyes while dribbling?" Is she using her finger tips or palm of her hand?" In this guided discovery teaching style, every child must be involved 100% of the time. If a manipulative skill is being taught, every child should have a piece of equipment. Children should be given plenty of time to develop the skill prior to moving on. The teacher should move around the room giving individual attention and praise when and where it is appropriate.

If there is some risk associated with skills such as gymnastics and tumbling, it may be necessary to use a task-style approach or command. Before any potentially dangerous skill is attempted, the teacher has a duty to provide adequate instruction. The instruction can be in the form of: (1) teacher demonstration, (2) pupil demonstration, or (3) media presentation (videotape, film or book).

There should be numerous opportunities to experiment and explore movement, using cognitive ability. The more students can be involved cognitively in the learning process, the better. The problem-solving, guided exploration and free exploration teaching styles provide cognitive involvement.

All children should not be required to achieve high ability levels in all areas. Individual differences, motivation and potential provide a wide variance in entrance and exit skill levels. The teacher's function is to provide opportunities for participation, give individual instruction and motivation. Hopefully the vast majority of children will gain in all areas, while others will have success in a few. Every child should experience some success during every class period. Daily lessons, therefore, should provide a variety of activities, particularly ones which give children a chance to work at their own level.

GOALS, OBJECTIVES AND DEVELOPMENTAL ACTIVITIES

SECTION OUTLINE

PSYCHOMOTOR DOMAIN, p. 201

Manipulative Ability, p. 201
    Goals and Objectives, p. 201
    Integrated Planning, p. 202
    Activities for Developing
    Manipulative Skills, p. 202

Hand-Eye Coordination, p. 203
    Games for Developing Hand-Eye Coordination, p. 203
    Games for Developing Catching Ability, p. 203
    Games for Developing Striking Ability, p. 203

Foot-Eye Coordination, p. 203
    Games for Developing Foot-Eye Coordination, p. 204

Rhythmic Goals & Objectives, p. 204
    Integrated Planning, p. 204
    Rhythmic Activities, p. 204

Creativity, p. 206
    Goals and Objectives, p. 206
    Integrated Planning, p. 206
    Creative Activities, p. 206

Fitness
    Goals and Objectives, p. 207
    Fitness Activities, p. 207

Tumbling & Gymnastics, p. 208
    Goals and Objectives, p. 208
    Tumbling & Gymnastics Activities, p. 208

Lead-Up Games to Team and
    Individual Sports, p. 211
    Body Image, p. 211

AFFECTIVE DOMAIN, p. 211

Self-Concept, p. 212
    Self-Concept Activities, p. 212

Team Loyalty, p. 212
    Team Activities, p. 212

Self-Discipline, p. 212
    Self-Discipline Activities, p. 212

Sportsmanship, p. 212
    Self-Respect & Respect for Others, p. 212

Sharing, p. 213
    Sharing Activities, p. 213

Respect for Authority, p. 213

Positive Attitudes, p. 213

Social Interaction, p. 213
    Social Interaction Activities, p. 212

COGNITIVE DOMAIN, p. 213

Creativity, p. 213
    Integrated Planning, p. 213
    Creative Activities, p. 213

Rules and Regulations, p. 214

Body Image, p. 214
    Body Image Activities, p. 214

Movement Terms, p. 214

Physiological and Movement Concepts, p. 214
    Integrated Planning, p. 214
    Concept Information, p. 214

GAMES, P. 215

EXAMPLE LESSON PLANS, p. 221

PSYCHOMOTOR DOMAIN

Manipulative Ability

Goals and Objectives

Hand-Eye Coordination

Goal: The child will improve hand-eye coordination.

Objectives:

1. Student will demonstrate the correct (left foot step when throwing with right hand and vice versa) throwing technique and hit a three foot diameter target 15 feet away 2 out of 3 times. This is to be done both overhand and underhand.

2. Student will be able to bounce a tennis ball with a paddle racket ten times in a row on a smooth hard surface.

3. Child will be able to catch a beanbag thrown overhand from a distance of fifteen feet using a scoop made from a plastic bottle or plastic milk container.

4. Child will be able to dribble an 8½" playground ball while walking in any direction.

5. Child will be able to hit a 7" sponge rubber ball into the air three times in a row using a paddle racket.

6. Child will be able to volley a 7" sponge rubber ball against a wall six times in a row.

7. Child will be able to catch two beanbags thrown simultaneously underhand from a distance of ten feet. Must catch one in each hand.

8. Child will be able to throw a beanbag through a rolling bicycle tire from a distance of 15 feet 1 out of 3 times.

Foot-Eye Coordination

Goal: The child will show improvement in eye-foot coordination.

Objectives:

1. The child will be able to kick an 8½" playground ball rolled at him on a smooth surface 9 out of 10 times.

2. Child will be able to punt an 8½" playground ball forward 2 out of 4 times.

3. Using an individual rope, child will be able to jump rope forward or backward four times in a row.

4. Using a long rope, child will be able to enter backdoor or frontdoor and jump three times in a row.

5. Child will be able to run and kick a slowly rolling 8½" playground ball and hit a goal area 8 feet wide from a distance of 15 feet three out of four times.

6. Child will be able to run and hurdle three, one and one-half foot high hurdles placed 10 feet apart.

7. Child will be able to dribble a soccer ball using the feet only through a series of marker cones placed seven feet apart. Child must pass on alternating sides of cones and use each foot equally.

Integrated Planning

Other subjects such as language arts, science, music, and math can be integrated with physical education while children are learning manipulative skills. For language arts, stations and learning centers (Chapter 5) can be used.

Music can be used for developing routines. During these routines, emphasis can be placed on moving according to phrasing, accents, and variations in the music can be used to provide variety particularly when playing classical selections. The children can be encouraged to recognize classical music by name while manipulating objects according to the mood created by the selection.

Math can be used in a stations approach by having children keep their score through a series of self-testing stations.

If introduced properly, science concepts such as receiving force, throwing objects at appropriate angles, balance, and levers can be learned during manipulative skill practice. Children can experiment with different angles of trajectory, various ways to catch or throw objects, and various levers of the body. A good source for science concepts which can be learned by children is *Knowledge and Understanding in Physical Education (9)*.

Paddle tennis develops manipulative skills

Activities for Developing Manipulative Skills

The eight and nine-year-old's hand-eye and foot-eye coordination is fairly well developed, but practice is needed in a variety of situations using various size balls and targets. Children should be capable of handling softball size balls (plastic ones are recommended). Targets should be either moving or a good distance away (15-25 feet). For motivation, targets should fall when hit (pins, plastic containers or old tennis cans).

Children like to be challenged at this age, and motivation is enhanced if low level competitive situations are established. Competition can be with self ("Can you throw up the ball, turn in a complete circle and catch it?") or with others ("Who can knock over the most pins in two rolls?").

Activities in which children can test their own ability also enhances motivation. These *self-testing* activities primarily focus on target activities (particularly targets that fall when hit), but can be activities such as: (1) the number of times the child can hit the ball in the air without a miss, (2) the number of catches made in a row, and (3) the distance he can throw or kick a ball.

Many of the same questions used with six and seven year olds can be asked of this older group.

How many ways can you throw and catch the ball by yourself?

How many ways can you throw and catch with a partner?

The difference is in the size of the ball and the skill level. Teachers must also be concerned with getting across the correct way to throw and catch. The *guided discovery approach*, therefore, is more valuable than the *problem-solving approach*. With the younger children (pre-school through second grade) questions were usually open-ended and not a great deal of time was spent on form although gross errors were always a concern. In the guided discovery approach children are led physically and cognitively toward a specific goal which is reflected in the type of question asked:

Let's watch Judy throw (Judy was selected because she was throwing correctly). With which foot is Judy stepping forward? Which hand is she throwing with? Does she follow through with her arm? Where does she look when she throws? How many of you can throw like Judy?

This type approach can be used with all skill activities where there is little danger of injury.

Hand-eye Coordination

Throwing — Throw varying size balls from 8½" playground ball to tennis ball for distance or at targets. Throws should be made overhand, underhand and sidearm. Children should learn to throw with either hand.

Throw at moving targets such as hoops, large balls, tires, or people.

Throw beanbags into barrels.

Throw deck tennis rings and try to hook them over pegs.

Shoot balls into eight foot high baskets.

Games for Developing Hand-Eye Coordination

1. Cowboys and Indians using beanbags to tag with (throw and hit), p. 182.
2. Tag games (using beanbags to tag).
3. Red Rover (center person uses beanbags to tag), p. 153.
4. Hit the Mat (or ball) Beanbag
5. Dodgeball, p. 221.
6. Bombardment, p. 219.

Catching — The emphasis should be on catching with the hands — thumbs together for high throws and little fingers together for low ones. Children should be taught to let their body give with the throw.

Catch different size balls thrown high and low.

Catch while in a high position (as tall as possible) and at a low position (on knees).

Catch while running including over the shoulder (back to thrower).

Use scoops to catch.

Catch two beanbags (one in each hand) simultaneously.

Games for Developing Catching Ability

1. Move Away — Partners begin six feet apart. With each successful catch of the beanbag, the catcher takes one step back. If missed, he must take two steps forward. The idea is to see how far away the partners can get and still throw and catch.
2. Bombardment (p. 219).
3. Modified Volleyball — Eight or nine people stand on each side of the seven foot high net. Six foam rubber balls are used (3 to side). Balls are thrown back and forth over the net with each one not caught counting as a point for the other team. Play is continuous until five points are scored by one team. The teacher keeps score on his fingers (one hand for each team). Children can play best out of five games.

Striking

Begin by having children strike with hands or arms.

Play one wall handball.

Volley foam rubber ball against wall or straight into air. "How many times in a row can you hit the ball in the air without a miss?"

After children have mastered striking ball with hand, give them an object such as a nylon racket, a wooden paddle, or a paddle racket. Children can bounce a yarn ball in the air or a tennis ball on the floor or against the wall.

Games for Developing Striking Ability

1. One wall handball or racketball — ball is served by bouncing it and hitting it again at the wall above a two foot high line. Ball must land inside the playing boundaries. Opponent must hit the ball before it bounces more than once and it must strike the wall in a prearranged boundary area. Points are scored each time a child is unable to play the ball properly.
2. Marathon — see which child can keep the ball in the air the longest or bounce it the most times without a miss.

Foot-Eye Coordination

1. As in the case of hand-eye coordination, targets which fall when hit should be used.

Bowling pins or plastic containers are best.

2. Move ball right, left, forward and backward as quickly as possible and still keep control.

3. Kick rolling ball for distance.

4. Stop rolling ball with feet.

5. Stop bouncing ball with legs.

6. Move ball around obstacle course — emphasize using both feet equally.

7. Punting foam balls or playground balls — if there is sufficient room for safety, the playground balls can be used. Punting is a two step skill — dropping the ball and swinging foot up to hit it before it reaches the ground. Many children have trouble coordinating the hands and feet and end up throwing the ball over their head or way into the air.

8. Obstacle courses requiring leaping over hurdles.

9. Rope jumping, see page 206.

Games for Developing Foot-Eye Coordination

1. Ball dribbling (with feet) races.

2. Obstacle course races — either dribbling, leaping or a combination of the two.

3. Area Soccer — children are assigned specific areas which they may not leave and may only play a ball which comes in their area. Positions are changed frequently and two or three children can be rovers and go anywhere on the field.

4. Kickety Pickety, p. 217.

5. Line Soccer — class is divided into two teams. Each team has active players (usually one-half of the team) while the other players form a line on one side of the field. If the ball comes to a player on the sideline, he is permitted to kick it toward the goal but may not score a goal. Only players in the middle of the two lines can score. The line and active players should switch places frequently. This is a good game when space is limited.

6. Crab Soccer (p. 217). If used indoors, a 10" foam rubber ball is recommended.

Rhythmic Goals & Objectives

Goal: Child will be willing to participate in creative rhythmic activities.

Objectives:

1. Children will work in pairs or small groups to design creative movements to both classical and modern music.

2. A child will design a unique rope jumping routine to music.

3. Children will demonstrate various moods and situations using their body while moving to various types of music. (Moods — happy, sad, gay, afraid, mad; situations — crowded bus, lonely dark road, haunted house, in the snow, on ice).

4. Children will be able to work together to create a unique lummi stick routine.

5. Children will learn five new folk and/or square dances per year.

Goal: Children will continue developing rhythmic ability.

1. The child will be able to bounce an 8½" playground ball in rhythm to various tempos.

2. The child will be able to keep time to music using the lummi sticks in a variety of ways either alone, with a partner or in a group.

3. The child will be able to jump rope rhythmically.

4. Children will be able to work together rhythmically using the parachute.

Goal: Children will learn five new dances a year.

Objective: Without the teacher's assistance, children will be able to perform five new dances a year from memory.

Integrated Planning

The obvious subject area which can be integrated with rhythmics is music, but so also can social studies and art. For music, children can learn accents, phrasing, and varying movements according to variations in the music. By using classical selections, children can learn the names of the classics while getting an excellent psychomotor experience.

To integrate social studies, children can do dances from other countries. For demonstration purposes, the children can dress in native costumes appropriate to the country from which the dance originated.

Art can be used to inspire movement. The children can react creatively to various styles of art from still life to modern. By combining music with the art, some fantastic creative movements may be elicited.

See Chapter 11 for additional ideas.

Rhythmic Activities

Rhythmic activities should be a combination of structured (primarily dances) and unstructured (creative) with an emphasis on creative movement. Many rhythmic activities from earlier years (Chapters 7 and 8) can be successfully

Swing your partner

used with this age group. One major adjustment from early years, however, is the move toward more group-oriented activities.

1. Work in pairs or small groups to create movement to classical or modern music.
2. Have children depict moods to suit various kinds of music.

"How does this music make you feel?"
"Can you move that way?"
Moods can include: happy, sad, joyful, mad, afraid, gay, unhappy.

3. Music can depict situations.

"What could you be doing when this music is playing?"
Situations could be: walking on a dark road, being in a haunted house, on a crowded street or bus, ice skating, or playing in a field.

4. Children can create lummi stick routines. Lummi sticks can be used in a variety of ways.
   a. Children keep time to music by hitting sticks on floor, together or a combination of the two.
   b. Children can also work in pairs to design ways to hit and pass sticks while keeping time to music.
   c. Small groups can be formed to create routines.
   d. Children can sit, kneel, be on their feet or combine a number of positions.
   e. The best music to use is that which has a distinctive beat and phrases which are easy to detect. The teacher should practice with the records before using them, to check their suitability.

Lummi sticks

f. At first children can follow the teacher who goes through a variety of different moves.

g. Children are then encouraged to create their own movements. "How many different ways can you pass the sticks with a partner (in a group) and still keep time with the music?"

"How many different levels can you use in a routine?"

"Can you keep time with your bodies and your sticks simultaneously?"

5. Children can all use other objects for rhythmic routines including: wands, balls, streamers, ropes and a parachute.

a. Rope jumping — rope should be long enough so that if a child stands on it with both feet, his arms could bend at less than 90%.

Jump rope forward and backward using double beat, then move to single beat (one jump for each rope turn).

Crossing rope in front — While jumping rope forward, arms are crossed until elbows touch and hands are on opposite sides. Child jumps through the crossed rope, uncrossing it as it goes up behind him.

Crossing rope in back — This is easier to do once learned, but is a harder skill for children to master. As the child is jumping rope backward the hands and arms are crossed as in front crossing above. The crossing should be made as the rope is in front of the child. The tendency is to attempt to take the crossed arms overhead along with the rope which is impossible to do. Although this is not a necessary lifetime skill, it is a challenge to children that keeps them jumping which is good for endurance development. It is also a good developer of coordination.

Front rope jumping to back rope jumping and vise versa without stopping the rope. "Can you go from front rope jumping to back rope jumping while continuing and vice versa without stopping the rope — "Can you go from front rope jumping to back rope jumping while continuing to make continuous circles with the rope in the same direction?" This is another problem-solving challenge which helps children become more coordinated and is an important skill to learn if routines are to be created. There is a trick to this one. After jumping forward, the rope is held to the side with fists together in a sort of praying position. The child keeps the rope going making full loops in the forward direction. The child then makes a 180° turn — turn forward the rope — and then again opens the rope and begins jumping backward.

Partner jumping — Pairs try to see how many different ways they can jump rope together using one rope — front to front, front to back, back to back, side to side facing the same or opposite directions, or one child jumps in while other is turning a single rope.

b. Parachute — see parachute activities, p. 139.

6. Folk dances (see page 395 for record sources) — A variety of folk dance records are available from a number of sources including: *The Methodist World of Fun, Honor Your Partner,* and *Dances Without Partners.* The Methodist World of Fun series has dances from many countries which helps in the integration of social studies with physical education. The other two series feature mostly American folk and square dances.

7. Simple square dances can be introduced at this level.

Creativity

Goals and Objectives

Goal: Children will continue to develop creativity.

Objectives:

1. Given various themes (A Day at the Circus, Going to the Zoo) children will create unique mimetic activities alone, with a partner, or in a group.

2. Given various situations (cold day, swimming in cold water, flying a plane, floating on a cloud, sky diving) children will demonstrate creative mimicry.

3. Children will move creatively to poems.

Integrated Planning

The easiest subject to integrate with creativity is science. As with creative rhythmics, children can move as if they were being affected by various weather conditions; they could also imagine being on other planets and move according to the gravity and weather conditions. Some creative activities can also be similar to the story plays done with younger children.

In the area of language arts, children can move to poetry. They could also create their own movement stories and poetry.

Other ideas can be found under creative rhythmic activities (p. 204) and in Chapter 11, Children's Dance.

Creative Activities

Although much of the creative activity focuses on rhythmics, the eight and nine-year-old children respond well to other creative activities.

1. Themes — Have children work in small groups around themes (the circus, the zoo, seaworld, a day on the farm, or life in the big city). After a few minutes of thought and practice, all children should demonstrate their creativity. Children can watch the other children as they do their interpretation. The teacher functions as a motivator and rewarder.

2. Mimicry is a good creative activity for this age group. Children can mimic slow motion, walking on a cold day, floating like a cloud, sky diving or swimming in cold water. The teacher must set a creative mood which is not always easy to do as children get older.

3. Mimicry can also be used in moving to a poem. A poem which has considerable movement in it is read while children act it out in their own way.

4. Also see creative activities in Chapters 7 and 8.

Fitness
Goals & Objectives

Goal: All children will show improvement on all test items from pre to post-test.

Objectives:
1. Child will be able to broad jump five inches beyond his own height.
2. Child will be able to do a flexed-arm hang for a minimum of ten seconds.
3. Child will be able to do 15 modified push-ups.
4. Child will be able to do a minimum of 15 bent knee sit-ups in 60 seconds.
5. Child will be able to climb a rope using hands and feet to one and one-half times his height.
6. In six minutes an eight-year-old child will be able to cover a minimum distance of 750 meters and the nine-year-old will be able to go 800 meters or more in nine minutes.
7. On a level course a child will be able to run 30 yards in 6.0 seconds or less.
8. At least 80% of the children will have an acceptable amount of body fat.

Fitness Activities

Fitness activities should focus on motor and physiological fitness. Read Chapter 6 before setting up a fitness program.

1. Provide a variety of fitness exercises.
    a. Sit-ups for abdominal strength and endurance.
    b. Push-ups for tricep and shoulder strength and endurance.
    c. Pull-ups and flexed-arm hand for bicep strength and endurance.
    d. Stretching exercises.
    e. Races for speed development.
    f. Timed runs 6, or 9 minutes, for cardiovascular endurance.
    g. Obstacle courses for agility.
    h. Standing and running broad jump for power.
    i. High jump for power.
2. Other fitness activities
    a. Rope jumping — Endurance and coordination.
    b. Rope climbing — Bicep strength.
    c. Rings — Arm strength.
    d. Tumbling — Flexibility.
    e. Balance stunts — Balance and strength.
    f. Balance beam — Balance.

Hurdlers stretch for flexibility development

208 *Grades Three and Four*

Individual tug-of-war using old bike tires

3. Maximum participation games which get children moving will also aid fitness development, see p. 207.
   a. Tagging games — Agility, speed and coordination.
   b. Crab Soccer — Strength.
   c. Tug of War — Strength.
   d. Combatives — Coordination, strength and agility.
   e. Pirate's Gold — Speed, agility, coordination
   f. Bombardment — Coordination, and agility
   g. Jump the Shot — Coordination
   h. Tether Ball — Coordination
4. Children with excess body fat, particularly those who are obviously overweight, can be very sensitive particularly if talked to individually about their weight problem. It is better to give general discussions to the entire class about proper diet and control of body fat. Body fat rather than weight should be the focus. Although fat and weight usually go hand in hand, it is not necessarily a perfect correlation. Many persons who are the proper weight (according to height-weight charts) for their height, often possess a high percentage of body fat.

Tumbling & Gymnastics Goals & Objectives

Goal: Child will develop tumbling and gymnastics ability.
Objective:
1. At least 80% of the children will be able to do at least 80% of the tumbling and gymnastics skills which follow.

Tumbling and Gymnastics Activities

1. Tumbling
   a. Review first and second grade activities.
   b. Handstand with spotter.
      Place hands shoulder-width apart with fingers straight ahead.
      Move shoulders over hands.
      Assume a push-up position with the rest of the body but draw one knee up under chest.
      Kick straight leg up to spotter while keeping head up with eyes looking straight down at mat.
      Slide other leg up beside the other.
   c. Cartwheel
      Lead-up — Place one hand on mat. Keep eyes on hand while jumping feet "around the corner." Second hand is placed down as the child jumps.
      Lead-up — stand sideways and do full cartwheel with spotter.
      Final — stand facing straight ahead. Kick as if going into a handstand but turn hand just before it touches mat and do a cartwheel.

Cartwheel

   d. Round-off
      Must be able to do a cartwheel first. Trick begins as cartwheel but at vertical position, feet are brought together while lower part of body (feet, legs and hips) makes a ¼ turn. The feet are then snapped down and the individual ends up facing the direction from which he came.

Balance beam

The flank vault position

The squat vault position

2. Gymnastics-Apparatus
   a. Balance beam — 8" high beam.
      Jump up and touch heels.
      Jump and make ½ turn.
      Pass another person without falling off.
      Make a full spin on one foot.
      Leap from one foot to the other.
      Do a cartwheel off.
      Do a round-off dismount.
   b. Vaulting
      (1) Front vault — front of the body passes over box. The right hand is placed on the near side of the box and the left is directly opposite on the far side. The feet stay together and the child lands facing sideways. The side of the body is next to the box. A lead-up is done by having children vaulting to a push-up position on box.
      (2) Flank vault — the side of the body passes over the box. Both hands are placed on the near side of the box and the feet are thrown out to one side or the other. The hand on the side where the feet must pass over is lifted and the weight is placed on one hand. The position is a side lean. The side of the body passes over the box, and the child ends up facing the same direction he was traveling with his back to the box. A lead-up activity is to have the children vault to the top of the box in a side learning position.
      (3) Squat vault — the feet are squated and passed between the hands which are placed in the middle of the box. Vaulter ends up facing away from the box.
   c. Rings
      (1) Inverted hang.
      (2) Bird's nest.
      (3) Skin the cat.
   d. Ropes
      (1) Climbing. Children should not be allowed to climb the rope until they demonstrate the ability to descend correctly. Limitations should also be set for the height which they can climb. They should not be allowed to go higher than ten feet off the ground.

210 *Grades Three and Four*

    (2) Descending. Children must be able to release from the climbing position and assume the descending technique before being allowed to climb.

    (3) Two Ropes. Two ropes closely spaced together can be used to do the same tricks as those listed under rings.

  e. Parallel Bars

    (1) Swing

    (2) Inverted hang

    (3) Straddle travel. Child gets into a straddle position and then releases and recatches in front. Legs are then swung between the bars to another straddle position. This continues until the child reaches the end of the bars.

    (4) Support travel. Child gets into a support position and then attempts to maintain that position while walking down the bars on his hands.

    (5) Front dismount. Child swings in a support position. On the back swing the legs are thrown over one of the bars while the hand on that side is released. The front of the body passes over the bar and the far hand is used to push off. The far hand is then released and re-

The support travel

catches the other bar to maintain balance as the child hits the floor facing in the same direction as when on the bars. The side of the body should face the bar.

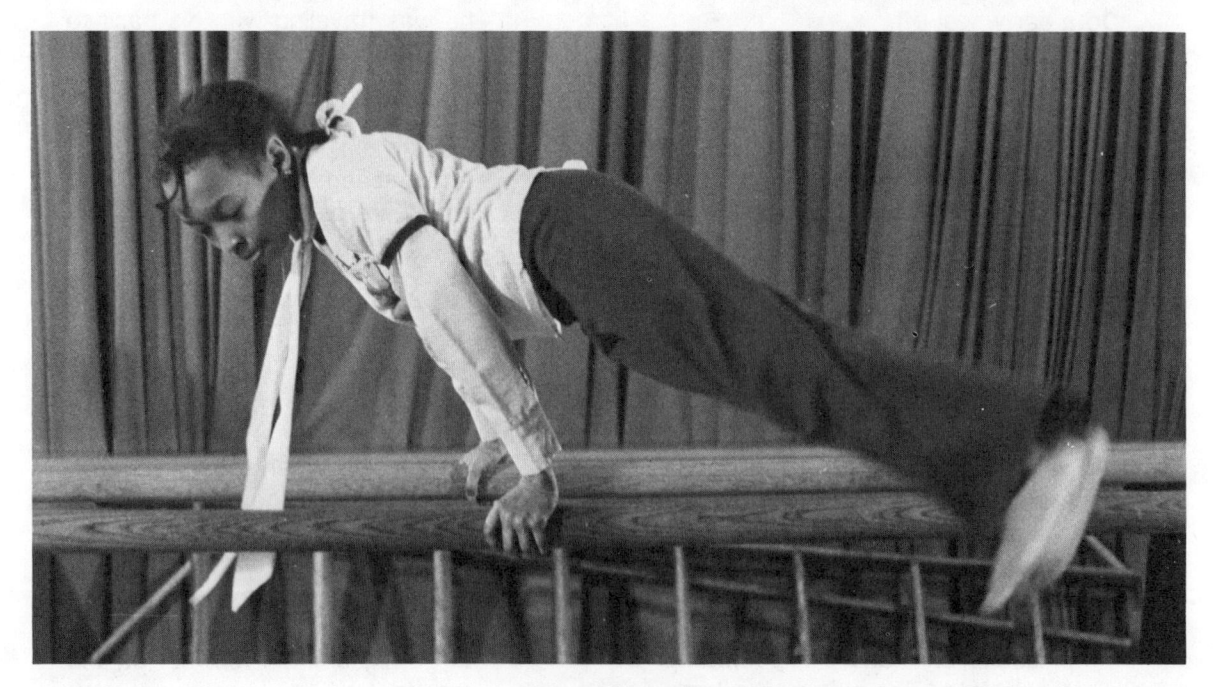

Front dismount

Lead-Up Games to Team and Individual Sports

Goal: Children will successfully play at least five new lead-up games each year.

1. Hockey
   a. Target Shoot — Plastic hockey stick is used to hit tennis ball, yarn ball or sponge rubber ball at target (plastic bottles, or some object which will fall). Game can be played one against one with each child keeping his own score.
   b. Zone Hockey — One child from each of two teams is assigned a specific zone on the field. They only play the ball when it enters their zone. Two players on each team are able to roam (go anywhere on the field). The roaming players are switched frequently and children change zones periodically.
2. Soccer, p. 236.
   a. Crab Soccer, p. 217.
   b. Kickety Pickety, p. 217.
   c. Scooter Soccer — Played like crab soccer except each child moves on a scooter. For safety, hands must be grasping the sides of the scooter at all times.
   d. Zone Soccer — Same as "Zone Hockey" except soccer skills are used.
3. Basketball, p. 255.
   a. Dribble Take Away.
   b. Monkey in the Middle — Soccer ball or volleyball is used to pass ball between two children while a third child tries to touch the ball. If the child in the middle touches the ball, the person passing it must take his place in the center. The idea is to stay out of the center.
   c. Circle Tag — Designed to develop the footwork required for basketball.
4. Volleyball, p. 240.
   a. Keep It Up — Each child tries to see how long he can keep up a sponge rubber ball.
   b. Over the Net — Class is divided in half, one team on each side of a six foot volleyball net. Each team has four sponge rubber balls (7½") each. Children throw balls back and forth over the net trying not to let any ball hit the floor. Each time a ball hits the floor, the team allowing it to touch the floor has one point scored against it. A scorekeeper on the sidelines keeps track of the score, since play is continuous (any ball hitting the floor is immediately picked up and thrown over the net). After a predetermined number of points or amount of time, the game is stopped. The team with the least number of points wins.
5. Bowling — Any size ball can be used, and plastic containers are used for pins. For variety, children can vary the distance, the number of pins, or the type of ball used.
6. Tennis, p. 244.
   a. One Wall Handball — Children play in pairs trying to hit a ball before it bounces more than once. The ball must hit inside a marked-off area of the wall and then bounce in a marked-off area of the floor.
   b. Nylon Balloon Tennis — Nylon racket (p. 373) is used to hit a balloon back and forth over a low net. Balloon may not touch the floor.
   c. Nylon Yarn Ball Tennis — Nylon racket (p. 373) is used to hit a yarnball (p. 373) back and forth over a net. A yarnball hitting the floor in a marked-off area is one point against the person allowing it to hit on his side of the floor.
   d. Paddle Racket Tennis — A paddle racket is used to hit a 7½" sponge rubber ball back and forth over a net. Ball may touch floor but may not bounce more than once.
   e. Four Square Tennis — Paddle racket is used to play Four Square (p. 219) with 8½" playground ball.
   f. One Wall Tennis — Same as "One Wall Handball," except paddle racket is used instead of hand.
7. Baseball, p. 220.
   a. Long Base, p. 220.
   b. Kickball, p. 220
   c. Plastic Bat and Ball — A variety of games can be devised using a safe plastic bat and ball. Regular baseball bats should not be used with this age group.

Body Image (See p. 214)

AFFECTIVE DOMAIN

The teacher must constantly observe students with the affective goals and objectives in mind. It is difficult to set up affective situations which will provide teachable moments, but any group of children in physical education will provide extemporaneous teaching opportunities in the affective domain. The teacher must be ready to handle such situations effectively.

Self-Concept

Goal. Children will improve their self-concept.
Objective:
All children will indicate they feel better about themselves after having participated in the physical education. This attitude will be measured using an anonymous questionnaire.

Self-Concept Activities

1. Provide a variety of psychomotor activities in which children experience success.
2. Give praise to each child verbally or nonverbally at least once during each class period.
3. Give children responsibility such as line leader, equipment person, door holder, etc.
4. Keep personal progress charts which each child can see periodically, but are not displayed for others to see.
5. Call children by name.
6. Work with children to reduce derogatory name-calling among children.

Team Loyalty

Goal. Children will begin developing team loyalty.
Objectives:
Children will work together and not argue with each other while working toward a common goal.

Team Activities

1. A group of 7 or 8 children get on their hands and knees under the "turtle shell" (a mat) and try to move in one direction. At first the children may move in different directions causing the mat to become unbalanced and fall off. Before long, it will become apparent to them that they must move together. The turtle can then move backwards, sidewards, etc., on cue. They can also try to manipulate an obstacle course.
2. Ships and Islands
Scatter hula hoops around the play area. Have children do various locomotor movements around and between the hoops. When the teacher yells "shipwreck," children can go to any hoop. There can be any number of people in a hoop. The number of hoops is gradually reduced requiring teamwork to get everyone inside the remaining hoops.
3. Cooperative Musical Chairs
Played like regular musical chairs except no one is eliminated. As chairs are removed, children sit on each other's laps. Eventually a long chain of lap sitting is required when there are only a couple of chairs left.

Self-Discipline

Goal: Children will develop self-discipline.
Objectives:
1. Children will be able to organize and conduct competitive games without fighting or arguing and without the teacher's direction.
2. Children will voluntarily help those who need it.
3. Children will not fight during a game.
4. Arguments which do occur will be resolved within 30 seconds.

Self-Discipline Activities

1. Choice Day — Children select the activities which they want to play. As many as three or four activities can be going on at one time depending upon the class interests. The teacher's role is to supervise. The students are responsible for organizing and running their game. The areas which should be developed are leadership, self-discipline, and interpersonal relationships.
2. Group Stations — Specific groups (teams) move from station (learning center) to station carrying out the activities. The group determines when each person knows enough to move on. This arrangement, hopefully, will foster leadership, group cooperation and interpersonal relationships.

Sportsmanship

Goal: Children will develop good sportsmanship.
Objectives:
1. Children will not fight with members of the other team or argue with an official during a team game situation.
2. As spectators, children will not boo.
3. Children will congratulate the other team whether they win or lose.
4. Children will call fouls on themselves voluntarily during games.

Self-Respect and Respect for Others

Goal: Children will demonstrate self-respect.

Objectives:
1. Children will not take drugs or alcohol.
2. Children will voluntarily carry out a home fitness program.
3. Children will practice good health habits: cleanliness, rest and diet.

Goal: Children will show respect for others.
Objectives:
1. Children will not call others names.
2. Children will not belittle others.
3. Children will not endanger others by violating safety rules.

Sharing

Goal: Children will demonstrate sharing
Objective:
Given a situation requiring sharing, children will voluntarily share with others.

Sharing Activities

The teacher sets up situations requiring sharing and then observes to see how well students are handling it. The arrangement can be stations with insufficient equipment to go around, thereby necessitating sharing.

Respect for Authority

Goal: Children will show respect for authority.
Objectives:
1. Children will listen when the teacher is talking.
2. Children will follow the teacher's directions.
3. Children and teacher will say "please" and "thank you."

Positive Attitudes

Goal: Children will develop positive attitudes toward fitness, health and safety.
Objective:
Children will follow all the safety rules established for the various activities.

Social Interaction

Goal: Children will effectively interact with others
Objectives:
1. Children will accept an assigned partner without complaining.
2. Children will not call others derrogatory names.

Social Interaction Activities

1. Gooey, Gooey
Gooey is a gentle, friendly creature that grows. Everybody wants to find and become part of the Gooey. To do this, everyone stands in a group, closes their eyes, and starts milling (moving) about. When you bump into someone ask "Gooey?" If the other child asks, "Gooey?" back, then you have *not* found the Gooey. Keeping your eyes closed, find another child to ask. When everybody is bumping about, with strains of "Gooey?" "Gooey?" "Gooey?" floating around the group, the teacher whispers to one of the players that he/she is the Gooey. Since the Gooey can see, that child opens his/her eyes and stands still. It seems that the Gooey is also a smiling mute, for when a child bumps into Gooey and asks that gentle question, "Gooey?" Gooey doesn't respond. Ask again, just to make sure: "Gooey?" No response. Eureka, you've found the Gooey at last! You take hold of the Gooey's hand or if you find you've bumped into two clasped hands, you know you've got the Gooey somewhere in the middle and you must feel your way to the end and join it and now you can open your eyes and stand still. This part should be demonstrated before the game begins. Soon enough, everybody's happily holding hands. The teacher should watch for children who may stray too far from the group and redirect them. When the last stray joins up and opens his/her eyes, the smiling Gooey usually breaks the silence by letting out a spontaneous cheer.

2. Double Walk
The first child stands on his partner's feet facing him. Partners grasp one another's upper arms. As the one child walks forward, the other shifts his weight from side to side in synchrony with his partner's movements. Partners can also stand back to back, elbows locked. One then tries to walk forward while the other must walk backward.

Also see the activities under "Team Activities."

COGNITIVE DOMAIN

Creativity

Goals: See Creativity, page 206 and Rhythmics, page 206.
Integrated Planning, p. 214.

Creative Activities

1. Creative Activities, p. 207.
2. Rhythmic Activities, p. 204.

Rules and Regulations

Goal: Child will learn five new games and five new dances each year.
Objective:
After appropriate instructions, children will be able to organize and play five new games a year and five new dances.

Body Image

Goal: Children will learn various body parts.
Objectives:
1. If asked, children will be able to touch the following body parts: stomach, abdominal region, thighs, shins, calf, and hips.
2. If shown a flashcard with the name of a body part, children will be able to identify the word and be able to touch the body part in question.

Body Image Activities
1. Simon Says, p. 152.
2. Flash cards, p. 148.

Movement Terms

Goal: Children will be able to recognize movement terms.
Objective:
If shown flash cards with movement terms on them, children will be able to do the appropriate movements without verbal assistance from the teacher. These movement terms include: catch, throw, punt, kick, jump, leap, roll, backward, forward and sideward.

Physiological and Movement Concepts

Integrated Planning

The sciences of movement and physiology should be an integral part of a physical education program. The information below should be learned by this age group.
Goal: Children will learn physiological and movement concepts.
Objective:
1. If asked, at least 80% of the children will be able to explain at least 80% of the following:
    a. How to absorb shock when jumping from a height.
    b. How to strengthen a muscle.
    c. How to improve cardiovascular efficiency.
    d. The best way to lift heavy objects.
    e. The best way to push and pull an object.
    f. The value of exercise.
    g. The importance of good posture.
    h. How to lose weight.
    i. The best way to throw and catch.

Concept Information

1. Absorbing shock — Children should be taught to bend their knees and roll forward if necessary when jumping from a height. This skill is required when coming off the vaulting box, parallel bars and when jumping for distance.
2. Strength Development — The muscle must be made to work harder than it is used to (overload). Various exercises should be given to point out how muscles can be developed.
3. Cardiovascular Development — Children should be taught to take their pulse, and then be given exercises to increase the heart rate. Fifteen minutes of daily vigorous exercise should be emphasized.
4. Residual Pain — The possible side effects of exercise (pain) should be made known to children. Knowledge should alleviate fears when such pain occurs during the early phases of a fitness program.
5. Warm-up and cool-down — Prior to a vigorous activity, one should gradually increase activity (warm-up); following vigorous activity, one should continue to move slowing down gradually (cool-down).
6. When lifting heavy objects, keep them close to the body and use the legs, not the back, to lift.
7. Push a heavy object using leg power.
8. Pull an object using the abdominal and leg muscles. Whenever possible, face away from the object being pulled so back muscles are not involved.
9. Exercise is beneficial to health.
10. Good posture is important to efficient movement and body functioning.
11. Proper diet is important to weight control — children should be taught the basic food groups, a balanced diet, and the concept of caloric intake and output.
12. Catching — To catch an object the force should be absorbed by the arms and body. The child should be taught to reach out for the oncoming object and then absorb the force by bending the arms as well as moving the body back away from the object.
13. Throwing — To get maximum distance, the object should be thrown at an angle of 45°.

Safety Rules

Goal: Children will learn safety rules.
Objectives:

1. If asked, children will be able to recite at least 90% of the safety rules established for class.
2. If asked, children will be able to give the reason for any safety rule which has been established.

Health Knowledge

Goal: Children will improve their health knowledge.
Objectives:

1. If asked, children will be able to give the reasons for each of the following.
    a. Being clean.
    b. Brushing their teeth.
    c. Being fit.
    d. Having the proper diet.
    e. Wearing proper clothing.

THIRD AND FOURTH GRADE GAMES

NAME	Page	Psychomotor	Affective	Cognitive	Grass	Multipurpose Room	Hardtop	Classroom	Can be Adapted to Any Area	Can be used for Evaluation
Sam Says	216	4	1	1					x	
Combatives	216	5	2	1	x	x				
Crab Soccer	217	5	1	1					x	
Kickety Pickety	217	2	1	1	x	x	x			
Pirate's Gold	218	3	2	1	x	x				
Small Group Dodgeball	184	3	2	1	x	x	x			
Relays	218	1	3	1					x	
Streets and Alleys	218	3	2	1	x	x	x			
Electric Shock	185	3	2	1	x	x				
Grab the Club	217	2	1	1					x	
Bombardment	219	5	1	1		x				
Target Games	219	5	1	1					x	
Tug of War	184	5	1	1	x	x				
Four Square	219	5	1	1			x			
Long Base	220	2	1	2	x	x	x			
Kick Ball	220	2	1	2	x		x			
Hand Baseball	220	2	1	2	x	x	x			
Plastic Baseball	220	2	1	2	x	x	x			
Jump the Shot	182	5	1	1					x	
Tether Ball	220	5	1	1	x		x			
Protect Me Tag	220	5	4	2	x	x				
Grabbing Sticks	220	4	2	2	x	x				
Running Dodgeball	221	3	1	1	x	x				
Catch the Dragon Tail	221	5	3	2	x	x				
Monkey in the Middle	221	5	1	1	x	x				

Game Code:
- N = Name of game
- DA = Developmental age for which game was designed
- DV = What the child should get from the game (developmental value)
- F = Formation
- E = Equipment required
- D = Description of the game

216 *Grades Three and Four*

N: Sam Says
DA: 8 - 12
DV: Fitness
 F: Free
 E: None
 D: This game is identical to Simon Says, except for the cue which now is "Sam Says." This makes the game more difficult and more fun for older children. The activities presented by "Sam" should focus on fitness.

N: Combatives
DA: 9 - 12
DV: Fitness
 F: Partners of nearly equal size and ability.
 E: Wands for toe fencing and mats for leg wrestling
 D: Combatives are usually one-on-one situations with pairs being of fairly equal size and ability. As the name implies, these are vigorous combative-type activities which children enjoy.

Crab Fight — Children get into a crab position and attempt to bump the other person until they sit down. The children are not allowed to kick with the feet or hit with the hands — they must bump or push the other person. This activity can also be done as a "free for all."

Crab fight

Chicken Fight — Children stand on one foot while holding the other foot behind them. Both hands must be held behind the back. Children then try to make the partner lose his balance and put both feet down. This activity should only be done in pairs of equal size and in a large cleared area.

Knee boxing

Knee Boxing — Children box with open hands attempting to hit the other person's knee. Each time a knee is hit, it counts as one point, and the first one with five to seven points is the winner.

Toe Fencing — Wands are used like fencing foils, except the tip may not leave the floor. The object is to touch the other child's toe with the end of the wand. This can be a dangerous activity if not controlled, particularly if the tips come off the floor and children start swinging the sticks.

Pull Across — Two children join one hand across a line. The object is to pull the other person across the line.

Pull across using old tires

Leg Wrestling — Two children lie on their backs with heads in opposite directions. They should be able to place their inside hand on the other person's shoulder. They both lift their inside leg and touch toes returning the leg to the floor. This toe

Grades Three and Four 217

touching is repeated a second time. On the third time up they lock knees and try to flip each other over backward. A mat should be used.

Indian Wrestling — Two children join their right hands while placing their right feet side by side, toes in opposite directions. By pulling or pushing with their hand and shoulder, they attempt to make the other person move his right foot. This activity can also be played where both feet must be stationary or from the left side.

Indian wrestling

Go Behind — One child tries to get behind and hold the other. This is a vigorous activity, and must be carefully controlled.

N: Crab Soccer
DA: 8 - 12
DV: Eye-Foot Coordination and Fitness
 F: Two teams
 E: Spongeballs or 8½" Playground balls.
 D: Players assume a crab position. A playground ball or sponge rubber ball of approximately 8½" to 10" is used. Ball is kicked until it crosses a goal line at one end of the play area (one goal line at each end). The team defending the goal line has one point scored against it each time the ball crosses its goal line. Children must move in a crab position and must have *both hands* in contact with the floor *behind* them when kicking the ball. Hands may not be used by anyone. Teams start on their half of the floor, but may travel to any part of the play area after ball has been put into play. Children with glasses must remove them or wear eyeglass protectors.

A variation of the game is the use of a 24" cageball. Because of the weight, no child can be permitted to roll onto his back to kick the ball with both feet. A misjudged ball could easily force a head onto the playing surface.

A 7½" or larger sponge rubber ball is the safest ball to use for this activity. A variation of the game is to have three or four sponge rubber balls going at once. Each time one crosses the goal line, it is taken to the leader who immediately puts it back in play. The game is continuous and is stopped only for rule violations.

N: Grab the Club
DA: 9 - 12
DV: Fun
 F: Two lines of six or seven children side by side.
 E: Plastic container with handle
 D: Each team counts off from left to right. An easy-to-grab object, plastic milk container, or Indian club, is placed midway between teams. When a player's number is called, he quickly goes to the center and tries to grab the object, and takes it back to his team (object may not be kicked, hit, or thrown). If successful, he gets two points for his team. If he is tagged, while holding the object, the tagging team gets one point. Players will quickly realize the need to jockey for the club rather than grabbing it right away since they will get tagged almost every time. Two or three numbers can be called at one time although players may not make physical contact while attempting to block for a teammate (screening is allowed).

N: Kickety Pickety
DA: 8 - 12
DV: Fun
 F: Two lines facing each other
 E: Soccerball or volleyball
 D: This game is almost the same as Grab the Club, except soccer skills are used. The two players try to get the ball *back* to their team using only the feet. The team must be able to pick up the ball with their hands. A ball which is kicked too hard and goes through the team receives no points. Children battle for the ball until one is successful at getting it *to* his team.

N: Pirate's Gold
DA: 8 - 10
DV: Agility
F: Two Teams
E: A nickel
D: Two teams, one the pirates and one the coast guard. The pirates get into a close huddle while the coast guard waits in the distance. A piece of gold (nickel) is given to one pirate although everyone pretends he has it. On the signal to go, the pirates try to cross the ocean (designated area), and the coast guard must try to tag them. Upon being tagged, a pirate must stop. The coast guard then asks, "Do you have the gold?" The pirate must give up the gold if he has it. If the coast guard catches the one with the gold, they get one point. If the pirate with the gold makes it to the safe base on the other side of the ocean, the pirates get a point. The two teams reverse roles and the game begins again. After each team has had equal chances to be pirates, the one with the most points wins.

N: Relays
DA: 8 - 12
DV: Fun
F: Varies
E: Marker Cones
D: Because they provide little activity, relays should not be offered too frequently nor should they be used as a formation for teaching skills. When relays are offered, lines should be kept short, with a limited amount of time alloted to them.

Standard Relay — On the signal to go, each child runs to a predetermined spot and returns, tagging the next person's right hand with his right hand who repeats the actions of the first. The team that finishes first is the winner.

Shuttle Relay — The team is divided in half with each half facing the other across a play area. When the go signal is given, the first person in one half of the line runs toward the other, tagging his teammate's right hand with his right hand. Each person runs when his hand is tagged until everyone has gone.

Rescue Relay — One person from each line stands at a marker about fifteen yards away from his team. On the go signal, this person runs to the first person in line and takes his hand, and both run back to the marker. The person who has been "rescued" then returns and rescues the next person and so on until everyone has been brought to the marker. No one rescues more than one person. Hands must remain joined during rescue.

Machine Relay — This is run like a regular relay, except that upon completion of the race, the group must make a machine with moving parts. Other groups guess what the machine is. Points can be awarded for fastest runners and for the best machines.

Math Relay — A classroom activity in which children must walk since they are moving toward a solid object, the chalkboard. Just before the go signal is given, numbers are given to each person in the line, i.e., the first person in each line has number 12, the second 3, etc. Each then writes the number on the board in turn, and the last person must add them up. The fastest team with the correct answer is the winner.

Monster Relay — Each person in the line is assigned a part of the monster to draw. Points are awarded for fastest team and for best monster (use chalkboard).

Airplane Relay — Parts of plane are assigned as in "monster." Points are awarded for fastest group and best plane. Artistic concepts can be pointed out, such as what could be seen depending upon the view — front, side, top, etc. Children and adults, too, will often incorrectly have wings coming out of top and bottom of plane when viewing from the side (use chalkboard).

N: Streets and Alleys
DA: 8 - 10
DV: Fun
F: About five even lines
E: None
D: Class is lined up in four of five even lines. Children join hands across lines to form alleys. When leader calls out, "streets," children all turn the same way and join hands down the line to form streets. When "alleys" is called they go to original position. Two players are chosen; one is the policeman and one is the robber. The robber begins running and is chased around the streets and alleys. The leader constantly changes from streets to alleys and back again. Runners may not break through hands nor may police reach across joined hands to tag. Game continues until robber is tagged or it is obvious that he will not be tagged. New players are selected, and old runners take their place in line.

N: Bombardment
DA: 8 - 12
DV: Hand-Eye Coordination and Agility
 F: Two teams on opposite sides of the play area
 E: Eight to ten playground or spongeballs and eight to ten plastic containers.
 D: A play area with a middle dividing line is marked off. About five markers are placed along each goal line at the ends of the area. The distance between the goal line and the center line should not be more than 15-20 yards. The markers should be easy to knock over — plastic bottles will do. Each team is given about five 8½" playground balls, which must be *rolled* at the targets. The teams may not cross the center line for any reason, and balls *must* be rolled. Anyone throwing a ball should be eliminated immediately from the activity. The object of the game is to knock down as many targets as possible. A scorekeeper records hits. Play is continuous and ends after a set number of points have been scored. Targets knocked over must be immediately set up by team members on the side of area where the target was located. Players may use hands or feet to stop the ball. No "guarding" of the targets, (standing closer than five feet), is allowed.

N: Target Games
DA: All ages
DV: Hand-Eye and Foot-Eye Coordination
 F: Varies — usually one person and one target
 E: Varies with game
 D: Children love target activities since they can immediately see results. They also love to knock things over which is often a part of target games. Children can use their hands or feet to propel the object — ball, beanbag, etc. — toward the target.

   Wastepaper Basket Toss — A good classroom activity requiring a couple of baskets or boxes and one beanbag, yarnball, or spongeball per child. Children stand behind a line and try to put beanbag in box.

   Basketball Shot — Children of all ages enjoy trying to put a ball in the basket. Basketball goals should be eight feet high for elementary children and balls should be light enough for children to get them to the basket.

   Bowling — Many objects can serve as pins — plastic bottles, plastic milk containers, or empty tennis ball cans. Children can keep score as they play.

N: Four Square
DA: 8 - 12
DV: Agility and Coordination
 F: Four people per square
 E: Playground ball (8½") or volleyball
 D: To begin the game, players stand in corners on numbers. Number 1 serves by bouncing ball and hitting it underhand with the palm of hand. The ball may be hit into any of the other three squares. When serving, the ball may not hit any inside line, but is considered good if it hits inside a square or on an outside line. A player in another square may play the ball only after it bounces in his square. He may play to any other square although the object is to get number "1" out so everyone else may move up. The object for number 1 is to stay in that position as long as possible. He gets one point each time he serves. After the serve, play continues until one player is unable to play the ball. That player must go to square 4 and everyone else moves up one square. Any ball hitting an inside line or the center circle is considered no good, and the player who hit the ball must go to position 4. Hits, except the serve, may be done in any way as long as ball is not caught and thrown. If a ball hits someone's square and begins traveling toward another player, he must not touch it until it bounces a second time, thus giving the player in the square where it bounced a chance to play it. If the other player does touch it, he must move to square 4. Play can continue indefinitely or to a set number of points. The ball may not touch any part of the player except the hands.

Four square

N: Long Base
DA: 8 - 10
DV: Fun
F: Two teams
E: 8½" Playground ball
D: One team is up to bat and one team is in the field. The pitched ball can either be hit with the hand or kicked with the foot, depending on size of the play area. Hitter then runs toward the long base which is placed in a second base position on a baseball field. Player may be gotten out only by hitting him below the waist with the ball. Fielders may not run with the ball, but can pass it to a team member who may have a better shot at getting the runner. The hitter can stay on the long base or try to come home. Any number of players can be on the long base at any one time, and all may try and get home at one time. As soon as everyone on a team has had a chance to bat, the teams switch places.

N: Kickball
DA: 8 - 10
DV: Fun and Lead-up Game
F: Two teams
E: 8½" Playground ball
D: Played much like regular baseball, except that the ball is kicked. Players can also be put out by hitting them below the waist with the ball.

N: Hand Baseball
DA: 8 - 10
DV: Fun and Lead-up Game
F: Two teams
E: 8½" Playground ball
D: Like kickball, except object is hit by hand. Is used indoors in a multipurpose room.

N: Plastic Baseball
DA: 9 - 12
DV: Fun and Lead-up Game
F: Two teams
E: Plastic bat and ball
D: Same as baseball, except bat and ball are plastic.

N: Tetherball
DA: 8 - 12
DV: Hand-Eye Coordination
F: One child on each side of pole
E: Tetherball poles and balls
D: A tetherball (special ball with loop) is attached by rope to an eight foot high pole. One child serves by hitting the ball and attempting to wrap the rope completely around the pole. The person on the other side tries to make the ball wrap around the other way. The first one to wrap the rope completely around the pole wins. There are variations of the game. In one, the ball can be caught by either player and then hit, while in the other, the ball must be in continuous motion (volleyball-type hits are allowed to get the ball in position to hit around the pole).

N: Protect Me Tag
DA: 8 - 12
DV: Teamwork, Basic Movement Development
F: Groups of Four — Three Form a Circle
E: None
D: Three members of the group make a circle by placing hands on each other's shoulders. The fourth group member then attempts to tag (back only) a predetermined person on the circle. The other two circle members try to "protect" the third person by moving in a circle always keeping the person to be tagged away from the tagger.

N: Grabbing Sticks
DA: 8 - 9
DV: Fitness
F: Two teams on opposite sides of a center line.
D: Each team has a prison area and another area for its four sticks. Both teams try to cross over the center line, run through their opponents' territory, and secure a stick without being tagged. Only one stick may be stolen at a time. Once a player crosses over the center line into opponents' territory, he may be tagged. A player successfully stealing a stick holds it high and may return to his team without danger of being tagged. A player tagged goes into his opponents' prison. Once there are prisoners, no stick may be stolen until all prisoners are free. If a player reaches one of his teammates held prisoner without being tagged, the two return to their team with hands joined to show their opponents that they may return without danger of being tagged. The team having the most sticks at the end of the playing time wins. Side line and end line boundaries should be well defined. Any player running out of bounds to avoid being tagged becomes a prisoner.

N: Running Dodgeball
DA: 8 - 9
DV: Running, throwing
 F: Two parallel lines facing each other
 E: 10 sponge balls (one per child who is a thrower)
 D: Two parallel lines are drawn about 40 feet apart to form a gauntlet which is about 60 feet long. Two teams of about 10 each. One team forms the gauntlet, and the other team tries to run through without getting hit by a ball. Each team must run the gauntlet a set number of times. Each successful hit gives the throwing team a point. No one is ever eliminated.

N: Catch the Dragon's Tail
DA: 8 - 9
DV: Balance, Strength, Cooperation
 F: Children form 3-person dragons
 E: Cloth ribbons
 D: The dragons are formed by holding on to each other's waist. The last person has a cloth ribbon of about 15 inches tucked into his or her waist. The dragons try to get each other's tail by grabbing the cloth strip. The dragon with the most number of tails is the winner. No dragon is eliminated even when he loses his tail; he just keeps going after others' tails.

N: Monkey in the Middle
DA: 8 - 9
DV: Throwing and Catching
 F: Groups of Threes
 E: One ball per group
 D: Two players stand across from each other at a distance dependent upon skill. One player stands between these two. The idea is for the person in the middle to intercept a pass between the other two.

EXAMPLE LESSON PLANS

1. 3rd and 4th

   Multipurpose Room

   Objectives:

   1. The students will be able to execute the step hop to the beat of the music and hold their balance to the different musical tones.
   2. The students will be able to create their own exercise and then perform 5 of them in repetition.

Activities   Formation

  I. Exercise Freeze game   I. Free

     The students skip around the room; when the whistle blows, they create an exercise and freeze. Then they perform 5 of the exercises. Repeat skipping again.

  II. Folk Dance — Seven Jumps   II. Small groups

     Seven step hops to right to left. Chorus Balance — Right left, left leg, one knee, both knees, right elbow, left elbow head. Between each repeat chorus.

  III. Back-to-Back Game (using music)   III. Free

     Students move around room to the beat of music. When the needle is removed students must get a partner quickly back-to-back, knee-to-knee, hand-to-hand, ear-to-ear, hip-to-hip.

Safety: No sliding.

2. 3rd and 4th

    Multipurpose Room

    Objectives:

    1. 80% of the students will be able to do forward, backward rolls, balances, tripods and tip ups as discussed in class.
    2. All students will be able to spot other students while attempting a tripod or tip up.

Activities	Formation
I. Stretching exercises	I. Free
II. Self-testing gymnastic skills.	II. 4-5 students at each mat.

    Forward and backward roll; front scale, front support and rear tripod, tip up, push up backbend cartwheel.

    III. Free practice — III. Small groups

    Students can practice any stunt gone over in class. With or without a spotter.

    Safety: No horse play on mats, no shoes; be careful of others.

3. 3rd and 4th

    Outside

    Objectives:

    1. The students will be able to do at least 5 different types of exercises, by being able to complete the station arrangement on physical fitness.
    2. If asked, 80% of the students could give examples of strength and flexibility exercises.

Activities	Formation
I. Exercises and jogging.	I. Free

    Students will job 1 minute and stop to feel pulse. We will then discuss fitness.

    II. Station arrangement with different exercises for students to do.   II. Small groups at stations

    Station 1

    Jump ropes — Can you jump 20 times without stopping? Can you jump 10 times backward? Can you jump alternating feet? Can you do hot pepper? Can you hop on one foot, on the other?

    Station 2

    Arm strength — Can you do 5 push-ups? Can you get a partner and do wheel barrows? Can you do the crab walk for 20 steps? Can you do a one hand push up?

Station 3

Leg strength — Standing broad jump — score recorded and analyzed to see level of fitness. Can you jump from 1 foot to 1 foot. Can you jump from 2 feet to 2 feet? Can you jump backwards? How far can you jump? How high can you jump?

Station 4

Agility — Can you run through the tires? Can you run to the cone, turn around and run back? Can you slide left and right without stopping?

Station 5

Flexibility — Can you touch your toes with straight legs? Can you touch the ground? Can you do a split? Can you do a push-up back bend? Can you touch your head to your feet?

   III. Free practice at last station.   III. Stations

4. 3rd and 4th

Multipurpose Room

Objectives:

1. The students will be able to perform a structured pattern and create their own pattern with lummi sticks, keeping in rhythm with the music.
2. When given lummi sticks, the students will be able to flip the stick in both the right and left hand while keeping in rhythm with the music.

Activities   Formation

  I. Warm-up exercises to music.   I. Free

Students will do warm-up exercises following the teacher to music.

  II. Lummi Sticks   II. Free

Teacher asks can you? Keep time to the music? Skip while beating your sticks? Do all locomotor skills while keeping beat to the music?

Structured pattern

Students keep time to the music by following a structured pattern with lummi sticks.

  III. Creative Groups   III. Small groups

Students can make up own routine in groups to the music.

Safety: No throwing sticks, no running, no sliding.

224 *Grades Three and Four*

5. 3rd and 4th

    Outside

    Objectives:

    1. The students will be able to move a playground ball with the inside of both the left and right foot for 10 feet without losing control of it.
    2. The students will be able to stop a moving ball with their foot and also their knees.

Activities	Formation
I. Running Exercise	I. Free

    Students follow teacher running all types of ways. High knees, straight legs, slow motion, fast motion, big steps — little steps, legs side ways.

    II. Eye-Foot coordination   II. Free

    Teacher asks can you? Move the ball with your foot while running? Place Kick the ball? Kick the ball to a partner using inside of foot? Trap or stop the ball using your feet? your knees? How else can you move the ball with your feet?

    III. Dribble Game   III. Straight line

    All students dribble ball with their foot and place kick to the finish line.

    Safety: No hard kicking.

6. 3rd and 4th

    Multipurpose Room

    Objectives:

    1. When given different pieces of equipment, the students will be able to make up some type of game at each station using that piece of equipment.
    2. The students will be able to complete each station by being able to execute the skills listed on the posters.

Activities	Formation
I. Brothers	I. Free

    Students run or skip, teacher yells back to back, knee to knee. Students find a partner.

    II. Stations Exploratory   II. Stations

    Station 1

    Jump Rope — What can you do with your rope?

    Station 2

Hula Hoops — What can you do with your hoop?

Station 3

Scoops — What can you do with your scoop?

Station 4

Nerf Balls — What can you do with your sponge rubber ball?

Station 5

Plastic Balls — What can you do with these balls?

  III. Make a game   III. Stations

Students will get together in their stations to make a game using that equipment.

Safety: Stay in your own station; no kicking the ball.

7. 3rd and 4th

Multipurpose Room

Objectives:
1. The students will be able to do 3 different dance steps well enough to stay in rhythm with the music.
2. The students will be able to create their own dance using 2 steps learned in class.

Activities   Formation

  I. Exercises to music following the teacher.   I. Free

  II. Disco Dance   II. Free

Students will learn the hustle, dig step and the 3 step turn. Dancing to disco music.

  III. Creative dance   III. Small groups

Students will make up own dance in small groups using their own steps and at least 2 steps learned in class.

Safety: No running, no sliding

REFERENCES

1. Arnheim, D. and R. Pestolesi. *Elementary Physical Education.* St. Louis: The C. V. Mosby Company, 1978.

2. Burton, E. *The New Physical Education for Elementary School Children.* Boston: Houghton Mifflin Co., 1977.

3. Cochran, N., et. al. *A Teacher's Guide to Elementary School Physical Education.* Dubuque: Kendall/Hunt, 1971.

4. Cochran, N., et. al. *Learning on the Move.* Dubuque: Kendall/Hunt Publishing Co., 1975.

5. Dauer, V. *Essential Movement Experiences for Preschool and Primary Children.* Minneapolis: Burgess Publishing Co., 1972.

6. Dauer, V. and R. Pangrazi. *Dynamic Physical Education for Elementary School Children.* Minneapolis: Burgess Publishing Co., 1975.

7. Fait, H. *Physical Education for the Elementary School Child.* Philadelphia: W. B. Saunders Co., 1976.

8. Kirchner, G. *Physical Education for Elementary School Children.* Dubuque: Wm. C. Brown Co., 1974.

9. Larson, L. (ed). *Knowledge and Understanding in Physical Education.* Washington: AAHPERD, 1973

10. Seagraves, M. *Move to Learn.* Winston-Salem: Hunter Publishing Co., 1979.

STUDENT ACTIVITIES

1. Write an original lesson plan for third or fourth grade children.

    Goal:

    Objective:

    Activity   Formation

Grades Three and Four

2. Observe a third or fourth grade class and record your observations of one child on the form below.

   Length of Class _____ Sex of observed child _____

   Activities presented:

   Number of interactions with other children _____

   Amount of time child spent in activity _____

   Behavior of child — record behavior being exhibited every 3 minutes or record all unique episodes of behavior.

CHAPTER 10
CURRICULUM FOR TEN- AND ELEVEN-YEAR-OLDS

After completing this chapter, the student should be able to:

1. Give the instructional implications for the growth and developmental characteristics in this chapter.
2. List and explain the curriculum emphasis for this age group.
3. Describe the most effective way to teach this age group.
4. Describe at least two activities which can be used to develop each of the curriculum objectives in the chapter.
5. Describe two integrated activities for each of the following areas: language arts, math, science, social studies, and music.
6. Design one original integrated activity appropriate for this age group for each of the areas listed in 5 above.

The curriculum presented in this chapter is designed for normal ten and eleven-year-old children. Not all children in this age group will be able to achieve 80% (the goal) of the objectives in this chapter. The wide variance of ability may necessitate using material objectives from the other curriculum chapters (7-9). Learning packages (Chapter 5) are a valuable aid in meeting the extensive ability range among children. Such packages are particularly useful since the curriculum contains more specific skills which can be stated in behavioral terms and children are able to read better, follow directions and assist each other. Teachers are encouraged, therefore, to use the objectives included in this chapter along with previously stated objectives (Chapters 7-9) to design learning packages which will meet the children's needs regardless of ability.

By the age of twelve, it is hoped that each child will be able to move efficiently, will possess a minimum fitness level and will have skills in at least one movement area be it dance, individual sports, team sports or recreational activities. By no means is it realistic to expect each child to be successful in every curriculum area. The children, however, should be exposed to all areas to provide a well-rounded movement experience.

Characteristics of Ten- and Eleven-Year-Olds and Implications for Instruction

The ten and eleven-year-old child is capable of a great deal of learning, much of which can be accomplished on an independent basis. With the ability to read, conceptualize and assist each other, much of the responsibility for learning can be placed on the child's shoulders. Most children in this age group enjoy physical education thereby providing a fertile environment for learning. By using movement as a medium, ten and eleven-year-olds can learn about fitness, safety, physiology and health. If properly presented, movement concepts can also be grasped by these children.

The relationship a teacher develops with this age group will determine, to a great extent, the amount learned. These children recognize the fallibility of adults and will take advantage of weak teachers, rejecting those they view as poor. The frequent mood changes of these children also require a teacher's understanding and skill. Often the ten and eleven-year-olds view themselves as being very sophisticated and very right. Although they have learned adult fallibility, often they view themselves as infallible. This feeling of infallibility is fostered by peer support in the form of cliques which are sociologically important to ten and eleven-year-olds. Reprimanding a clique member can often lead to a revolt by others in the alliance. Reasoning through discussion is often successful but is not a guaranteed strategy when problems do arise.

Problems for this age group can include sexual changes, rebelliousness and drugs. Concerns once reserved for junior and senior high school, have become realities for the elementary child, parent, and teacher. Changing morality has resulted in pregnancies, venereal disease and psychological harm for elementary children. The rush to adulthood has been thrust on children much to their detriment. Sex and drug problems have been brushed under the rug by many educators either in ignorance or fear. Since many physical educators have good health backgrounds, they can play a major role in facing these problems and devising means of coping with them.

The following characteristics and their implications should assist the reader in understanding ten and eleven-year-old children.

Physical Characteristics

1. Posture can be a problem.

Implication — Continue to emphasize posture and give reasons for standing correctly. This age group is capable of understanding information about muscles, bone structure, digestion, etc. The understanding of the reasons may go a long way toward bringing about a positive attitude toward good posture.

2. Fitness is poor in many children.

Implication — Give both exercises for, as well as reasons for, physical fitness. A fifteen-minute discussion on the importance of fitness may be more helpful than two hours of physical fitness activities. Areas which usually need considerable work are upper body strength, abdominal strength and cardiovascular endurance.

Abdominal strength needs to be developed

3. Girls are often larger than boys.

Implication — Size usually causes a problem only in dance activities requiring a partner. When there is a marked difference in height, both parties seem embarrassed. Some girls will attempt to slump down if they hit their growth spurt before others, and this may lead to postural problems.

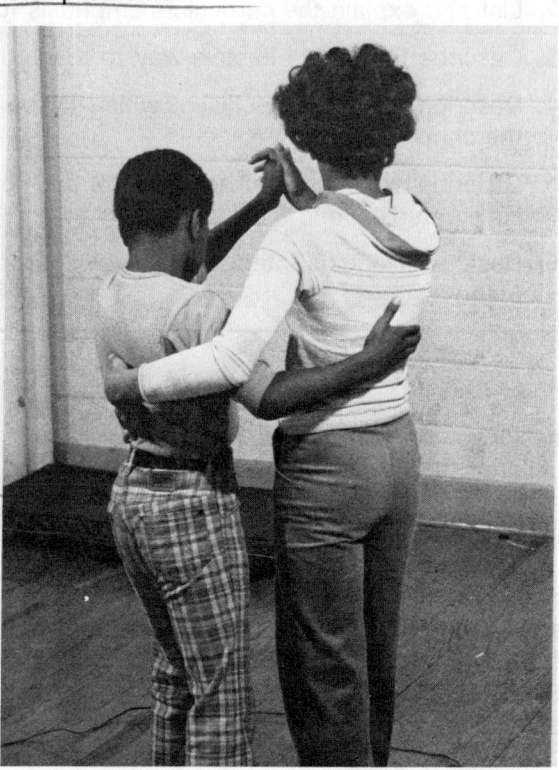

Differences in size can be a problem in rhythmic activities.

4. Menstruation may begin.

Implication — This is mainly a psychological problem for some girls although painful menstruation is a physical problem. Physical participation is not harmful to the child during menstruation, although many parents still believe it is. Communication on this subject is difficult at times due to old taboos. Male teachers must be cautious when dealing with girls who will not participate during menstruation, since undue pressure at this time can have psychological implications.

5. Skills are well developed in some children.

Implication — The teacher should set up a program which allows both superior and poor students to maintain interest and achieve success. Strategies for individualizing instruction are more important as the difference in abilities becomes more apparent.

6. Children like to be active.

Implication — Although this age group is capable of sitting and listening to explanations and demonstrations, they want to be up and doing. In the psychomotor domain, children learn best by doing, no matter what the age level, so the teacher should use less talk and more action.

7. Awkwardness may accompany growth spurt.

Implication — Teachers should be able to recognize reasons for changes in physical performance, and be sensitive to the psychological problems which may be caused by clumsiness. Children who are awkward should be constantly encouraged and not punished by sarcastic remarks or by failing grades.

8. Boys tend to be rougher than girls.

Implication — In any game situation, caution must be exercised to avoid any child being hurt by very aggressive children. For the most part, boys tend to cause the most injuries to others as well as themselves. Rough children can also cause other children to withdraw from activity out of fear. Set and enforce rules in which elimination from an activity will be the penalty for rough behavior by anyone.

Social and Emotional

1. Children can see fallibility of adults.

Implication — Children will not accept incompetency in teachers. They will take advantage of poor teachers, and are more willing to complain about unfair teachers. Although their evaluations are not always valid, they are more willing to go against adults than they were in the past.

2. Team loyalty is well developed.

Implication — Lead-up games to team sports should be successful at this age level. Children are much better able to understand and practice the team concept.

3. Children's interests are peer-centered.

Implication — Children at this age have entered a world where peer status is much more important than the adult-child relationship. A child should not be confronted by an adult in front of peers, since it puts the child in a difficult emotional situation. Problem children should be taken aside for discussion without calling undue attention to the confrontation. Children should not be asked or pressured into telling on a peer. "Squealing" on a peer is actually a sign of immature behavior and may earn the child a beating from his peers. Only in extremely serious offenses, such as destruction of school property, stealing or serious physical injury to a child, should a child be pressured into revealing the guilty party.

4. Children can be reasoned with.

Implication — Frank discussions can be helpful in dealing with this age group. The reasoning ability and intellectual capacity of many children exceed that of the teacher. Hopefully the teacher's training and background experience, however, will control the situation during a confrontation. Teachers must be ready to justify their actions when questioned by students. "Because I said so" is not sufficient.

5. Rebellious behavior may occur.

Implication — Rebellious behavior is more characteristic of the upper range in this age group, although the school arrangement can make a difference. If the fifth grade is the highest grade in this school, the fifth-graders will often exhibit a superior attitude because they are the oldest and biggest children in school (senioritis). When the upper elementary grade is sixth, the problems seem to be most apparent near the end of the year. Some people blame the age, others the teachers, and still others the weather. No matter what the cause, there is a definite rebellious attitude which can take the form of talking back, boycotts, and general civil disobedience. Although children cannot be allowed to control the school or dominate the learning environment, teachers must recognize this as normal behavior and not deal with it too harshly.

6. Boy-girl relationships are beginning.

Implication — Many problems once reserved for junior high school or middle schools are now part of the elementary level. Giggling, note passing, hand holding or arguments over who belongs to whom can disrupt learning. Any emotional situation, particularly when "love" is involved, must be handled cautiously. The prime movers in this area are usually the girls who talk and fight over the boys, while the boys desperately try to maintain an air of cool detachment. This behavior knows no bounds and may be a cause for unrest during physical education, particularly in pairing for rhythmic activities. A teacher must be aware of all this and handle it in the best manner possible, keeping in mind the delicacy of the situation.

7. Sexual problems can affect behavior.

Implication — Seek out the underlying causes of behavior before taking any drastic action.

232 *Grades Five and Six*

The new morality has invaded the elementary school and such things as venereal disease, pregnancy and sexual intimacy are no longer uncommon to this age group. Children with sexual problems are often withdrawn and may not want to participate.

8. Drugs may alter behavior.

Implication — Another sociological problem apparent at the elementary level is the use of mind-altering drugs. Such drugs can cause either hypoactive or hyperactive behavior, or may trigger violent behavior. Teachers should learn to recognize characteristics of drug use and refer suspected children to the school nurse or psychologist. Use of certain drugs can cause respiratory and heart failure, so teachers should be proficient in the use of lifesaving first-aid procedures.

9. Alcohol may be a problem.

Implication — Teachers should be able to recognize children with behavior problems which may be caused by alcohol abuse. Alcohol is the leading drug used by children and teenagers.

10. Boys and girls may be self-conscious together.

Implication — Where ability levels differ so greatly as to cause embarrassment, children should be grouped accordingly and separated for individual instruction. Often such differences are primarily characteristic of one sex. Children, however, should not be separated at any level solely on the basis of sex.

11. The unskilled may withdraw.

Implication — A program should be set up which gives every child success. Even with such a program, the unskilled child must be given individual attention. Since everyone can see physical performance, children are more sensitive in this area than in an area like math, where a score on a quiz can be hidden. Poorly skilled children may also develop psychosomatic illnesses, such as headaches and sick stomachs. These children should be encouraged to participate, although undue pressure will cause further withdrawal.

12. Moods change quickly.

Implication — Rapid changes in behavior are not abnormal.

Intellectual

1. Children can learn easily.

Implication — For the child of normal intelligence, this can be a productive period of learning. Sports skills, rhythms and dance, and gymnastics are learned with only short explanations and lots of practice. Keep explanations brief and to the point.

2. Children may be discouraged if unsuccessful.

Implication — A positive learning environment is important. Failure breeds failure and success fosters more success. The emphasis should be on success and learning, not grading.

3. Children can think conceptually.

Implication — The learning of concepts of movement and fitness should play a major role at this level.

4. Children can be very creative.

Implication — Creative thought should be a part of the physical education curriculum. Children should be given the opportunity to create routines and shows and to take part in the planning and evaluation of curriculum. Some of the best ideas come from the children. Give them the opportunity to participate cognitively.

Curriculum Emphases

Many persons feel that the fifth and sixth grade curriculum should consist only of sports and fitness activities. This is unfortunate since there are many other important activities which should be offered to the ten and eleven-year-old child. These additional activities include dance, creative activities including creative rhythmics, movement efficiency particularly in the area of running and self-testing activities. Attitude development should also play a major role in the fifth and sixth grade curriculum. These children are more capable of reasoning than younger children and are therefore more apt to understand the need for sportsmanship, interpersonal relationships and other values. Outside influence from the peer group, television, and adults often negatively influence value judgments in such areas as honesty and respect for self and others. The teacher, by example and discussion, can play a positive role in attitude development.

The children's increased cognitive ability provides opportunities to pass on concepts particularly in the areas of movement and physiology. Balance concepts such as generating and receiving of force and exercise and aging can be learned through a combination of movement experiences and discussion.

Integrated Planning

Integrated activities should be a part of the ten and eleven year olds curriculum. Subject areas which can be included are: science, language arts, social studies, art, and math. Ideas for integrated activities are included throughout this chapter and can be found by checking the section outline.

Grades Five and Six 233

For a better understanding of integrated activities, see the Section II explanation, p. 110.

Teaching Approaches

The child's ability to read opens up new avenues of instruction heretofore less feasible. These avenues include self-instruction through written materials which give each child the opportunity to work at his own level. The teacher's role is to prepare materials, motivate, evaluate, and give individual attention where necessary. The nucleus for this approach is the learning packet (Chapter 5) which is designed to guide a child through a sequence of activities from simple to complex. Such packets are not easy to develop, but once complete they can be used over and over again.

Not all activities lend themselves to learning packets nor should a curriculum focus only on individual skill acquisition. Rhythmics, creativity and team activities necessitate other organizational patterns such as small group work. The group approach also aids the development of leadership skills and interpersonal relationships.

The teaching approach which must be avoided is the command style of explanation/demonstration to the entire class. Some children need an explanation and demonstration, but to use the command approach with the whole class presupposes the equalization of all children. By using this teaching style, a teacher assumes all children are at the same ability level, learn at the same rate and learn in the same way. Such thinking violates numerous learning principles.

Children want and need instruction. There are, however, numerous media besides the teacher which can be used for instruction. Loop films, videotapes, audiotapes, films, slides, books and learning packets or a combination of these media can be used to get the material across to students. The teacher has a duty to provide instruction, but that instruction does not have to come only by way of the teacher's vocal cords.

Where is the place of movement education in the fifth and sixth grade curriculum? Some advocates of movement education suggest free exploration as an approach to skill development. Although exploration can be beneficial to the development of creativity, it is of questionable value in skill development. Movement education as it relates to creative development, rhythmic ability, movement efficiency and problem-solving ability should be an integral part of the fifth and sixth grade curriculum.

The teaching approaches to use with ten and eleven year olds are task, and guided discovery (Chapter 4). The latter is favored when dealing with relatively safe sports skills such as basketball, hockey and soccer. In this style the children could be asked such questions as "How many ways can you dribble the ball using your hands?" or "Can you dribble the ball like a basketball player?" Skillful children can then be selected to demonstrate their ability while the teacher asks such questions as "Is he slapping the ball or pushing it?" "Is it bouncing high or low?" or "Where should he look while dribbling?" These questions could be followed by, "Who else can dribble as well as Billy?" or "Who has another way to dribble?" When asking questions, one must be cautious not to set up a situation in which the solution could cause injury. This concern is particularly true in tumbling and gymnastics which must be carefully controlled to avoid injuries.

By using the guided discovery approach, children will become cognitively involved in the learning process; they have more opportunity to show their skills; and the teacher does not have to demonstrate. The teacher's role is one of evaluation, guidance and motivation.

Safety

The primary safety concern for ten and eleven-year-olds should be in the areas of sports participation and gymnastics. Although contact sports are not a part of the elementary curriculum, any team sport has injury potential. Soccer, touch football, hockey, baseball, and basketball although non-contact sports can often lead to injury if not controlled. Certain popular activities such as flag football and football games which allow contact blocking should not be played. Special precautions must be taken in hockey and baseball due to the implements used.

Glasses are of particular concern as both a potential danger to the eye as well as the replacement expense. Any game in which a ball (except sponge rubber balls) is used can lead to an injury or breakage. Eye glass protectors should be used or if feasible, the glasses should be removed and placed in a safe area. Some children dislike the protectors and will opt to remove the glasses even though it significantly reduces their vision. Such folly can also lead to injury. At times, teachers must take prudent action to protect children from themselves and insist upon the glasses and the guards if the child wishes to participate.

Gymnastics is the most potentially dangerous area if not properly taught and controlled. The

234 *Grades Five and Six*

unusual and often inverted positions in gymnastics expose the head and neck to injury. The implications are obvious. A background in gymnastics instruction should precede offering this activity and when presented, extreme student control must be exercised. Children love gymnastics, but are not always cognizant of the dangers even when forewarned. Horseplay including pushing, tickling and lack of attention to spotting are common in an uncontrolled gymnastic activity.

The fifth and sixth grader is often susceptible to "dares" which may extend him beyond his ability. Such potentially dangerous situations may occur during physical education as children attempt to physically outdo each other. Again, gymnastics tends to lend itself more to dangerous "dares" than other curriculum offerings. Strict limitations must be placed on activities which can be attempted on the mats or other pieces of gymnastic equipment. The trampoline seems to be a piece which is often violated. Although the trampoline is a good developmental piece of equipment, the risks outweigh the potential benefits and it should, therefore, not be included as a piece of gymnastics equipment for the elementary level.

GOALS, OBJECTIVES, AND DEVELOPMENTAL ACTIVITIES

SECTION OUTLINE

PSYCHOMOTOR DOMAIN, p. 235

Sports Skills, p. 235
   Integrated Planning, p. 235
   Softball Objectives, p. 235
      Softball Activities, p. 235
   Soccer Objectives, p. 236
      Soccer Activities, p. 236
   Football Objectives, p. 237
      Football Activities, p. 237
   Hockey Objectives, p. 238
      Hockey Activities, p. 238
   Basketball Objectives, p. 238
      Basketball Activities, p. 238
   Volleyball Objectives, p. 239
      Volleyball Activities, p. 240
   Tumbling and Gymnastics Objectives, p. 241
      Tumbling Activities, p. 241
      Gymnastics Activities, p. 242
   Tennis Objectives, p. 244
      Tennis Activities, p. 244
   Track and Field Objectives, p. 245
      Track and Field Activities, p. 245

Fitness, p. 246
   Integrated Planning, p. 246
   Fitness Activities, p. 246

Rhythmics, p. 247
   Integrated Planning, p. 247
   Folk and Square Dance, p. 247
      Terms, p. 248
   Creative Rhythmic Activities, p. 248

Creativity, p. 249
   Integrated Planning, p. 249
   Creative Activities, p. 249

Self-Testing Objectives, p. 250
   Self-Testing Activities, p. 251

AFFECTIVE DOMAIN, p. 251

Self-Concept p. 251
   Self-Concept Activities p. 251

Sportsmanship p. 251

Team Concept p. 251

Leading & Following, p. 251

Interpersonal Relationships, p. 251

Safety, p. 251

Fitness, p. 251

Health, p. 252
   Affective Domain Activities, p. 252

COGNITIVE DOMAIN, p. 252

Integrated Planning p. 252

Rules and Regulations p. 252

Knowledge of Body Parts, p. 252

Fitness, p. 252
   Short Term Effects of Exercise, p. 253
   Long Term Effects of Exercise, p. 253

Health Knowledge, p. 253

Cognitive Activities, p. 253

GAMES, p. 254

EXAMPLE LESSON PLANS, p. 258

PSYCHOMOTOR DOMAIN
Sports Skills

Goal: Children will develop a variety of skills which can be used in various individual and team games and recreational activities.

Integrated Planning

The education value of learning sports skills is enhanced through integration with other subjects. Language arts for example can be integrated by using learning packets and stations (Chapter 5). Through these two individualized approaches the teacher can use written instructions which provides reinforcement of reading skills and can allow for the introduction of new sight vocabulary. The physical educator should consult the classroom teacher to determine appropriate words to introduce. As with younger children, a combination of pictures and words can be effective in learning new vocabulary. The better readers can also assist those whose language arts skills are not as well developed.

Physical Science can also be integrated with sports skills. Such concepts as analyzing and receiving force, balance, laws of motion, levers, trajectories, and others can be learned. An excellent source for some concepts appropriate for elementary children is *Knowledge and Understanding in Physical Education* (9).

Math can be integrated by having students keep score in a stations approach in which self-testing activities are used. Point values can be given for number of hits, hitting certain areas of a target, knocking over pins, or putting the ball in a basket. Fractions can be used on some targets to increase the degree of math difficulty.

Softball Objectives:

1. Children will be able to throw a softball underhand a distance of 20 feet to another child.
2. With a bat, hit 3 out of 6 softballs pitched in the strike zone.
3. Catch a softball thrown overhand from a distance of 20 feet 3 out of 6 trials.
4. Catch a softball thrown 25 feet into the air 3 out of 6 times.

Softball Activities:

Hand-eye coordination is the key to initial success in softball, and it is a skill which should be fairly well developed if children have had a developmental physical education program over the years. The following activities, however, should be helpful in refining hand-eye coordination to the level required for a team game.

1. Throwing and catching plastic softballs or tennis balls.
2. Have children catch low balls or balls coming over the shoulder with both hands keeping the little fingers together, and high balls with both hands keeping the thumbs together.

Over the shoulder catching position

3. Catching pop flies is a difficult perceptual skill and should be practiced frequently.

Catching the fly ball

4. All forms of throwing should be practiced — underhand, overhand and sidearm. Children should be taught to follow-through and aim at specific targets. Target games in which objects fall when hit are particularly motivating.
5. Control of force should be emphasized when throwing between partners. The distance between partners should vary and children should use all types of throws.

Getting down on a ground ball

6. Sliding right and left should be practiced as it relates to fielding a ground ball. Children should learn to get their body in front of the grounder bending at the knees and waist to field it.

7. The batting skill can be practiced by nearly everyone at one time if plastic bats and balls are used. This safe approach to developing hand-eye coordination will transfer to the use of a regular bat and ball. If space permits, children can work in groups of threes using regular softball equipment to practice pitching, batting and fielding skills. This drill should be reserved for those who have demonstrated fairly high skills alone or in pairs.

8. Children should learn the names and locations of various positions. Sophisticated strategy of position play, however, should be reserved for later years.

9. Children love to play a regular game and time should be allotted for team play. Since the physical participation level is low, emphasis should be placed on developing sportsmanship.

10. Lead-up games such as Must Swing Baseball, page 255, should be played rather than attempting a regular softball game.

Soccer Objectives:

1. Kick a slowly rolling soccer ball into an 8 foot goal area 35 feet away 3 out of 4 times.

2. Dribble a soccer ball alternating feet in and out of eight marker cones set 10 feet apart within a 20 second time limit without losing control of the ball.

3. Execute a moving leg trap of a soccer ball kicked from a distance of 15 feet.

4. Head a soccer ball thrown from a distance of five feet two out of three times.

5. Successfully pass a soccer ball to a partner 10 feet away while both players are moving in the same direction.

Soccer Activities:

Soccer is one of the simpler team games which allows maximum participation and can be enjoyed by children of various ability levels. It is a highly recommended team game for all elementary aged children. The primary skill required is foot-eye coordination which is not usually as well developed in American children as hand-eye coordination.

1. Manipulate an 8½ inch ball using both feet equally around obstacles or to commands.

2. Both the inside and outside of the foot should be used to dribble and kick the ball.

3. The bottom of the foot and heel should be used to stop and maneuver the ball while dribbling.

4. The main trapping skill to emphasize is the leg trap which is executed by turning the foot outward allowing the ball to strike the inside of the leg below the knee. The ball should rebound in the direction the player wishes to travel. The ball should not be stopped dead.

5. The chest trap can be used by the boys but should not be used by girls. The girls are allowed to use their forearms to protect the chest. Boys should learn to absorb the shock of the oncoming ball by moving the shoulders forward and pulling the chest back just as the ball makes body contact.

6. Heading the ball should be done with the forehead. The ball should contact the head at the hairline. The neck must be rigid when the ball is struck and the head should move forward or sidewards (depending upon the ball's direction) to contact the ball (keep eyes on ball at all times). This skill should first be practiced with the child throwing the ball to himself and then having someone else throw it from a short distance. This skill should only be used in a game situation if sufficient skill is demonstrated in controlled practice. *Children with glasses must wear eyeglass protectors during soccer.*

7. Dribbling and passing the ball while on the move should be practiced in pairs emphasizing the use of the inside and outside of each foot as well as leading the partner with the pass.

8. Tackling (taking the ball away) is an important skill to ultimate success in soccer but should not be overemphasized at the elementary level due to potential injury.

9. Lead-up games include Zone Soccer in which children must stay in certain zones during play; Alley Soccer in which children can move up

and down the field in designated alleys running the field's length; and Five on Five Soccer played with teams of five children on a small soccer field.

Football Objectives:

1. Successfully throw a spiral pass using a junior football to a running partner 10 yards away.
2. While running, catch a junior sponge rubber football thrown from a distance of 10 yards 2 out of 3 times.
3. Kick a junior football off a tee a distance of 20 yards.
4. Punt a junior football a distance of 15 yards.

Football Activities:

Although football was once exclusively for males, touch football has fast become a sport played by both sexes.

1. Initial training for football should consist of throwing and catching a sponge rubber football. Until sufficient hand-eye coordination is developed, a hard rubber football should not be used; the pointed end of a misjudged ball can injure the child. Children should catch the sponge ball high (thumbs together), low (little fingers together), and over the shoulder (little fingers together) while standing with their back to the thrower.
2. There are two ways to place kick the football, regular and soccer style. The soccer style is done by approaching the ball from a semicircular run and kicking with the instep (shoelaces) of the foot. The toe should be pointed down and slightly to the outside edge of the ball.

The regular placekick involves approaching from directly behind the ball and swinging the foot primarily from the knee joint with the ankle locked at a 90° angle to the leg. The ball should be struck just below the middle with the toes.

3. Punting is a two part skill; the ball drop and the contact between the foot and the ball. Both must be executed correctly for any success. The ball should be dropped flat so that it would bound straight up if allowed to strike the ground. If either end is tilted it will result in a poor kick. The point of the ball farthest from the kicker should point in slightly. The normal procedure is to take two or three steps and drop the ball as the kicking foot is behind the body. The lead (non-kicking foot) is planted and the other foot is swung forward and upward to contact the ball when is is about two feet off the ground. The foot then drives up and through the ball using the instep to kick. The toe should be

Punting

Catching a high throw

The proper way to carry a football

pointed and the leg straight when the ball is struck.

4. Lead-up games include:
Punt Across — One child kicks off by punting the ball from the "40 yard line" on a reduced (40 yard) field. The opponent must retrieve the ball and punt it from where it stopped or, if caught in the air, he can take three giant steps toward the other goal prior to punting. A point is scored each time an uncaught ball is punted over the goal line (rollers do not count). Two players on a side. No player may punt the ball two times in a row.

Small games, 2 on 2, or 3 on 3, can be played to increase participation. Positions should be rotated on every play to eliminate dominance by a few players.

Field Goal Contests and Punt, Pass and Kick Contests — Individual skills can be used to set up contests among children.

Hockey Objectives:

1. Dribble a hockeyball in and out of eight marker cones set 10 feet apart in less than 20 seconds without losing control of the ball.

2. Hit a hockeyball into a four foot goal area from a distance of twenty feet 3 out of 4 times.

3. Successfully pass the hockeyball to a partner 10 feet away while both are moving in the same direction.

Hockey Activities:

Field hockey is an international sport played primarily by men. Although dominated by women in the United States, Olympic field hockey is for men only.

1. Dribbling should be done with one side of the stick only. One hand should be at the top of the stick while the other is in the middle of the handle. Dribbling is done primarily by a flexion and extension of the top arm with the lower arm acting more as a fulcrum. The ball should be kept in front at all times while dribbling.

2. Stopping an oncoming ball is done by straightening the top arm and creating a closed angle between the ground and the face of the stick with the stick touching the ground.

3. The drive shot is done from a forward stride position with the ball to one side of the body. The stick is drawn back beside the body with one hand slightly higher than center and one on the top. The shot is executed with a drive motion forward while flicking the ball by quickly pulling the top hand back and pushing the bottom hand forward. The stick may not come higher than the waist on the follow-through.

4. Passing the ball to a partner should be practiced while moving up and down the field in the same direction. Leading the partner with the ball should be stressed.

5. Lead-up games to hockey are the same as those used for soccer.

Basketball Objectives:

1. Dribble a junior size basketball in and out of eight marker cones set ten feet apart in less than 15 seconds without losing control of the ball.

2. Dribble a junior basketball thirty feet in ten seconds while alternating hands and keeping control of the ball.

3. Make two out of three layups using a junior basketball and an eight foot basket.

4. Make one out of three set shots from a distance of ten feet using a junior basketball and an eight foot basket.

5. Demonstrate a bounce pass and a chest pass to a partner ten feet away.

Basketball Activities:

1. Dribbling should be done with the fingers by pushing the ball toward the ground not allowing it to touch the palm of the hand. Children should learn to dribble the ball with either hand without looking directly at the ball. They should learn how to protect the ball by dribbling low and by placing their body between the opponent and the ball. Junior basketballs, soccer balls, volley balls or playground balls can be used to practice the skill.

2. The layup should be done by taking off on the foot opposite from the hand which is shooting. The ball should be aimed at the backboard just above and slightly to the near side of the basket's center. The one hand should guide the ball while the other shoots it. A volleyball or soccerball should be used with an eight foot basket during the initial stages of learning. A junior basketball can be substituted after success with the smaller ball. Ten foot baskets should never be used with elementary age children since bad habits will be developed getting the ball up to the high basket. These incorrect habits will be difficult to break later on.

After learning the layup in the stationary (near the basket) position, the child can dribble, jump and shoot. This, however, is a highly coordinated activity which should be practiced slowly.

3. The set shot is usually taken with one hand while the other hand guides the ball. The body is turned slightly away from the shooting side placing the shooting hand and arm closer to the basket. The foot on the same side of the

The one-hand set shot

The two-hand set shot

shooting hand is in a forward stride position. The shot is done by bending both the arms and legs and then uncoiling them simultaneously with a follow-through of the shooting hand and arm toward the basket. A good arch should be placed on the ball.

4. The ball may be passed in many ways between players although the most frequent and efficient way of passing is the bounce pass. This pass is done by holding the ball with the palms of the hands on opposite sides of the ball (not behind). The thumbs should be spread, but should not be placed behind the ball so as to raise the palms off the ball. The ball is pushed from the chest toward the ground with a slight backspin. The ball should strike the ground about ¾ the distance between the players and closer to the receiving player so the ball bounces up to his waist. A step should be taken by the passer while executing this skill.

The chest pass is identical to the bounce pass except the ball goes directly from the passer's chest to the receiver without striking the ground.

5. Lead-up games: Basketball is one of the most difficult team games to teach elementary children and few are able to master even a good approximation of the game during the limited time allotted for physical education. Some lead-up games will meet with limited success.

No Dribble Basketball — best played 3 on 3, with no dribbling allowed. Children are free to move when they do not have the ball, but must remain in place when they receive it. The ball may be passed or shot.

2 on 2 or 3 on 3 — Games with a limited number of players are more successful than 5 on 5, but even with only a couple of players, such concepts as defense and rules such as walking are difficult to get across.

Dribble Take Away — Each child is given a ball which is dribbled around the floor. While dribbling the ball, the child can attempt to knock someone else's away. If someone loses a ball, he may not touch anyone else's until he retrieves his and begins dribbling again. At the end of a given time, those who have lost their balls the least are declared the best dribblers.

Volleyball Objectives:

1. Hit a volleyball two times in a row using the overhand hit and not have to move more than five feet to make the second hit.

2. Bump a volleyball thrown underhand from a distance of five feet straight into the air and catch it without having to move more than five feet.

3. Execute an underhand serve over a six foot high net from a distance of fifteen feet and have it land inside the boundaries.

4. With a partner, hit a volleyball back and forth over a six foot high net three times without a miss.

Volleyball Activities:

Volleyball is one of the fastest growing sports in the United States and can be enjoyed by upper elementary age children if played in a modified form. The modified games will be discussed under leadup games to volleyball, game 256.

1. The set and bump can be practiced initially by using sponge rubber balls followed by playground balls or volleyballs. The set is done with the end of the fingers and thumb. It is a very controlled skill and children should practice setting the ball to themselves rather than hitting it over the net. The ball should be hit right in front of the face. The elbows should be pointed outward, the knees bent and the eyes on the ball. The ball must be struck by uncoiling the body and following-through. The ball is not allowed to touch the palm of the hand nor may it be hit to the right or left of the striking player. The set should be used whenever possible.

2. The bump is used for balls too low to set. The hands are clasped and the ball is struck with the forearms. The bump, like the set, is a controlled hit and children should practice bumping to themselves. The hands must be together when bumping or a violation will be called during a game. Children should not be allowed to hit the ball with one hand or their fist during play except for serving.

3. There are two types of volleyball serves, the underhand and overhand. Elementary children will have most success with the former. The underhand serve is done by hitting the ball out of one hand with the heel of the other. The child should step forward with the opposite foot and keep the fingers of the hitting hand curled up. The ball should *not* be tossed into the air and then hit. Serves should be attempted from about fifteen feet over a six foot high net.

The underhand serve

Preparing to set the ball

Executing the set

Tumbling and Gymnastics Objectives:

1. Be able to perform five new tumbling activities each year.
2. Be able to do a three stunt routine on each of two different pieces of equipment.
3. Perform two new vaults each year.

Tumbling and Gymnastics Activities:

Ability levels and past experience will necessitate the use of individualized techniques (Chapter 1) for tumbling and gymnastics. With a good background, however, the fifth and sixth grade child is capable of fairly difficult stunts. Mats are essential to all gymnastic and tumbling activities.

Tumbling

1. Front Walkover — Child kicks into a handstand but rather than going into a hold position, one leg leads the other as the child arches his/her back to come up on his/her feet in a walking type motion. This skill requires extreme lower back flexibility and is usually easier for girls.

2. Back Walkover — Like the front walkover, back flexibility is essential. The child must bow the back and legs as much as possible reaching back with the hands and head while simultaneously swinging one leg up followed by the other. Both hands should be nearly touching the floor as the leg is swung up. One leg hits the floor followed by the other.

Back walkover

3. Kip — The kipping skill is essential to a number of stunts and should be learned from a supine position prior to attempting its use in a skill like the front handspring. To do the kip one must be on his back. Both legs are then pulled up over the head while the hands are placed flat next to the ears (identical to a backward roll). The feet are then allowed to begin returning to their original position, but when they get to an angle of approximately 45° to the floor, the child punches the bottoms of his feet straight out at the 45° angle. This punch is accompanied by a simultaneous push with the hands. If executed properly, the child will land on his feet. The punch with the feet is achieved by an explosive straightening of the legs at the knee and hip joints.

4. Front handspring — The front handspring is done from a run. The child kicks into a handstand from a run, allowing the feet to continue over. Just past the center or what would be the balance position, the kip is performed to cause the child to land on both feet simultaneously. Most children do not execute the kip properly and land on their backs necessitating spotters to avoid injury.

5. Back handspring — The back handspring is not particularly difficult but there is a fear factor when executing backward stunts. The child pretends he is going to sit in a chair by bending the knees while simultaneously leaning back. As soon as he senses a loss of balance, he jumps both up and back while throwing the head and arms backward reaching toward the mat with both hands while looking for the back wall. The feet continue over together and land

Spotting the back handspring

Executing the back handspring

together on the mat. This skill must be spotted with the spotter giving support and lift behind the small of back and lift and rotation with one hand on the back of the thigh.

Gymnastics

Vaulting Box Activities (with Reuther Board):

1. Squat vault — After take off, hands are placed about shoulder width apart on the center of the box. The feet are drawn up by bending the knees and go between the hands. The feet land together on the opposite side of the box with the child facing away from the box.

2. Straddle vault — Hand placement is the same for the straddle vault as in the squat vault. The legs, however, are spread and straight. The body is piked slightly at the waist just prior to removing the hands from the box to allow the legs to go over the box. The feet come together on the far side of the box prior to landing which is accomplished with the back to the box.

Straddle vault

3. The neck spring — Two spotters, one on each end of the box, should be used for this vault. The child does a forward roll over the box using a kip to spring to the feet on the far side of the box. The spotters each grab an arm with their far arm as soon as the vaulter places his hands on the box. The spotters can then lift or push the vaulter with the near arm if necessary.

4. Handspring — Identical to the neck spring, but arms are kept straight throughout. No child should be allowed to attempt this vault unless he has mastered the neck spring. Even then, two spotters are essential. Some children will duck their head too soon which would cause them to fall down the near side of the box onto their neck. The spotters can push them over to safety with little difficulty.

Squat vault

Spotting the handspring

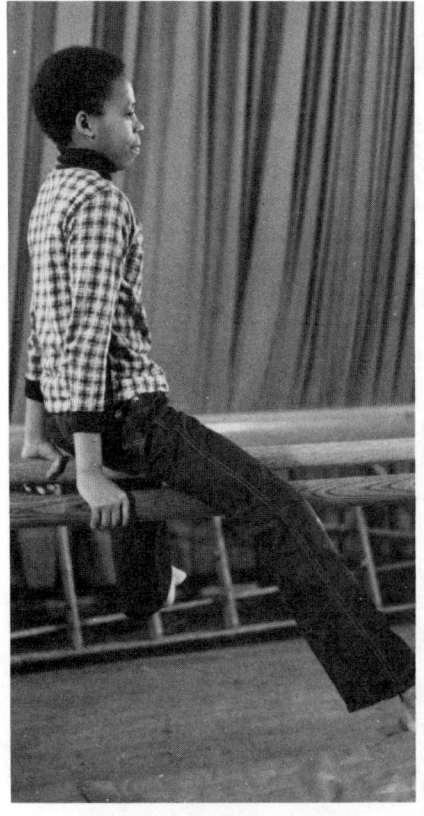

Straddle position 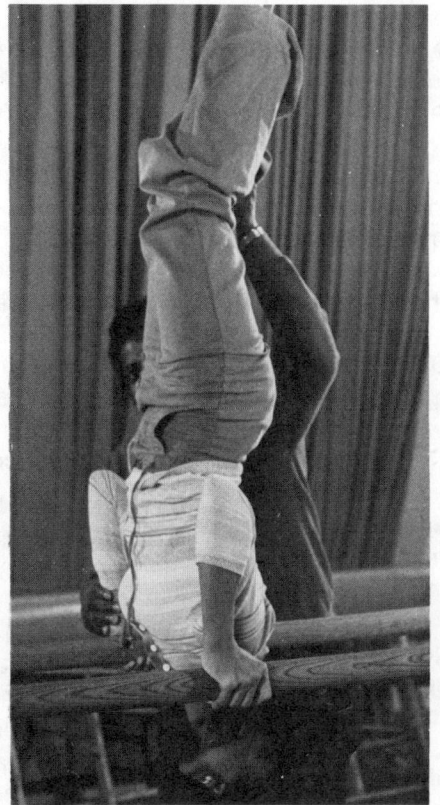   *Shoulder stand*    *Inverted hang*

Parallel Bars:

1. Swing — While in a support position, swing forward and backward from the shoulder joint. The body should be kept straight during the swing.

2. Swing to Straddle — During the forward part of the swing the legs are split and come to rest one leg on each bar in a straddle position. The legs should be kept straight.

3. Forward Roll — From the straddle position the child does a forward roll between the bars using the arms to rotate on and ending in a straddle position. The elbows must remain out during this roll.

4. Backward Roll — Do the same as a forward roll except going backward.

5. Shoulder stand — From a straddle position the child slowly rotates to a balance position with the feet straight in the air. A mat can be placed across the bars to catch children who fall while practicing this stunt.

6. Rear Dismount — From a swing, both legs are thrown off one side during the forward part of the swing so the rear part of the body is passing over the bar. The hand on the side where the legs are going is released while the other pushes off. The child should land facing the same direction he started at with the far

Rear dismount

hand regrasping the bar for balance.

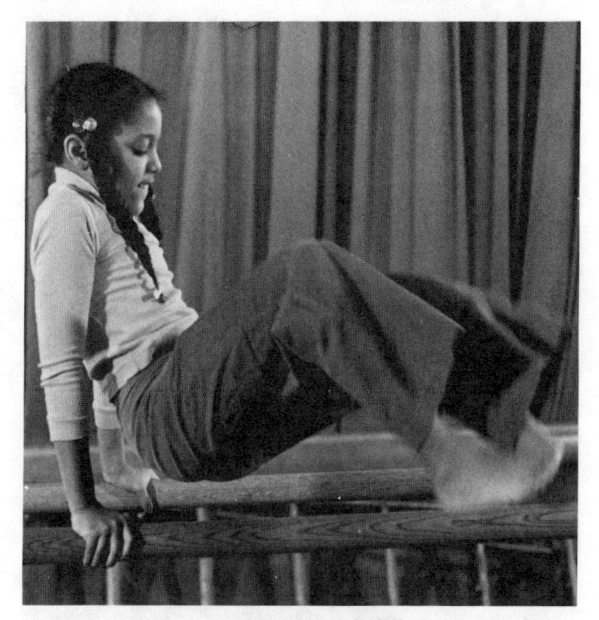

7. Front Dismount — Same as the rear except it is executed on the back part of the swing. The front part of the body crosses over the bar.

8. Inverted Hang — This is a head down, feet up position.

Balance Beam Activities — All balance beam activities should first be practiced on the low beam. Only those who are proficient on the low beam should be allowed on the high beam which should not be higher than three feet off the floor.

1. Full Turn — The full turn is done on one foot using the other foot along with the head and arms to provide the force needed to turn. A complete 360° turn is done.

2. Jump and Half Turn — The child jumps off both feet and turns 180°.

3. One Leg Squat — The child squats down on one leg with the other leg straight and returns to a standing position without losing his balance.

4. Squad Turn — The child takes a squat position with one leg straight and the heel of the foot resting on the beam in front of the child. The child then rotates 180° assuming the same position again.

5. Jump Tuck — The child jumps into the air and tucks by pulling up and grasping the knees with his arms. The child untucks and lands on the bar in a balance position.

6. Forward Roll — The roll is done on one shoulder with support coming from the hands grasping below the beam. The child should end up with one foot on the beam and the other swinging beside the beam to provide the momentum to come into the upright position (high beam only).

7. Shoulder Balance — Child balances on shoulder while holding onto the bottom of the beam with both hands.

8. Back Walk Over — This stunt is done the same as a back walk over on a mat (p. 241).

9. Turns — Children should learn one-half and full turns in as many ways as possible.

10. Leaping — The child takes off on one foot with a long suspension in the air and lands on the other foot.

11. Cartwheel — The cartwheel can be performed on the beam or as a dismount.

12. Roundoff Dismount — A roundoff is executed from the end of the beam.

13. Rope jumping on the low beam is good balance practice.

Tennis Objectives:

1. Using a paddle racket, bounce a tennis ball off the ground 30 times in a row without a miss.

2. Using a forehand stroke, bounce and hit a ball off the wall and then hit it to the wall again after it has bounced once.

3. Using a backhand stroke, bounce and hit a tennis ball against the wall.

4. Demonstrate the proper stroke technique for the serve and hit a tennis ball at least 40 feet using the serve.

Tennis Activities:

For children, the best practice is done using a paddle racket and ball in combination with a wall to hit the ball against. A court is not necessary and even if available it should be used on a limited basis during the initial phases of skill learning.

1. Forehand stroke — The child should shake hands with the racket handle to assume the forehand grip. The "V" between the thumb and first finger should be on the top of the handle with the racket face perpendicular to the ground. To execute the stroke, the child should stand sideways to the intended path of the ball with the racket back, arm bent slightly and racket head slightly higher than the hand. A small step can be taken with the lead foot as the racket is swung forward (shift weight from rear foot to front foot) making contact with the ball just off the lead foot. The child should hit through the ball and follow-through bringing the racket head higher than the non-hitting shoulder. The racket face should be perpendicular to the ground at ball contact and close during the follow-through. This closing action will put a topspin on the ball. The aiming point on the wall should be three to five feet over the net which is three feet in the center and three feet, six inches at the poles.

Rope jumping on the low balance beam

2. Backhand — The backhand grip is a ¼ turn of the racket which places the knuckle of the first finger on the top of the racket handle. A more pronounced body turn is made as compared with the forehand which will result in the back of the hitting arm's shoulder being closest to the wall or net. The racket which is back is swung forward as the weight is shifted from the rear to front foot. The ball should be contacted slightly forward of the lead foot. The racket face should be flat upon contact and open during follow-through which will create backspin on the ball.

3. The Service — The service grip is midway between the forehand and backhand. The child should stand slightly sideways to the net with the lead foot pointing toward the netpost. The racket arm motion is nearly identical to the throwing motion. The ball toss which is critical, is up, slightly away from and in front of the body. If allowed to fall, the ball should hit the ground just in front of and away from the lead foot. The difficulty with the serve is coordinating the two arms. Both arms start in front and then both go down and then up at the same time. The ball is pushed (not thrown) up by one hand while the racket makes a loop behind the head (throwing action), and finally the arm is fully extended so the racket makes contact with the ball as high as possible. The weight goes from rear foot to lead foot and both feet are together at ball contact.

Track and Field Objectives:

1. Run the 50-yard dash in 12 seconds or less.
2. Each child will be able to high jump at least ½ his height and at least 60% of the children will be able to clear ¾ of their height.
3. Will demonstrate visual baton passing skill as demonstrated in class without dropping the baton.
4. Will shotput a softball at least 15 feet.
5. Will do a standing broad jump at least ¾ of their height.
6. Will be able to triple jump at least 2 times their height.

Track and Field Activities:

1. Sprints — The children should be taught to use their arms, legs and body properly when sprinting. The arms should drive straight ahead while keeping a 90° angle at the elbow joint. The legs should reach out on each stride with a high leg lift behind the body (the heel should nearly hit the buttocks). The feet should be pointed straight ahead and the child should run on his toes. The head should be held even neither leaning forward or backward. All motions such as shaking the head, which do not assist in moving forward should be minimized or eliminated. All sprinting activities should be preceded by a warm-up including leg stretching and running.

2. High jumping should only be done if a very soft landing surface can be provided. Even with a soft surface, the flop style jump in which the child lands on his shoulders and neck should not be allowed. The scissors and rolls should be taught. In the scissors, the child runs at about a 30° angle to the bar and kicks the foot closest to the bar up first. The child goes over the bar in a sitting position with the legs doing a scissor motion. The roll is done by approaching the bar at a moderate speed on a 45° angle. The heel nearest the bar is planted while the other leg kicks up to provide lift. The child then rolls over the bar with the belly nearest the bar.

3. Baton passing for relays should be taught using visual passes. The approaching child places the baton with the left hand. The receiving child stands sideways extending the right hand back toward the approaching runner. The lead runner should begin moving before the other child arrives so the pass is made on the run. The palm of the hand can either be up or down depending on the type of pass desired. The underhand pass (palm down) is faster.

4. To put the softball, it should be held by the fingers not in the palm of the hand. It should be held beside the ear and pushed (put) not thrown by extending the arm out at a 45° angle with drive from the leg. The child who masters the pushing motion can practice the move and put. To move, the child turns his back to the eventual direction of flight. The first move is to take a backward hop on the same leg as the arm which is putting the shot. The child then drives off this foot while turning his body. The drive produces another hop as the child is turning and upon landing, the child must learn to keep his balance and not fall forward.

5. The standing broad jump should be used to develop leg power. If a suitable landing area (soft) is available, the running broad jump (takeoff on one foot and land on two) can be practiced.

6. The triple jump is a hop followed by a step and then a jump. This skill requires a lot of practice to learn the sequence. All three must be done consecutively without any stopping in between phases.

7. Distance Running — For the elementary child anything over 200 yards can be considered distance running, and children should be taught

how running distances differs from sprints. The body motion and pace are two factors which children must learn. The arms are carried so hands are near the shoulders when running. Rather than driving straight ahead as in the sprint, the arms should be moved back and forth across the chest in a very relaxed fashion. The hands should be loose. The feet should hit either flat or on the heels rather than on the toes. The head should be level and still with the jaw relaxed. The pace must be determined by the distance to be covered and will vary according to the individual.

Fitness

Goal: Each child will improve his fitness level.
Objectives:
1. The children will improve on all five of the VCU Fitness Text items.
2. The child will be able to touch his toes without bending his knees.

Integrated Planning

Both science and mathematics can be integrated with fitness. The science concepts associated with short and long term effects of exercise many of which are included in this chapter should be an integral part of a fitness program.

Another way to integrate science is through "Compass Exercises" which help older children, nine to twelve, understand directions. After a classroom discussion, a large cardboard compass is placed in the middle of the play area and task cards are spread over the entire area. The task cards include both exercises to be accomplished as well as directions to the next station. To begin the activity, children go to *any* task card, but after that they must go in sequence until all cards have been covered. A task card might read: #4, DO TEN BENT KNEE SIT-UPS AND THEN GO 50 GIANT STEPS NORTHWEST TO FIND CARD #5. Children should be encouraged to move quickly, but do all the exercises correctly. Emphasis should also be placed on using a natural compass, such as the sun, to determine direction.

Math can be used by the child to determine his percentile rank on a fitness test; it can also be used to calculate miles per hour in the 9-minute run; and laps can be mathematically converted to meters in the Running for Life Program (Appendix A).

Fitness Activities

As was pointed out in Chapter 6, physical fitness will usually be developed outside physical education time. The physical educator, however, must provide the knowledge and motivation to carry out a home fitness program. The knowledge usually consists of activities which can be incorporated into the home program and motivation can be in the form of fun activities in class which foster fitness. The activities below are a combination of exercises for home and activities for class time.

1. Sit-ups — Sit-ups can be done in a progression from easy to difficult. The easiest are those done with the legs slightly bent and the hardest are done with the knees fully bent.

2. Push-ups — The push-up is one of the better developmental exercises since it involves muscles in the arms, shoulders, chest and abdominal region. It can be done using the knees or the toes as the fulcrum. The latter is more difficult.

3. Pull-ups — The biceps are developed through use of the pull-up. This can be done from a bar hang or can be modified by placing the heels on the floor and leaning the body back under a low bar and pulling the bar to the chest.

4. Running — To develop the cardiovascular system, running must elevate the heart rate to a sufficient level and maintain that level for 15-18 minutes (Chapter 6). Such long runs are possible but not practical during physical education class. Children should be taught to take their pulse, calculate the proper conditioning heart rate and follow a fitness program featuring cardiovascular development.

5. Rope Jumping — If done long enough, rope jumping can be a good cardiovascular activity. It is also good for developing coordination and rhythmic ability.

6. Other good fitness activities:
Gymnastics, p. 242.
Crab Soccer, p. 217.
Combatives, p. 216.

Rhythmics

Goal: Each child will learn a variety of dances and dance steps. (Also see Chapter 11.)

Objectives:

1. The child will be able to perform the following dance steps: polka, schottische and bleking.

2. Without assistance the children will be able to do five new folk dances a year.

3. The children will demonstrate knowledge of the following square dance terms by correctly executing them doing a square dance: do si do, allemande, grand right and left, star, ladies' chain promenade and swing.

4. The children will be able to perform two new square dances a year.

Goal: Children will demonstrate creative rhythmic ability.

1. The children will move creatively to various types of music — classical and modern.

2. The children working alone or in a small group will develop a creative dance routine to their own music incorporating all four of the movement qualities — force, time, space and level — in their routine.

3. The children will develop original rhythmic routines alone or in small groups using each of the following pieces of equipment: jump ropes, lummi sticks, tinikling poles, wands, and streamers.

Integrated Planning

Integrating social studies with rhythmics is highly recommended. By learning dances from other countries, children may gain understanding about people from other countries. A good record series for dances from other countries is *The Methodist World of Fun Series.*

Folk and Square Dance

1. Polka — The polka can be developed from a two step which is relatively easy for children to learn. Have children form a single circle. When music starts all begin doing a slide (side gallop) counterclockwise while facing the center of the circle. On the teacher's command "change," the lead foot is changed by having the children face away from the center while still moving counterclockwise. The time between "changes" can gradually be shortened to the point the children are changing the lead foot every time thus creating the two step. The sequence is step, together, step, turn. To create the polka step, ask the children to vigorously lift their knee as they change the lead foot. This lift will usually cause the hop required to change the two step to the polka.

2. The Schottische — The schottische step consists of three steps and a hop. The three steps are taken with the hop coming on the foot which leads on the third step. Beginning with the right foot, it would be step forward right, step forward left, step forward right and hop on right foot. The side schottische can be done either left or right. To the right, it would be step right on the right foot, close left foot to right, step sideward on the right foot and hop on the right foot.

3. The Bleking — The bleking is sometimes referred to as the Mexican hat dance step. It is a quick alternating of the feet with heel of the lead foot striking the floor in front of and slightly to the right or left of center of the body. The bleking is done in a series of three steps, right, left and right with a slight pause between series of threes.

4. Partners — The most difficult thing to do when teaching folk and square dancing to ten and eleven year olds is getting them into a partner arrangement. Although there is a whole series of *Dances Without Partners (p. 395),* children will miss valuable rhythmic experiences if they never have partners. Most children enjoy partners of the opposite sex, but cannot acknowledge the fact because of peer pressure. No matter how hard one tries, children have to put on a show when pairing up. This normal behavior which is disruptive can be minimized by promising them a favorite activity for their cooperation. Such a tactic is justified because rhythmic activities requiring partners are valuable and children enjoy them even though they usually will not admit it.

A grand march can be used with the girls on one side of the floor and the boys on the other coming together at the top of the hall two at a time in a kind of follow the leader. The random selection minimizes the picking process which can cause hurt feelings if someone is rejected.

Another method is to have the girls make a circle and then have the boys stand between two girls. The girl on the boy's right then be-

A squared set

comes the boy's partner.

5. Folk Dances — There are a variety of folk dances ranging from simple to complex which can be taught to children. The children's past experience and ability dictate which to use. The best series for folk dances is *The Methodist World of Fun* (p. 395). With dances for all ability levels and from numerous countries, this series will provide hours of fun. The *Dances Without Partners* (p. 395) series also provides a wide range of rhythmic experiences. Both of these series come with complete dance instructions. The *Dances Without Partners* — records have verbal instructions on them.

6. Square Dancing — Square dancing is usually done in a four couple square with the head or number one couple being the one with their backs to the music. Couple two is on their right, three is across from them and four is to their left. The lead couples are one and three, the side couples are two and four. The boy is on his partner's left side and the girl to the boy's left is the corner lady.

Terms

Do si do — The do si do is done either with the partner or corner lady and is executed by moving towards each other arms folded across the chest. The two pass right shoulders, go back to back and then move backwards into place (can be done right or left).

Allemande — The allemande is done with the corner gent and lady taking left hands and making a half turn moving past each other returning to their original positions.

Grand Right and Left — The grand right and left is begun by facing one's partner joining right hands. The two pull past each other extending their left hand to the person coming toward them. This right, left, right continues until partners meet again at which time they usually take hands and promenade back home. The grand right and left is almost always preceded by an allemande left which usually confuses children. Some prefer to teach the grand right and left in a large circle, but more success may be possible teaching it in the regular square. Most times only one or two persons are having difficulty and they are easily identified and helped in the small groups. By creating a little competition among square, motivation and thus learning can be increased.

Star — The star is formed by four persons extending the same hand and grasping another's wrist to form a square. This can be done either right or left and the four usually circle in the direction they are facing.

Ladies Chain — The ladies chain is done between any two ladies by grasping right hands and going past each other extending their left to the opposite gent (boy). The gent takes the left hand and places his right hand on the girl's back making a half circle in place. These ladies have thus switched positions and partners. Frequently, they will chain back again right away.

Promenade — There are a variety of ways to promenade with the most popular one being the holding of both hands right to right and left to left in front of the couple. The boy is on the inside.

Home Position — The home position is always where the boy began the dance. When partners are switched, they return to the boy's home position.

Calling — The caller is the person responsible for telling the dancers what to do. Some records have the callers on them, but these are not recommended during the early stages or learning. When mistakes are made, the record must be stopped and begun again. With the high noise level usually associated with early learning, the record caller is often difficult to hear. By using a microphone and calling one's own square dances, the teacher is able to control the pace. Those records with instructions on them are also difficult for children to understand. The teacher should teach the dance and rely only on the record for music.

Creative Rhythmics
(Also see Chapter 11.)

Creative activities and particularly creative

rhythmics are too frequently limited to younger children. The 10 and 11 year old can gain valuable movement experiences while developing creative ability using rhythmics.

1. Modern dance to commercially available music or to music produced by the children can be successful with 10 and 11 year old children. The movement qualities of force, time, space and level can be used to establish guidelines to aid children in the development of original dance routines. Children can work together in pairs or small groups to develop dances.

2. For children unaccustomed to creative activities, familiar activities such as ropes, lummi sticks, tinikling poles, wands, and streamers can be used to foster creative rhythmic routines. Rope, wand and streamer routines can be done alone or in a group while lummi stick activities and tinikling are usually group activities. Establishing criteria for routines provides guidance during the early phases of creative development. Criteria for various activities could be as follows:

Ropes:
1. Jump both single beat and double beat.
2. Have both front rope jumping and back rope jumping.
3. Move around while jumping.
4. Use the rope in some other rhythmic way which does not require jumping.

Lummi sticks:
1. Do an activity while sitting or kneeling.
2. Do a move while on your feet and moving around.
3. Have one pass in which everyone's sticks are being passed at the same time.
4. Keep rhythm with your body as well as the sticks during one phase of the routine.

Tinikling:
1. Work with a partner who is doing a mirror image of your move.
2. Have a part in which partners are moving in opposite directions.
3. Have a part in which you follow each other through the sticks.

Creativity

Goal: Children will develop creative ability.

1. Children alone or in small groups will imitate machines which have moving parts.
2. Children will creatively act out various movement themes through pantomime such as:

Tinikling

the circus, famous events, the city, sporting events and weather.

3. Children will move creatively to various poems which have movement activities in them.
4. Also see creative rhythmics.

Integrated Planning

As with younger children, science can be integrated with creativity. Older children can be asked to move as if they were in various weather situations. They can also work in groups to be machines which have various moving parts.

For integrating language arts, children can write out routines, make up games using written rules, and create their own shows with scripts.

Creative Activities:

Although the creative activities for ten and eleven year-old children are similar if not identical to those suggested for younger children, this older group hopefully will be more advanced in their movement activities. The ten and eleven-year-old child should also be better able to work in small groups.

1. A good way to get children moving creatively is to set themes for them to act out. These can be: (1) Moving in a heavy snow, (2) moving on another planet, (3) being made of rubber, metal or plastic, (4) moving in different moods or like different people, (5) moving in slow motion while acting out sports activities, (6) moving to music and (7) moving to poems. Most creative rhythmic activities will be successful if presented properly. Children's inhibition is usually created by the teacher's inhibition.

2. Gravity and Planets can be studied with a trip to outer space, stopping at different planets. Children can act out how they would move and how they would react to the climate and surface.

3. A good way to encourage creativity in upper elementary children is to ask them to create musical routines using equipment. A ball routine, for example, could be done to modern or classical music, in which fast and slow portions of the music, accents, and phrases are highlighted by some change in the routine, i.e., bouncing ball hard on accent, switching the skill at the end of each phrase, moving slowly or quickly according to the tempo.

4. See creative rhythmics, p. 249.

5. Many activities from the curriculum for eight- and nine-year-olds can be used with older children.

Self-Testing Objectives

Goal: Children will learn a variety of self-testing activities each year.

Objective:

Children will learn at least ten new activities a year for which they can test themselves.

Self-Testing Activities:

As the name implies, self-testing activities are those in which the child is able to test his own ability without assistance from the teacher. A child knows, for example, when he has jumped the rope, pulled or pushed himself up, jumped over a bar, thrown a ball, hit a target or run a given distance. Such activities are intrinsically motivating and therefore enjoyed by children. Whenever possible, learning activities should be self-testing in nature which will allow children to self pace their activities by testing their own ability.

1. Rope jumping — Rope jumping is not only a self-testing activity, it also aids the development of coordination, rhythmic ability and fitness. The skills described in the following list can be mastered by a number of ten and eleven year olds.

    a. Double jump — In the double jump the rope passes under the feet twice in one jump. This skill requires a quick double turn of the rope while jumping higher than usual. Most children try to enter the double jump from a very fast single rope jumping speed. Only rope speed is necessary when the double jump is attempted. Some children will be able to master it from a single jump, returning to a single jump speed without losing control of the rope turn. Others will make it under the feet twice but fall or lose their balance causing them to stop jumping.

Long rope jumping is a favorite activity of upper elementary children.

    b. Routines to music — Rope jumping routines combining a number of skills put to music is a valuable developmental activity.

    c. Short rope jumping while long rope jumping — jumping a short rope while at the same time jumping a long rope requires body coordination and coordination of three people — the long rope turners and the short rope turner.

    d. The long rope crisscross — Two long ropes are turned simultaneously while crossed at a 90° angle. Children try to jump in after the ropes have begun moving.

    e. Double Dutch and Irish — To turn Double Dutch, two ropes are turned simultaneously by two turners holding one rope in each hand. In Double Dutch the turner's hands travel up toward the turner's chin and away from the body. Full arm circles are required. Double Irish is the same as Double Dutch ex-

Double Dutch requires considerable skill.

cept the turner's hands begin moving down toward the feet and away from the body. The biggest difficulty initially with these two skills is getting the turners working properly. After the ropes are going, children try to jump in. Usually only a small percentage of children can do these double rope activities.
f. Disco rope jumping — Children attempt to do disco dancing while jumping rope. Appropriate disco music should be provided.

Other Self-Testing Activities:
Tumbling and Gymnastics, page 241.
Sports Skills, page 235.

AFFECTIVE DOMAIN

Objectives in the affective domain are specified in unit and yearly plans but not on lesson plans. Since attitudes are only changed over long periods, affective objectives would be inappropriate as short term objectives such as those usually specified on lesson plans. Many of the objectives stated below are idealistic and will not be accomplished fully during a year or even in many years, but they serve as guides for teachers.

Self-Concept

Goal: Each child will improve his self-concept.
Objective:
1. Given an anonymous questionnaire children will respond positively to questions regarding their self-concept as a result of physical education participation.

Self-Concept Activities:
1. Call children by name.
2. Use a humanistic approach.
3. Give students input into curriculum design by administering anonymous questionnaires.
4. Provide success for all children.
5. Do not confront children in front of their peers.
6. Do not correct students in front of their peers.

Sportsmanship

Goal: Children will improve their sportsmanship.
Objectives:
1. No child will physically fight with another child during a game situation.
2. Children will not boo for any reason.
3. Children will congratulate the other team win or lose.
4. Children will call rule violations on themselves.

Team Concept

Goal: Children will learn how to work as a team toward a common goal.
Objectives:
1. All children, no matter what their ability, will be given an equal chance to play by the team captain.
2. Children will not openly ridicule members of their own team.
3. Children will verbally encourage members of their team no matter what the circumstances.

Leading and Following

Goal: Children will learn to be both leaders and followers.
Objective:
Children will be able to organize and conduct their own games with teacher supervision but not help.

Interpersonal Relationships

Goal: Children will learn to get along with each other.
Objectives:
1. Children will not call each other derogatory names during physical education.
2. Children will show respect for the right of others by not violating safety rules which endanger others.
3. Children will accept partners of the opposite sex for rhythmic activities with sufficient ease that the rhythmic activity can be successfully conducted.

Safety

Goal: Children will follow safety rules.
Objective:
During all activities children will not deliberately violate safety rules.

Fitness

Goal: Children will carry out a personal fitness program at home.
Objective:
At least 70% of the children will carry on a home fitness program as evaluated by their response to fitness questions on an anonymous questionnaire.

Health

Goal: Children will have good health habits.
Objectives:

1. Given an anonymous questionnaire, children will respond positively to those questions dealing with good health habits.

2. Most children will show self-respect by not using dangerous drugs including alcohol and cigarettes.

Affective Domain Activities:

1. Choice Day — Children should frequently be given the opportunity to choose and conduct their own activities under the teacher's supervision. By conducting their own activities children will get the chance to develop leadership and followship qualities.

2. Choosing Sides — Children like to choose and be chosen. By giving them a chance to select their own teams, a teacher can fulfill this need. Care must be exercised to give many different children the chance to be choosers. Caution must also be taken to avoid children being hurt by being chosen last. One way to handle this problem is to have children choose from a class list in secret. Another way is to have each captain choose two children and assign the rest.

3. Discussion — Incidences in class will provide the motivation for class discussions regarding affective topics. These discussions must be skillfully conducted by the teacher to get the most out of them. Controversial issues must be carefully handled or avoided. These issues include sex and religious beliefs. Sex education is a part of some elementary curriculums and is, therefore, less sensitive to discuss. Religious discussions except those related to the acceptance of others and tolerance of others' beliefs have no place in public schools.

4. Questionnaires — Valuable affective data can be obtained through use of an anonymous questionnaire such as the one on page 10.

5. Attitude Development — Affective domain behavior is determined by attitudes. Positive or negative attitudes can be developed in physical education depending upon the teacher. The teacher can serve as an example by practicing good health (being fit and not smoking) and safety habits. Children will give little credence to a discussion on health from an overweight individual who is knocking them over with cigarette breath.

COGNITIVE DOMAIN

The educational foundation and increased ability of ten and eleven year olds to conceptualize provides a fertile area for learning movement and physiological concepts. Properly presented, many important bits of information can be learned and utilized by children on a daily basis.

Integrated Planning

The cognitive domain as would be expected provides numerous opportunities for integrated activities, particularly in the area of science. Science concepts such as those listed under short and long term effects of exercise should be an integral part of a physical education program. Closely linked to exercise concepts are those in health. Knowledge of internal and external body parts and how they function is another way to integrate science.

Rules and Regulations

Goal: Children will learn a variety of sport and game rules and regulations.
Objectives:

1. If asked, children will be able to organize and conduct at least five new games per year.

2. Without assistance, children should be able to organize and conduct at least 15 different games.

Goal: Children will be able to do dances from memory.
Objective:
Children should be able to do at least five new dances per year from memory and a total of 15 different dances (old and new) in any year.

Knowledge of Body Parts

Goal: Children will know a variety of body parts.
Objective:

1. Besides those learned in earlier years (see Chapters 7-9) children will be able to identify the following body parts by touching them or indicating their approximate location if they are internal organs: biceps, triceps, abdominal area, stomach, heart, forearm, sternum and clavical.

Fitness

Goal: Children will learn fitness information which can apply to their daily lives.
Objective:

1. If asked, at least 80% of the children will be able to indicate the meaning and importance of the following information:

Short Term Effects of Exercise

a. When peak physical performance is desired, a warm-up which produces sweating is desirable. A warm-up is also necessary if the activity will require all out muscular activity such as sprinting or broad jumping.
b. To facilitate recovery, a cool-down period should follow strenuous exercise.
c. One should continue to walk after vigorous running so leg muscles can massage the blood from the legs thus avoiding the blood pooling in this area.
d. Fluids should be taken before, during and following exercise as needed. During hot weather when large quantities of fluid are lost, an extra 8 to 16 ounces of water should be ingested even after thirst is quenched.
e. Suitable clothing should be worn during exercise including proper footwear. Rubber suits which hasten weight loss through sweating are extremely dangerous and could cause *death* under certain circumstances.
f. Judgment must be exercised regarding activity and climate — extreme hot or cold. Fluid loss during heat can lead to heat stroke or exhaustion and frostbite can occur rapidly to exposed skin in cold weather.
g. Exercising when fatigued significantly increases the likelihood of injury.
h. No safe drug will improve fitness or increase skill performance.
i. Heart rate increases with exercise and will recover within two to three minutes following most exercise bouts.
j. A heart rate of 60 to 80% of the predicted maximum heart rate should be used for cardiovascular training. For elementary children this conditioning rate is about 160-170 beats per minute.
k. Muscle soreness will follow within 24 hours an exercise bout which uses unconditioned muscles.
l. Vigorous exercise will produce the following conditions: sweat, increased respiration, decreased appetite, increased need for fluids and increased body temperature.

Long Term Effects of Exercise

a. A muscle will grow in size (hypertrophy) with use and decrease in size with disuse (atrophy).
b. Hormonal differences and body composition preclude the development of muscle definition on a female as compared with a male. Girls need not fear the development of bulging muscles as a result of exercise.
c. The cardiovascular system becomes more efficient with appropriate exercise (Chapter 6). A decreased resting heart rate is one noticeable effect of a cardiovascular development program.
d. Weight can be controlled or reduced by combining diet and exercise.
e. Strength and endurance training are activity specific, i.e., training in one activity will have minimal transfer to others.
f. Good posture is dependent upon muscle strength.
g. Fitness programs should progress gradually.
h. Fitness will: (1) improve the ability to relax, and (2) improve health.

Also see movement information in Chapter 9.

Health Knowledge

There is a great deal of health knowledge which a fifth and sixth grader should know, some of which is possible to teach during physical education. Such subjects as the effects of smoking, and use of alcohol and drugs lend themselves to discussion as they relate to physical performance and fitness.

Goal: Children will learn health information as it relates to physical education.

Objective:

Children will be able to answer at least 80% of the questions relating to alcohol, drugs and smoking which were discussed in class. Evaluation can be a written test or oral questioning.

1. There is no *safe* drug which improves physical performance.
2. Alcohol has a detrimental effect on physical performance.
3. Long term use of alcohol can lead to serious disease.
4. Alcohol is a depressant.
5. Smoking will decrease physical performance particularly in the area of cardiovascular efficiency.
6. Smoking has been related to cancer, emphysema, heart disease and a number of other debilitating diseases.

Cognitive Activities:

Most of the cognitive objectives are fairly self-explanatory, and there are no specific activities other than participation and discussion to aid in the accomplishment of them. A few ideas on when discussion could take place are listed below.

1. Fitness — Children can be told about fitness while they are doing various exercises. As the children exercise, the teacher can ask such questions as, "Why should you exercise?", "What muscle groups are being developed?", "If you develop muscles using these exercises, what will you be able to do better?", or "How often should you exercise?"

2. Running — As children are running in a circle around the teacher, he can direct them to do different things such as shaking the head, running on the toes, holding the hands down at their sides, or running while swinging the feet out to the side. These activities can be followed by questions (while the children continue to run) such as, "How should you hold your head when running?", "Is it better to run on the toes or heels when running slowly?" or "Should you take big steps or little ones?"

3. Discussion — Since children learn best by doing, cognitive concepts should be learned through direct purposeful experience although discussion without movement may be valuable in some cases.

FIFTH AND SIXTH GRADE GAMES

NAME	Page	Psychomotor	Affective	Cognitive	Grass	Multipurpose Room	Hardtop	Classroom	Can be Adapted to Any Area	Can be used for Evaluation
Chain Tag	255	5	3	2	x	x				
Jump the Shot	182	5	1	1					x	
Sam Says	216	5	1	1					x	
Combatives	216	5	2	1	x	x				
Tug of War	184	5	1	1	x	x				
Four Square	219	5	1	1			x			
Tetherball	220	5	1	1	x		x			
Crab Soccer	217	5	1	1					x	
Grab the Club	217	2	1	1					x	
Relays	218	1	3	1					x	
Plastic Hockey	255	4	3	2	x	x				
Must Swing Baseball	255	2	3	2	x	x	x			
Football Kick Across	255	3	3	1	x		x			
2-on-2 Basketball	255	5	3	2		x	x			
No Dribble Basketball	255	4	3	2	x	x	x			
Volleyball Games	256	4	3	2	x	x	x			
Frisbee Golf	256	4	2	2	x		x			
Pillo Polo	256	5	3	1	x	x				
Circle Tag	256	2	2	1	x					
Protect Me Tag	220	5	4	2	x	x				
Triangle Dodgeball	257	3	1	1	x	x	x			
Soccer Keep Away	257	3	1	1	x	x	x			
Balloon Ball	257	4	2	1	x	x				
Balloon Bucket	257	5	2	1	x	x	x			
Frisbee Toss	257	4	1	1	x	x	x			
Wall Ball	257	5	1	1		x				

Game Code: N= Name of game
DA= Developmental age for which game was designed
DV= What the child should get from the game (developmental value)
F= Formation
E= Equipment required
D= Description of the game

Grades Five and Six

N: Chain Tag
DA: 11 - 12
DV: Teamwork and Agility
F: Free
E: None
D: One person is "it." As soon as he tags another person, they join hands, and must go together to tag others. As others are caught, the chain grows. Only the ends of the chain can tag. If the chain breaks, no one may tag. Players not tagged can go around the chain or break through. As soon as almost everyone is caught, game ends or can be played again.

N: Plastic Hockey
DA: 8 - 12
DV: Fitness
F: Two teams
E: Hockey sticks, puck or ball, and eyeglass guards
D: Plastic ice hockey-type sticks can be used both indoors and out. Children love this very vigorous game, particularly in a large indoor area. The cheaper plastic sticks work well indoors, but are of little value on grass.
Area Hockey — children are assigned areas which they cannot leave. Two or three players on each team are permitted to go anywhere in the area. This arrangement prevents all the children from gathering around the ball or puck, which can lead to an injury. Children must be instructed to keep the head of the sticks below their waist, and must wear protective goggles over eyeglasses.

N: Must Swing Baseball
DA: 9 - 12
DV: Teamwork
F: Two teams
E: Bat and ball
D: Played like regular baseball, except that the pitcher is a member of the team at bat. All pitches, therefore, are strikes no matter where they go. This arrangement eliminates both the need for an umpire as well as a long wait as the batter looks for the perfect pitch. The number of outs is usually increased from three to six, or everyone gets one chance to bat and then the teams switch sides.

N: Football Kick Across
DA: 11 - 12
DV: Eye-Foot Coordination
F: Two players and one ball
E: Junior size football
D: Children are paired up with one football or round ball (soccer ball or playground ball) between them. Goal lines are established and each person tries to punt the ball in the air over the goal line. The first kick is made from the "40 yard line." If the ball is caught in the air, the catcher can take five giant steps toward his opponent's goal line before punting the ball. All other balls must be punted from where they are stopped. If there are only a few footballs, they should be traded off with other players using the round balls, so that everyone gets a chance to use the football (junior-size football only).

N: Two-on-Two or Three-on-Three Basketball
DA: 10 - 12
DV: Teamwork and Coordination
F: Teams of two or three
E: Junior size basketballs and eight foot baskets
D: Basketball is probably the most difficult game for elementary children to play, so lead-up games must be used. By making the teams smaller than the usual five, children get more playing time. Even with small teams, however, rules must be greatly modified (see next game). The equipment must also be modified. Balls can be soccer size, and the basket should be lowered to seven or eight feet. Children playing with regulation equipment and ten-foot baskets develop incorrect habits in order to have success — getting the ball in the basket. These habits are often hard to break later on. By modifying equipment and rules, children will have success and skills will carry over.

N: No Dribble Basketball
DA: 10 - 12
DV: Teamwork
F: Two or three on a team
E: Junior size basketballs and eight foot baskets
D: The ball may not be dribbled and can only be moved by passing off to teammates who can move freely when they do not have the ball. Emphasis can be placed on the walking rule during this game and what to do when you do not have the ball.

256 Grades Five and Six

N: Volleyball
DA: 10 - 12
DV: Teamwork and Coordination
F: One team of six players on each side of the net
E: Volleyballs and six foot high net
D: It is very difficult for children, if not specially trained, to play a regulation game of volleyball. Modified games, however, are fun and use the same skills required for regular play.

One Bounce Volleyball — the ball may bounce one time between each hit and any number of hits are allowed to get the ball back over the net.

Three Hit Volleyball — same as "One Bounce" above, but the ball must be hit a minimum of three times before it can go back over the net.

Multiple Hit Volleyball — one person may hit the ball more than once in a row.

Other arrangements such as shortening the distance required for serving, lowering the net, and banning the spike can all be added to any of the above games. The rules from the different games can also be combined to give the children success.

N: Frisbee Golf
DA: 9 - 12
DV: Hand-Eye Coordination

Frisbee Golf

F: One frisbee per person
E: Frisbees and hoops
D: A golf course is laid out using hoops (lying on the ground) and some kind of marker flags. Holes should be placed so as to avoid the possibility of children being hit by the frisbee. Each throw counts as one point. The frisbee must be completely inside the hoop to be successful. Children continue to throw from where the frisbee stopped until they get it in the hoop. If the frisbee is across the hoop, one additional point is added to the score. The one with the lowest score at the end is the winner. Distances between holes should vary, and hazards should be included to increase the difficulty.

N: Pillo Polo
DA: 9 - 12
DV: Hand-Eye Coordination, Fitness, and Teamwork
F: Two teams
E: Pillo Polo set and eyeglass guards
D: This activity is similar to the polo played on horseback, without the horse. The game comes with specific directions, although variations due to equipment and space are easy to design. The object of the game is to get the ball into a goal which should, like ice hockey, allow for play behind the goal. The reader is referred to the directions that come with the Pillo Polo set. It is a vigorous activity and fairly safe.

N: Circle Tag
DA: 10 - 12
DV: Fun
F: Circle
E: None
D: Students hold hands to form a circle and then take five or six giant steps backward to enlarge the circle. All then face in the same direction to run around the circle. The object is to tag the person immediately in front. The tagged player leaves the circle and the tagger continues after the next runner. The circle continues to get smaller as the game progresses. The game ends when one player is left. Any player running outside the circle to avoid being tagged is automatically out. Since this is an elimination activity, it should be saved for the end of a class period, and even then, it should not be given more than three to four minutes of class time.

N: Triangle Dodgeball
DA: 10 - 11
DV: Agility, working together in small groups
 F: Groups of 4
 E: A ball for each group
 D: The class will get into groups of 4 children. Three of these children will form a large triangle. The children should be about 8 yards apart. The fourth child will be "it." The person who is "it" must stay within the triangle. You may only hit "it" below the waist. "It" may move any way he wishes. If the thrower hits the child who is "it," the thrower becomes the new dodger. The game moves quickly and involves the entire class. It may be played inside, but the game needs more room — outside.

N: Soccer Keepaway
DA: 10 - 11
DV: Kicking, eye-foot coordination
 F: Triangle and one in center
 E: Soccer ball
 D: Three players for a triangle, each about 30 feet apart. One player stands in the middle. The players kick the ball to one another while the center person attempts to steal the pass or break it up. The ball is kicked in a clockwise fashion. If the center is successful, he changes places with the passer. Each child should get a turn in the middle eventually. This activity should be done outside for adequate space.

N: Balloon Ball
DA: 10 - 11
DV: Eye-Hand Coordination
 F: Two Teams
 E: Balloons
 D: Divide the class into two teams. Half the players on each team have balloons. When the teacher starts the game, they try to bat their balloons to a goal behind the other team. Those without balloons will try to take them away from the other team by batting toward the other goal. Balloons must be kept in the air at all times and may not be grabbed.

N: Balloon Bucket
DA: 10 - 11
DV: Hand-Eye Coordination
 F: Partners
 E: Balloons and Hula Hoops
 D: One balloon is given to each pair. Hoops are spread around the floor. The students bat the balloon toward a hoop (no one partner can bat the balloon twice in a row) which must then be picked up and the balloon batted through it. The object is to see how many hoops the team can get through in a given amount of time. A pair may not go through the same hoop twice, nor can they move the hoop around the room while batting the balloon through.

N: Frisbee Toss
DA: 10 - 11
DV: Eye-Hand Coordination
 F: Target Stations
 E: Frisbees and Hula Hoops
 D: Each student has two frisbees. He stands behind the restraining line 10 feet away. He scores one point each time he tosses the frisbee in the circle.

N: Wall Ball
DA: 10 - 11
DV: Hand-Eye Coordination
 F: Scattered around a wall
 E: One ball per child.
 D: Children hit ball with their hand (emphasize using each hand) and make it hit the wall. They then must hit it before it bounces twice. This game can be played in pairs in which they must alternate hits. The opponent scores one point each time a child misses the ball.

EXAMPLE LESSON PLANS

1. 5th and 6th

    Multipurpose Room

    Objectives:

    1. The students will be able to do single and double underhand turns and the 3 step hustle with a partner.
    2. After instructions, the students will be able to create their own dance using the turns and steps taught in class with a partner.

Activities	Formation
I. Jump rope to music. Students will jump rope anyway they can to popular music.	I. Free
II. Disco Dance with partner Students will hustle step with a partner, and the single/double underhand turn.	II. Partners
III. Create Dance Students will practice and make up own dance with a partner using the steps learned in class and those they might already know.	III. Partner

    Safety: No pushing or pulling partners.

2. 5th & 6th

    Multipurpose Room

    Objectives:

    1. The students will be able to do the single underhand turn and the double turn with a partner.
    2. The students will be able to do 5 different dance steps while keeping in time with the music.

Activities	Formation
I. Move to popular music. Students do exercises to music.	I. Free
II. Disco dance single/partners Students will learn *Saturday Night Fever* line dance with six different dance steps with partners; will learn underhand turn, double turn with 2 hands.	II. Free with Partner
III. Creative Dance Students make up own dance with a partner or by themselves.	III. Free with partners

    Safety: No running, no sliding.

3. 5th and 6th

   Multipurpose Room

   Objectives:

   1. The students will be able to do cartwheels, forward and backward rolls in succession.
   2. The students will be able to hold a headstand and a handstand for 3 seconds with a spotter.

Activities	Formation
I. Exercises working on stretching and flexibility.	I. In groups around mats.
II. Tumbling skills Forward rolls in succession, backward rolls in succession, tripod balance to headstand, handstand with spotter, cartwheels in succession, backbends — standing or lying down, round-offs, diving forward roll on crash mat.	II. Small groups at mats.
III. Free tumbling practice working on stunts learned in class.	III. Same groups at the mats

4. 5th and 6th

   Gymnasium

   Objectives:

   1. The students will be able to execute 5 consecutive bumps and sets to themselves.
   2. If asked, the students will be able to demonstrate both the underhand and overhand serve and the spiking approach.

Activities	Formation
I. Students show 10 different exercises that they think would develop their body for good volleyball play.	I. Free
II. Introduction to volleyball skills — bump, set spike, serve. Students practice by themselves, then with partners.	II. Free — partners
III. Volley Game Students are divided into 4 groups. When told to go, they must keep the ball in the air by bump, sets. Everytime the ball hits the ground 1 point. Team with the *least* points wins.	III. Small groups

   Safety: No running, sliding. Be careful when spiking.

260   *Grades Five and Six*

5. 5th and 6th

    Outside/multipurpose room

    Objectives:

    1. The students will be able to do the underhand serve well enough to get it to their partner.
    2. When given a volleyball, 80% of the students will be able to execute 5 consecutive bumps and sets to themself.

Activities	Formation
I. Do This, Do That	I. Free

    Teacher will say do this, do that and the student must do it when she says do this.

    II. Introduction to volleyball — II. Free

    Each student will have a ball and executive bumps and sets to self. Teacher asks can you? Do 5 bumps to yourself? Do 5 sets to yourself? Do bumps and sets to your partner without the ball hitting the ground? Do the underhand serve to your partner?

    III. Volley Net Game — III. 4 teams

    Using sponge rubber balls, students will volley the balls back and forth until the whistle blows. The team with the least number of balls on their side wins.

    Safety: No kicking balls or throwing balls out at people.

6. 5th and 6th

    Outside

    Objectives:

    1. The students will be able to do 5 bumps and sets to themselves.
    2. The students will be able to complete all stations by being able to bump, set, spike and serve.

Activity	Formation
I. Students lead different exercises	I. Free
II. Spiking: Get a partner, or groups of three	II. Stations

    One person throws the ball up and the others run up using the spiking approach and spikes the ball. Switch back and forth.

    Station 2
    Divide into 2 groups. One group on each side of the net. Keep the ball in the air as long as possible using bumps and sets.

Station 3
Practice serving overhand and underhand. Use a partner.

Station 4
Can you? Do 10 bumps to yourself? Do 10 sets to yourself? Do bumps, sets to yourself? Throw the ball up and spike it?

III. Shower Serve Volleyball Game   III. Two teams

Three balls to a team. Players serve and opposite team tries to catch the ball. If ball is caught that player goes to service area. If the ball is dropped the other team gets a point.

7. 5th and 6th

Outside

Objectives:

1. The students will be able to do 5 bumps and sets to themselves without the ball hitting the ground.
2. The students will be able to spike and execute the underhand serve using large plastic balls.

Activities   Formation

I. Jump ropes — students jump anyway they   I. Free
can for 3 minutes.

II. Station arrangement using volleyball   II. Stations
skills.

Station 1
Spiking: Get a partner or groups of 3. One person throws the ball up and the other runs up, using the spiking approach and spikes the ball. Switch back and forth, one spiking, one throwing.

Station 2
Divide group in half. One group on each side of the string. Keep the ball up in the air as long as possible by bumping and setting.

Station 3
With a partner, practice serving overhand and underhand. How many can you get to your partner?

Station 4
Can You? Do 10 bumps to yourself? Do 10 sets to yourself? Throw the ball up and spike it?

III. Modified Volleyball Game   III. Four teams — two games

262 *Grades Five and Six*

8. 5th and 6th

    Outside or Gym

    Objectives:

    1. All students will be able to interact in a group situation by practicing and playing together during a game.
    2. Students will be able to bump, set and serve well enough to keep the ball in action during game play.

Activities	Formation
I. Warm-up for volleyball play. Students will be divided into 4 teams. Each team will do their own warm-up exercises and practice the bump, set and serve within their own group.	I. Teams
II. Volleyball Play	II. Four Teams
Modified rules and rotation procedures will be taught. Four teams play until one team wins.	
III. Tournament Play	III. Four Teams
The two winners of the previous game will play each other for the championship. The two losers will also play each other.	

9. 5th and 6th

    Gym

    Objective:

    1. The students will be able to dribble with either hand while walking, running and changing directions without losing control of the ball.
    2. The students will be able to execute and receive a chest and bounce pass from 10 feet away.

Activities	Formation
I. Ball Handling Exercise	I. Free
Students do movement exploration with the balls. When the whistle blows they must freeze. When told to start they must continue doing something completely different than what they were doing.	
II. Specific Dribbling	II. Free
Can you?	
Can you dribble while walking forward (right and left hand), while walking backwards, while running with your finger tip, in a circle, high and low, or while sliding left and right?	

2nd Part

Passing with partners. Chest pass — starting close, then moving apart. Bounce pass — starting close, then moving apart. Free

III. Dribble Tag III. Free

First person is "it." All people have a ball and dribble around the room. The person who is "it" runs around and tries to tag someone. If you are tagged you become "it."

11. 5th and 6th

Outside or Gym

Objectives:

1. The students will be able to make 1 out of 3 baskets using the two hand shot and the underhand shot.
2. The students will show understanding of basketball terms by completing each station.

Activity Formation

I. Basketball mimetics I. Free

Students will run in place. When the teacher calls out different basketball skills they must respond by doing that skill without a ball.

II. Station Arrangement, working on shooting, dribbling and passing. II. Stations

Station I
Can you make *8* baskets using the two hand and underhand shot?

Station II
How many shots can you make from the foul line?

Station III
Can you dribble around the outside of these cones with your right hand? Your left hand? Can you dribble in and out of the cones switching hands?

Station IV
Make a circle and do chest and bounce passes. How far apart can you get?

III. Hands-Up Basketball Game III. Two teams

One team lines up on outside boundaries, other team spreads out in between. Using 5 balls, the outside team tries to get the ball across to other team members while the team in the middle tries to get the ball. Must use chest or bounce pass. One point is scored each time the ball successfully gets to the other side.

Safety: No kicking the ball.

264 *Grades Five and Six*

11. 5th and 6th

    Outside or Gym

    Objective:

    1. The students will be able to guard and gain possession of the ball when working with a partner.
    2. The students will have some concept of basketball game play by being able to play a modified basketball game.

Activity	Formation
I. Jump rope. Students must jump rope for 3 minutes.	I. Free
II. Basketball skills with a partner. Practicing dribbling, guarding, passing and gaining possession of the ball. Students will be shown the guarding position and they will practice with their partner taking turns.	
III. Modified basketball game 3 on 3 or 4 on 4 will play at the baskets keeping score.	II. Small groups

Safety: No horse play, no slapping the balls or kicking.

References

1. Arnheim, D. and R. Pestolesi. *Elementary Physical Education*. St. Louis: The C. V. Mosby Company, 1978.
2. Burton, E. *The New Physical Education for Elementary School Children*. Boston: Houghton Mifflin Co., 1977.
3. Cochran, N., et. al. *A Teacher's Guide to Elementary School Physical Education*. Dubuque: Kendall/Hunt, 1971.
4. Cochran, N., et. al. *Learning on the Move*. Dubuque: Kendall/Hunt Publishing Co., 1975.
5. Dauer, V. *Essential Movement Experiences for Preschool and Primary Children*. Minneapolis: Burgess Publishing Co., 1972.
6. Dauer, V. and R. Pangrazi. *Dynamic Physical Education for Elementary School Children*. Minneapolis: Burgess Publishing Co., 1975.
7. Fait, H. *Physical Education for the Elementary School Child*. Philadelphia: W. B. Saunders Co., 1976.
8. Kirchner, G. *Physical Education for Elementary School Children*. Dubuque: Wm. C. Brown Co., 1974.
9. Larson, L. (Ed.) *Knowledge and Understanding in Physical Education*. Washington: AAHPERD, 1973.
10. Seagraves, M. *Move to Learn*. Winston-Salem: Hunter Publishing Co., 1979.

STUDENT ACTIVITIES

1. Write an original lesson plan for fifth or sixth grade children.

   Goal:

   Objective:

   Activity   Formation

2. Observe a fifth or sixth grade class and record your observations of one child on the form below.

   Length of Class _____ Sex of observed child _____

   Activities presented:

   Number of interactions with other children _____

   Amount of time child spent in activity _____

   Behavior of child — record behavior being exhibited every 3 minutes or record all unique episodes of behavior.

CHAPTER 11
CHILDREN'S DANCE
by
Fran Meyer
Hugh Mercer Elementary School
Fredericksburg, Virginia

    This chapter is devoted to children's dance for grades one through six. Dance and particularly dance for upper elementary children is an often neglected area in elementary physical education. The activities presented in this chapter were used by the author with children in a normal public school setting. There are three age groupings, first and second graders, third and fourth graders, and fifth and sixth graders. Activities, however, can cut across all three age divisions. Children who complete the activities presented in this chapter should be able to accomplish the following goals:
1. Perform a self-designed creative dance composition which coordinates movement, spatial, and rhythmic elements.
2. Develop flexibility, muscular strength and endurance, balance and body coordination through various styles of movement, i.e., mime, modern dance, and jazz dance.
3. Develop social skills through small and large group interaction.
4. Learn how dance/movement correlates with subject areas such as art, music, language arts, health, mathematics, and science.

DANCE ACTIVITIES
1st and 2nd Grade Level

Goal	Skills	Activities
The student will demonstrate a knowledge of the body parts relating to movement	The ability to touch and move each body part: head, ear, eye, nose, mouth, neck, shoulder, arm, elbow, wrist, hand, finger, palm, thumb, torso, back, chest, waist, stomach, hip, leg, thigh, knee, calf, ankle, foot, toe	Following cues from the teacher, the child will place a hand on each body part named. As the child becomes familiar with the body, the speed of touching and naming each body part may be increased, the activity may be done with the eyes closed, and a variety of ways to move each body part may be experienced. Chants or songs may be used to reinforce the vocabulary, improve movement of each isolated body part, and help children understand the relationship of one part to another; "The toe bone is connected to the foot bone, the foot bone is connected to the ankle bone, the ankle bone is connected to the leg bone, etc." (continue until all the parts have been named) This chant may be repeated for as many body parts as desirable: "Here is my head, here is my head. I can move it this way, I can move it that way. I can keep it moving, then I'll stop." GAME: RAGGEDY ANN AND ANDY The child will position the body parts and "freeze" following the visual or tactual cues of the teacher. As the body part is moved, the child will call out the name of the part. GAME: BODY SCULPTURE Each child has a partner. The teacher, or leader, makes a call to form a body sculpture while touching knee to knee, right hand to right hand, head to head, etc. Signal a change to a new partner.
The student will develop a movement vocabulary while experiencing movement through space	The ability to jump, hop, leap, walk, run, gallop, slide, skip	Following cues from the teacher, the child will perform each skill moving in and through the spaces of the room. Each skill may be practiced many ways. "Move as though you are walking through deep snow (quick sand, water, oil, hot sand, on eggs, on a tight rope, on the moon, etc.)." "Jump with both feet as high (low, quietly, loudly, or far apart, etc.) as possible."
The student will develop a movement vocabulary while experiencing movement in space	The ability to swing, bend, stretch, push, pull, twist, turn, shake, bounce	Following cues from the teacher, the child will perform each skill while moving within space. "How far can you stretch each part of the body?" "Bend one body part (a second, third, etc.). Stretch each part, one at a time, on the drum signal."

Goal	Skills	Activities
		"Can you make one body part into a very twisted position? Can you move the body part while it is twisted?"
The student will perform compositions which use variations of locomotor and non-locomotor movements	The ability to manipulate the body and remember movement patterns	The child will select one locomotor and/or non-locomotor skill to create a movement pattern. The skill will be varied many ways. A drum beat will signal a change: "Can you run very fast? Can you make very big running steps? How low to the floor can you run? Can you run using very small steps?" Repeat the running pattern.

"How can you swing one body part? Can you swing a second body part? Try to swing two body parts which are on opposite sides of the body." Repeat the movement pattern. "Can you hop? (Can you hop a different way on the other foot?) Can you twist an arm and move it? Can and you twist and move a leg while doing a low hop? Try to twist and move the torso." Repeat the movement pattern.

GAME: SKATING PARTY The children will hold hands in groups of 2's or 3's. A movement composition will be created using variations of hops, slides, gallops, skips, etc. (for example, slide 8 steps, hop 4 times on each foot, skip in a circle.) The children move through the spaces among the other sets of skaters. |
| The student will demonstrate a knowledge of the spatial elements relating to movement | The ability to move the body in a variety of directions: up, down, forward, backward, sideward — right and left | The child will experience directional changes while practicing various locomotor and non-locomotor skills: "Can you walk backward while moving (weaving) around your classmates without touching anyone?" "Can you run while moving in a sideward direction?" "While moving the body forward, can you move the arms up and down?"

GAME: SKATING PARTY This activity may be reviewed. |
| | The ability to vary the range of movement | The child will vary the degree of movement while performing movement patterns: "Can you reach high for the sun and pull it closer to your body?" "The body is a gigantic balloon that can enlarge and shrink at varying speeds." Emphasize differences in the body extensions with the speed changes. "Make the body as large as possible. How can you move across the floor?" "Can you move with a very small body?" |

270 Dance

Goal	Skills	Activities
		Select two body parts. Attempt to stretch the parts away from each other. Repeat the stretches with several different body parts.
	The ability to move in and through space on various levels and planes	Following cues from the teacher, the child will practice locomotor and non-locomotor skills on low, medium, and high levels: "While staying in one place, can you 'freeze' the body on a high level?" What about a low level? A medium level? Continue the questioning to vary movement of each body part on different levels. "Begin movement on a medium level. On the signal (drum beat, clap, etc.) change the movement to a different level." Repeat several times. "Begin moving through the spaces around your classmates (weaving). Change to a different level of movement when you pass a classmate that is on the same level as you."
	The ability to establish a direction by focusing the eyes at a particular point in the room or area in space	Various body parts may be used as focal points while moving through or in space: "Watch the hand carefully as it moves up, down, away from your body, or toward you. Give the hand movement your full attention." "Watch your partner's hands as you move around the room. Though you may change levels, continue looking at the same place."
		Various points in the room or in space may be used as a focal point: "Choose a corner in the room. Look at the corner as you move toward it." Focusing away from an area while moving toward it may also be experienced. "Watch an imaginary ball as it rolls to you and away from you. Continue to watch it as it bounces across the ground or moves through the air. Can you watch the imaginary ball while you and a partner throw it back and forth?"
	The ability to perceive a floor pattern using lines in straight and circular forms	The child will select a non-locomotor activity which will move a body part in a straight (then circular) pattern.
		The teacher may show a flashcard of a locomotor movement that may be used to describe a selected path.
		Individually or with a partner, the child will use a rope on the floor to demonstrate a straight path, curved path, and/or geometric shape (square,

Goal	Skills	Activities
		circle, triangle, rectangle) which can be described through non-locomotor and locomotor movements. The floor patterns may vary in size.
	The ability to perceive the body as a three-dimensional object which can make sharp, angular shapes or smooth, curved shapes	Using a rope or heavy cord, the child will make a rounded shape (or angular figure) on the floor. The body will be molded to fit the shape. Each child will then form the shape again away from the rope. The child will experience other ways to demonstrate the same form (i.e., lying on the back or stomach, kneeling, squatting, standing, etc.).
		A child will lie on the floor and model many angular (rounded or a combination of the two) shapes. A partner will outline the body with the rope and then attempt to make the same form in another way (standing, sitting, or kneeling). The model may compare the shapes left by the rope form and the partner.
The student will identify the rhythmic elements of time and force as they relate to movement/dance	The ability to recognize the move in slow, fast, and moderate speed patterns	The child will experience changes in tempo while practicing non-locomotor movements: "Perform a swing at a moderate speed. Perform it slowly and then quickly." Level and directional changes may vary the movement.
		In partners, one child will move very slowly while the other moves fast. Percussive sounds or recorded accompaniment may stimulate interest.
		GAME: FOLLOW ME One child leads the group (of 4-6) in a variety of movements around the room, often changing the tempo of the movement. Each child has the opportunity to be the leader.
		GAME: ME AND MY SHADOW One child is the leader with the partner (shadow) beside or behind. The leader will move in place and through the spaces of the room, varying the tempo of the movements. Each child will be the leader and the shadow. Percussive sounds or recorded accompaniment may modify the activity.
		GAME: SLOW MOTION DODGEBALL One half the class forms a large circle around the other half of the class. One child acts as the ball being thrown at the targets in the center of the circle. All movements must be in slow motion.
	The ability to recognize the amount of force needed to perform specific movements	The child will describe these words through movement: light, heavy, strong, weak, loud, soft, jerky, smooth, etc.

Goal	Skills	Activities
		Varying degrees of intensity will be performed through tense and relaxation activities. While lying on the floor, specific body parts are tightened four to six seconds then released (relaxed). Later, start with the head, tighten each body part moving down the body to the toes. Relax the muscles in reverse. This will be done with the eyes opened and closed.
		Divide the class into two groups. One group will yell loudly, "Hello!" to a second group that will softly say "hello." The groups will demonstrate the contrast of loud (strong) and soft (weak) through movement. The groups will switch roles.
		GAME: WIND-UP TOY The child's body has become a mechanical toy that must be wound to move. The toy moves very strong and fast at first. As it winds down, the movements are slower and weaker.
	The ability to recognize the pulse (underlying beat) of a movement and music pattern	Using a steady drum beat, have the children clap on every beat. A tap on the floor, slap on a body part, or a silent clap can modify the activity. Change the tempo of the drum beat.
		Using a steady drum beat, the child will perform a non-locomotor movement or a locomotor step on every beat.
		Select a familiar song (i.e., "Old MacDonald Had A Farm," "Twinkle, Twinkle, Little Star," etc.) and clap, tap, or slap the underlying beat.
		GAME: PASS IT ON The class is seated in a circle with an object placed in front of each child. On the beat, each person places an object in front of the person to the left. Continue until the signal is given to pass the objects to the right. The children place the objects and change directions without missing a beat.
	The ability to identify and move even and uneven rhythmic patterns (duration)	The children will repeat the even and uneven rhythmic patterns clapped by the teacher. (i.e., claps; claps; body slaps; body slaps)
		The children will clap the repeated rhythmic pattern of their classmates names, as well as their own (i.e., *Da mi an Sams; Chris to pher Clue; Ma ri anne Cling er*). The children will think of movements to go with their name (i.e., DA-MI-AN SAMS might be: jump hop hop leap).

Goal	Skills	Activities
		GAME: SPOTLIGHT A child will be selected to demonstrate a repeating movement pattern to go with his name while the classmates clap the rhythmic pattern several times. The performer then selects the next classmate to be "spotlighted." The group size may vary.
		The child will clap the rhythmic pattern of a favorite song or nursery rhyme.
	The ability to recognize and perform movement in measures.	Select a grouping of beats, possibly 3, 4, or 5. Listen to the rhythm. The children will clap for one grouping of beats. Repeat it several times. Substitute a non-locomotor or locomotor movement for the claps: "Walk forward as the drum beats. Stop when the drum beat stops." Repeat several times. "The next time the drum beat stops continue the movement for the same number of beats." Repeat several times. "During the next set, walk forward on the first grouping of beats, backward on the second grouping, low on the third set, and high on the fourth set." Vary the movement for each measure: "Jump backward on the first set, turn low on the second set, jump forward on the third set."
		Chants or action songs which call for a new movement with each measure may be created and experienced (for example, "I can move high; I can move low; 'round and 'round and then up and down"). The child will have an opportunity to create many ways to move high, low, around, up and down.
	The ability to perform accented measures of movement.	Listen to an accented meter with a drum beat. The children will tell which beat is emphasized the most. Hand claps, body slaps, cymbals, bells, etc. may be substituted for the drum beat. The children may compose their own accented meter.
		In small groups, each child will select non-locomotor and locomotor movements to perform in accented measures. Others in the group will watch and listen to determine the accented beat.
	The ability to recognize and perform movement in phrases.	The child will select a locomotor skill to develop a measure of movement. There will be a directional change with each measure (3 or 4). Repeat the movement pattern. "Run forward 4 beats, backward 4 beats, in a circle 4 beats, Repeat." "Jump to the right 4 times, forward 4 times, backward 4 times, to the left 4 times. Repeat."

274 Dance

Goal	Skills	Activities
		Each child will compose a measure of movement (3, 4, or 5 beats) to teach the others in their group of 3 or 4 students. The group will perform each child's meter consecutively.
The student will participate in a variety of movement/dance activities.	The ability to move efficiently while performing activities to develop balance, strength, flexibility, and coordination.	"Can you stand with the arms by the side and raise the body to a balance on the toes of both feet? How long can you balance? Try it with the arms out from the sides. Try it with the eyes closed." The balances will be attempted using each foot separately.

"How many body parts can you swing while continuing to balance?" Vary the tempo and direction of the swing.

"Can you swing an arm and a leg on the same side of the body?" Try swings with an arm and a leg on the opposite sides of the body." Vary the level of the body while experiencing the swings.

The children experience non-locomotor movement with a bean bag balanced on the head. Level, tempo, and directional changes will be practiced.

"While lying on the stomach, can you raise the arms and legs off the floor as though you are a plane taking off and moving through the air?"

"From the stomach-lying position, can you think of a way to stand and return to the floor without bending the knees?"

"Can you make your body like a piece of elastic? Stretch each body part away from the center of the body." Each part may be stretched separately or with two or more simultaneously. The stretches may be performed in the standing, kneeling, sitting, or lying positions.

"Grasp the hands very tightly and pull them apart slowly." Try it with each finger and thumb. "Grasp the foot with the hand and slowly pull them apart." Allow one, two, or three body parts to come together and move away from each other as far as possible. Repeat each movement several times.

"Can you let your body fall almost to the floor and then suddenly pull it back up to a stand?" Discover many ways to collapse and rise.

"How many ways can you roll your body? Can you roll several times and stop on the stomach (back, etc.)?" "How many different rolls can

Goal	Skills	Activities
		you do across the room without touching another classmate?"
		"Can you move one part of the body without moving any other part?" Try it several times at varying levels and speeds.
		"The body can become many different shapes, forms, and sizes. Can you describe the shape of a rock (tree, balloon, ball, pancake, arrow, log, etc.) with your body?" Flashcards with pictures or names may enhance the experience.
	The ability to move efficiently through the spaces and across the room	Traveling across the floor may be done many ways. WALK: slowly, quickly, heavily, lightly, high, low, happily, sadly, or thinly; on the toes, heels, sides of the feet; through water, deep snow, mud; as a puppet, glass man, robot, skater; or combine the walk with a clap in the front (back), a knee slap, a pointed toe and a stretched foot, etc. JUMPS: high, low, quietly, loudly, small, big; as a frog, rabbit, grasshopper; with the legs straight, body twisted, feet crossed, knees lifted on the jump, or with the feet apart (front and back, sideward). Other traveling steps will include the hop, leap, run, slide, gallop, and skip.
		Non-locomotor movements may be combined with the traveling steps: Jump and turn; skip and swing; run and collapse; hop and clap; walk and stretch, etc. The size of the action, tempo, force, direction, and level of movement will modify the activity.
	The ability to compose interpretive responses	Action words may be described through movement: push, pull, freeze, melt, shrivel, shrink, grow, lift, explode, strike, twirl, spin, dart, fly, swoop, shake, rocking, vibrate, etc.
		Poems, fairytales, nursery rhymes, and songs may offer stimuli for interpretation.
		The children will guess which community helper (police officer, fire fighter, mechanic, dentist, postal carrier, etc.) is being described by a classmate. Other environmental situations may be interpreted: drifting in the wind, shoveling snow, digging, ironing, climbing ladders, sawing wood, hammering nails, or playing games.
	The ability to solve problems and create situations	*The Toy Store* The children are toys that have come to life when the toymaker goes to sleep.

Goal	Skills	Activities
		The Bakery One partner is the baker and the other is the cookie mix. The batter is made into a cookie person that comes to life to dance with the baker. Each group creates a different ending for the dance.
		The Slinky After watching the movement of a toy slinky, the children will attempt to move the same way.
		The Fire Individually, with a partner, or in small groups, the movement of a fire will be described.
		The Present Describe, through movement, the contents of a beautifully wrapped present.
		GAME: FIVE QUESTIONS This game may be played in small groups or as a class. Place an object into a large bag. The leader handles the object without looking at it. Five questions are then asked by the group to determine the contents of the bag (i.e., How does it feel? What is the size? What is the shape? What noise can it make? What is it used for?). Responses are made through movement and verbal sounds, though talking is not allowed. Following the questions, each player is allowed one guess. The first child with the correct guess is the new leader. If no one solves the problem, the leader selects the next person to proceed.
The student will demonstrate an understanding of himself and a respect for others	The ability to understand emotions and moods	The children will describe, through movement, situations that have been happy (sad, painful, angry, scared, excited). If students also wish to verbalize the emotional experience, small group settings may be organized.
		In a large group, make a list of happy (sad, painful, angry, scared, excited) occasions. Divide the class into groups of two, three, or four students. Each group selects an occasion to describe through movement.
	The ability to show respect to another individual	List different ways that "Hello!" ("Good bye") might be demonstrated through movement. Walk to each classmate and demonstrate a "Hello" (or "Good bye").
		GAME: PLEASE AND THANK YOU Several props (i.e., hula hoop, scarf, wand, box, sack, hat, balloon, jump rope, etc.) are placed in the center of each small group. There should be one object per child. Each pupil in turn may obtain a prop by asking "John, may I *please* have the _____?" Upon receiving the prop a "Thank you" is stated.

Goal	Skills	Activities
		The person passing out the props responds with "You are welcome." The dialogue continues until each child has received a prop. Two to three minutes will be allowed for exploration and experimentation with the prop. The objects are placed in the center again. The children ask for a different prop each successive turn.
		GAME: EXCUSE ME Children travel in and through the spaces among the classmates. Each time a person moves in front of someone "Excuse me" must be stated. "I'm sorry" is stated when an accidental touching occurs. A child must sit out of the game if he neglects to say "Excuse me" or if he collects two "I'm sorry." A new game is started every two to three minutes. The object is for each child to play every game and stay in the game as long as possible.
	The ability to cooperate	GAME: RAFTING Carpet squares may be used as a raft. Start with a large raft and take squares away to make it smaller. The idea is to get all the children on the smallest raft possible. A story can be created to explain the decreasing raft size and the importance of keeping everyone on the raft.
		GAME: THE ROBOT Partners are needed for this activity. A humming robot has been built by the clever scientist in one of the laboratories. The robot cannot see and must be taken around many obstacles (boxes, chairs, tables, etc.) to reach a second laboratory to receive the eyes. The scientist must tell the robot how to progress (forward, backward, right, left, stop, go, etc.) in order to reach the described goal. The robot does not hum when stationary. If the robot touches an obstacle it will break apart and cannot continue. Each child will play both roles. Try it with other classmates.
		GAME: LINE UP The class is divided into several groups which form lines by placing the hands on the waist or shoulder of the person in front. The group moves in unison (forward, backward, sideward, or in a circle). Lines may also be formed with the children standing side by side.
Safety will be demonstrated throughout the school term	The ability to listen and follow directions	The student will respond to the teacher's questions, problems, and commands as carefully as possible.
		Props and equipment will be used in the designated areas.

Goal	Skills	Activities
	The ability to recognize ways to create a safe environment	Make a list of things that can be done to create a safe environment in the community, at home, or at school. In small groups, select an item to portray for the class: putting toys in the proper place, cleaning the dishes, keeping books and paper out of the walking areas, crossing the streets and roads carefully, playing away from traffic, or riding one person on a bike.
		Make a list of community people who work to create a safe environment (sanitation worker, police officer, fire fighter, rescue squad member, county agent — farm and home consultant, etc.). Discuss the importance of the individuals in these careers. Select a job and demonstrate it through movement.
The student will explore the use of props and sounds in movement/dance compositions.	The ability to create movement sequences from themes involving props	Props such as chairs, chorus risers, sturdy wooden boxes, cardboard boxes, towels, small soft scarfs, crepe paper streamers, chinese jump ropes, beach balls, hats, hula hoops, lumni sticks, benches, balloons, sacks, carpet squares, costumes, etc. may be used. There will be a prop for each child. Allow time for exploring the qualities of the prop: the shape, size, feel, the spaces created with the prop, or possibly the sounds derived from the object. Explore the movement possibilities: "Can the prop be moved?" "Can the body move with, over, under, around, in, or through the prop?" Discovering the potential use of a prop may be enhanced through a variety of questions and problems.
		Ask the children to remember some of the movements they have discovered while exploring the props. Share three, four, or five of the favorite movements with the class.
		Explore the effect on movement quality when the speed, direction, and level of activity is changed.
		Experience the use of one prop for two children.
	The ability to create a movement sequence involving verbal sounds, sticks or wands, songs, chants, poems, etc.	Discover movements of the body that can create sounds (i.e., hands clap, body slap, finger snap, foot stamp, hand tap on the floor or desk, etc.) "Can you add a traveling movement to the sound?" "How many traveling movements can you add to one sound?" (hand clap on each step of a walk, run, jump, leap, slide) "Make a sound with each step of your favorite locomotor movements. Change the sound when you do a different locomotor skill."

Goal	Skills	Activities
		Axial and traveling movements may be combined with verbal sounds (clucking, lip flap — caused by expelling air through the closed mouth, tongue roll, etc.) and a variety of lumni stick sounds (tapping on the side and end, hitting on the floor, brushes along the stick, etc.). "Think of a movement that will describe each sound you have discovered."
		A chant may be created as a stimulus for movement. "Walk, walk, walk, walk, all around the room. Jump, jump, jump, jump. Then make a great big BOOM. (Sit on the BOOM) Leap, leap, leap, leap, all around the room. Run, run, run, run. Then make a great big BOOM." Other locomotor movements and non-locomotor skills may be performed. Songs may be developed from the chants.
		Familiar songs may motivate children to move: "London Bridge," "Hokey Pokey," "Old MacDonald Had a Farm," "Three Blind Mice"
		Poetry and verse also foster creative movement. Selections from A.A. Milne's "When We Were Very Young" and "Now We Are Six" motivate children to move.
The student will perform many movement studies and dances within an informal situation (regular class meeting).	The ability to remember sequences and perform in front of peers	The student will perform at least once during each class period individually, with a partner, or in a small group. The performance may be structured or improvisational.
The student will perform a minimum of two formal movement study/ dance presentations.	The ability to remember sequences, move with quality, and perform for the community and peers.	Schedule times for 2-3 classes to share their compositions.
		Schedule assemblies in which students may show their work to the entire student body.
		Schedule afternoon or evening performances that will allow the parents and community to view the movement studies and dance compositions.
The student will be exposed to movement and dance styles on various levels of performance.	The ability to evaluate the quality of movement.	Brief question-answer sessions will follow slide shows, films, and videotapes of professional, collegiate, high school, and elementary performers.
		Resource people (community, collegiate, or professional) may enhance the dance curriculum by presenting assembly programs which allow the children to actively participate.

280　*Dance*

Goal	Skills	Activities
The students will demonstrate respect for entertainers during all performances, informal (classroom) and formal (inter-class, assemblies, and concerts).	The ability to remain seated and quiet during performances	Constant reminders by the classroom teachers, administrators, and parents are necessary. Stress audience behavior within the classroom setting for the informal performances. Performances should be applicable for the age level.
	The ability to react appropriately to situations which are comical and those which can be demoralizing	Class discussion and sensitivity talks will be held. Emphasis on the positive aspects of skill performance, creative composing, and general attitude will be paramount.
The student will identify relationships between dance and art.	The ability to recognize lines as they relate to the body and movement	Use paper and pencil, rope, or string to form a straight (or curved) line. Move the body in the path designated by the line. Change the level of movement.
	The ability to relate movement to concepts	Geometric shapes (circle, square, triangle, rectangle) or abstract forms may be designated with the string, rope, or pencil and paper. "How can you describe the shape or form with the body?" "How can you describe the design through movement?" Flashcards of shapes and forms may be used to initiate movement. The children will divide themselves into groups according to the color of their shoes (shirts, pants, hair, eyes). Each group will select a geometric shape or abstract form and draw it on a sheet of paper. Every group, in turn, will describe the shape through movement. The children will divide the class into groups of three or four according to height. The groups will develop a body sculpture that will represent far away (close together, large, small, etc.). The sculpture may also be formed with children of very different sizes. GAME: THE PICTURE Divide the class into groups. Each group will receive a picture to describe as a still life using the bodies as parts of the picture. The picture should have simple lines and figures. If there is a picture of goats on a hillside, the children may portray the goats, rock, and plant life. Allow the class to see each group's still life, the picture, and the still life again. Compare the line, sizes, and shapes of the picture and the still life.

Goal	Skills	Activities
The student will identify relationships between physical performance and music	Skills for this are listed throughout the curriculum	Activities for this are listed throughout the curriculum.
The student will demonstrate relationships between dance and language arts	The ability to identify letters of the alphabet	Individually, with a partner, or in small groups, the children will form each letter of the alphabet. Flashcards may be used to stimulate the students.

The children will move through space to form each letter of the alphabet. Letters of the child's name may also be formed in and through space. |
| | The ability to follow directions and to arrange movement into a logical sequence | Following the one-step directions of the teacher, the children will sit in a chair, move to the left of it, to the right of it, over, under, and around the chair. The sequence may be continued and varied.

GAME: ECHO The children will repeat the movement pattern (three to four movements within a series) demonstrated by the teacher or a student.

The sequence of a favorite fairytale, nursery rhyme, Aesop fable, walk through the school, or visit to the zoo may be described through movement: "Goldilocks and the Three Bears" "Little Red Riding Hood" "The Three Little Pigs" "Little Miss Muffet" "Humpty Dumpty" "While walking around and through the school, many things were seen. Trees were swaying to and fro, ants were marching by the walk, leaves were moving across the ground. The custodian was working hard and the secretary typed a letter. Children were working at the desk, some were having recess and others were eating lunch." The story may be as long as desired.

GAME: LION HUNT The teacher will begin telling the story. The children will repeat each line of the story and describe the actions of the story through movement. Teacher: "Let's go on a lion hunt." Children: "Let's go on a lion hunt." Teacher: "Ready, let's go." Children: "Ready, let's go." Experiences encountered along the way may include: swimming a wide river; sloshing through the swamp; getting stuck in the quicksand; sneaking past a rhino, snake, and a panther; climbing a tree for nuts; reaching for fruit and berries; going through the hot jungle; all of this just to be chased back to the camp by a family of lions (quickly reverse all the previously taken actions). |

Goal	Skills	Activities
	The ability to recognize words by sight	The children will demonstrate action words listed on flashcards: run, walk, jump, leap, skip, gallop, slide, swing, bounce, shake, twist, turn, bent, stretch, fly, swoop, rock, vibrate, melt, freeze, etc.
	The ability to identify similarities and differences	GAME: SOUNDS LIKE The teacher or leader will call out a word, "HAT." The children will act out a word that sounds like hat (sat, fat, flat, etc.) Other examples might be: Letter — sweater, feather, weather Fair — bear, hair, chair, care Hour — flower, tower, sour Lip — clip, sip, flip, whip
		GAME: RAGDOLL AND STIFFMAN The ragdoll and the stiffman are the best of friends. Describe many everyday things they can do. Show how differently each might do the same activity, such as walking down the street, or moving up stairs.
		GAME: ANIMAL CRACKERS The leader will whisper in each child's ear either "cow" or "duck." On the signal, each child closes the eyes and makes the appropriate sound of the assigned animal. Like animals try to group themselves. VARIATION: Other types of animal sounds, musical instrument sounds, environmental sounds, or phonetic sounds may be used.
The student will identify relationships between dance and health.	The ability to identify nutritious foods	Class discussion concerning the importance of a good diet will be held.
		Make a "good food" list. Each child will select a food from the list and describe it for a small group. After guessing the chosen food, the children will name the food group to which it belongs.
		The class will make a list of good health habits that will be described through movement individually or in small groups.
The student will demonstrate relationships between science and dance activities.	The ability to determine the effects of the weather	"How would you walk if the weather was: sunny, windy, raining, very hot, very cold, stormy, or snowy?"
		"If you were a big balloon, how would you be affected by gusts of wind, a hard rain, or the bright warm sun.
	The ability to recognize like things in the environment	Each child selects an animal picture or name from a box. A movement to describe the animal is decided. The children attempt to group them-

Goal	Skills	Activities
		selves by watching each classmate's movement. Do not change the movement once the "search" for like animals has begun. Auditory cues may not be used. When everyone is in the group, show the picture or name selected and discuss the movement patterns which affected the child's decision to select the group they did. VARIATION: Plants, machines, or appliances with moving parts may be substituted for animals.
The student will identify relationships between mathematical concepts and dance activities	The ability to identify and form numerals	The children will be grouped by two, three, or four students. The leader will select a number from the hat. The groups will form a body sculpture of the numeral.
		GAME: SCRAMBLE The children will randomly walk (hop, jump, skip, etc.) through the spaces among the classmates. The teacher or leader holds up a card of a single digit number. The children must get with other students to form a group of that number before the leader says, "Scramble, scramble, get to your number. Scramble, scramble, then you stop." Everyone stops. Any student who is not in a correctly numbered group must sit out until the next number appears for the scramble. The leader will call out the new movement to be performed before the next number appears.
		"How far can you count while balancing three body parts on the floor?" Try balancing one, two, four, five or more body parts on the floor while counting as high as possible on each balance.
	The ability to identify the relationship between two numbers	GAME: COMING HOME Each child is assigned a number and a home spot. The leader will make an assignment to the group: "All numbers greater than four (or less than four) gallop to the opposite wall and return home." "All numbers less than two perform a locomotor movement and a non-locomotor movement and return home." The leader will assign a new movement for each "greater than" and "less than" relationship.
	The ability to count by 5's and 10's	A set of numbers will be assigned to each child. The numbers, which go to 100 by 5's (or 10's) will be scattered on the floor. As each child progresses to each number consecutively, a new movement is performed (skip to 5, leap to 10, slide to 15, etc.) Movement to each number may be reversed.
	The ability to tell time to the nearest hour and half hour	Each child will form a circle with a rope, string, or chalk drawn line on the floor. The numbers will be placed at the boundary to make the face of the

Goal	Skills	Activities
		clock. While sitting in the center, the child will use the right arm as the hour hand and the left arm as the minute hand. The leader will direct the children to demonstrate various times to the nearest hour and half hour.
		The class will compose a "Clock Dance." Children will stand in the position of the clock numbers. Two classmates will stand in the center to represent the hands of a clock. The "hands" will move around the clock. When the hands stop, everyone will call out the time. The children representing the time will perform and improvise dance movement or a previously choreographed movement. Recorded accompaniment may be used.
The student will demonstrate a relationship between creative dance experiences and social studies.	The ability to understand and describe customs of the community	There will be a class discussion of the pioneers of the local community. The children may compose dances to describe the struggles and happy times of the forefathers.
		The children will describe methods of communication (or transportation) that are important to the individuals within the community. "How can you describe a telephone, newspaper, radio, television, or postal carrier through movement?" "Choose one form of communication, can you show how it is important to the everyday life?"
		School and resource individuals can assist children to understand the similarities and differences in the customs of farm, city, or seaside communities. The lifestyle of the various communities may be described through movement.

EVALUATION

Teacher observation, checklists, videotape recordings and student observations may be utilized to evaluate student responses.

DANCE ACTIVITIES
3rd and 4th Grade Level

Goal	Skills	Activities
Review terminology for the basic non-locomotor and locomotor movements.	Walk, jump, hop, leap, swing, bend, stretch, push, pull, twist, turn, shake, bounce	Following cues of the teacher, the child will perform each skill moving randomly in and through spaces of the room and in structured lines across the room.
Review combinations of basic non-locomotor and locomotor movement.	The ability skip, gallop, slide, prance, rise, fall, roll, bounce and walk, skip and shake, hop and turn, swing and jump, run and twist, etc.	Following cues from the teacher, the child will perform each combination moving randomly in and through spaces of the room and/or in structured lines across the room.
The student will perform compositions individually and with a partner using at least two locomotor skills within a movement pattern.	The ability to manipulate the body in sequential movement patterns	The child will create and perform his own movement pattern: "Skip 3 steps, shake the hand 4 times, twist the torso 4 times, prance 6 steps."
	The ability to manipulate the body in a sequential movement pattern with another student	The child will teach his movement pattern to another student, learn the other student's movement pattern. The two will simultaneously perform each movement pattern.
The student will demonstrate a knowledge of the spatial elements relating to movement.	The ability to move the body in and through space: forward, backward, sideward—right and left, and in a circle	The child will experience directional changes while practicing various combinations of non-locomotor and locomotor skills: "Can you bend the body forward, skip and move backward?" "Can you twist the body, slide to the left, then the right?" "Swing one leg sideward, and hop forward." "With the elbows forward and moving in a circle, gallop around your classmates."
	The ability to vary the range of movement	The child will vary the degree of movement while performing movement combinations: "Can you make a circle with the arms?" "Extend the arms to make the circle larger." "Stretch the foot and leg forward to make the steps larger." "As you make a turn, open the legs and arms as wide as possible." "Perform the twist with a narrow movement, then a wide movement."
	The ability to move in and through space on various levels and planes.	The child will experience movement on a high, low, and medium level while performing variations of locomotor and non-locomotor movements: "Can you move backward on a medium level, with the elbow leading the movement?" "How can

Goal	Skills	Activities
		you move on a low level from one point to another point?" "Can you move on a high level using one locomotor and one non-locomotor movement simultaneously?" "How can you move from one point to another point using all levels and a different movement for each level?"
		GAME: STATUE Each child becomes a "statue" which uses all body parts. At the sound of the drum beat, a new statue is formed on a different level. No statue may be repeated two times consecutively. Lively background music may be added as a variation.
	The ability to establish a direction by focusing the eyes at a particular point in the room or area in space	The child will focus the eyes on a particular point and move toward it. Each time the focus is changed use a different locomotor and non-locomotor movement.
		As the children move across the floor the teacher will beat a loud sound on a drum to signal a change of focus.
		The children will focus on a particular body part as it leads movement through space: "Focus on the arm as it moves upward. Raise the body higher as a continuation of the movement." "Allow the arm to lead your movement on different levels in and through space."
	The ability to perceive a floor pattern using lines in straight, circular, square, or zigzag forms	The child will repeat a floor pattern demonstrated by the teacher.
		The child will repeat a floor pattern demonstrated by another student.
		The child will use paper and pencil to draw a floor pattern which has been demonstrated.
		The child will draw a floor pattern and compose movements that will move him through the pattern.
	The ability to perceive the body as a three-dimensional object which can make sharp, angular shapes or smooth, curved shapes.	Stand, sit, or kneel so the body can make as many corners as possible, count the angles. Release the angles and repeat them to the beat of the drum several times.
		Curve the limbs and torso to make the body round and smooth. Release the curves and repeat them to the sound of the drum (bells, tamborine, etc.) several times.
		Change the body from the angular to the round shapes, and back again. Feel the difference in

Goal	Skills	Activities
		the body spaces as the changes are made quickly, then slowly.
		Use the body to form geometric shapes of circles, ovals, squares, triangles, rectangles, and diamonds.
		Use partners and/or small groups to describe stationary and moving geometric shapes.
		The angular and curved shapes may vary direction and level as they move through space.
The student will identify the rhythmic elements of time and force as they relate to movement/dance.	The ability to recognize and move in slow, fast, and moderate speed patterns.	GAME: ECHO The child will repeat the rhythmic pattern clapped, stomped, body slapped, or finger snapped by the teacher or another student. VARIATION: The child will repeat a movement pattern by the teacher or another student.
		GAME: MIRROR IMAGERY Two children face each other. One is the leader, the other is the mirror. The mirror moves simultaneously with the leader performing locomotor and non-locomotor skills at varying speeds. The leader and mirror switch roles on cue from the teacher.
		The child will perform movement to nursery rhymes or story plays created by the teacher and/or students which demonstrate tempo variations.
		The child will perform a movement pattern created of locomotor and non-locomotor skills at a moderate, fast, and then slow tempo.
	The ability to recognize the pulse (underlying beat) of a movement and music pattern	Using a steady drum beat, have the children clap, snap, tap the floor, or slap a body part on every beat. Then combine sounds: clap on the first beat, snap on the second, tap the floor on the third and slap the body on the fourth beat. Change the rate of speed for the beats.
		Using a steady drum beat, have the children step on every beat. Vary the locomotor movement. Then combine movements: step on the first two beats, jump on the next two beats. Change the tempo.
		Use a disco or march record to move and/or step on every beat.
		GAME: POLICEMAN The police officer uses hand signals to direct the movement of the class. Children change directions without losing a beat. Changes in level and speed may vary the game.

Goal	Skills	Activities
		Instrumental or recorded accompaniment may be used.
	The ability to identify and move in even and uneven rhythmic patterns (duration)	Using two speed patterns, have the children sound out the pattern with claps, snaps, stamps, or slaps (i.e., *snap snap claps*).
		Using two speed patterns, have the children combine non-locomotor movement patterns (i.e., *stretch stretch 2 twists; bend bend 2 shakes*). Then use combinations of locomotor movements (walks and runs, jumps, and leaps, and/or walks and hops).
		GAME: ECHO The teacher claps or sound a rhythmic pattern and the children must echo the pattern. Non-locomotor and locomotor movements may be substituted for the sounds. Students may compose the patterns to be echoed.
	The ability to recognize and perform movement in measures	Select a grouping of drum beats, possibly 4, 6, or 8. Listen to the rhythm. The children will clap for one group of beats. Repeat it several times. Substitute other movements for the claps (slaps, snaps, stamps). Combine the sounds for the next responses: clap one measure, stamp a measure, snap the fingers another, and slap for another measure. Then allow the children to compose the order of the measures of sound.
		Repeat the above activity using locomotor and non-locomotor movements: "Walk forward 4 steps, skip backward 4 steps, leap sideward 4 times, and run 4 steps." "Swing 4 beats, jump 4 beats, turn 4 beats, and bend 4 beats." The children may compose their own measures of sound and movement.
		GAME: THIS IS WHAT I CAN DO This activity may be done with a partner, in small groups, or large groups. Each group creates a movement, sound, or a combination of movement and sounds to perform while chanting: This is what I can do. Everybody do it too. This is what I can do. Now, let's see you do it too." All other partners and/or groups say the chant and repeat the movement. New leaders are chosen until each group has the opportunity to perform.
	The ability to perform accented measures of movement	Select a meter with a drum beat, or disco record. Accent the first beat in each measure with a clap, stamp, or finger snap.
		Clap, stamp, or finger snap on each beat except the accented beat.
		Use locomotor and non-locomotor movements

Goal	Skills	Activities

to accent the beat: "clap, clap, clap, jump." "arm push, stamp, stamp, stamp."

Use locomotor movements on the non-accented beat with strong non-locomotor movements on the accented beat: "arm jab, walk, walk, walk." "jump, jump, jump, torso twist." Reverse the use of locomotor and non-locomotor movements: "swing, swing, slide, swing." "arm shake, jab three times, leap."

Direction may be changed on the accent. Level of movement may change on the accent.

GAME: THIS IS WHAT I CAN DO Divide the class into groups and assign each group a different beat to accent. Each group will perform the accented measures and say the chant (listed above). All other groups will perform the movement pattern without losing the beat.

| | The ability to recognize and perform movement in phrases | Listen to a record and clap at the end of each phrase. |

Put several measures of movement together into phrases: "Leap four steps, raise one leg for three beats and replace it on one beat, walk backward four steps." Repeat each phrase.

Using locomotor and non-locomotor movements the children may compose their own movement phrase. Alternate locomotor and non-locomotor movements each phrase.

Change levels and direction of movement with each phrase.

GAME SHADOW IMAGERY One person is the leader (standing, sitting, kneeling, or lying) with another person (the shadow) beside or behind. Using body sounds, locomotor, and non-locomotor movements, the leader performs a phrase of movement. The "shadow" performs simultaneously. At the end of each phrase, the leader and shadow switch roles.

| The student will learn a variety of movement/dance activities. | The ability to move efficiently while performing a series of mime movements to warm-up the body, develop flexibility, strength, balance, and coordination. | "Can you lie on the back and curl the knees to the chest? Now, stretch the legs straight out (about 6-inches off the floor) and lower the heels slowly." Repeat several times. |

"Kneel so you are sitting on the heels. Try to stretch the arms up and pull the body up on the knees. Now, sit and bring the arms by the side." Repeat several times.

Goal	Skills	Activities

"Can you sit so that one leg is straight in front and the other is bent at the knee beside the body? Try to stretch the torso over the straight leg so the nose will be as close to the knee as possible." This stretch may be done 4-8 times for each leg.

"Kneeling on all fours, can you contract the stomach (abdominal) muscles so the back is rounded? Release the back to straighten the spine." Repeat several times.

"See if you can stretch the neck muscles while performing a series of 'yes' and 'no' movements with the head."

"Raise and lower the eyebrows; wiggle the nose; move the eyeballs side to side, up and down; show a big smile, then a half smile."

"Shrug the shoulders up and down as though expressing 'I don't know'; move the shoulders in a circle forward and backward. Can you move each shoulder separately, then simultaneously?"

"Can you sit in tailor fashion with the arms at the side and move only the chest side to side several times? Can you move the chest forward and backward?"

"While standing, can you bend at the waist to touch the fingers or palms to the toes? See if you can get close to the toes with each long stretch."

"Can you stand with the arms outstretched and swing each leg forward, backward, and side to side? Can you do it wihtout moving any other part of the body?"

The ability to interpret words, moods, animal movements, jobs, nature, objects, etc., through movement

These interpretations may be performed individually, with a partner, or in small groups: Think of a movement or series of movements to describe the words: zap, pop, pow, zip, bang, tingle, ding, pluck, etc.

What movement or series of movements can be used to describe various moods: happy, sad, fear, pain, love, jealousy, etc.

How can animals be described through movement, such as the lion, ape, snake, dog, bird, elephant, etc.

Choose a job or career and describe it through movement.

Goal	Skills	Activities
		Describe the wonders of nature through a movement or series of movements: wind, rain, sun, stars, tornado.
		Select an object and describe it through movement: elevator, row boat, lawn mower, washing machines, etc.
	The ability to solve problems and create situations	Create and explore an imaginary wall.
		Move into and out of a box.
		Walk in place. Run in place.
		Individually, with a partner, or in groups, perform sport events in slow motion.
		Become a robot or mechanical person.
		Interpret nursery rhymes: "Jack Be Nimble," "Mary Had A Little Lamb," "There Was A Crooked Little Man," etc.
	The ability to move efficiently while performing a series of modern dance warm-up techniques to develop flexibility, balance, strength, and coordination.	FLOOR MOVEMENTS: "Can you sit with the soles of the feet touching and round the back to touch the head to the heels? Try to release (stretch) the back on a forward diagonal and move backward to a straight sitting position." Repeat the movement several times.
		"When you sit with the legs together and straight in front of you, can you stretch the torso over the thighs? Try holding the nose close to the knees for 6-8 counts. Return to a sitting position and repeat 5-6 times."
		"While lying on your back, can you pull in (contract) the stomach (abdominal) muscles so the lower spine will touch the floor? Hold the contraction several beats and release it. Try it several times."
		"In a kneeling position, with the arms by the side, try to contract the abdominal muscles, then release. Simultaneously with the release, circle the arms overhead."
		"Can you sit with the legs in an open position and stretch the torso over the thigh? Hold the nose close to the knee several beats (or counts). Release (straighten) the back and repeat the stretch to the other leg and to the center position. Try it several times."

Goal	Skills	Activities
		"While sitting with straight legs and the arms behind the back for support, point and flex the feet. Rotate the feet around the ankle. Repeat several times."
		STANDING MOVEMENTS: Knee Bends "With the arms curved in front of the body, twist the legs in the hip socket so the knees are 'turned outward.' Tuck the hips to straighten the spine and keep the heels close together, touching the floor. Remembering all this, bend and straighten the knees several times. Repeat the knee bends while circling the arms overhead. Remember to keep the legs turned out in hip socket."
		"Can you brush the foot along the floor til the toe is pointed and touching the floor? With the knee straight, slide the foot back to the beginning position and repeat it several times. Try the movement with each leg. Can you do it with each leg twisted in the hip socket so the foot is turned out? At a low level, a medium level, and a higher level?"
		"Can you jump and land very quietly with the feet close together and then open, side by side?" Try it several times with the legs twisted from the hip socket.
		"See if you can coordinate a torso twist and arm movement using a 6 count: 1, raise the curved arms overhead; 2, twist the torso to the left; 3, open the arms and stretch sideward; 4, return the torso to the front; 5 & 6, curve the arms to the front again. Repeat the torso twist to each side several times."
	The ability to move efficiently across the floor	"Try to walk forward with straight legs, stepping toe-heel and holding the body erect. The arms may be curved in front, stretched to the side, or moved in a circle." Similarly, a backward walk may be performed. "Can you stretch the leg backward and point the toe with each step?"
		Allow students to compose movement sequences combining locomotor and non-locomotor skills which travel across the floor. The feet and toes should be stretched and pointed during the movements. Instruments or recorded music may be used to accompany movement.
	The ability to perform controlled (quiet) falls and rolls	Perform a forward fall in slow motion, then sideward and backward.
		Perform rolls with the body as small as possible, as large as possible, as long as possible, etc.

Goal	Skills	Activities
		Combine the falls and rolls in a movement pattern: "Combine a sideward fall with a large roll." "Combine a backward fall with a small roll."
		Combine locomotor and non-locomotor movements with the falls and rolls: "Use a four beat meter to: slide 4 beats, fall sideward 4 beats, long roll for 4 beats, turn and rise for 4 beats, and repeat." "Compose a sequence of your own."
	The ability to move efficiently while performing a series of jazz warm-up activities, to develop flexibility, strength, balance, and coordination.	FLOOR MOVEMENTS: "Can you isolate the movements of the head and neck from the rest of the body? Move the head forward, backward, side to side several times. Now try it with the arms outstretched."
		"Can you sit in the tailor position and move only the shoulders up, down, forward, backward, and even in circles? Can you move them separately and simultaneously?"
		"Can you isolate the movement of the hands up, down, and side to side several times?"
		"While lying on the floor with the arms outstretched, can you lift both knees to the chest and return them to the beginning position? Try to repeat the movement 4-6 times with the toes pointed."
		"If you are lying on the floor, can you lift the chest (sternum) so it is the first body part to move upward and forward to a sitting position? Curve the back and return to the floor. Repeat the movement several times.
		"Try to bend and stretch the body so that it becomes a moving pretzel. Allow the chest (sternum) to lead the body movement up then forward so the nose is close to the knee. Stretch up to a sitting position, then curve the back to lie down. Lift both straight legs over the head so the pointed toe may touch the floor. Slowly and quietly return the straight legs and pointed toes back to the lying position."
		STANDING MOVEMENTS: "While standing with the arms comfortably at the side, the feet together in a parallel position, the heels on the floor, and the back straight—try to bend the knees and straighten the legs several times. Repeat the movement with the feet open comfortably to the side. Again, repeat the knee bends with the feet comfortably open one foot in front of the other."

Goal	Skills	Activities
		"When you stand with the feet apart and the hands on the front and side of the abdomen (pelvis), can you move only the hips (pelvis): side to side, forward and backward, in a circle? Now, try to lift the right hip and move it forward and back. Repeat it with the left hip."
		"While standing with the feet in a parallel position, try to move each knee front and back several times. Repeat the knee isolations with the feet in an open and parallel position. Can you move each knee separately, alternately, and in a circular motion?"
		"While standing with the hands on the waist, can you move only the rib cage side to side several times? Then try forward and backward movements. Can you move the rib cage in a circle?"
		"Stand straight and tall. Can you raise the heels to a high balance? Try raising and lowering the heels with the feet in a parallel turned out position. Try it with the feet close together and in an open position."
		"See if you can brush one leg forward and lunge onto the front foot. Point the toe as you do it. Push the front foot off the floor (try pointing the toe) and return to the beginning position. Try the lunges forward, sideward, and backward."
	The ability to move efficiently across the floor	Bounce walk using a hand clap or finger snap with each step.
		With each step of a walk, perform a pushing movement with the opposite hand. Vary the tempo. Then, push the same hand as the stepping foot. Vary the speed so a push using both hands may be done with each step.
		Tap Step Walk: tap the right foot by the left and step forward on the right foot. Tap the left foot by the right and step forward on the left foot. Vary the tempo.
		Hip Lift Walk: keep the stepping leg straight and the toe pointed as the hip is raised for the step forward.
		Prance: lift the knee high and point the toe with each hopping step. Prance 8 steps fast and 4 slow. Adding shoulder isolations and head movements may vary the movement.

Goal	Skills	Activities
		Add locomotor movements to various walks. The students can develop compositions consisting of walks with non-locomotor movements which emphasize isolating particular body parts.
The student will demonstrate an understanding of himself and a respect for others.	The ability to set realistic goals	The child will choose an admirable person and describe the emotional, social, and intellectual qualities of the individual through movement.
		In groups, a chant (which may be written in the classroom) and movement will be composed to explain "why rules exist."
		Several short and long term projects will be assigned which require varying degrees of self-discipline and organization.
	The ability to respect an individual's capabilities.	Compose a movement phrase in which all movement is performed backward or using the non-dominant side.
		After watching one or several student composition, the children will tell one good thing about each performance.
		Describe through movement your reaction to a person or group that: is physically handicapped, is not as intelligent as you, does not have as much money as your family, etc.
		Describe through movement how you react toward another person or group demonstrating anger, fear, loneliness, hate, jealousy, happiness, love, generosity, etc.?
	The ability to cooperate	In groups, the children will make the largest moving statue they can possibly make.
		In groups, the children will choose aparticular machine, animal, or mode of transportation to describe through movement.
		Assign each child a separate set of movements to perform within a small area. Students must decide how to share the practice space.
		Three to five minutes will be allowed for groups of 3-6 to compose a movement sequence 45-60 seconds long.
Good safety practices will be demonstrated.	The ability to listen and follow directions	The children will respond to the teacher's problems, questions, and commands as closely as possible.
		Props and equipment will be used in assigned areas.

Goal	Skills	Activities
	The ability to recognize and make judgement about creating safe environments	Falls, collapses, balances, and rolls will be controlled.
		While moving within a group, look for the open spaces.
		GAME: BUMPER CARS Each child is a special car. The computer which controls the special car has malfunctioned. The cars are bumping into the sides of other cars, rebounding, and bumping into another. It is a good idea to limit the points of contact for the bumper cars.
The student will learn activities which use props, sounds, and visuals of varying dimensions.	The ability to create movement sequences from themes involving props.	Props such as chairs, chorus risers, sturdy wooden boxes, Chinese jump ropes, beach balls, hats, small soft scarfs, hula hoops, lumni sticks, benches, balloons, sacks, carpet squares, transparent plastic wrap, etc., may be used: "The scarf may be held in one hand. Move it in a variety of circular and waving patterns. Change the direction, speed, and level of movement. Toss the scarf overhead, let go. Allow the body to drift downward with the scarf. The scarf may flow as locomotor movements are performed." Again, speed, direction, and level of movement may vary.
		Individually, with a partner, or in a small group, compose a movement study using combinations of these patterns. "Using your magic carpet square, compose a dance containing a series of twists, swings, bends, stretches, and turns, with 4-6 counts per movement." Limit the movement pattern to 6-8 measures. "Perform locomotor, non-locomotor, and combinations of the basic movements, using a selected prop." Limit the study to possibly 6-8 movements.
		GAME: MIRROR IMAGERY May be done with a partner or in a small group. It may be done in silence or with musical accompaniment. One person is the leader. The other person(s) will be the mirror(s). The leader and the mirror switch roles often. Encourage slow locomotor and non-locomotor movements at first so the mirror can easily follow the leader's movement.
		What story can be told through movement involving a selected prop?
	The ability to create movement sequences with imaginary props.	Compose a dance using sport skills which generally require a piece of equipment (i.e., basketball, tennis, soccer, fencing, etc.).
		List the movements a carpenter or farmer might go through during a day's activity and create a dance using the movements.

Goal	Skills	Activities
	The ability to create a movement sequence involving verbal sounds, sticks or wands, songs, chants, poems, readings, etc.	Think of movements to describe words like crack, zoom, bubble, punch, pow, ting, boom, zap. The child can make the sound while performing the movement. Create a dance of sounds.
		Children can perform movements to describe the action of a chant, song, reading, or poem. "Wands! Wands! Look at the wands! This is what we do with our wands!"
	The ability to use visuals to enhance dance movement	The child will use construction paper to make shapes and designs to be projected by an overhead projector as a background for a movement study/dance.
		Colored cellophane covering various shaped holes cut from construction paper and reflected by an overhead projector can be a background set: curved and/or angular shapes may be designed as a background for a dance about geometric shapes.
		Murals on a large sheet of paper can be a background for a dance.
		A clear glass dish with water and food coloring mixed (and maybe oil drops) can be projected as a background for a dance about water, microscopic life, etc.
The student will perform many movement studies and dances within an informal situation (regular class setting).	The ability to remember sequences and perform in front of peers.	The student will perform at least once during each class period individually, with a partner, or in a small group. The performance may be structured or improvisational.
The student will perform a minimum of two formal movement study/dance presentations.	The ability to remember sequences, move with quality, and perform for the community and peers.	Schedule times for 2-3 classes to share their compositions.
		Schedule assemblies in which students may show their work to the entire student body.
		Schedule afternoon or evening performances that will allow the parents and community to view the movement studies and dance compositions.
The student will explore movement and dance styles on various levels of performance.	The ability to evaluate the quality of movement.	Appropriate magazines and books concerning the various styles of movement will be on display in the gym, classroom, and/or library for required and/or enrichment reading.
		Question-Answer sessions will follow slide shows, films, and videotapes of professional, collegiate, high school, and elementary performers.

298 *Dance*

Goal	Skills	Activities
		Appropriate dance programs by professional and semi-professional groups with active participation by the students will be scheduled.
The student will demonstrate respect for entertainers during all performances, informal (classroom) and formal (inter-class, assemblies, and concerts)	The ability to remain seated and quiet during performances	Constant reminders by the classroom teachers, administrators, and parents are necessary. Stress audience behavior within the classroom setting for the informal performances. Performances should be applicable for the age level.
	The ability to react appropriately to situations which are comical and those which can be demoralizing	Class discussion and sensitivity talks will be held.
The student will identify relationships between dance and art	The ability to recognize and describe lines in movement	While moving through spaces, make many straight lines in the floor pattern. Now, make straight lines with the body while moving in straight lines through the room. Substitute curved, zig-zagged, dotted, dashed, or broken lines for straight lines.
	The ability to recognize and describe forms in and through movement	Choose a shape (circle, oval, square, triangle, or rectangle). "Can you use 3 body parts to draw the shape in space?" Use 2 locomotor movements to draw the shape through space, then make the form with the body. Add a second shape to the above composition. The movements may be combined by varying the tempo, direction, and level of movement.
	The ability to assign a movement to concepts	Choose a color. Think of 6-8 movements that might describe the color. Combine these movements into a dance. In partners, select a contrast (up-down, small-large, light-heavy, rough-smooth, etc.) and move to illustrate it.
The student will demonstrate a relationship between dance and language arts	The ability to organize and sequence movements/events	The children are given a list of movements or actions which must be placed into a logical order (i.e., perform a turn on the middle level, 8 jumps, melting fall, body sway, crawl, slow motion run, quick rise, roll).

Goal	Skills	Activities
	The ability to enhance word recognition and reading for comprehension	Station work requires children to read and translate the problems to be solved.
	The ability to improve writing skills (penmanship, spelling, punctuation, sentence structure)	The children will write, in sequential order, the movements of the study or dance. The children will write a story and compose a movement sequence which will tell the story. The children will write a chant, song, or poem to initiate or accompany dance movement.
	The ability to increase the creative thinking process	The teacher poses many problems which can be solved in a variety of ways.
The student will identify relationships between dance and health.	The knowledge and good health habits and posture are important in the quality of movement	Children will perform a movement sequence without any postural cues, then with postural cues. Class discussion will be held concerning the most efficient method for control. The children will be divided into groups. Each group makes a list of 4-5 good health practices, then describes them through movement. The rest of the class attempts to guess each group's list of good habits.
	The ability to identify anatomical parts: quadriceps, biceps, abdomin, hamstrings, gastrocnemius, skull, spine, ribs, humerus, carpals, pelvis, femur, tarsals	Identify the bones and muscles while chanting, touching, and moving the body part: "This is my ____. This is my ____. This is how I move (flex, stretch) my ____." Each child has an opportunity to name an anatomical part and decide a movement for the body part.
The student will demonstrate a relationship between mathematical concepts and dance activities.	The ability to know geometric shapes	Compose a movement sequence which includes a floor pattern consisting of a circle, square, triangle, and/or rectangle. This may be done individually or in small groups.
	The ability to judge fractions of a whole	Of the assigned dance area, one child is allowed to use the whole area as the stage, another is allowed ⅔ the area and another is allowed ⅓ the area. All perform their compositions simultaneously. Repeat the activity using different size groups, see if the child can accurately designate the movement areas.

Goal	Skills	Activities
	The ability to demonstrate competency in measurement.	Compose a study that must end at a given time. Compose a study describing large, small, long, short, heavy, light, etc.
The student will demonstrate the relationship between dance activities and science.	The ability to apply the physical concepts of balance, leverage, weight factor, resistance, and direction of force	Perform activities which will vary the base of support, height, range, and direction of movement: "Squat, place the feet together and rock. How far can the body rock and maintain balance?" Repeat the movement at different heights with the feet in a variety of positions. "Working with a partner, explore a variety of ways to climb and balance on each other; roll with and over each other; and fall or rise against each other."
	The ability to interpret the environment	Four groups within the class are assigned a season (fall, winter, spring, summer) to interpret. Select an area or region to interpret (jungle, desert, mountain, seashore, etc.) through movement. In groups, select an idea for interpretation: movement of the solar system; weather condition(s); bird, fish, animal, insect lifestyle; jobs of individuals which are involved with sciences (i.e., chemist, physicist, biologist, physiologists, etc.).
The student will demonstrate a relationship between creative dance experiences and social studies	The ability to describe characteristics of historical and present-day American cultures	The basic Indian dance step pattern will be taught. Write a chant about something important to the American Indian culture (weather, food, communication system, family, etc.) Create hand and body gestures to combine with the basic step and chant. Costumes may also be constructed. Other cultures, regions, and periods may be examined through creative dance activities (i.e., Appalachian mountain culture; the deep south, north, west, and the melting pot of the mid-west; the colonial period, Civil War years, and the world war periods).

EVALUATION

Teacher observation, checklists, videotape recordings and student observations may be utilized to evaluate student responses.

DANCE ACTIVITIES
5th and 6th Grade Level

Goal	Skills	Activities
Review terminology for the basic non-locomotor and locomotor movements and combinations of the movements	The ability to manipulate the body in sequential movement patterns individually and with others	The student will create and perform a movement pattern consisting of non-locomotor skills, locomotor skills, falls, and rolls: "Jump 4 times, slide 4 steps, a 2-hand push twice, swing 4 times, turn 2 times, run 8 steps, one backward fall, and a sideward roll." The student will teach the movement pattern to another student, learn the other student's movement pattern. The two will simultaneously perform each movement pattern. GAME: ROUND OR CANON MOVEMENT The group will perform the learned movement pattern as a round. Each student in the group performs the composition to the end without stopping. Each person in turn begins the first movement of the series when the person ahead has completed the first movement and begun the second (as in the round, "Row, Row Row Your Boat").
Review the spatial elements relating to movement	The ability to move the body in and through space: forward, sideward—right and left, diagonally, and in a circle	The student will experience directional changes while practicing various combinations of locomotor and non-locomotor skills: "Run on a diagonal, changing the diagonal every 4 steps, then twist the left arm and make a turn to the left." "Shake the hand and hop forward, skip and turn moving backward." "Leap sideward 4 steps, bend and stretch on a diagonal, and gallop backward in a circle."
	The ability to vary the range of movement	The student will perform activities which improve joint flexibility so the degree of movement may be increased. "Can you stretch the left arm overhead, bend the arm over and around the head? Attempt to touch the left earlobe with the left hand. Repeat the movement with the right hand." This may be done several times. "In a frog sitting position (soles of the feet together), round the back so the head is over the feet. Stretch back to the vertical position." Try it several times. "Sit with the legs straight in front and arms by the side. Round the back and then straighten it. Try this 4-5 times." "Stand with the feet shoulder width apart and arms by the sides. Lean sideward so the body weight is supported by the right leg; simultaneously lift the left leg forward." Repeat the movement to each side several

Goal	Skills	Activities
		times. "Perform leg swings forward, backward, and sideward with each leg. Swing the arms forward, backward, and sideward."
		Compose a movement study utilizing combinations of arm and leg swings.
	The ability to move in and through space on various levels and planes	The student will experience movement on high, medium, and low levels while performing variations of non-locomotor and locomotor movements: "Can you skip and turn on a medium level?" "Can you leap and swing the arms while moving on a high level?" "Can you stretch and roll on a low level?"
		GAME: MOVING STATUE Music may set the tempo for the activity. Each person becomes a "moving statue" which uses many body parts while moving slowly from one position to another. The level is changed with each measure of movement. VARIATION: In small groups the students form a moving statue which remains in contact with another person throughout the activity (at the hand, arms, head, leg, etc.).
		GAME: MIRROR IMAGERY One person is a leader, the other is a mirror. A variety of locomotor and non-locomotor movements are experienced as the leader changes the level of movement every 4, 6, or 8 beats.
	The ability to establish a direction by focusing the eyes at a particular point in the room or area in space	The student will move across the floor (walk, prance, leap, skip, gallop, slide) changing the focus with each step left to right, down, up, straight forward. Repeat.
		GAME: MOVING STATUE As the statue moves from pose to pose, the focus is in the direction of the movement. Level and direction may be changed with each movement. Sharp (percussive) or slow (sustained) movements, with or without accompaniment, may be performed.
		The student created a movement pattern. The focus will be in opposition to the movement. For example, if the arm is stretched sideward to the right, the focus will be sideward to the left; if the leg swings forward, twist the upper torso and focus backward.
	The ability to perceive a floor pattern using lines in straight, circular, square, or zig-zag forms	The student will compose a movement study covering a designated area (20' x 20') which consists of many lines and shapes (zig-zag, circle, triangle, scalloped).
		GAME: MATCH The student(s) will select one of several abstract drawings, prints, posters, or

Goal	Skills	Activities
		paintings. Examine the work closely, and compose a movement sequence describing the lines and shapes.
		Other student(s) will guess which art work was described by class discussion, secret ballot, or a show of hands.
		Select several pieces of equipment or props to place around the room (chairs, table, door frame, chorus risers). Students may develop a floor pattern under, through, over and around the apparatus.
	The ability to perceive the body as a three-dimensional object which can make sharp, angular shapes or smooth, curved shapes	Make many angular shapes with the body while moving across the floor. Moving rounded shapes may be explored. Level changes, directional changes, and a variety of locomotor movements may be explored while making angular and curved shapes.
		Within small groups, students may experience contrasting movements. Simultaneously, one student may describe angular movements, a second may describe curved movements, and a third may describe a combination of angles and curves.
The student will demonstrate a knowledge of the rhythmic elements of time and force as they relate to movement and dance.	The ability to move in a variety of speed patterns and combinations of speed	Begin with the head and move each body part, in sequence, at a slow, moderate, and fast tempo.
		Create a pattern of non-locomotor movements and perform it at a slow, moderate, and fast speed. Perform individually, with a partner, or a small group.
		Combine speed variations within a single movement: "Twist the hand very fast as the arm makes a large slow circle." "With the hands on the waist, bounce the knees at the moderate speed and make a slow circle of the upper torso."
		"While moving the feet in place very fast, perform a slow half fall and rise several times. The movement may travel."
		In small groups, compose a movement sequence involving three variations of speed. Have a group perform a sequence at a fast tempo, then separate to perform a slow movement sequence individually, and re-group to perform a moderate speed activity.
	The ability to demonstrate the pulse (underlying beat) of a movement and music pattern	Using a steady drum beat, have the students perform a movement on every beat: "Walk on the first beat, kick on the second, walk on the third, and kick on the fourth beat." "Leap and twist the arm and shoulder on each beat."

Goal	Skills	Activities
		Students may provide a steady pulse by using body sounds (claps, finger snaps, body slaps, foot taps), vocal sounds (tongue roll, cheek pops, low chest moan, swoosh sound, hum), or instrumental sounds (sticks, triangles, tambourines). Experiment with tempo changes.
		Combine movement and sound on each beat.: "Jump and make a low chest moan." "Tongue roll and arm twist." "Walk, push the arms forward, and swoosh sound." "Clap, hop (leap, jump, walk), and low chest moan on each beat."
		Group composition: while half the group provides a steady beat using body, vocal, or instrumental sounds, the other half performs a group dance composition. The sounds may be recorded on a cassette tape.
	The ability to demonstrate even and uneven rhythmic and movement patterns	Using two speed patterns, have the students sound out the pattern of claps, snaps, stamps, or slaps (_stamp stamp snap snap_). Add three speed variations (_stamp stamp claps snap snap_).
		Students may combine non-locomotor movements using two and three speed patterns (_twists swing fall twists_). Then, use combinations of locomotor and non-locomotor movements (_walks fall rise_) (_turn & swing run & clap bend & stretch_).
		Compose and perform a sound or movement sequence using a two or three speed rhythmic pattern. This may be done individually or in groups.
		GAME: QUESTION-ANSWER One person "composes the question" through movement and/or sound. A partner must repeat the question (movement/sound composition) and give a different movement pattern as an answer. Other "questions" are asked. Each person performs in both positions.
	The ability to recognize and perform movement in measures	Listen to a record, determine the number of beats per measure, and perform a different locomotor and non-locomotor movement for each measure. An entire measure may also be used to perform one movement.
		Change direction, level, tempo, or focus with each measure.
		With a partner or in small groups, compose a movement sequence emphasizing a change with each measure. The dance may be performed as a canon.

Goal	Skills	Activities
	The ability to perform accented measures of movement	Select a meter with a drum beat or recorded accompaniment. Designate the beat(s) to be accented with a clap, stamp, or finger snap (i.e., first, third or fifth). Then sound each beat except the accented beat.
		Move across the floor and accent with non-locomotor movements or sounds: "Walk, walk, walk, backward kick. Now, repeat." "Finger snap, leap, leap, leap." Find different movements (or pause) for the accented beat.
		Change level or direction on the accented beat.
		GAME: SHADOW IMAGERY One person is the leader (standing, sitting, kneeling, or lying) with another person (the shadow) beside or behind. Using body sounds, locomotor, and non-locomotor movements, the leader performs a measure of movement. The "shadow" performs simultaneously. At the end of several measures, the leader and shadow switch roles.
	The ability to recognize and perform movement in phrases	Using body and vocal sounds, put several measures together into a phrase: "Deep chest moan 4 counts, 4 hums, 4 finger snaps, and 4 hand claps." "Three swoosh sounds, 3 bops, 3 stamps, 3 body slaps." Vary the sound and the number of beats within a measure.
		Using locomotor and non-locomotor activities, compose a movement phrase, 4 counts per measure and 4 measures per phrase. Repeat it. Tempo, direction and level may be changed with each repetition.
		GAME: CRAZY PHRASES Each student selects a number (2-8) which will determine the beats per measure and the number of measures per phrase. The teacher may limit the number by suggesting odd (or even) numbers be chosen. The student(s) compose a movement study consisting of one phrase. If the number 5 was selected, a study might be: long stretch and lunge sideward for 5 beats; a fall, roll, and rise during the second 5 beats; run quickly for 5 beats; swing and turn for 5 beats; and a slow backward pull for 5 beats. Repeat the phrase. Two students with the same number may perform their studies simultaneously. Then, students with odd and even numbers may perform together.
The student will learn a variety of movement styles.	The ability to move efficiently while performing a series of mime warm-up activities to	"Can you curl the head and knees toward the chest, stretch the body into a V-sit position, then slowly return to a straight lying position?" Try it several times.

Goal	Skills	Activities
	develop flexibility, strength, balance and coordination.	"Kneel and sit on the heels. Place the hands on the floor behind the body. Try to push the abdomin forward and up, drop the head back to arch the body as much as possible. Return to the kneeling position and repeat it several more times."
		"In a squat position, place the palms on the floor. Try to straighten the legs without moving the hands. Hold the stretch 5-6 seconds and return to a squat. Repeat it several times."
		"How can you perform a half turn without moving the feet off the floor? How many levels can you perform the half turns? Can you jump into the air and turn around before landing?"
		"How high can the arms swing forward and backward? How high can they swing sideward and across the front of the body?"
		"How much can you stretch the neck muscles while performing a series of 'yes' and 'no' movements with the head? Can you tilt the head sideward to touch the ear to the shoulder without raising the shoulder? Try it several times to each side."
		"When you stand with the hands on the waist, can you move only the chest to each side several times? How far forward, backward can you move the chest? Can you move the chest in a circle?"
		"Stand with the hands on the waist to see how far you can move only the hips (pelvis) to each side. Try to move the hips (pelvis) diagonally forward and backward to each side 3-4 times."
		"Try to move the shoulders separately, simultaneously, and in opposition: up, down, forward, backward, in a circle."
		"As you stand with the arms by the side, try to raise the elbows even with the shoulders and control the release downward several times. On the last raise, hold the elbow position and see how many body parts you can isolate and move (swing the forearm in a pendulum motion, then in a circular motion, bend and stretch the fingers; wave the hand back and forth, etc.)."
		"What are some other ways to isolate the movement of the hands, fingers, and elbows?"
		"With both feet on the floor, how can you move one knee (forward, backward, side to side)? Can you move both at the same time?"

Goal	Skills	Activities
		"Stand with the feet shoulder width apart. Lean as far forward, backward, and sideward as possible."
	The ability to interpret feelings, abstract words, things in the environment, or events	These interpretations may be performed individually, with a partner, or in small groups. "Think of a movement or series of movements to describe abstract words: twinkle, glow, bump, spin, grumble, float, etc." "What movements can be used to describe feelings (pride, friendliness, caring, shyness, disappointment, bewilderment, etc.)?" "How can events or happenings be described through movement (a child at Christmas, a family at the zoo, walking on the moon, the witch making brew, the life of the cookie monster, etc.)?" "How can things in the environment be described through movement (a table, chairs, sports equipment, cars bikes, trucks, etc.)?"
	The ability to create illusions that can be used in interpretive situations	These activities may be performed individually, with a partner, in small groups as station activities, or within a large group situation. Create illusions such as: climbing a rope, ladder, or steps; walking or running in place; pushing heavy and light objects sideward, backward, up, down; pulling heavy and light objects from sideward, forward, backward, upward, downward positions; walking boldly, tired, scared, rubbery, stiffly, limping, silly; moving in a car, airplane, stagecoach, on a sailboat, skateboard, camel, etc.; moving through the desert, jungle, crowded streets, etc.
	The ability to create a story and portray many characters	*The Sculptor and the Clay* One student is the sculptor, another is a huge piece of clay. The sculptor molds each part of the clay: the legs, feet, torso, shoulders, arms, hands, neck, head and face. *The Big Race* Two, three, or more students have a slow motion foot (row boat, car) race. Concentrate on good movement rather than winning. *The World Championship* This could be tennis, ball game, boxing, etc. Concentrate on facial control, as well as limb control. This may be performed effectively in slow motion. *The Traffic Policeman* Guide cars through a busy intersection and pedestrians across the street. This can be comical or dramatic.

Goal	Skills	Activities
		The Ultimate Fairy Tale Create a tale that includes witches, goblins, dwarfs, giants, pixies, monsters, dragons. This may be discussed before movement begins or the story could be improvised after the characters are chosen.
		The students will suggest ideas for other stories to be told.
	The ability to move efficiently while performing a series of modern dance movements to warm up the body, develop flexibility, strenght, coordination, and balance	FLOOR MOVEMENTS: "Sit with a straight back and the knees bent. Extend one leg forward, the other leg forward, then attempt to touch the chest to the legs. Return the back to a vertical position and drag the pointed feet along the floor to bend the knees. How far can you stretch each time the movement is repeated?"
		"While sitting with the legs together and the arms curved in front of the body, how far can the feet and toes be stretched, then flexed? Can you feel the muscles stretch as the feet rotate around the ankles?"
		"While sitting with the legs in an open position and the arms stretched overhead and slightly curved, how far can the torso stretch sideward over the leg, to the center of the legs, and to the other side? How much further can you stretch with each attempt?"
		"Attempt controlled half knee bends (the heels remain in contact with the floor) and full knee bends with the feet in a closed position and open position. How far can the legs be twisted in the hip socket and still allow the pelvis to be in a straight line with the back while performing the knee bends?"
		"How far can the leg be stretched forward and upward (sideward and upward, backward and upward) without losing the balance? Show how the torso can be stretched upward while performing the leg movements?"
		"With both legs straight, how far can you swing one leg forward and backward without losing the balance? Try the swings with each leg while holding the arms sideward for balance and slightly curved."
	The ability to efficiently change level and direction while moving across the floor	"Point the toe, alternate knee lifts, and add a slight bounce on the weight shift to perform a prance in place. The prance may be done with the legs in a turned out or parallel position. Move across the floor with a prance. Change the tempo and direction."

Goal	Skills	Activities

"Use good posture to walk forward, stepping toe-heel. Change levels—combine the high and low walks—using a 4 count, bend the knees to walk low on the first 2 beats, on the toes the second 2 beats (down, down, up, up). Then use a 3 count (down, up, up). Reverse the order (up, down, down). Add a circle to the floor pattern: walk straight (down, down, up, up. Repeat), walk in a circle (down, down, up, up. Repeat), walk straight." Repeat as a triplet (down, up, up).

Perform a half turn on the first beat of each measure and continue moving toward the same point in the room: "Forward—down, down, up up; backward—down, down, up, up; forward—down, down, up, up."

Use a variety of locomotor movements, directional and level changes to move across the floor: "Slide 4 steps, turn and slide 4 steps, etc." "Run 8 steps, turn and run backward 8 steps." "Run 8 steps, turn and run backward on a middle level 8 steps. Repeat."

Review combinations of locomotor and non-locomotor movements with a variety of falls and rolls added.

The students compose a dance sequence which includes four locomotor movements, four non-locomotor movements, a fall, a roll, and 2-3 directional changes.

The ability to move efficiently while performing a series of jazz dance movements which develop flexibility, strength, balance, and coordination

FLOOR MOVEMENTS: "While sitting in the tailor position with the hands resting on the knees, roll the head sideward, forward, sideward, backward and repeat."

"How can you move each shoulder in a circle forward, then backward? Try to alternate the circles—move the right shoulder forward and the left backward. Reverse the movement."

"While lying on the back with the knees bent and the hands on the ankles, push the pelvis as high in the air as possible. How high can you get with each stretch?"

"While lying, lift the knee and grab the foot. How straight can you stretch the leg? Release the-grip and slowly lower the straight leg to the floor. Try the stretch with each leg several times."

"With the hands and knees on the floor, pull in (contract) the abdomin so the back is curved. Release the contraction to a straight back. How much can you curve the back?"

Goal	Skills	Activities

Goal	Skills	Activities
		"While kneeling with the arms by the side, how far forward and backward can you lean without losing control?"
		STANDING MOVEMENTS: "If you stand with the feet together and the hands behind the head, can you bend forward from the hips and keep a straight back? How far forward and downward can you lean with a straight back?"
		"Try to control this series of knee bends and heel raises: 1) keep the body straight, bend only the knees; 2) lift the heels without moving any other body part; 3) return the heels to the floor; and 4) slowly straighten the leg to the beginning position.
		Reverse the movement on the next 4 counts: 1) keep the body straight, raise the heels; 2) bend only the knees; 3) lower the heels to the floor without moving any other body part; and 4) straighten the legs to the initial position. Try the series several times with the feet in an open position." The students may create their own series of knee bends and heel raises.
		"Discover ways to isolate movement of the knees without moving the feet: roll (circle) each knee right, forward, left, and back several times; move the right knee forward (lift the heel so it can move more), return the heel to the floor, and straighten the knee."
		"How high (forward and backward) can the turned out leg swings be performed while maintaining body control? Try it with each leg while the torso is stretched upward. Try it with a turned out, bent-knee, and a pointed toe."
		"Compose a set of finger, wrist, and hand movements to work each part separately. Then combine some of the movements."
		"How far around the waist can the torso be twisted?" Add a hand clap or finger snap to each twist: clap the hands at chest height. Simultaneously, push the right arm and shoulder forward, the left arm and shoulder backward—twisting only the upper torso. Clap the hands and push the left arm and shoulder forward and the right backward.
	The ability to move efficiently across the floor	"Keep the knees bent and walk forward on a middle level. Swing the arms in opposition to the stepping foot." Repeat. Move backward on a middle level.

Goal	Skills	Activities
		"Shake the head and shoulders while walking forward at a set tempo. Snap the fingers with each step (or alternating step)." Repeat the movement sideward and backward.
		Tap, clap, and step: use 4 beats for one set of steps—1) tap the right toe in front of the body; 2) simultaneously, clap the hands and step on the flat right foot; 3) tap the left toe in front of the body; and 4) simultaneously, clap the hands and step on the flat left foot. Repeat across the floor. Vary the step by moving throughout the room and around classmates.
		Jump, clap, walk: use 6 beats—1) jump; 2) clap hands; 3, 4, 5) walk forward (backward, sideward); and 6) pause.
		Walk and box step: step on the right foot to walk four times and make a box—step the right foot across the left, step straight backward with the left foot, move the right foot backward and sideward, then step forward with the left to complete the box pattern. Start again with the walks. Vary the movement by starting with the left foot, changing tempo, making larger steps, adding claps and finger snaps, etc.
		The student will compose a movement study/dance which includes walks, body isolations, and percussive sounds.
The student will demonstrate an understanding of himself and a respect for others	The ability to set realistic goals	Individual and group projects varying in length and complexity will require self-discipline and good organizational practices.
		The student will develop a project for performance. Prior to composition, the style of movement, the length of the study, and the expected time of completion will be decided by each individual, written in contract form, and signed by the student and the teacher. After the performance, the student will evaluate (discussion or written) the quality of the performance and whether the expectations had been realistically set.
	The ability to respect individual capabilities	Students will list good points about performances of the classmates.
		Within a group each person choreographs a movement phrase that can be performed by each person in the group. The group will in turn perform each movement phrase.
		Each student will select a handicapping condition from a prepared list and compose a quality

Goal	Skills	Activities
		movement sequence while "experiencing" the handicap: the dancer has no use of one arm, is confined to a wheelchair, has a broken leg, is blind, etc.
	The ability to cooperate	In partners, students will compose a movement sequence to teach another set of partners.
		In groups, select a popular quotation concerning cooperation and sociability. Describe it through movement: "Two heads are better than one." John Heywood "Politeness costs nothing and gains everything." Lady Mary Wortley Montague "Good manners never intrude." Edward Moore "The only way to have a friend is to be one." Ralph Waldo Emerson
		GAME: PICK IT UP In groups, one person begins a dance and freezes. The next person picks up the last movement, adds another before freezing. The movement continues until each person in the group has added to the dance. VARIATION: The first person could begin a story through movement then freezes. The second person picks up the movement, adds to the story, and freezes. Each person in the group adds to the story.
Good safety practices will be demonstrated.	The ability to listen and follow directions	The student will respond to the questions, problems, and commands as carefully as possible.
		Props and equipment will have properly designated areas.
	The ability to recognize and make judgements about creating safe environments	Body and prop control will be demonstrated when performing balances, falls, and rolls, as well as working with sticks, chairs, tables, etc.
		The importance of strength and flexibility for safety will be emphasized as the students compose a set of exercises to develop strength within the large muscle groups and flexibility of each joint.
The student will demonstrate a minimum of four movement study/dance compositions using props.	The ability to create movement sequences from themes involving props such as: elastic strips, paper cups, candles, chairs, stools, sturdy wooden boxes, beach balls, bandanas, bats, small scarfs (12" x 18"), large scarfs (54" x 72"), hula hoops, lumni	Perform many combinations of non-locomotor and locomotor movements with a selected prop.
		Compose a movement sequence using a prop, perform it in a reverse order (on a different level, at another speed, or using a different body part).
		Examine a prop. Use approximately 30 seconds of movement to describe the qualities of the prop (shape, weight, texture, etc.).

Goal	Skills	Activities
	sticks, wands, carpet squares, door frames, etc.	GAMES: ECHO, MIRROR IMAGERY, SHADOW IMAGERY, ROUND OR CANON, or any combination of these may be utilized for a composition involving prop(s).
	The ability to create a movement sequence involving sounds (body sounds, verbal sounds, sticks, songs, chants, poems, readings, etc.)	Compose a dance to be accompanied by a cassette recording of sounds: body sounds (stomps, finger snaps, finger thumps, claps, body slaps), verbal sounds (clucking, tongue rolls, cheek pops, various chest and throat sounds), abstract action words (wop, blap, zing, woo-oo-oo, zip, bang, ping, yack, booing), homemade instrumental sounds (sticks, wands, drums, tin cans, pie pans, bean shakers), environmental sounds (door closing, walking on tile, car starting, dog bark, cat cry, running water, doorbell), or any combination of the sounds.
	The ability to use visuals to enhance dance movement	Design a background scene for a dance which can be displayed by an overhead projector.
		Make a slide or filmstrip to visually accompany a mime or dance.
		Compose a dance which the student must use a special light source: flashlight, blacklight, strobe light, sparklers, candles, etc.
The student will perform many movement studies and dances within an informal situation (regular class setting).	The ability to remember sequences and perform in front of peers	A student should perform at least once, individually, with a partner, or in a group, during each class period. The performance will vary in length. It may be structured or improvisational.
The student will perform a minimum of two formal dance presentations.	The ability to remember sequences, move with quality, and perform for the community and friends	Schedule times in which 2-3 homerooms may share their compositions.
		Schedule assemblies so the students may show their work to the student body.
		Schedule afternoon or evening performances that will allow parents and the community to view the student compositions.
The student will be exposed to movement and dance styles on various levels of performance	The ability to evaluate the quality of movement	Brief class discussions concerning individual and group performances.
		Magazines and books will be on display for examination and study.

Goal	Skills	Activities
		At least one dance concert by a professional or semi-professional group will be presented followed by a question-answer session.
		Students will view slides, films, and videotapes of professional, collegiate, high school, and elementary age performers. Class discussion and group evaluations will follow.
	The ability to remain seated and quiet during performances	Reminders by the classroom teachers, administrators, and parents are necessary.
		Audience behavior will be stressed within the classroom performance setting.
		Plan appropriate length performances.
	The ability to react appropriately to situations which are comical or possibly demoralizing	Class discussion and sensitivity talks.
		Individually or in small groups, the student will perform a situation that can be described seriously and/or comically: a robbery, a step into a hole, bumping into a tree, fainting, etc.
The student will identify a relationship between design and art.	The ability to recognize and describe lines through movement	Compose a movement study/dance that includes the shape of a diamond, hexagon, pentagon, octagan, and/or a parallelogram within the floor pattern.
	The ability to recognize and describe forms in and through movement.	Interpret textures (smooth, slippery, soft, silky, bumpy, rough, hard, scratchy) through movement.
		The student will be given an object to describe through movement. "How would you describe the form, shape, and feel of feathers, driftwood, coconuts, pineapple, scarfs, etc.?"
		Students will make masks (clown skeletal, warrior, funeral) and describe a situation through movement that would involve the mask.
	The ability to assign movement to concepts and abstractions	Individually or in groups, students compose dance movement to illustrate symmetry and assymetry.
		Students will paint, tie dye, or draw a design on a large bedsheet. Movements will be created to describe the design. Then a dance will be performed using the art work as a back drop.
The student will identify relationships between physical performance and music.	Skills for this are listed throughout the curriculum	Activities for this are listed throughout the curriculum.

Dance 315

Goal	Skills	Activities
The student will demonstrate a relationship between movement/dance and language art.	The ability to enhance word recognition, reading for comprehension, and following directions	Students will participate in station work which will require reading and translating problems to be solved.
	The ability to improve writing skills (spelling, punctuation, sentence structure and penmanship)	Compose a movement sequence and describe it on paper.
		Write a research paper concerning a particular style of movement or dance.
	The ability to increase the creative thinking process	The teacher will pose many problems which can be solved in a variety of ways.
		Communicate the theme or message which might be found on a greeting card (or poster).
		Within one dance, describe contrasts and similarities.
The student will identify relationships between dance and health.	The ability to use proper body mechanics	Discuss the importance of a strong, well-balanced framework and the importance of muscle strength to control the framework.
		Use correct posture in all movements.
	The ability to identify anatomical parts: skull, rib, scapula, spine, humerus, femur, pelvis, carpals, tibia, fibula, tarsals, metarsals, deltoid, triceps, trapezius	Locate the body parts on a teacher prepared diagram.
		Compose a movement sequence accompanied by a poem, chant, song, or story that uses the anatomical names.
The student will demonstrate relationships between science and dance activities.	The ability to apply the physical concepts of the environment	With a partner or in small groups, compose a movement sequence that: requires students to balance on each other; requires lifting, pushing, or pulling; describes centrifugal and centripetal force; describes the force of a magnet; etc.
The student will idenitfy a relationship between mathematical concepts and dance activities	The ability to demonstrate geometric shapes and their properties	Compose a dance using a pair of lines that parallel, intersect, and are perpendicular.
	The ability to demonstrate competency in measurement	Design and make a set to accompany dance movement.
	The ability to organize a set of numbers	In groups of 5-6, use many stage entrances and exits to compose a dance about sets of odd or even numbers. Students in the "even" group may only enter and exit the stage with an even

316 *Dance*

Goal	Skills	Activities
		number of dancers. The same even number may not be repeated two times consecutively: in a group of 6, for example, 4 enter, then 2 exit; 4 enter, and 2 exit; 4 exit, then 6 enter, and 2 exit, etc.
The student will demonstrate a relationship between creative dance experiences and social studies	The ability to understand and appreciate the customs and contributions of others	Select individuals who have had a great effect on society and describe, through movement, their contribution (George Washington Carver, Henry Ford, Thomas Edison, etc.). Compose dances which describe characteristics of European (Asian, African, etc.) cultures.

EVALUATION

Teacher observation, checklists, videotape recordings and student observations may be utilized to evaluate student responses.

REFERENCES

1. Boorman, Joyce. *Creative Dance in the First Three Grades.* Ontario, Canada: Longman Canada Limited, 1969.
2. Cayou, Dolores K. *Modern Jazz Dance.* Palo Alto, California: National Press Books, 1971.
3. Dimonstein, Geraldine. *Children Dance in the Classroom.* New York: The Macmillan Company, 1971.
4. Fleming, Gladys A., ed. *Children's Dance.* Washington, D.C.: AAHPER, 1973.
5. Fleming, Gladys A. *Creative Rhythmic Movement — Boys and Girls Dancing.* Englewood Cliffs, New Jersey: Prentice-Hall, Inc., 1976.
6. Giordano, Gus. *Anthology of American Jazz Dance,* 2nd ed. Evanston, Illinois: Orion Publishing House, 1978.
7. Schurr, Evelyn L. *Movement Experiences for Children,* 3rd ed. Englewood Cliffs, New Jersey: Prentice-Hall, Inc., 1980.
8. Shephard, Richmond. *Mime the Technique of Silence.* New York: Drama Book Specials (Publishers), 1971.
9. Sherbon, Elizabeth. *On the Count of One: Modern Dance Methods,* 2nd ed. Palo Alto, California: Mayfield Publishing Company, 1975.
10. Stonzenberg, Mark. *Exploring Mime,* 3rd ed. New York: Sterling Publishing Co., Inc., 1980.
11. Winters, Shirley J. *Creative Rhythmic Movement.* Dubuque, Iowa: Wm. C. Brown Company Publishers, 1975.

STUDENT ACTIVITIES

1. Design and teach a dance lesson to children or peers.
2. Observe children in a variety of dance activities and analyze the activity by pointing out similarities between the dance activities seen and the objectives in this chapter.

CHAPTER 12
ADAPTIVE PHYSICAL EDUCATION
by
Mark Runac
Virginia Commonwealth University

After completing this chapter, the student should be able to:

1. Define physical education as it relates to handicapped individuals. P.319
2. Discuss the effects P.L. 94-142 has had on adaptive physical education.
3. List and explain the components of the IEP.
4. Design an IEP having been given data on a handicapped child.
5. Explain the importance of each learning principle listed in the chapter. — p.323
6. Analyze a motor task into its three phases: preparation, execution, and follow-through.
7. Design a hypothetical behavior modification program.
8. Discuss the teaching styles most effective with each handicapping condition. p.325
9. Design a developmental activity for each handicapping condition discussed in the chapter.

Most children, from the elite athlete to the uncoordinated child, have the basic need to engage in physical activities. In the past, children with special needs were denied physical education or were given non-participating roles such as scorers or equipment dispensers. The growth of humanism and instructional technologies of the late 1960s brought forth an era in which many handicapped individuals' needs were identified and served through physical education programs. This chapter is an overview of physical education for handicapped children.

Before proceeding, a definition of handicapped children must be provided. A handicapped child is defined for physical education purposes as an individual with psychomotor dysfunctions that necessitates specialized instructional strategies. Our educational system traditionally has labeled children according to their intelligence quotients (IQs) or the degree of their impairment (e.g., total blindness and partially sighted). These classification systems have shortcomings in programming in adapted physical education. The physical educator must view children as individuals who possess different strengths and weaknesses.

Education is an ongoing process in which total growth and development proceeds in a predictable and organized fashion. The rate in which children progress along the developmental continuum, however, varies with each child. The educator therefore, must employ an individualized and humanistic approach to maximize the benefits derived from any program. Individualized instruction is achieved when a child's position on the developmental continuum is pinpointed and experiences are offered that enhance each child's future development. This approach underlies recent legislation and instructional technology related to education for handicapped children.

PAST, PRESENT, AND FUTURE OF PHYSICAL EDUCATION FOR THE HANDICAPPED

Our American educational philosophy is based on each child's right to a free public education. Equal opportunity for all children was articulated through a statement issued from the Supreme Court in 1954. The statement reads:

> Education is required in the performance of our most basic responsibilities. In these days, it is doubtful that any child may reasonably be expected to succeed in life if he is denied the opportunity of an education. Such an opportunity where the state has undertaken to provide it, is a right which must be made available to all on equal terms.

The principle later was supported specifically for handicapped children in the court case of PARC, etc. vs. Commonwealth of Pennsylvania, et.al. The decree stemming from this case mandated that a public and appropriate education should be provided to all handicapped children.

The 1975 passage of Public Law 94-142, Education for All Handicapped Children Act, revealed a growing public concern for appropriate educational opportunities for handicapped children. The major legislation provisions are: 1) a handicapped child is entitled to an educational setting that is least restrictive or most normalized, and is designed to meet his or her needs, 2) education is provided at no cost to the parent, 3) the child where appropriate and his parents are involved in educational decisions, 4) the evaluation process is objective and non-discriminatory, and 5) clear management procedures are utilized in planning for a child's education program.

P.L. 94-142 specifically mentions physical education as a required curriculum area. Physical education is seen as an avenue which may lead to self-sufficiency in the community through the attainment of leisure and domestic skills. Physical education for special students is defined as:

(i) ... the development of:
 (A) physiological and motor fitness; (B) fundamental motor skills and patterns; and (C) skills in aquatics, dance and individual and group games and sports (including intramural and lifetime sports).
(ii) The term includes special physical education, adapted physical education, movement education, and motor development.

The future of adaptive physical education is presently uncertain. The federal government is relinquishing many of its educational responsibilities to state authorities. Many educators fear that the state governments will fail to support education for handicapped children as the federal government has in the past. Despite the uncertainties, many positive movements are apt to continue; (1) the knowledge base derived from recent research in physical education for handicapped children will stimulate additional research; (2) as the research knowledge base expands, instructional strategies and technologies will evolve that will allow for individualized instruction; and (3) the advancement in instructional technologies and a greater acceptance of handicapped children will enable more handicapped children to be mainstreamed with their normal peers.

Greater emphasis will be placed upon the multidisciplinary approach in formulating educational programs for handicapped children. In multidisciplinary approaches, the child's total personality is examined thus insuring a balanced program. Increasingly, more disciplines will be included in programs for handicapped children. If the physical educator is to become a contributing member of a multidisciplinary staff, he or she must have a general understanding of all educational areas and be able to interact with other professional staff.

Decategorization of handicap labels is a trend of the 1970s that will continue to grow in the 1980s. Labeling often increases the stigmatism attached to possessing a handicap without providing additional information to the teacher. Furthermore, many educators believe that the factors underlying human development are common for all children and that children differ because they are at various positions on the developmental continuum. As a result, teaching models have evolved that develop generic teaching competencies in assessing, planning, teaching, and evaluating handicapped children. According to these teaching models, the educator observes the child's behavior, diagnoses any problems, prescribes activities to alleviate the problems, implements the teaching plan, and evaluates the child's progress.

PUBLIC LAW 94-142

In drafting 94-142, Congress established guidelines and policies that required states to employ practices that insure equal educational opportunities for handicapped students in a least restrictive environment. The IEP is an integral part of P.L. 94-142 and provides the mechanism to assure that the states are meeting the law's provisions.

Individualized Educational Plan (IEP)

The IEP is formulated by a multidisciplinary staff consisting of a school representative, teacher, parents, and the child, if appropriate. Through staff meetings, the parents take part in decisions that will affect their child. Many potential problems between the parents and professional staff are alleviated if both parties are involved in the initial planning process. Additionally, rapport between the parent and teacher is frequently a direct result of the multidisciplinary meetings.

P.L. 94-142 requires that the following components, but not exclusive of others, be addressed in each child's IEP:

(1) *A statement of the present level of educational performance.* Assessment instruments must be valid and reliable, and measure content areas relevant to the child's needs, if sound educational decisions are to be made. The decision process may be further enhanced if two or more tests or observations are administered. A child's motor performance may be measured with a variety of assessment techniques, such as teacher observation, developmental scales, standardized fitness and motor tests, and teacher-made behavioral objectives.

(2) *A statement of annual goals and short term instructional objectives.* Physical education goals are listed in P.L. 94-142 definition of physical education. These goals are generic to all children, handicapped or not. The physical educator must identify behavioral objectives that reflect specific goal areas that are essential to a child's well-being in his community. After each child is assessed on relevant objectives, the physical educator places those objectives in order of priority and establishes timeliness for their attainment.

(3) *A statement of the specific education services to be provided and the extent to which the child will participate in regular physical education.* All special education and related services required to meet the child's needs should be described. Furthermore, the percentage of time that the child will receive instruction with his normal peers should be specified. If a child is unable to participate in a regular class, justification for alternate placement must be provided.

(4) *A statement of appropriate objective criteria and evaluation procedures and schedules for determining, on at least an annual basis, whether instructional objectives are being achieved.* A child's progress in the education program should be monitored periodically. P.L. 94-142 guidelines suggest evaluation should take place quarterly. The information obtained from these evaluations should be submitted to other multidisciplinary staff members because it forms the basis for subsequent educational decisions.

An Example IEP

In attempting to write an IEP both expediently and thoroughly, the teacher is often caught in a dilemma. The planning time afforded teachers for individual programming generally is limited. A partial solution to this dilemma is through use of a curriculum guide designed for local school district needs. By referring to the guide, the teacher is able to save valuable time that would have been wasted in replication and writing. For example, a teacher in many cases could refer to an instructional objective by number rather than formulating a new objective. The effectiveness of this process hinges on the comprehensiveness of the curriculum guide. The guide must address motor skills in a developmental connotation. That is, behavioral objectives should reflect performances at various points along the skill continuum. In cases when motor skills to be developed are unique to a child and are not included in the guide, the teacher must write his own instructional objectives. See Chapter 5 for information on writing behavioral objectives.

Figure 12-1 illustrates an example IEP. The required components of an IEP are addressed in the columns directly under the student information.

Goals appear in the first column. These goal areas which are common to all children include physical fitness, fundamental motor skills, sport skills, dance, and aquatics. In columns 2, 3, and 4, present and targeted performance levels are described in terms of instructional objectives. Behavioral objectives can be obtained from a curriculum guide. If the teacher is referring to the curriculum guide, he lists the design number that corresponds to the intended objective. In the example IEP, objectives for the overhand throw and catch are indicated by their curriculum guide number. Timeliness for the initiation and termination of instruction for each objective are given in columns 5 and 6. The remaining columns are employed to describe the type of placement and support personnel needed to deliver physical education services. Total time or percent of time may be used to indicate the proportion of time spent in each placement.

Least Restrictive Environment

P.L. 94-142 mandates that handicapped children are placed in a setting that enhances their chances for optimal educational development. Many authorities believe that an integrative rather than a segregative approach is imperative to maximum development, and that any

Figure 12-1
I CAN PHYSICAL EDUCATION IEP FORM

School District/School __Demuke__

Student Name or Number __John Smith__

Recommended Total Time in Physical Education __3__ days/weeks __30__ minutes/day

Current Placement __Special Education__

Date Submitted __9/10/81__

Date of Planning Meeting __9/29/81__

Date(s) of Review _____ (Listed when Scheduled)

Teachers __Mr. Monk__

	Program Goal Areas in Physical Education	Present level(s) of Performance	Annual Student Goals	Short Term Objectives	Time Required (min/day)	Duration Dates Begin	Duration Dates End	Regular Education Placement	Special Designed Instruction	Support Personnel Needed (See back)
Area 1	Physical Fitness	A. Sit-ups-5th %'l B. 9-min run 20th %'l	A. Sit-ups 20th %'l B. 9-min run 25th %'l	A. Increase 1 rep per week B. Dec. 2 sec. per week	10 min a day	9/1/81	6/1/82	100%	0%	None
Area 2	Fundamental Motor Skills	A. Overhand Throw (Obj. 1.1.2) B. Catch (Obj. 1.2.4.)	A. O. Throw (Obj. 1.1.5) B. Catch (Obj. 1.2.6)	A. Obj. 1.1.3 1.1.4 1.1.5 B. Obj. 1.2.5 1.2.6	10 min a day	4/3/82	5/26/82	50%	50%	None
Area 3	Aquatics	The student was able to swim 5 yards without stopping	The student will be able to swim 25 yds.	The student will increase 5 yds a wk.	20 min/day 2 days/wk	1/4/82	3/28/82	0%	100%	YMCA
Area 4										
Area 5										

type of segregation will further widen the gap in normalizing handicapped children. The basis for their belief stems from the educational benefits derived from pupil interaction. This interaction, if planned appropriately, can result in a transfer of values and behaviors, and a decrease in the stigmatism attached to possessing a handicap.

The law maintains that the placement must be least restrictive to the child, with placement decisions made from a continuum of alternatives. The placement may be a special class, a regular class with special help, a regular class, or a combination of the three. The IEP committee must determine the time the child should spend in each placement alternative. The child, however, should be in a regular classroom as much as possible.

Several factors need to be considered prior to making placement decisions. The teacher must first ascertain the child's physical, social, cognitive, and emotional performance levels. A child who deviates significantly from other class members often possess problems to others in the instructional setting. If individualized instruction is practiced, the heterogenity effect of performance levels is greatly diminished. Problems associated with teaching physical education to a diversified group generally occur in game situations rather than in skill development oriented activities. Rules and strategies of games may be changed to include the children with lower performance levels. If the modifications make the games unrealistic or less challenging for other class members, however, the teacher has done a disservice to the class. Some teachers who are aware of difficulties in integrating handicapped children in complex games often group children according to ability level during these activities. If this segregation becomes common place, the teacher must reexamine the curriculum to insure that all children are being served.

Before the child is placed, the teacher must consider the possible effects the handicapped child will have on other class members. Protection of optimal educational development should extend to all students. If the handicapped child will have an adverse effect on other class members, separate programming may be warranted.

Teachers face three major stumbling blocks in their efforts to place children in the least restrictive environment. First, schools have failed to provide additional resources and staff necessary to integrate handicapped children. This problem will persist in light of recent budget cuts. To compensate for the inadequate staff, the teacher must employ strategies such as individualized instruction, peer tutoring, squad leaders, and the utilization of older children to aid in physical education. Second, the needed instructional technology is not readily available to physical educators. The reader is referred to Chapter 5 of this book and "Principles of Methods of Adapted Physical Education and Recreation," by Walter C. Crowe, David Auxter, and Jean Pyfer for furthering reading related to strategies utilizing an individualized instructional approach. Third, many physical educators were inadequately trained to employ new instructional techniques for individualizing instruction. To compensate, many universities and state education departments offer courses and inservice training programs in physical education. One course or a workshop, however, is not sufficient to develop competencies necessary to implement a successful physical education program.

LEARNING PRINCIPLES

The teacher must arrange the classroom conditions to change a child's behavior. Certain concepts, if applied appropriately, will enhance learning. To apply these concepts, the teacher must first determine the cause of the behavior by observing the surrounding events that cause the behavior. Once the cause is identified, the conditions can be altered and the child's behavior changed. To be most effective, a teacher should practice the principles of learning which follow:

1. Task Analysis — breaking down a skill into teachable units and proceeding to teach children the units that they do not possess. An example of task analysis is provided in Figure 12-2.
2. Shaping — reinforcing a response that closely approximates or represents improvement toward a desired behavior. A teacher uses the shaping principle by developing a sequence of activities that gradually increase in difficulty and enable the child to move toward the desired goal. For example, a child could be rewarded for trapping a ball with the chest and arms before he is required to catch a ball solely with his hands.
3. Prompting — assisting the child in performing a response with verbal, visual, or manipulative cues. Holding a child's hand while he is learning to walk up stairs is an example of a prompt.
4. Fading — withdrawing the prompts gradu-

Figure 12-2. Task Analysis of a Kick

Objective: To kick a stationary 10" playground ball a distance of 20 feet, two out of three times, with a mature kicking skill.

PHASE	PHASE COMPONENTS
Preparation	a. The approach involves one or more steps with the last step being a leap.
	b. The swing leg is hyperextended at the hip and flexed at the knee.
	c. The support leg is planted slightly to the side of the ball.
Force Production (execution)	d. As the support leg contacts the ground, the shoulders are retracted and trunk is inclined backward.
	e. The forward swing of the leg is initiated at the hip.
	f. Prior to ball contact, the speed of the thigh is diminished and the knee extends rapidly.
	g. The arm and leg move in position.
Follow-through	h. The leg continues its pendular motion.
	i. The kicker lands by hopping on the support leg.

Kicking could be analyzed further by identifying prerequisite motor and cognitive skills. For example, dynamic lateral balance is needed to successfully perform kicking.

---

ally as the child improves. The next step after physically assisting a child walking up stairs may be to provide a hand railing.

5. Time out — isolating the child from his classmates when he exhibits inappropriate behaviors. The teacher would require a child to sit out of a game if he misbehaves. The child should return to the activity after he demonstrated appropriate behavior or indicates he will follow class rules.

6. Knowledge of Results — providing information concerning the child's performance. In most cases, this information should be given concisely and immediately following a response. A child who is throwing well except the incorrect foot is placed forward quickly should be told "You are throwing well, but place your left foot forward before releasing the ball." The teacher may also demonstrate a correct throw or place foot prints on the floor to aid the child's understanding of the throwing skill.

See Chapter 2 for additional principles of learning which can be applied to the handicapped child.

BEHAVIOR MODIFICATION

Children with handicapping conditions frequently require a different approach to control as compared with the normal child. Motor dysfunction, disfigurement, and/or lower mental capacity among handicapped children are often misunderstood by their normal peers. These handicaps and how people respond to them often lead to undesirable compensatory behavior by the handicapped child in the form of disruptive behavior.

How disruptive behavior is handled depends on the child. Children of normal mental capacity who exhibit emotionally unacceptable behavior might possibly be dealt with using techniques discussed in Chapter 4. Those with lower mental capacity as well as those with severe emotional problems seem to respond well to behavior modification.

By using behavior modification, the teacher seeks to eliminate the undesired behavior; it will not eliminate the cause. For this reason, behavior modification has been maligned by many. It must be emphasized, therefore, that modifying the behavior is only the beginning; the long range goal is to find and cure the behaviors underlying cause.

The components of a behavior modification program are:

1. Identify the behavior to be eliminated.
2. Begin immediately to find the behavior's underlying cause.
3. Count the frequency of the behavior.
4. Establish a program objective including a time frame for accomplishment.
5. Design a program to bring about the desired change.
6. Assess the results.
7. Make appropriate changes.

An Actual Case Study

A large third grade boy is beating up his smaller peers. The frequency and severity is sufficient to call it a major behavior problem. The school personnel have an obligation to protect others from the child, and must, therefore, seek ways to change the disruptive child's behavior quickly. The objective was to eliminate all physical fights initiated by the child within three weeks. A committee was immediately established to seek the underlying cause for the fighting.

In consultation with the child, his love for basketball and physical activity in general was discovered, and this became the key to the program. Initially only a short period of time in which no fights occurred was sufficient to win extra activity time. The physical educator and classroom teacher worked out the cooperative program so the boy could join any physical education class or could have supervised play in the gym. The good behavior time required for the reward was gradually lengthened. The behavior modification program combined with the committee's work were sufficient to meet the program's objective.

Some key elements to remember in designing and conducting a behavior modification program are:
1. Focus on only one behavior at a time.
2. Award points for good behavior but never subtract points when the child falters.
3. Gradually increase the number of points required to obtain the reward.
4. Rewards can be anything positive which motivates the child. Activity time is highly recommended. Any form of candy is just as highly discouraged. Fruits can be used if the child does not have a weight problem. Whenever possible the reward should be getting something (positive reinforcement) rather than losing something (negative reinforcement). One emotionally disturbed and retarded girl who was also grossly obese responded only to threats of not being fed (which at times she was not).
5. Other negative reinforcers such as time out must also be handled carefully. Some-parents have sued schools because their child was placed in special time out areas. One school actually placed children in locked wooden cabinets similar to upright coffins. Although the technique worked in changing behavior, such techniques are highly questionable.

TEACHING TECHNIQUES FOR THOSE WITH REDUCED MENTAL CAPACITY

Certain teaching styles seem to be better than others when working with various handicapping conditions. Unlike the normal child, children with reduced mental capacity respond best to a command style approach (Chapter 4). A firm but positive approach is recommended. Individual attention along with the command style is also required by many moderately retarded children. Lessons with these children will usually have fewer activities and less maximum participation as compared to those for the mildly handicapped and normal children. It is frequently difficult, therefore, to mainstream more than a few moderately retarded children into any one physical education class. The extent to which mainstreaming can take place is dependent upon the degree of attention required by any one or group of children.

ACTIVITIES

Since each child's needs are different, it is difficult to cover every handicapping condition. The activities in this section cover a wide variety of handicapping conditions most frequently encountered by physical educators.

Lack of Strength

Certain principles should be applied in developing a strength program. They are:
(1) Specificity — only muscles directly involved in a specific movement are strengthened.
(2) overload — gains in strength result from placing stress on the muscles.
(3) safety — excessive stress placed on the bones of pre-adolescents may retard bone growth or cause injury.

A strength program for elementary children should be designed to gradually develop moderate rather than maximum strength levels because the growth centers of pre-adolescents have not yet ossified. Injuries to these growth centers will often have a detrimental effect on the child's future development.

Strength Activities

1. Title of Activity: Curl-up
   Objective: To develop abdominal muscles
   Formation: Scattered
   Equipment: Mats
   Procedure: The child lies supine with his arms crossed in front of the chest and the legs are bent 90 degrees at the knees. The head and shoulders are lifted four to six inches off the floor while keeping the lower back on the floor. After the upper

body is held in this up position for two seconds, the entire upper body is rotated at the waist to one side and then to the other side. Each position should be held for two seconds. The upper body is slowly lowered to the floor before another repetition is started. The curl-up is effective because the abdominal muscles perform a majority of the work and undue stress to the lower back is avoided.

2. Title: Down hill sit ups
   Objective: To develop abdominal muscles
   Formation: Incline or slope of a hillside
   Procedure: The downhill sit-up is appropriate for children who cannot perform one sit-up on a flat surface. The sit-up is performed as the child lies on a slope with the feet downhill and the head uphill. As the child performs more sit-ups, the slope should be decreased.

3. Title: Roll weights
   Objective: To develop wrist strength
   Equipment: String, weight, tubing from wax paper roll
   Procedure: a weight (sand bag) is attached to a paper tubing from a wax paper roll by a string (See Figure 12-3). The ends of the roll are held with the hands and the weight is elevated to the tubing by rolling the wrists.

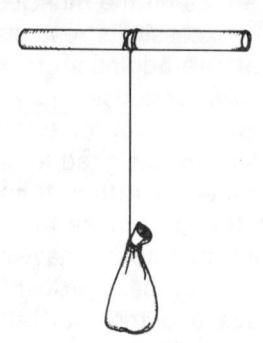

Place tube around feet straighten legs, pull toward chest.

Sit down, place tube around feet, spread legs apart laterally.

Step on tube, flex arm at elbow.

Place tube around hands above the head and pull outward.

Place tube around hands at chest level and pull outward.

Place tube around hands at chest level and pull as if pulling a bow in archery.

Place tube around head and arms, hold arms stable and move head at the neck.

Place tube around knees, pull knees outward.

Lie prone and place tube around ankles and hands, extend legs at knees.

Place tube around the back and hands, extend arms at elbows.

Figure 12-3. Roll Weight

4. Title: Inner tube activities
   Objective: To develop strength (depends on the specific movement)
   Formation: Scattered
   Equipment: Inner tubes
   Procedure: a discarded bike inner tube is used to provide resistance. The resistance can be altered by using various width inner tubes. The following activiites (Figure 12-4) illustrate the different tube exercises.

Tug-of-War (May have to use more than one inner tube for safety)

Figure 12-4. Innertube Activities

Adaptive 327

5. Title: Plastic milk carton pulley
   Objective: To develop strength (depends on specific movement)
   Formation: Scattered
   Equipment: Rope, pulley, sand, plastic milk carton
   Procedure: A rope is attached to a plastic milk carton loaded with sand. The weight is altered by the amount of sand in the milk carton. The rope is placed through a pulley anchored to a post or tree. Figure 12-5 illustrates different pulley exercises.

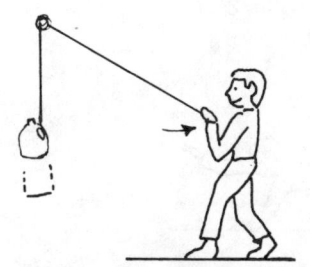

Face pulley, pull rope toward chest by flexing at the elbows.

Face away from pulley with arms upright, bring arms forward and downward.

Face away from pulley, hold arms straight and bring arms together in front of the body.

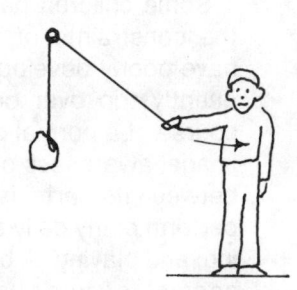

Stand with side facing pulley, bring arms in front and across the body.

Face pulley, bend downward at the waist.

Figure 12-5. Pulley Exercises

Balance Problems

Balance is a key component in many skills. Children with poor balance often perform skills mechanically or inefficiently. Programs for these children should encompass all facets of balance: static, dynamic, and flight balances along the three body axis. The child should be required to maintain his balance as he stands, walks, runs, jumps, and hops.

Activities

6. Title: Beam walking and standing
   Objective: To develop static and dynamic balance
   Formation: Lines or a balance beam for each child.
   Equipment: Boards of various widths
   Procedure: Children stand or move forward or backward on a balance beam. Different locomotor skills should be used to cross the beam. The arms may be held outward or the hands may be placed on the hips, as the children perform. The eyes may focus on the beam, up toward the ceiling, or closed. The width of the beam should be decreased gradually as the child's balancing ability improves.

7. Title: Flight balance
   Objective: To develop flight balance
   Formation: Lines
   Equipment: Spring board, mini-tramp (inner tube with canvas cover), mats
   Procedure: The following movements are performed, while the child is airborne:
   1) tuck
   2) pike
   3) Visit
   4) straddle
   5) twist
   6) scissors
   7) touch various body parts
   8) side kick

8. Title: Balance stunts
   Objective: To develop static balance
   Formation: Scattered
   Equipment: Mats
   Procedure: The child performs the stunts depicted in Figure 12-6.

Poor Body Coordination

Body coordination is the ability to integrate motor patterns of different body parts for a planned motor act. A clumsy child often has poor body coordination. A body coordination program should include activities that necessitate movements as the child assumes various positions.

328 Adaptive

Tripod   Frog Stand   Head Stand   Push-up

Stork Stand   Needle Scale   Single Squat Balance

Knee Scale   One Foot Scale   Two-point Balance

Figure 12-6. Balance Stunts

9. Title: Scooter
   Objective: To develop ability to move the scooter in various positions.
   Formation: Scattered
   Equipment: Scooter
   Procedure: The child moves the scooter forward, backward, and sideward as he assumes prone sitting, kneeling, or standing positions on the scooter. A maze or obstacle course should be added as the child can move on the scooter with efficiency.

10. Title: Animal Walks
    Objectives: To develop the ability to move the body in various movements
    Formation: Scattered
    Equipment: Mats
    Procedure: The following activities should be performed forward, backward, and sideward:

    1) crab walk
    2) inch worm
    3) duck walk (half squat)
    4) bear walk
    5) monkey run
    6) seal crawl
    7) rabbit jump
    8) hop
    9) snake crawl

Poor Body Image

Some children have difficulty moving within the constraints of their space because they have poorly-developed body images. They frequently trip over or walk into objects in the course of a normal day. A well-developed body image, awareness of the body and relationship between its parts, is necessary to successfully perform many daily skills, such as walking, eating, and playing. A body image program should consist of various locomotor movements through different environmental spaces.

11. Title: Cardboard Box Obstacle Course
    Objective: To develop the ability to perform various movements through an obstacle course.
    Formation: Children in lines and different size cardboard boxes scattered throughout the gym.
    Procedure: The children form a single file line and play follow-the-leader through the obstacle course. The leader should use various locomotor skills: walking, crawling, creeping, crab walking, inch worming, monkey running, jumping, and hopping, and various directions: forward, backward, sideward, over, and through. Children can also assume a position so the open ends of the boxes are at their sides and they can creep in the boxes like a tank.

12. Title: Hoop Jungle Gym
    Objective: To develop the ability to perform various movements through a hoop jungle gym.
    Formation: Jungle gyms are scattered throughout the gym with children in lines or scattered.
    Equipment: Hoop Jungle Gym — hoops are taped to each other so they are standing upright and form different shapes.
    Procedure: Children form lines and play follow-the-leader through the hoop jungle gym. The leader should use various locomotor skills and directions (same as activity 11, cardboard box obstacle course) and when going through the hoop.

13. Hoop-scotch
    Objective: To develop the ability to perform various locomotor skills through a hoop maze.
    Formation: Children in lines, hoops are placed flat on the floor in two rows next to each other. (Figure 12-7) Three different colors are alternated in serial order.
    Procedure: Children form a line and play follow-the-leader through the hoop maze. Children can go down the maze in the following ways:
    1) walking or running with one foot per hoop
    2) jumping with one foot per hoop
    3) jumping with two feet per hoop
    4) hopping
    5) skipping
    6) bear walking or crawling
    7) jumping up with ½ twist
    8) activities 1-6, backward
    9) activities 1-8 stepping in only one color of hoops

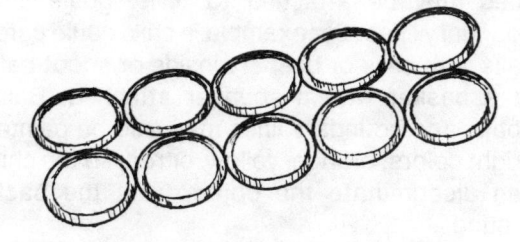

Figure 12-7. Hoop Formation

Poor Hand-eye Coordination

Children with poor hand-eye skills such as catching, striking, and kicking, are at a distinct disadvantage in most activities. The physical educator must use a developmental approach to teach these skills. For example, trapping the ball should be taught before children attempt to catch a ball solely with the hands. Balloons enable children to track and react to a moving object more accurately due to the decreased speed. Children with cerebral palsy or loss of an upper limb may require prosthetic catching or striking devices.

14. Title: Balloon activities
    Objective: To develop hand-eye coordination
    Formation: Scattered or in a circle, each child has a balloon.
    Equipment: Balloons
    Procedure: Children perform the following activities:
    1) toss balloon up and trap it
    2) toss balloon up and catch it with the hands
    3) tap the balloon in the air, 10 times with your hands
    4) tap the balloon in the air with the:
       a. head
       b. shoulder
       c. knee
       d. elbow
       e. foot
       f. two, three, four, etc. body parts
    5) toss balloon up and:
       a. clap your hands and catch it
       b. touch your head and catch it
       c. touch your shoulders and catch it
       d. touch your elbows and catch it
       e. touch your stomach and catch it
       f. touch your knees and catch it
       g. touch your ankle and catch it
       h. touch 2, 3, or 4, etc. body parts and catch it
    6) with a partner:
       a. toss and trap balloon
       b. toss and catch balloon with hands
       c. taps the balloon back and forth
    7) with a partner, place the balloon between various body parts and move forward or backward:
       a. between your partner's hip and yours

330 *Adaptive*

b. between your partner's shoulder and yours
c. between your partner's chest and yours
d. between your partner's head and yours
e. between your partner's back and yours
f. between your partner's knee and yours
g. between your partner's ankle and yours

15. Paper Plate Catching
Objective: To develop hand-eye or foot-eye coordination
Formation: Scattered with a partner
Equipment: Paper plates, paper fasteners, elastic cords, light weight bean bags
Procedure: The paper plate catcher can be used with children who are missing hands or do not have use of the hands. Bean bags are passed between partners and caught by the paper plate catchers. The paper plate catcher (Figure 12-8) is constructed by: a) cutting a slice to the center of the paper plate, b) overlapping the edges, c) attaching paper fasteners to secure the edges in that position, and d) attaching another paper fastener and a loop of elastic cord (6") to the plate's center. The catcher can be attached to the arms or legs.

16. Title: Velcro catching mitt
Objective: To develop hand-eye coordination
Formation: Scattered individually or with a partner
Procedure: A ball with Velcro strips glued across its diameter is tossed in the air. A mit shaped like a hand and constructed with two felt pieces sewn together is used to catch the ball. The ball sticks to the mitt upon contact.

17. Title: Badminton striking
Objective: To develop striking skills
Formation: With a partner
Equipment: Badminton racket, shuttle cock, velcro strips
Procedure: A badminton racket is attached to a child's arm with Velcro strips. The Velcro strips should be tightly secured to the racket to prevent rotation or propulsion of racket from arm.

Visual Problems

Children with visual problems often have diffi-

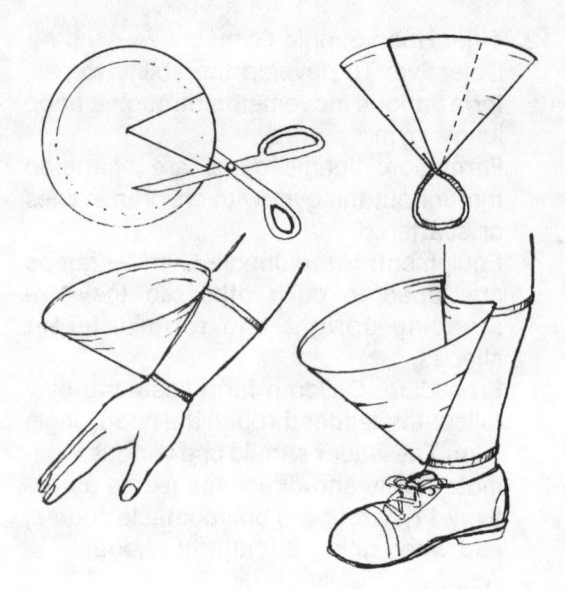

Figure 12-8. Paper Plate Catcher

culty understanding instructions because demonstration, a powerful teaching tool, is ineffective with these children. The teacher must utilize other instructional tools more effectively when introducing motor skills. Clear and concise verbal instruction paired with kinesthetic prompts enable the child to develop a mental picture of a skill. This mental picture enables the child to reproduce the intended movements accurately and independently. Some children with visual problems benefit if they can feel dolls that the teacher is manipulating to perform the desired movements. This method allows a child to get an idea of the whole skill instead of segments of a skill. Scaled-down models of gyms, locker rooms, classrooms, and pools are also helpful because the child learns his environment as related rather than isolated parts.

Stimuli that elicit responses often have to be strengthened if the child with visual problems is to respond properly. Aural or stronger visual cues may be attached to balls, goals, and boundary lines. For example, a child could catch balls with bells or beepers inside or shoot balls at a basket with a sounder attached. Balls, goals, and boundary lines may also be painted bright colors, orange, yellow, or red, so the child can discriminate the object from the background.

18. Title: Line Goal Ball
Objective: To develop underhand roll and goal keeping skills
Formation: Two teams, each team is spread out across their goal line; space children so they cannot reach other teammates.

Equipment: Goal ball or ball (15" in diameter) with beeper/bells, and goal lines
Procedure: The game is played on a rectangular field with two goals located on opposite sides. Each team attempts to *roll* the ball across the opponents' goal while protecting their goal by intercepting the ball before it crosses the end line. All participants must keep the feet in a fixed position when goal tending and must always remain within a playing zone that extends one meter in front of the goal line. Sounder can be attached to the goals to provide directional cues. The referee must reposition any participant too close to another teammate. A penalty, one point added to opponent's score, results if: 1) a participant steps out of the playing zone, 2) a participant throws rather than rolls the ball, and 3) a participant touches a teammate or moves their feet while goal tending.

19. Title: Toss Over (modified volleyball)
    Objective: To develop throwing skills
    Formation: Two teams, one team on each side of the net
    Equipment: Audio nerf ball, standards, and net placed at regulation volleyball height
    Procedure: The rules are the same as volleyball except team members throw rather than volley an audio, brightly colored ball over the net into opponent's court. The ball is permitted to hit the floor and roll before the receiving participant gathers the ball for play. Only one throw is allowed to cross the net. Bright colors or beepers should be added to the net to provide directional cues.

20. Title: Guidewire or Tandem Running
    Objective: To develop running skills and endurance
    Formation: Child holding guidewire or is paired with a sighted partner
    Equipment: Wire or rope (minimum of 25 yards), 1" diameter metal ring and strap (optional)
    Procedure: The rope or wire is suspended from a post or tree at waist height. Two rubber balls are attached to designate the end points so the child knows when to change directions. The child can use gloves or hold a strap and metal ring attached to the rope while running. A sighted person may also be used for running. The child with visual problems holds his sighted partner's arm slightly above the elbow and runs a half pace behind his partner.

Hearing Problems

The physical educator must arrange the gymnasium so children with hearing problems can utilize their vision or remaining hearing skills. Class demonstrations should be conducted so these children can easily observe the demonstrator. Directions should be given with the child directly facing the teacher. The use of signing may be required to communicate to a deaf child.

Most children with hearing problems can be integrated with hearing children with few adaptations to specialized activities. One activity designed for children with a little hearing is movements to rhythmic beats. The child may run, clap, skip, march, or beat a drum to various beats.

Respiratory Problems

Children who suffer from asthma, bronchitis, and emphysema are included in this group. The child's physician should be consulted prior to planning a physical education program. The physical educator must be aware that some children with respiratory problems are sensitive to pollens; the gym should be as dustfree as possible. Gym floors and tumbling mats should be cleaned frequently, and dustless chalk should be used when writing on a chalkboard. The physical educator needs to be attentive to the child on days when the weather is changing, the humidity is high, or the child is required to perform strenuous activities. If they become thirsty during class, these children should be encouraged to drink water (not cold).

21. Title: Ping pong golf
    Objective: To develop more efficient breathing patterns
    Formation: Scattered
    Equipment: Ping pong ball for each child, carpet with 3' diameter hole cut out of one end of the carpet
    Procedure: The child attempts to blow the ping pong ball into the hole. The child is assessed one stroke for each breath. The ball must come to a complete stop prior to the next breath. Sand traps and obstacles may be added to make the activity realistic.

22. Title: Balloon Races
    Objective: To develop more efficient breathing patterns
    Formation: All children behind a starting line
    Equipment: Balloons
    Procedure: Children on all fours line up behind the starting line with a balloon. Upon a start signal, the children blow the balloons to the finish line. A maze may also be utilized in the races.

23. Title: Bending breathing exercises
    Objective: To develop more efficient breathing patterns
    Formation: Scattered
    Equipment: None
    Procedure: The child assumes a standing position with feet shoulder width apart. The child breathes out as he slowly bends at the waist to the right, left, or in front. All muscles are relaxed in the down position except the abdominal muscles should be contracted. The child inhales as he raises upward. The abdominal muscles are relaxed during the inhaling phase.

Ambulatory Problems

Children who use crutches, braces, wheelchairs, or have difficulty moving due to inefficient locomotor skills need an accessible environment. These children should not be eliminated from activities because the setting was inaccessible. Ramps, easy open doors, and wide doorways should be incorporated into the design of the gymnasium and outdoor facilities. The physical educator should consult with the child's physician to learn transfers needed to move the child and to discuss movements or activities that may be harmful to the child.

If available, an aquatics program should be provided to the child with poor ambulation. Many skills can be performed more easily in the water than on land because less weight is placed on the joints and less balance is required due to the body's buoyancy.

24. Title: Flexibility Exercises
    Objective: To stretch muscles that are tight due to specific disabilities or confinement to a wheelchair, bed, or braces.
    Formation: Scattered
    Equipment: Mats
    Procedure: Contractures occur if children confined to restricted positions or have cerebral palsy do not perform range of motion exercises daily. Tight muscles must be identified and moved throughout a wide range, actively or passively. Movements should be smooth and slow and the stretch should be held for 5 seconds. Flexibility develops gradually so excessive force should never be applied to a joint or muscle.

25. Title: Ramp Bowling
    Objective: To develop pushing and aiming skills
    Formation: Children face bowling pins
    Equipment: Commercial ramp or carpet roll (diameter larger than the bowling ball), bowling pins, and balls.
    Procedure: A commercial ramp or carpet roll is placed near child/wheelchair. The child aims the ramp in the direction of the bowling pins set on the floor. The bowling ball is lifted, placed on the ramp/roll and pushed down the ramp. A point is awarded for every pin knocked down.

26. Title: Table Top Tether Ball
    Objective: To develop striking and hand-eye skills
    Formation: Two children, one on each side of the tether pole
    Equipment: Ball or balloon, dowel rod (36" length), string, and base (20" x 20")
    Procedure: The activity is played on a table top tether ball model. Each player attempts to wind the ball/balloon around the pole by striking it in the opposite direction of his opponent. Paddles can be introduced after the children learn the game.

27. Title: Alley Ping Pong
    Objective: To develop striking and hand-eye skills
    Formation: Two children, one on each side of a ping pong table.
    Equipment: Ping pong table, balls, and paddles/bihandle paddle
    Procedure: Ping pong rules apply to this activity except a two foot high wall is placed at the table's side to prevent the ball from leaving the table. The ball must cross over the net and land on opponent's side. A player is permitted one swing; the ball, however, may bounce more than once before the ball is hit. A point is awarded if after the ball strikes the table, it lands on the floor. A bihandle paddle should be used by children who have insufficient hand-eye skills or arm/shoulder strength to control regulation paddle.

STUDENT ACTIVITIES

1. Using the form on the next page, write an IEP based on the hypothetical data described below. You are to generate annual goals, short term objectives, time requirements, duration dates, placements, and support personnel for each objective.

   Student's Name: John Doe

   Age: 10 Years Old

   Student's Goal Areas/Objectives: Physical Fitness/abdominal strength and cardiovascular endurance

   Aquatics/floating and swimming

   Present Status: 1) John performed 13 sit-ups on the President's Physical Fitness Test (10th percentile).

   2) John ran a distance of 750 meters in 6 minutes (5th percentile).

   3) John is unable to float or swim without flotation devices.

   Time Available: 1) 18 weeks; 3 days per week; 30 minutes per class period.

   2) YMCA has offered the use of the pool for 12 weeks; 2 days per week.

   Other Considerations: 1) John is able to participate successfully with non-handicapped students in the gym.

   2) One-on-one instruction is needed in the pool.

Worksheet for project #1

I CAN PHYSICAL EDUCATION IEP FORM

School District/School _____　　Date Submitted _____

Student Name or Number _____　　Date of Planning Meeting _____

Recommended Total Time
in Physical Education _____ days/weeks _____ minutes/day　　Date(s) of Review (Listed when Scheduled) _____

Current Placement _____　　Teachers _____

Program Goal Areas in Physical Education	Present level(s) of Performance	Annual Student Goals	Short Term Objectives	Time Required (min/day)	Duration Dates Begin / End	Regular Education Placement	Special Designed Instruction	Support Personnel Needed (See back)
Area 1								
Area 2								
Area 3								
Area 4								
Area 5								

ELEMENTARY PHYSICAL EDUCATION

SECTION 3
OTHER IMPORTANT CONSIDERATIONS

In this section, the focus will be on those additional considerations necessary to successfully implement a curriculum. Such matters as legal liability, the role of competition, and equipment will be discussed. Also included is a cognitive learning-through-movement chapter designed for the classroom teacher who may wish to use this proven approach to teaching the 3 R's. The physical educator may glean ideas from the cognitive chapter in order to create additional integrated activities which can be included in physical education.

CHAPTER 13
PHYSICAL EDUCATION AND THE LAW

After completing this chapter, the student will be able to:

1. Discuss the two reasons why one should study legal liability.
2. Define and give an example of at least 80 percent of the legal terms presented in the chapter.
3. Describe potential hazards usually associated with a movement-oriented environment.
4. Describe safeguards for each of the potential hazards.
5. Explain each defense for negligence.
6. List the important information which should be included on an accident report form.

Few people are aware of legal suits involving teachers and legitimately wonder, therefore, why it is necessary to spend time studying legal liability. Although the percentage of suits is not high, the number is continuing to increase daily in this age of litigation. A suit, even if won by the teacher, can frequently ruin a career, and losing can mean depletion of one's entire life savings. Even under the worst of circumstances, however, the chances of being sued are slim, which brings us back to the original question. Knowledge of legal liability, hopefully, will make a teacher more aware of safety factors, which if adhered to, will protect children. The concerned, knowledgeable teacher will create a safer learning environment. Children, too, must be made safety conscious, but the teacher is mainly responsible for safety. Injuries to children are the leading cause of suits in public schools. The two reasons for studying legal liability, therefore, are: (1) to protect the children, and (2) to protect the teacher.

People who teach physical education are no more liable than anyone else, but opportunities for injuries which might lead to suits are greater during physical education than during most other activities. Nearly half of the early childhood injuries during school happen in organized games. This frequency is far too high and can be reduced by reasonable and prudent teacher action.

Organized games such as Paul Revere Relay have a high possibility of injury, particularly if played on a hard surface.

Ignorance of the law is not a valid excuse for failing to act in accordance with the law. The first step toward improving one's legal I.Q. is to become familiar with legal terms. Hopefully, the definitions and examples to follow will provide a foundation for developing a basic understanding of the law.

Selected Legal Terms

Corporal punishment is any type of physical punishment inflicted on the body.

Example: A Washington State physical educator punished rule violators by requiring them to run between two lines of their classmates while being hit by their peers (2).

Assault is intentional force directed toward an individual such as a threat which could potentially be carried out.

Example: An adult teacher threatens to spank a small child if the child does not follow class rules.

Battery is the actual use of unlawful physical force against another individual.

Example: The adult teacher who threatens to spank the small child actually strikes the child.

In Loco Parentis infers that one is acting in place of a parent or legal guardian.

Example: While on a field trip to another school's athletic field, a child strays from the group and is hit by a car while attempting to cross a street. The teacher is negligent for failing to keep the child in the group.

Negligence is a key word which is defined as not acting as a reasonable and prudent person should have acted under the given circumstances.

Example: During a kickball game, the ball is accidently kicked onto the school's roof. The teacher directs one of the children to climb onto the roof to retrieve the ball. The child falls and breaks a leg. The teacher failed to act as a reasonable and prudent person should have acted. The ball should have been allowed to remain on the roof and retrieved later by the school's janitor.

Attractive nuisance implies that on the school's premises exists an apparatus or piece of equipment which may naturally attract the attention of an individual. Due to the individual's inexperience, his unsupervised participation on this apparatus can foreseeably be dangerous.

Example: The physical education teacher forgot to fold, lock-up, and put away the trampoline following a gymnastics lesson. While passing the gymnasium, several children noticed the trampoline (an attractive nuisance) and proceeded to play on the apparatus. One child falls off and injures his back. The teacher would be charged with negligence because a reasonable and prudent person should have foreseen the danger of leaving the trampoline unlocked and unsupervised. There was one case where students broke into a school, found a trampoline set up and were subsequently injured on the apparatus. In this case the court ruled against the teacher who left the equipment up.

Omission implies that one has failed to act as the law requires.

Example: A student is injured on the playground. An individual arrives who has first-aid training, but fails to administer. This person is negligent, since it would have been reasonable for this person to utilize his ability to administer the first-aid.

POTENTIAL HAZARDS

Accidents, as previously mentioned, are going to occur. The safety minded teacher, however, can avoid many accidents. The purpose of this section is to identify potential hazards and offer suggestions on how to correct these dangerous situations. Selected court decisions are presented to emphasize the point.

Unsafe Facilities and/or Equipment

Teachers should establish a routine for inspecting instructional areas prior to class meeting times. Playground equipment as well as indoor equipment should also be inspected periodically. To ensure a safe environment one should follow the guidelines presented below.

A. Playgrounds
1. Inspect playground for holes, broken glass and other trash.
2. Inspect wood structures, such as seesaws, for warpage and splinters.
3. Inspect jungle gyms and other climbing apparatus for missing bolts and sharp edges.
4. Determine if protective material should be placed under climbing apparatus.
5. Inspect ladders and slides for missing or loose rungs.
6. Inspect swings for worn and/or rusty chains.

Note the hard and uneven surface under this high horizontal ladder.

The same piece of equipment with the horizontal ladder lowered — Note the soft sandy surface below the apparatus.

High injury risk and low developmental value

B. Indoor Facilities
1. Inspect floors for loose or raised boards and/or missing tiles.
2. Inspect walls for protrusions such as coat hooks or fire boxes.
3. Determine if protective mats are needed to help guard against injury.
4. Inspect the floor surface for slippery spots caused by dust build-up or spilled water.

Court decision. A high court awarded damages to a young boy who was injured while playing football in the school's gymnasium (7). The parents of the boy contended that their son's injury was not the result of being shoved by another student, but instead was the result of several of the boards in the gymnasium floor being elevated above the rest. Damages were awarded because the school district was negligent for failing to provide a safe environment.

342   Liability

Objects protruding from the wall should be padded.

Generally, protective matting should be used when students are in inverted positions.

Lack of Supervision

Supervision is defined here as the ability to see and control children, and the lack of supervision is the most frequent reason for suits. The frequency is based on the ease of proving that a teacher was or was not present at the time of an injury. Even when one is not present, however, the prosecution must prove that the injury would not have occurred had the teacher been present. To ensure proper supervision teachers should avoid:

1. leaving their class to answer a phone call.
2. leaving their class unattended while going to the rest room.
3. leaving their class to speak with another teacher.
4. allowing class to go outside for recess while they remain inside to grade papers.

Court decision. Aileen and a small group of girls always played a hiding game each day at lunch (6). One day a group of boys was playing in their usual play area so the girls moved to another location. The girls used poor judgment

A potentially unsafe instructional environment

Note unpadded pillars and exposed overhead lights.

in selecting a glass door as a base. While running toward the base, Aileen pushed her arm through the glass, severing a major artery. Being scared, the injured child ran wildly around the playground before another child caught Aileen and took her to the school nurse. Aileen had lost so much blood that she later died. If a teacher had been present, he would have either stopped the game or would have been able to calm the child down before so much blood was lost.

Inadequate Control Measures

Rules are essentially limitations imposed on games and/or general classroom procedures to facilitate both fair play and a safe instructional environment. Failure to adhere to the rules of a game can cause rough play and subsequent injury. In fact, in many instances, innocent bystanders have been injured by individuals failing to follow established classroom procedures. The following guidelines are means of keeping law and order in the gymnasium.
   A. General Rules
      1. Post all rules.
      2. Deal with all rule violators.
   B. Rules Involving Games
      1. Provide instruction on the rules of the game.
      2. Question students periodically on the rules of the game.
      3. Have consequences for all rule violations.

Court decision. A young girl received injuries during a game of line soccer (4). The activity primarily involves kicking skills. Specific rules have been developed forbidding rough play and uncontrolled, severe kicking. During the conduct of the game, the teacher failed to enforce the rules outlined in the syllabus. The court found the teacher negligent for not adhering to the established rules which cautioned the teacher to penalize violators.

Inadequate Instruction

Teachers are required to give adequate instruction before a child is asked to perform. This legal obligation has been interpreted by some as requiring a command style of teaching — explanation and demonstration by the teacher. Instruction, however, can come from any media including the teacher. These media include films, slides, tape recorders, videotapes, books, computers, and T.V. No matter what medium is used, this aspect of the law only applies to those activities in which an injury is likely if children are not adequately prepared. Tumbling and apparatus-type activities fall in this category, so teachers must exercise caution during this phase of the program. Ball handling, movement skills, and other basic psychomotor skills can be handled with less caution since the injury possibilities are far less. Teaching styles such as problem-solving and exploration, therefore, should be used with care. A question such as, "Can you show me some different ways you can throw the ball?" is safe while a question such as "Can you show me your tumbling skills?" can lead to some real problems.

To guard against inadequate instruction, it is advisable for the teacher to prepare a checklist of activities for each program area to be included in the curriculum. This checklist should be constructed in a hierarchical fashion, listing activities from simple to complex. This procedure will provide a safeguard against forgetting to teach appropriate lead-up activities before complex skills are attempted. For instance, the "back rocker" (lie on back, hug knees and rock back and forth like a rocking chair) should be taught as a lead-up before introducing the tumbling skill — the backward roll. Within recent years, a guided exploratory approach of teaching tumbling and apparatus skills has become widely known as educational gymnastics. As previously mentioned, instructors should be very careful how they word their guided questions. The practice of instructing students with open ended questions could prove to be dangerous. For instance, one teacher asked her group of students to find five different ways to roll their bodies. One child attempted to perform a front flip off the stage.

Court decision. In the case LaValley v. Stanford, the court ruled that the teacher was negligent for allowing two boys to take part in a potentially dangerous activity in which the teacher failed to warn the boys of the danger involved and also failed to provide instruction in the art of the activity. (5).

DEFENSES

No matter how knowledgeable or careful a teacher is, accidents will occur. To prove an injury was a result of teacher negligence, the prosecution must show that the teacher's actions led directly to the student injury. If it is possible to show that something occurred between the teacher's actions and the injury, negligence cannot be proven. These intervening actions are termed defenses against negligence and include (1) act of God, (2) contributory negligence, (3) assumption of risk, and (4) sudden emergency.

Act of God

Injuries due to uncontrollable forces are termed acts of God. Examples would be a child hit by lightning, or children injured due to hurricanes, tornadoes, or floods. A gymnasium roof falling, fire, or natural causes could all be classified under this category. None of these examples, however, is a sure defense since each may have additional circumstances associated with it. Suppose, for example, children were allowed to continue practicing golf while a thunderstorm was approaching and a child was hit by lightning. A reasonable and prudent person would have gotten the clubs out of hand and sought appropriate shelter. Lightning has killed more people in this country than all other storms combined. It is a killer and must be respected. People who teach in hurricane, tornado, or flood areas must also exercise prudent judgment if they have any hope of using the act of God defense.

Contributory Negligence

If it can be shown that the actions of the injured child rather than the teacher's actions caused the injury, the defense is called contributory negligence. For example, suppose the teacher instructs all the children on trampoline usage and forbids flips. The child in defiance of the teacher does a flip and is injured. The teacher is not liable. If the teacher had talked only with the injured child about not doing flips and had not given the rule to the rest of the class, then they could not have come forward in the teacher's defense. Spotting rules and do's and don'ts should be covered with all students prior to gymnastics. Rules should also be posted for those who can read.

Assumption of Risk

Injury in certain activities is more likely to occur than in others. Any contact sport, of course, is inherently more dangerous than a non-contact activity. Many activities which are classified as non-contact, however, do cause their share of accidents. To participate in any contact activity requires a certain assumption of risk, and parental permission is absolutely essential. Since contact sports should not be part of an elementary curriculum, teachers should not be concerned with this aspect of participation. For other activities, though, proper precautions should be taken. Accidents will happen, and as long as negligence cannot be proven, assumption of risk could apply. A teacher must be extremely cautions about forcing a child to participate against his will. Fear can be a deadly companion to children, particularly in gymnastics and tumbling. A prudent teacher will not force children to participate in any activity where injury risk is a factor. Encourage, yes — force, no.

Sudden Emergency

In a life or death situation, a teacher can be relieved of normal supervisory duties. However, the situation must be truly life threatening. Example: A child falls and badly cuts her chin. Direct pressure is immediately applied by the teacher, who then leaves 29 children unsupervised to take the child to the office. Horseplay among the children results in serious injury to a child and his parents sue. The judgment goes against the teacher. The teacher should not have left the class; a child should have gone for the nurse. The bleeding child was in no immediate danger, and the teacher's actions, therefore, could not be covered by "sudden emergency."

PRECAUTIONS

Chambless and Mangin (1) list a number of precautions a teacher should take for self-protection as well as for child protection:

Insurance

Low cost liability insurance is available to members of the National Education Assocaition (NEA), the American Alliance for Health, Physical Education, Recreation, and Dance (AAHPERD) and some state professional associations. A prudent individual will have insurance. The NEA will also provide lawyers at no cost to members who are sued. A person without insurance who loses a judgment can be wiped out financially, and his salary can be attached.

Know the Health of Students

Classroom teachers should be able to keep up with their students' health status, but a physical educator with larger teacher/pupil loads has more difficulty. A classroom teacher can be extremely helpful by keeping the physical education teacher informed of the children's health problems. Anyone teaching physical education must know a child's limitations and restrictions.

Administer First Aid Only

The American Red Cross is considered the first aid authority, and all teachers who want to act reasonably and prudently should have a Red Cross First Aid certification. Physical educators and classroom teachers are frequently guilty of practicing medicine, diagnosing injuries and prescribing treatment. This is a hazardous practice and one need only see how much liability insurance costs a doctor to realize it. "It's just a sprain; soak it in hot water tonight." "Get up, you'll be all right." "Walk it off." These frequently heard expressions could lead directly to a suit if a child is seriously injured as a result. Know what to do when an accident occurs, follow proper procedures when treating the victim, and leave the medical practice to those properly trained.

Keep Accident Records

Records can be a valuable aid in a court case. Such things as time, place, circumstances, witnesses, and actions taken should all be recorded as soon after an accident as possible. Do not rely on someone else, such as the nurse, to keep records. Figure 13.1 illustrates a sample acident report form.

Permission Slips

Teachers who conduct special activities, such as trips and athletic participation after school, should obtain a permission slip or waiver from a parent. Some teachers feel such slips make them immune to suits. Parents also believe such documents restrict their rights and will not, therefore, sign them. The only value of such slips is the parents' acknowledgement that their child is participating. In no way does a permission slip relieve the teacher's legal obligations. Parents may not sign away their child's rights. In fact, no person may sign away another individual's rights, except through court action. A permission slip or waiver, therefore, is worth nothing if negligence can be proved.

REFERENCES

1. Chambless, J. and C. Mangin, "Legal Liability and the Physical Educator." *JOHPER,* 44: 42-43, April, 1973
2. "Children Removed to Protest 'Gauntlet'." *Richmond News Leader,* April 20, 1977.
3. "Court Denies Recourse to Paddled Students." *Richmond News Leader,* April 19, 1977.
4. *Keesee v. Board of Education of City of N.Y.,* 235 N.Y.S.2d 300 (1927). Cited in H. Appenzeller. *From the Gym to the Jury.* Charlottesville, Va.: The Michie Company, 1970, p. 81.
5. *LaValley v. Stanford,* 70 N.Y.S.2d 460 (N.Y., 1947). Cited in H. Appenzeller. *From the Gym to the Jury.* Charlottesville, Va.: The Michie Company, 1970, p. 81.
6. *Ogando v. Carquenez Grammer School District.* 75p.2d 641 (Cal., 1938). Cited in H. Appenzeller. *From the Gym to the Jury.* Charlottesville, Va.: The Michie Company, 1970, p. 39.
7. *Read v. School District No. 211 of Lewis County.* 110 P.2d 179 (Washington, 1941). Cited in H. Appenzeller. *From the Gym to the Jury.* Charlottesville, Va.: The Michie Company, 1970, p. 107.

Figure 13.1
SAMPLE ACCIDENT REPORT FORM

Name: _____ Date: _____

Place of accident: _____

Time of accident: _____

Nature of injuries sustained: _____

_____

_____

Circumstances surrounding injury _____

_____

_____

Was first-aid administered: _____

If yes, explain actions taken: _____

_____

_____

_____

_____
Witness

_____
Witness

_____
Instructor

STUDENT ACTIVITIES

1A. Make a tour of an indoor physical education facility and note potential hazards which exist.

1B. How would you correct the potential hazards that you found during your tour of an indoor physical education facility?

2A. Make a tour of a local playground. Note any potential hazards which exist.

2B. How would you correct the potential hazards that you found during your tour of a local playground?

CHAPTER 14
UNDERSTANDING COMPETITION

After completing this chapter, the student will be able to:

1. Describe the role of competition in the elementary physical education curriculum.
2. Describe the extent to which youth sport injuries may be detrimental to the growth and development process.
3. Describe problems associated with utilizing age-group records to motivate young children.
4. Discuss dietary concerns of the young athlete and associated problems.
5. Describe the role of youth sports as a contributor to physical fitness.

Competition is an inherent part of American life. This fact is frequently used to justify high levels of competition among children's groups such as Little League. Like any other aspect of growth and development, however, competition must be introduced gradually. There are those who will advocate no competition among children in early childhood. Children will, however, create their own competitive situations. Any attempt to eliminate competition will probably be futile; control and amount are the keys to introducing competition.

COMPETITION IN SCHOOL

Teachers should be aware of the need to introduce competition gradually. Activities in early childhood should stress competition with self-testing activities and reward coming internally when each person has done his best. Open competition among children in the academic area can lead to frustration and discouragement among the poorly skilled or slow learner. Such practices as posting grades, displaying progress charts with children's names, and ridiculing certain children should be eliminated. Any technique which could embarrass a child should not be used.

COMPETITION IN PHYSICAL EDUCATION

Unlike classroom work, a child's physical performance is hard to hide. The early childhood curriculum, therefore, should consist primarily of activities which focus on individual physical development and non-competitive group interaction. Highly competitive activities have no place in the curriculum for young children. Low key competitive activities, such as simple games and relays, can be played with a minimum of emphasis on winning and losing.

After third grade, children will have been exposed to considerable competition both in and out of school. They are ready, therefore, to participate in more highly competitive sports activities. This is not to suggest extremely high levels

The standing long jump is an excellent self-testing activity.

351

Simple games provide low-key competition.

of competition, only more intensive levels than in early childhood. Lead-up games to team sports and individual sports, therefore, can be included in the physical education curriculum.

COMPETITION IN ATHLETICS

The number of young athletes participating in organized youth sports continues to accelerate. In a recent survey, researchers estimate that the number of youth sport participants now exceeds 20 million (12). This means that on the average, more than 50 percent of the children in any elementary school classroom are participating in an organized youth sports program.

Controversy has surrounded competition, particularly with the advent of highly competitive athletics for elementary children. In early years, teams were directed by poorly qualified people, there were few meaningful rules to protect the children, and coaches emphasized winning over the joy of playing. Despite some changes for the better, there are still some disturbing trends. One trend is toward earlier involvement. Just a few years ago, growth and development specialists shuttered at the fact that children as young as five or six years of age were participating in team activities such as "T" baseball. Today, a four-year-old holds an age group record for running a marathon in six hours and three seconds—a distance of over 26 miles (11). There has in fact been attempts to conduct an "Infants Olympics" (10). Thus, in the near future, there may be national and international records for creeping and crawling.

Like it or not, competition for young children is no longer an issue—it is a fact. Since competition is here to stay, the schools need to focus their efforts toward educating parents, coaches, and even the young children about competition. Reviewing the literature makes one aware of the many concerns regarding competition for preadolescent children. Presented below are a selected group of frequently asked questions regarding competition. An understanding of these physiological and psychological concerns will hopefully lead to better supervised competitive youth programs.

Question: To what extent are sport related injuries detrimental to the growth and development of young participants?

Answer: The physiological effects of athletic participation have been fairly well-documented. On the positive side, any vigorous physical activity, except long distance running, is physically beneficial. There is some evidence to indicate that long distance running by children can adversely affect long bone growth. Although running is a good cardiovascular development activity, it is the opinion of some that children should not run continuously for more than fifteen minutes a day (11).

Some negative physiological effects may occur as a result of contact sports and other activities which stress certain areas, such as the elbow and shoulder. Damage can occur to the epiphyseal (growth portion) ends of the long bones as a result of trauma. Trauma can occur from a severe blow in a contact sport or, more subtly, by constant irritation, the common cause of "Little League elbow" or shoulder. Increased interest in tennis has also created "tennis elbow," which is medically the same condition as Little League elbow. Both problems are created by irritation of the elbow joint while throwing curves in baseball or putting spin on the tennis ball. While traumatic injuries to the growth portion of the bone (epiphyseal) may have some long term effects on the growth and development of some children, recent research evidence indicates that such injuries are infrequent. One doctor notes that about one-half of all athletic fractures he sees involves injury to the growth portion of the bone. He also noted, however, that about one-half of all free play fractures involved the epiphyseal. Furthermore,

98 percent of the epiphyseal injuries were uneventful (1). Similar findings have been reported by other researchers (4).

Question: What can be done to reduce the number of youth sport injuries?
Answer: Researchers have concluded that many youth sport injuries are avoidable (7). Selected guidelines for avoiding youth sport injuries follow:

1. Use quality constructed and proper fitting protective gear (9).
2. Match teams for competition on the basis of physical fitness, skill level and physical maturation (biological age) — not chronological age only.
3. Children should not be forced into sport participation. "Children who don't want to be involved in a sport are at high risk for injury" (13).
4. Young participants should be encouraged to play different sports and experience different positions within a given activity. This practice tends to reduce injuries which may be a result of overstressing a particular movement pattern.
5. Pay close attention to signs of physical fatigue. Many injuries occur late in a game or practice session when the children are tired. Unfortunately, the image conveyed by some coaches, "to be tough," keeps many young athletes from telling the coach of their fatigue.

Question: At what age should children be allowed to participate in training programs?
Answer: Authorities generally agree that young children are capable of learning and practicing sport skills around six years of age (2). The emphasis at this time should, however, be on self-improvement, not success in regard to "out-doing" an opponent. Intensive training programs have no place in the life of the average preadolescent child.

Question: Is winning essential if one is to enjoy youth sports?
Answer: From an adult perspective, the final outcome — winning — tends to be the most important variable of an athletic contest. Children's perspective on winning and losing is, however, quite different from that of an adult. In a survey of youth football players, 72 percent of the young athletes indicated that they would rather play and lose the game, than sit on the bench and win the game (8). Such evidence indicates that the priorities of youth sports organizers, in some cases, conflict with the priorities of the young participants.

At what age should children begin learning sport skills? How young is too young?

Question: Should the juvenile athlete be given special nutritional considerations?
Answer: The nutritional requirements of the young athlete are essentially the same as for any other active youngster. For the most part, an individual's appetite is an indicator of caloric needs. Thus, parents should provide well-balanced meals, being sure that portions are served from each of the four basic food groups. It appears that problems arise when parents alter children's diets in an attempt to give their child an additional competitive edge. For instance, many youth sports leagues are organized according to "weight classes" — not age. Some parents have been known to place their children on diets, even periods of fasting, so their child will be able to compete in a lower weight class. Such practices are to be avoided. Dietary supplements have also been a source of nutritional problems. It appears that some parents are not aware that certain vitamins when taken in large dosages are toxic. Dr. Nathan Smith, a well noted pediatrician, has recently reported five cases of Vitamin A poisoning. In one case, parents of a young tennis player who had experienced Vitamin A poisoning, repeat-

edly kept putting their child back on the vitamin (1). Vitamin supplements are not necessary when the young athlete is eating balanced meals.

Question: When young children are placed in training programs at an early age and become successful at their sport, will this competitive edge carry over into the high school and college years?

Answer: Not necessarily. Researchers who conducted the Medford, Oregon, Boys Growth Study found that many individuals who were competitively successful during the elementary and junior high school ages were later surpassed by the skilled abilities of their peers in the adolescent years. While early maturers may have a competitive edge during the elementary years, they are often smaller and weaker than their late maturing peers during the adolescent years.

Question: What is "Psychological Burn-out?"

Answer: When young children are required to adhere to strict training schedules, year after year, many tend to lose interest in their sport activity. Many young swimmers, for instance, train two hours before school and several hours after school throughout the year. Allowing children to participate in many different sports as well as playing different positions in a given sport is one method of reducing psychological burn-out.

Question: Does participation in a contact or otherwise aggressive sport make children more aggressive in other phases of their life?

Answer: Researchers have not been able to distinguish whether an individual selects a particular sport because of his personality or whether one's personality is created by the sport.

Question: At what age should "age group records" be kept as a means of motivating children to push themselves to reach higher goals?

Answer: It has been suggested that age group records should not be kept until the child is capable of abstract thinking — generally around eleven or twelve years of age. At this age, the youngster is more capable of intrinsic motivation. Prior to this age, the danger lies with the psychologically immature child who may push himself beyond his capabilities just to obtain adult approval.

Question: Will participation in youth sport programs improve physical fitness?

Answer: Yes and no. It appears that participation in youth sports programs is accompanied by improvements in motor fitness. Its effect, however, on health related fitness is questionable. Recent evidence indicates that the most popular youth sport activities such as baseball and football are primarily motor fitness oriented (6). Many believe that children would be better off selecting activities which would significantly elevate their heart rate high enough to obtain a training effect (See Chapter 6). Youth programs in soccer, track and swimming tend to emphasize health-related fitness.

Children are not going to obtain optimal personality development from youth sports participation until adult organizers stop trying to turn children's play into work. Thus it becomes the job of the professional community to educate their coaches concerning the physiological and psychological needs of the young participants. Positive steps toward accomplishing these goals are now being taken in states such as New York and Michigan where specific "Volunteer Coaches Training Clinics" have been developed. In the near future, several states will also require all volunteer coaches to be certified by the State's Athletic Commission.

REFERENCES

1. Barnes, L. "Preadolescent Training — How Young is Too Young?" *The Physician and Sportsmedicine,* 10:114-119, Oct., 1979.
2. Bharadwaja, K. "Early Sports Training: Is It Worth The Price?" *The Phsyician and Sportsmedicine,* April, 1977, pp. 37-52.
3. Bula, M. "Competition for Children: The Real Issue." *JOHPER,* Sept., 1971, p. 40.
4. Francis, R., T. Bunch and G. Chandler. "Little League Elbow: A Decade Later", *The Physician and Sportsmedicine,* April, 1978, pp. 88-94.
5. Gerber, S. "Are Kids Too Young To Avoid Sports Injuries?" *Science Digest,* Oct., 1975, pp. 44-51.
6. Gilliam, T. "Fitness Through Youth Sports: Myth or Reality?" *JOPER,* 49: March, 1978.
7. Goldberg, B., P. Witman, G. Gleim, and J. Nicholas "Children's Sports Injuries: Are They Avoidable?" *The Physician and Sportsmedicine,* 7:93-97, Sept., 1977.
8. Griffin, L. and K. Henschen "Attitudes Toward and Values of Little League Football Competition." *APAHER — Update,* June, 1976, p. 4.
9. Hale, C. "Protective Equipment for Baseball." *The Physician and Sportsmedicine,* 7:59-63, July, 1979.
10. "Infant Olympians Sought." *Richmond Times-Dispatch,* Dec. 2, 1979, p. A-22.
11. Jeffers, P. "A Marathon Runner: Thoughts on Children's Running." *The Main Artery,* Feb. — March, 1980, p. 2.
12. Seefeldt, V. and J. Haubenstricker, "Competitive Athletics for Children — The Michigan Study." *JOPER,* 49:38-41, March, 1978.
13. Williams, R. "Why Children Get Hurt." *Sport Scene,* 7:1, Feb., 1980.

STUDENT ACTIVITIES

1. Observe a youth sports competitive athletic contest and make the following observations:
   A. Did all children get to play in the game?

   B. How many children were injured during the course of the game?

   C. Were the young athletes successful in achieving the goals of their sport? For example: During a basketball game chart or make a frequency tally of the following:
      A. Number of shots attempted: _____
      b. Number of shots made: _____
      c. Number of shots which hit the rim but failed to go in the basketball goal: _____
      d. Number of shots which failed to even contact the basketball goal structure: _____
      Determine the percentage of total for each of the categories. What can you say about the young athletes' success-failure in this activity?

2. Interview the coach of both the winning and losing teams. Compare the two coaches' viewpoints about the game. To help you make a comparison, asking the following questions may be helpful:

   a. Do you have a systemic approach for determining how much playing time each child receives?

   b. How do you prepare the children for the games?

   c. Are you a volunteer coach, and if so what are your goals or intrinsic rewards for coaching?

3. During the course of the athletic contest, observe parents of the young participants. You should note their gestures, comments to their team, and comments to opposing team. Are they offering instruction to their child or his/her teammates? Record your findings below.

CHAPTER 15
THE COGNITIVE DOMAIN AND MOVEMENT

After completing this chapter, the student should be able to:

1. Differentiate between Integrated Physical Education and Cognitive Physical Education.
2. Describe the three reasons according to Humphrey why Cognitive Physical Education is successful.
3. Describe the AMAV technique for teaching reading.
4. Design a cognitive learning activity which meets the standards established for such activities.

The use of games as a learning media has gained in popularity within recent years. The concept, however, that children learn better through movement or play activities has been recognized for centuries. Piaget has shown that the child's activity is responsible for his intellectual development (2). Piaget believes that children acquire knowledge not by sitting at a desk, but by moving about and interacting with their environment.

In an article entitled, "Education or Imprisonment," Rappaport (10) notes that children are more comfortable and efficient when they are allowed to perform in a manner to which they are accustomed (moving). Under our present educational system, however, when children reach the magic age of six, they are generally expected to learn better when sitting quietly at a desk listening to teacher verbalization. Humphrey (5) has recognized that verbal learning involves almost complete abstract symbolic manipulation. The ability of young children to interpret many abstract symbols must be questioned.

If a child is to grasp a specific cognitive concept, the concept must be internalized. Internalization is best acquired when the individual is required to learn the concept in context to practical application. The games media for teaching academic concepts is not only adaptable to practical application, but also lends itself to inherent learning facilitators, namely (1) increased motivation; (2) proprioception; and (3) knowledge of results (9). Children are motivated because the activity is fun, they get immediate knowledge of results, and they like the competition. Since the answer comes immediately during the activity, children do not have to wait to find out if they have answered a question correctly. Proprioception is sensory feedback from the muscles. It has been suggested "that sensory experiences arising from muscle action acts as a kind of coordinating process that aids in the integration of visual and auditory input, forming a holistic kind of perceptual experience . . ." (5). Thus the perceptual modalities appear to be the "tools" needed for cognitive learning. Only recently has proprioception been promoted as an important part of cognitive learning even though its importance in psychomotor behavior has long been known. This total involvement of the body in cognitive learning has been emphasized by Humphrey (7) and Asher (1). The third reason listed by Humphrey is reinforcement. A strong stimulus response bond is formed when the reinforcement closely follows the response. As mentioned earlier, the answer is apparent almost immediately after the response. The correctness of the answer by the student is not important in the reinforcement theory as long as the correct response is given.

A word of caution. Some of the activities appearing in the curriculum chapters (7-10) of this text have been referred to as Integrated Physical Education Activities (8). While children who play these activities may learn academic concepts, the primary objective of these activities is a physical one. The concept learning related to another subject area is merely a bonus, like getting two things for the price of one. These activities like any other good physical education activity should provide for maximum participation and total physical involvement.

The activities which appear in this chapter have been referred to as Cognitive Learning Through Movement Activities. Although many of these activities may seem similar to those found in the curriculum chapters, the objectives of the activities are different. The major objective in these activities is the reinforcement or learning of an academic concept. The medium is movement, either creative or in the form of a game requiring large muscle movement. Unlike a developmental activity or a game, not all children are moving, but all must be thinking.

Now that a distinction has been made between the two types of activities, it should be clear that the activities in this chapter should be conducted during the time set aside for the subject in question and should not be done during physical education. Children should be given a well-rounded curriculum, including physical education, and to take time away from this important aspect of education to teach academic skills and concepts would be unfortunate.

LANGUAGE ARTS

Speedy Spelling

In the traditional spelling bee, teams were formed and children took their turn at trying to spell a word. Unsuccessful spellers were often ridiculed by teammates, or at the least, embarrassed. Another approach was to call out words which any person could answer, with correct spellers getting points. Only the best spellers worried about the spelling; the other children tried to keep from being called on.

In speedy spelling, everyone must think about how to spell the word. Two teams are formed and identical packages of letters are given to each team (two or more letters for each child). Teams stand behind a starting line next to each other. The teacher calls out a word which everyone must spell in their head to see if they have a letter in the word. If they do, they run to a predetermined location and put their letter in the proper place to spell the word. Slow learners can be assisted by teammates. The values of this activity are: (1) everyone must think of the answer; (2) children get immediate knowledge of results; (3) they are motivated by the game aspect; (4) they are totally involved in learning through movement. This game, and the two which follow, can be played at every grade level with the degree of difficulty being determined by the words used.

Speedy Antonyms

The rules are the same as for Speedy Spelling, except children must think of an antonym (opposite word meaning) of the word called out and then spell the antonym.

Speedy Homonym

Again, the rules are the same as for Speedy Spelling, except children must think of a word pronounced like the assigned word but which has a different meaning and spelling.

Twister Spelling

Selected letters of the alphabet are drawn on a sheet as shown below.

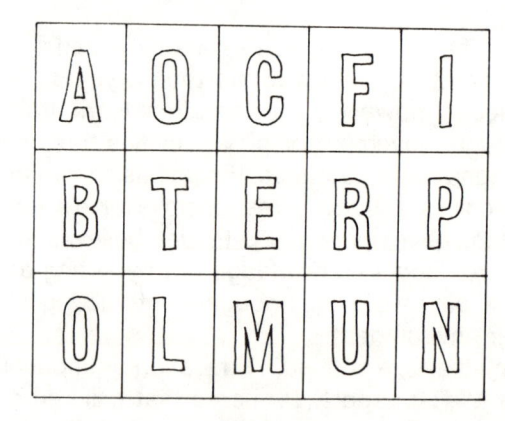

A	O	C	F	I
B	T	E	R	P
O	L	M	U	N

Figure 15-1.

The teacher calls out a two, three, or four letter spelling word. The child must touch a body part to each of the letters contained in the word.

Body Spelling

Divide the class into small groups. Teacher calls out a three letter word and students must make the appropriate alphabetical shapes with their body in order to spell the word.

Verbs In Motion

Similar to the traditional spelling bee but instead of the teacher calling out a word, the children must "act out" the word. Sample action verbs are provided in Figure 15-2.

Talking Alphabet

The purpose of this activity is to develop auditory discrimination in reference to the sounds of letters in the alphabet. Before playing this activity with students, the teacher will need to make an audio tape recording of alphabetical sounds.

Action Verbs	
run	gallop
hop	slide
skip	walk
roll	leap

Figure 15-2. Action Verbs

For example, with the recorder running the teacher will randomly make the sounds of the letters, i.e. AAAAAA DDD PPPPP etc. Each child is then assigned a letter sound. The tape is played and when students recognize their sound, they jump in place.

Alphabet Race

A set of flash cards containing all the letters of the alphabet are passed out to each of two teams. The teacher or student leader from team #1 randomly selects five of team #2's cards, while team #2 collects an equal number of cards from team #1. On the signal "Go," each team is to arrange their cards in alphabetical order and then determine which five letters their opponents selected from their deck. The first team to correctly write on the board their five missing letters are the winners. Teachers should vary the types of locomotor movements the children use to get to the board.

Do This, Do That

This activity is useful for helping children learn to follow directions. The teacher or student leader stands in front of the class and performs various fundamental movements (hop, jump, etc.). The leader has two flash cards, one stating "Do This," the other, "Do That." These cards are periodically flashed to the class. While the leader will always be in motion, class members are to model the leader's movements only when the card "Do This" is being shown. Any class member caught moving when the "Do That" card is shown will receive one penalty point.

Circuit Training Dictionary

Construct several task cards and place them around the classroom. On the task card should be written the directions to simple exercises. Within the exercise's description, however, the teacher should use words that are not familiar to the students. Thus in order for the students to understand the exercises they will need to look up the unfamiliar words in a dictionary. A dictionary or two should be placed at each station.

Human Punctuation

The teacher writes a sentence on the board: " [1] where have you been [2] [3] lucy [4] " The teacher then asks children what must be done to make number one correct, number two, etc. The students answer by forming the correct answer with their body.

AMAV Technique for Teaching Reading

AMAV, as defined by Humphrey (7) is a successful technique using movement to teach reading. The first "A" stands for auditory, which is the beginning point of learning to read. Children hear words and can speak many of them, even though they cannot read. The written word must be decoded to reach the audio-visual stage which is reading ("AV"). This decoding is facilitated, according to Humphrey, by movement, "M". The movement activities, therefore, act as a bridge between the known, listening and speaking vocabulary (A) and reading ability (AV).

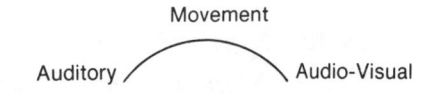

Movement
Auditory ⌒ Audio-Visual

The steps in the AMAV technique include: (1) listening to a story read by the teacher or on a record (6); (2) acting out th story through creative movement; and (3) hearing the story read again while following along in a book or prepared sheet. Stories can be purchased commercially (6) or prepared by the teacher. When choosing stories, the teacher must be sure that they lend themselves to movement.

After the story is read, children take different parts (all children must be involved) and act out the story through movement. Children can be trees or objects as well as people or animals. The important thing is for the children to follow the story and enjoy the creative movement.

The last step is to have the children sit and listen to the story again while following in a book or sheet identical to the one the teacher reads. Certain vocabulary words can be emphasized by recalling the movement phase of the technique, i.e., "Who was the tree?", "How is 'tree' spelled?", and "How did the tree move?"

MATH

Speedy Math

This game is organized like Speedy Spelling, page 360. The cards given to students, however, contain numbers rather than letters. Each team should also have one plus (+) sign, one minus (-) sign, and one equals (=) sign. A person should have only one sign at most and at least one number. The game has several variations with different degrees of difficulty.

Equation. The left side of the equation, i.e., 5 + 3, is given. Students must run to a specified area placing 5 + 3 = 8. The first team to have the equation down correctly is the winner.

Answer. In this variation, only the answer is given and the left side of the equation must be determined. The left and right sides of the equation must be equal.

Plus and Minus. Again, the answer is given, but this time the left side of the equation must contain both the plus (+) and the minus (-) sign, i.e., 5 + 4 - 1 = 8.

Double Trouble. A number is given, and both the left side and the right side of the equation must equal the number. One side of the equation must use the minus (-) sign and the other the plus (+) sign.

Grab the Club Math

Set up this game as Grab the Club, page 217. A math problem is called out (5 - 2) and the person with the same number as the answer tries to get the club back to his team.

Call Ball Math

Eight to ten children stand in a circle with one child in the middle. Each child has a number from one to eight or ten. The child in the middle calls out a math problem (5 + 2 or 4 + 4) and the child with the same number as the answer tries to catch a ball which has been thrown up by the center child just after calling out the equation. If the ball is caught before it bounces more than once, the child who caught it gets to throw the ball up next. If unsuccessful, the child who threw it up gets one more turn. After two turns with no catches, the center child picks a new thrower. This is a very low participation game, but all children must be cognitively involved in solving the math problem. There is also immediate feedback regarding the correct answer.

Crows and Cranes Math

Set up the game as Crows and Cranes, page 183. A math problem is called out (5 - 2). If the answer is odd, one group (designated the "Odd Group") must run to safe base; if the answer is even, the other group runs.

Twister Math

A series of discs with numbers are drawn on a sheet as shown:

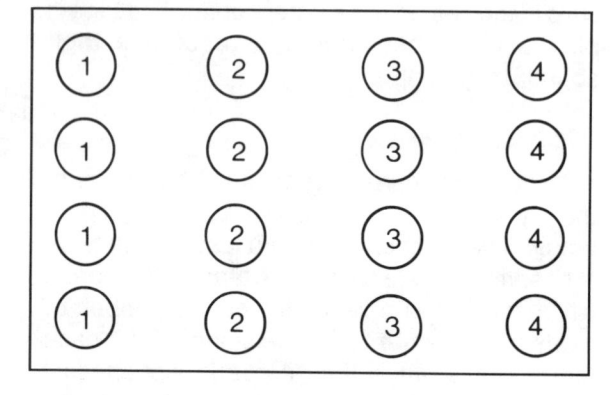

Figure 15-3

Three to four children can play at a time on the same sheet. The leader calls out "right hand 2 - 1" or "left foot 2 + 1." Children must solve the problem and place the proper part on the correct number. This is a balance activity with each person trying to cause the others to lose their balance and fall. No pushing, shoving, or bumping is allowed. Children merely try to get into a favorable balance position by getting numbers close to them, thus forcing others to make long, unbalanced stretches to other numbers. Only one person can be on any one disc at a time. The last one left is the winner. In this variation, all answers to problems must be between the numbers one and four. The game can be made more difficult by using larger numbers.

Stew Pot Math

Children line up in two lines facing each other about ten to fifteen feet apart. Each person has a number on the floor in front of him. One child stands between the two lines (in the stew pot). The leader holds up two equations — one for each line. The child who has the solution to the problem in front of him must change places with the child in the other line. The person in the center tries to tag one of them as they go through the stew pot. If successful, he takes that child's place on the line. If unsuccessful after two or three turns, the center person can be replaced. The center person can also solve the problem and tag the person while he is still in line — the center person does not have to wait for the people changing places to move.

Human Math

Divide class into three equal teams. Each team stands shoulder to shoulder behind a restraining line. An answer line is drawn about five feet in front of each team. The teacher or student leader calls out a math problem. The object of the game is for each team to move to their answer line and be the first to display the answer by the number of children standing. All others must squat down, i.e., with ten people on a team, and an equation of 10 - 4 = ??, four people must squat down leaving six standing.

Human Math Groups

The leader has students perform different types of locomotor movements around the room. The leader holds up a card on which is written a certain number. Students are to hold hands and sit in groups corresponding to the flashed number. Odd numbered students unable to get into a correctly numbered group receive one point against them.

Human Equations

Two teams stand behind a starting line. An answer is called out. Each team then must run to a predetermined area and make the equation, including the answer with their bodies (must have plus or minus sign and equals sign). Variations such as those for Speedy Math can also be used.

Multiplication Throw

Place the class into two equal lines standing approximately three yards from one another. Give children in one line a tennis ball which has written on it a multiplication problem. Have the child throw the ball to the child opposite him. Once the child has caught the thrown ball he must run to a designated area and search through a pile of flash cards for the correct answer. The first four children to stand with the correct answer held over head are the winners.

Select a Problem

In small groups of three or four, students take turns at tossing a bean bag toward a numbered square. The child then selects a math problem from a deck of flash cards. If the child answers the problem correctly, he is awarded the number of points corresponding to where his toss landed in the numbered square. The first child to accumulate 50 points wins.

Body Math

Have the children, individually or in small groups, lie on the floor and position their body(s) to resemble the numbers called out by the teacher. This same activity can be played using Roman numerals instead of Arabic numerals.

Dribble Math

One playground ball is given to each group of three students. The first child bounces the ball from 1-8 times, the second student performs the same task. The third student bounces the sum. The teacher can designate the type of problem, i.e., addition, subtraction, etc.

Count Down

Children stand tall and count from ten backwards, by ones. Each time a number is counted off, the children squat lower and lower. After children reach the number one, they shout, "Take-Off" and jump high as possible into the air. Have children count backwards by twos, threes, fours, fives, etc.

Fraction Line

Divide class into two equal teams. Mark a straight line on the floor in front of each team. When the leader calls out a fraction the players are to group themselves above and below the fraction line according to how many should be in the numerator and how many should be in the denominator. Any extra players should squat. The maximum number of players must be utilized. For example: ½ should be 5/10 with two squatting if there are 17 players on each team.

Metric Long Jump

Children take turns performing the standing long jump. Partner measures the distance of jump using meter stick. If a meter stick is not available, measures can be made with the traditional yard stick and converted to metric standards. Most dictionaries contain metric conversion tables.

SCIENCE
Simon Says Globe

Each child must envision himself as a globe of the world. Playing by the rules of Simon Says, page 152, children are asked to touch the equator (waist usually), the North Pole, South Pole, etc. Children can begin to get the relationships between the countries. This is also an interesting game to play with adults.

Electric Shock

Two teams of equal numbers stand on each side of a leader and form a semicircle. Children hold hands with teammates and the leader. The leader sends an electric shock by squeezing the first person's hand on each team (leader should hold hands behind his back). The current is then sent by squeezing until it gets to the last person, who upon receiving the current, raises his hand. No person can squeeze someone else's hand unless his hand is squeezed. The first team to raise their hand is the winner. The teacher can talk about broken circuits (hands not held) and short circuits (someone forgetting to squeeze).

Weather Vane

A leader calls out directions, i.e., North, South, Northeast, etc. Children must jump in place and face the proper direction. Each proper jump receives one point. Those with the most points at the end are the winners.

Momentum Roll

Roller skates and scooter boards can be utilized to teach the concept that momentum is influenced by the object's speed and object's weight. Two children of unequal size and weight skate side by side (at the same speed) for a distance of 15 feet. Without applying further force both coast to a stop. Children should note that the lighter person coasted the greater distance, i.e. greater momentum.

Head Stand

The head stand can be used to illustrate the concept, "A body at rest is more stable if it has a wide base of support." On a tumbling mat, outline with tape or draw the head and hand positions illustrated in Figures 15-4 A and B. Allow child to perform the head stand utilizing each of the two positions. Ask the child why it was easier for him to balance when his head and hands were positioned like that illustrated in Figure 15-4 B.

Electric shock

Cognitive Domain 365

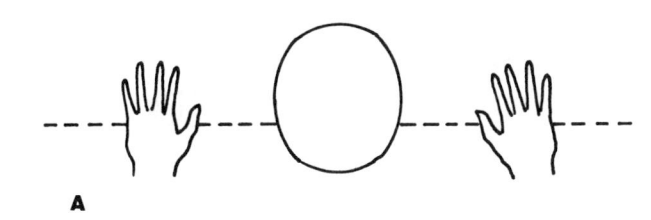

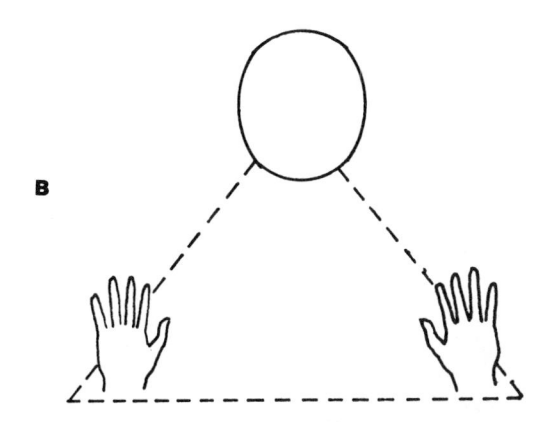

Figure 15-4

REFERENCES

1. Asher, J. "The Total Physical Response Approach to Second Language Learning." *The Modern Language Journal,* LIII, January, 1969.

2. Case, R. "Piaget's Theory of Child Development and Its Implications." *Phi Deta Kappan,* 1973, Sept., 20-25.

3. Gallahue, D., P. Werner and G. Luedke. *Moving and Learning.* Dubuque: Kendall/Hunt Publishing Company, 1972.

4. Gilbert, A. *Teaching the Three Rs Through Movement Experiences.* Minneapolis: Burgess Publishing Company, 1977.

5. Humphrey, J. "Active Games as a Learning Medium." *Academic Therapy Quarterly,* 1969, 5(1), p. 22.

6. Humphrey, J. *Teaching Reading Through Creative Movement — The AMAV Technique,* LP 5070, Kimbo Educational Records, Long Island, New York, 1969.

7. Humphrey, J. "The Use of Total Physical Response Motor Learning in the Development of Academic Skills and Concepts with Elementary School Children." Paper presented to the Third Psycho-Motor Learning and Sports Psychology Symposium, Vancouver, B.C., October 25-27, 1971.

8. Humphrey, J. *Child Learning Through Elementary School Physical Education.* Dubuque: WM. C. Brown Company, 1974.

9. Humphrey, J. *Education of Children Through Motor Activity.* Springfield: Charles C. Thomas, 1975.

10. Rappaport, S. "Education or Imprisonment." In *Foundation and Practices in Perceptual Motor Learning — A Quest for Understanding.* American Association for Health, Physical Education and Recreation, 1971, p. 4-8.

11. Werner, P. and E. Burton, *Learning Through Movement.* St. Louis: The C.V. Mosby Company, 1979.

CHAPTER 16
HOMEMADE EQUIPMENT

by

John P. Bennett, Ph.D.

George Mason University

After completing this chapter, the student should be able to:

1. List at least five sources for obtaining elementary physical education equipment.

2. Design and make a homemade piece of equipment from scrap materials around the home.

Physical education budgets rarely are sufficient to meet children's equipment needs. Administrative knowledge and attitudes are frequently reflected in their commitment toward physical education. Even where there are sympathetic principals, budgetary constraints have created problems in all curricular areas. To minimize the limitations created by fiscal problems, one must seek alternatives to school purchased equipment and supplies. These alternatives include using homemade equipment and supplies, having a junk day, getting parents involved, seeking funds from the P.T.A., and/or having senior high industrial arts classes make elementary physical education equipment.

Jump ropes can be made from no. 8 or no. 10 sash cord.

Much of this chapter will be devoted to the first suggestion, homemade materials. Small items such as beanbags, pinnies, scoops, and targets are easily made from scrap materials. Other items such as balance beams, balance boards, wands and lummi sticks can be inexpensively constructed with minimal mechanical knowledge and effort on the teacher's part.

A carefully-organized junk day can bring in a number of useful items from students' homes. A list of items which might be considered useless at home, but useful at school could be prepared and sent home with the children. Such items as old tennis rackets, badminton rackets, used milk containers, and cloth for beanbags might be included on the list. Care must be exercised to guarantee that children do not bring valuable items from home to please the teacher. By analyzing needs and specifying items as well as requiring parental permission to bring such items, the junk day can be very successful.

Parents frequently volunteer their services to schools and are seeking opportunities to aid children and teachers. These willing parents can be asked to make beanbags, streamers, yarnballs and other easily constructed supplies. Funds for materials can often be obtained from the P.T.A.

An industrial arts class or students at the vocational technical center can be asked to build the larger pieces of equipment — a vaulting box, or materials for creative playground. Such equipment can be as good, if not better, than commercially produced materials and can be constructed inexpensively.

Seeking alternative resources for equipment and supplies takes a little more teacher time and effort, but seeing the rapid growth and development of children when each child has a piece of equipment makes it worthwhile. Maximum participation can become a reality with a little knowledge and minimal effort.

372 *Equipment*

A vaulting box made by industrial arts class.

There are some distinct values that evolve within the school setting from the use of homemade equipment. They are as follows:
1. Students that have input into their learning are more motivated to participate in activities.
2. Cooperation and communication channels are enhanced between parents and P.T.A.s, high schools, elementary schools and the community.
3. The opportunity for innovation through creative efforts does a great deal to promote student and parent interest in the program.

When one is making or designing homemade equipment that will be for use in the classroom, one must consider a variety of factors. These factors listed below have become increasingly important in light of legal suits that have appeared on the educational scene today for a variety of reasons:
1. Above all — BE SURE IT'S SAFE!
2. To insure safety, make certain that it's sturdy, use non-toxic paint, and keep the equipment clean.
3. Have a regular maintenance system and do not hesitate to discard a piece of equipment when it can no longer be used safely.

A big advantage of using homemade equipment over commercially made equipment is that it often permits the teacher to satisfy the special need of each and every child to a higher degree.

Equipment should be designed with the idea in mind that regardless of the skill level of a child, he or she can find a place for entry into the activity without experiencing any problems. Then the equipment or any activity can truly meet the needs of every child, regardless of where the child is on the spectrum of development. Entry level according to ability requires extra planning and work, but homemade equipment can assist greatly in making this concept a reality.

The remainder of this chapter is devoted to the explanation of equipment construction for use in individualized physical education instructional settings.

Item: *Paper-tape balls.*
Materials: Newspapers, masking tape.
Directions: "Ball-up" sheets of newspaper and secure in a round shape by wrapping with masking tape.
Suggested Uses: Throwing, catching, and striking.

Item: *Foam balls.*
Materials: Four or seven-inch squares of heavy duty foam.
Directions: Cut off edges of squares to make round balls.
Suggested Uses: Throwing, catching, striking, and bouncing.

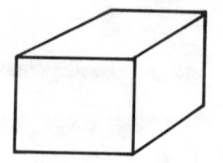

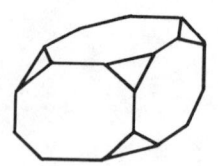

Figure 16-1. Making a foam ball

Item: *Bean bags.*
Materials: Heavy fabric, heavy duty thread, dried beans or peas.
Directions: Cut 4 ½ to 6 ½ inch squares of cloth; double hem on three sides of two squares.

Turn inside out and fill halfway with navy beans or birdseed; double hem open end.

Suggested Uses: Throwing, catching, kicking, and directionality activities.

Note: Bags of various colors, shapes and textures lend themselves to a larger variety of uses.

Item: *Coat hanger rackets*
Materials: Heavy duty coat hangers, nylon stockings.
Directions: Bend coat hangers to shape of a racket. Tie a knot just above the heel of the stocking; cut off the foot portion (save this piece), and turn the stocking inside out. Slip the stocking over the hanger and tie another knot at the opposite end, preferably the handle end, so that the remainder of the stocking and pieces may serve as cushioning around the handle. Finish off the handle by wrapping it with athletic tape.

Note: Strength and durability of the racket may be increased by using two coat hangers and two nylon stockings.

Suggested Uses: Nearly all racket activities.

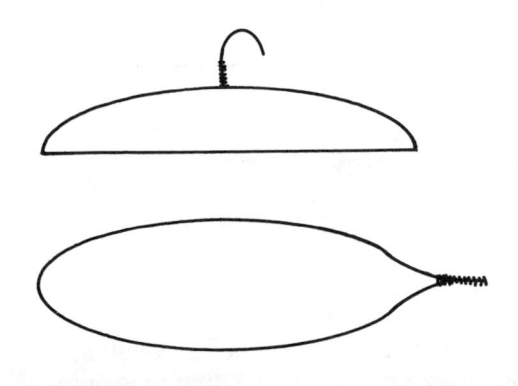

Figure 16-2. Coat hanger racket

Item: *Yarn ball.*
Materials: Heavy yarn, cardboard, twine, crochet hook.
Directions: Draw and cut out two circle patterns of cardboard; eight inch outside diameter and five inch inside diameter. Cut a hole in the center of the circle. Holding circle patterns together, wind yarn (cut out into short lengths) around them. Start winding from outer circle edge to center hole, keeping yarn evenly spaced. Tuck yarn ends under wound strands. Wind yarn around pattern in layers until center hole is completely filled. As the hole fills, use crochet hook to pull yarn through. Cut yarn along outer edge of pattern with razor blade or scissors. Tie yarn between cardboards with strong twine. Pull twine very tight and tie it securely to make sure no strands of yarn escape. Tear out the cardboards. Hold ball by the twine ends and shake it vigorously to fluff it and to remove any loose pieces of yarn. Trim off the uneven ends of yarn and the excess twine.

Suggested Uses: Throwing, catching, and striking.

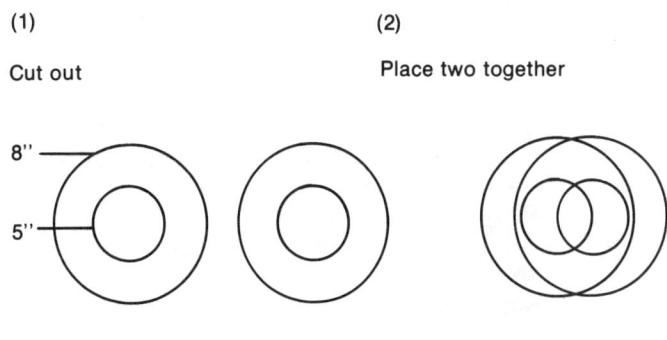

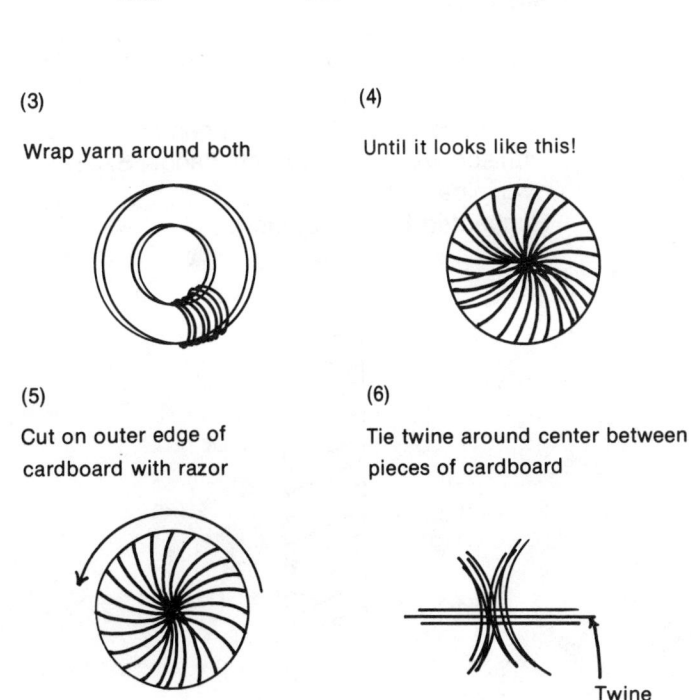

(1) Cut out

(2) Place two together

(3) Wrap yarn around both

(4) Until it looks like this!

(5) Cut on outer edge of cardboard with razor

(6) Tie twine around center between pieces of cardboard

Twine

(7) Shake and fluff up and trim ends of yarn and twine

Figure 16-3. Process for making yarn balls

Item: *"Bleach Bottle" scoops.*
Materials: One gallon size plastic bottles, scissors.
Directions: Cut away the shaded area following a design similar to that of the dotted line.
Suggested Uses: Throwing and catching.

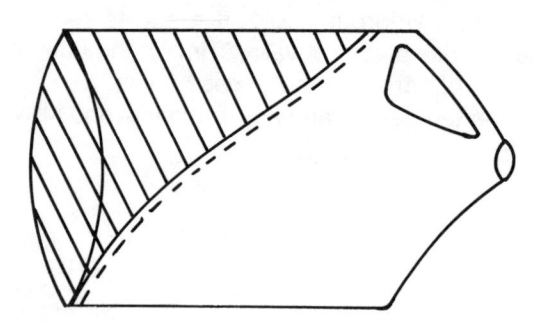

Figure 16-4. Bleach bottle scoop

Item: *Batting tee.*
Materials: Radiator hose 1-12" by 18", pipe (threaded out at one end), 1" by 12" floor flange 1" in diameter, wooden base 2" by 12" by 18", wood screws.
Directions: Attach flange in center of board with screws; screw pipe into flange. Slip hose over pipe.
Suggested Uses: Batting.

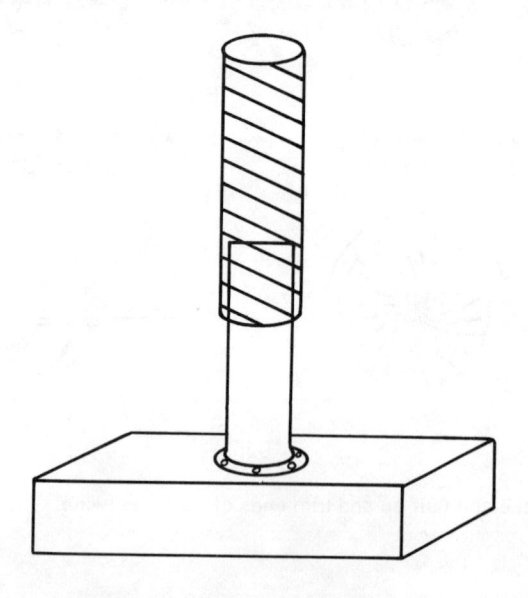

Figure 16-5. Batting tee

Item: *Paddle.*
Materials: ¼" or ½" plywood for handle and paddle head; half-round molding for handle; glue.
Directions: Cut head of paddle to 7 ½" wide and 10" long with rounded edges and a 5" handle. Cut half-round molding into 5" lengths. Glue molding onto handle. Drill a ¼" hold through handle to attach a safety line.
Suggested Uses: All racket activities.

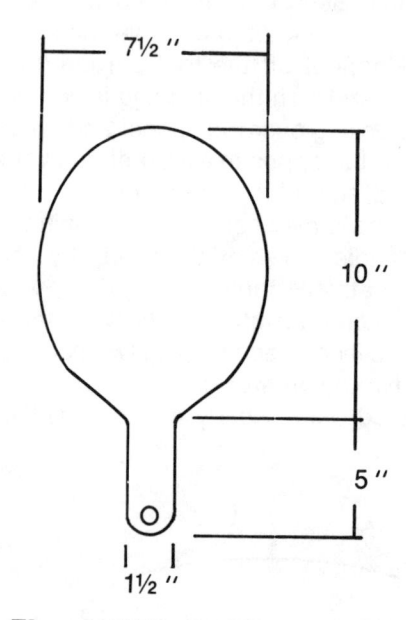

Figure 16-6. Paddle

Item: *Jump ropes.*
Materials: ⁵⁄₁₆" or ⅜" diameter rope.
Directions: Cut into 7', 8', or 9' lengths, depending on the age group. Either tape or burn the ends of the rope if it is nylon to prevent unraveling of the rope.
Suggested Uses: Locomotor movements, combination movements, coordination development, flexibility and creative dance.

Item: *Plastic hoops.*
Materials: Seven to eight lengths of flexible plastic pipe, such as PVC pipe found at the hardware store, approximately ½" in diameter; ½" nylon or wooden dowels about 3" long; saw and a knife; access to very hot water.
Directions: Put ends of pipe in hot water until soft. Insert dowel in one end of pipe joining the other end at the dowel, thus forming a circle.

Equipment 375

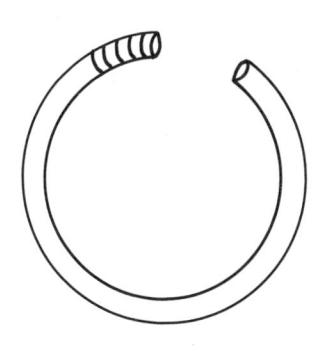

Figure 16-7. Plastic Hoop

Suggested Uses: Movement routines, targets, locomotor activities, creative dance, and combination movements.

Item: *Sticks.*
Materials: 5'8" wooden dowels or broom handles.
Directions: Cut to desired length for particular stick activities.
Suggested Uses: Rhythms, hurdles, and games.

Item: *Scooter and stand.*
Materials: *Scooter* — Square of plywood 1" by 12" by 12"; four ball bearing casters 1 ¼" in diameter; sixteen wood screws; rubber inner tubes. *Stand* — Pipe threaded at one end 1" by 4"; one inch floor flange; four wood screws; square of wood 2" by 18" by 18".
Directions: *Scooter* — Attach casters to corners of square. Drill a 1½" hole through scooter for storage. Tack a strip of rubber tubing all the way around scooter to act as a bumper. Note: Rounded edges on scooters will improve safety. *Stand* — Attach flange to middle of square with screws; screw in pipe for scooter storage.
Suggested Uses: Upper and lower body development.

Item: *Paper strip streamers.*
Materials: Crepe paper or newspaper; tips of fishing rods or thin branch or thin stick of bamboo.
Directions: Cut strips that are 1" to 2" in width and 4' to 10' in length. Attach strips to sticks or use unattached.
Suggested Uses: Rhythmic Activities.

Item: *Skittles.*
Materials: 4" by 4" wooden posts for uprights; ¾" plywood for base; screws to attach posts to bases.
Directions: Cut 4" by 4" posts in pairs 12" or 18" or 24" long. Cut plywood into 10" squares and attach with screws to post. Note: Notch top of post to rest a wand or pose on.
Suggested Uses: Obstacle courses, hurdles, and markers.

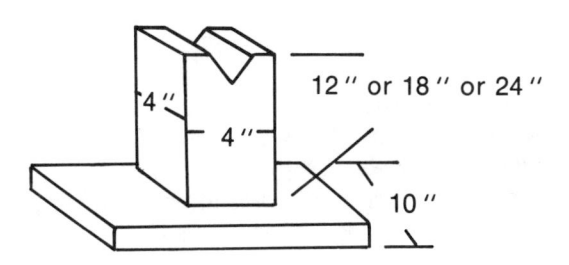

Figure 16-9. Skittles

Item: *"Bleach Bottle" markers.*
Materials: One gallon size plastic bottles.
Directions: Weight bottles for outdoor use by partially filling them with sand or gravel. Paint for increased visibility and varying meanings.
Suggested Uses: Boundary markers.

Item: *Blocks and cones.*
Materials: Wooden blocks 4" by 4" by 12" or 4" by 4" by 8"; ¾" or 1" dowels cut to 4' lengths; traffic cones.
Directions: Notch blocks for width of wands on side and end. Notch cone on top for wand.
Suggested Uses: Place dowel in notch for obstacle courses, hurdles, and markers.

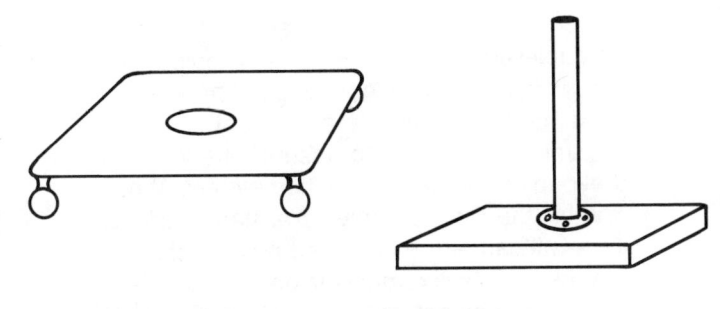

Figure 16-8. Scooter and stand.

376   Equipment

Item: *Pinnies.*
Materials: Old towels.
Directions: Cut hole in center of towel to put over head like a poncho. Attach snaps or velcro fasteners at sides. Dye towels for teams. Sew on numbers if needed.
Suggested Uses: Determination of teams for team play.

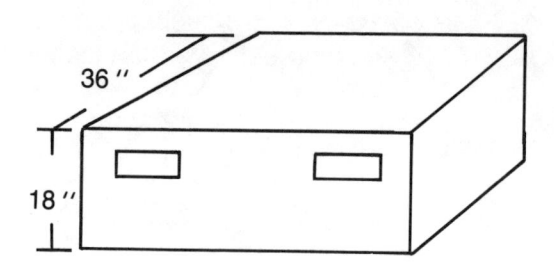

Figure 16-12. Box

Figure 16-10. Pinnies

Item: *Box.*
Materials: Two 36" squares of ¾" plywood; two 18" by 36" rectangles of ¾" plywood; two 18" by 34 ½" rectangles of ¾" plywood; 1 ½" wood screws and glue.
Directions: Cut hand holes in the 34 ½" long rectangles; glue and screw pieces together to form a box.
Suggested Uses: Gymnastic activities.

Item: *Sashes and bandannas.*
Materials: Two different colors of material, i.e., red and blue.
Directions: Cut materials into circles or triangles; sashes 2" wide and 36" circumference; bandannas — half or a 26" square.
Suggested Uses: To determine opposite teams or partners in dance.

Item: *Pegboards.*
Materials: 2" by 10" by 8' wooden board; two wooden dowels 1" by 6".
Directions: Drill 1 ½" holes in board in a zigzag pattern; hang board on wall.
Suggested Uses: Upper body development.

Item: *Maracas (Shakers)*
Materials: Two large, burned-out light bulbs; wheat paste (wallpaper paste — ½ cup); strips of newspaper or paper towel; two or three pints of water; tempera paint; plastic spray.
Directions: Mix wheat paste and water (same as papier-mache) and cover light bulbs with six or more complete coverings of paper towels dipped in wheat paste. At least six coats of paper are needed to assure safety. Allow the papier-mache to dry completely. When dry, hit the bulb sharply on a hard surface. This will cause the enclosed bulb to shatter, but the glass will remain inside the paper and rattle. Paint as desired and spray with plastic for permanence.
Suggested Uses: Rhythmic activities.

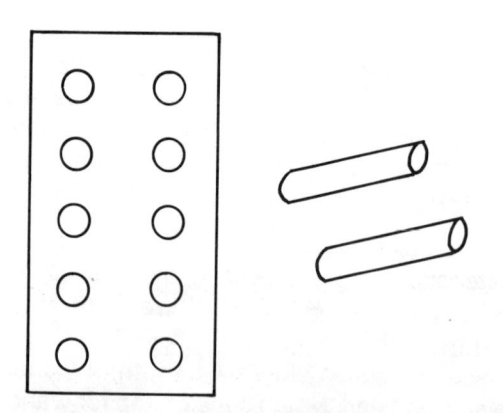

Figure 16-11. Pegboard

Item: *Balance beam.*
Materials: Five 2″ by 4″ by 8′ boards.
Directions: Cut 2″ by 4″ by 8′ boards to fit the 2″ by 4″ by 8′ board as shown in diagram. Attach the 2″ by 4″ by 8″ board to the 2″ by 4″ by 8″ board as shown in the diagram with screws and glue.
Suggested Uses: Balance and gymnastic activities.

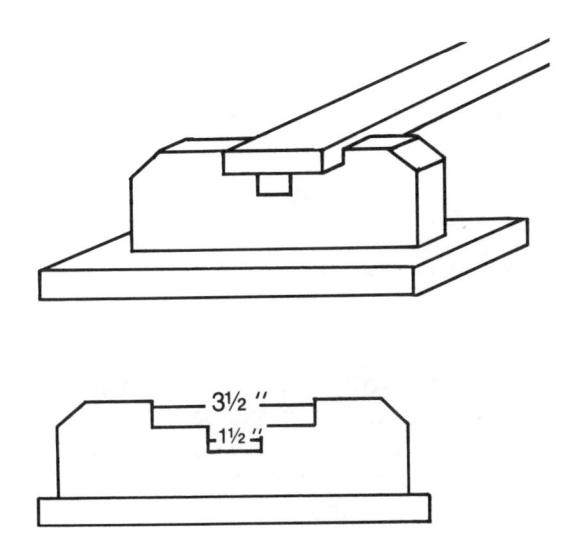

Figure 16-13. Balance Beam

Item: *Drums.*
Materials: 1 pound, 2 pound, and 3 pound coffee cans; contact paper, chamois, rawhide strings, mallet or stick.
Directions: Cover cans with contact paper; stretch chamois across bottom and top and connect with rawhide. Mallet is a pencil covered with leftover pieces of the skin.
Suggested Uses: Rhythmic activities.

Item: *Drum.*
Materials: Wooden powder keg or nail keg; calf's hide; rawhide; metal eyelets.
Directions: Cut the calf's hide into a circle. Put holes every two inches and insert metal eyelet. After all the eyelets are in, weave the rawhide through the holes. Place the hide on top and bottom and pull as tightly as possible (wetting leather slightly will help make it tighter).
Suggested Uses: Rhythmic activities.

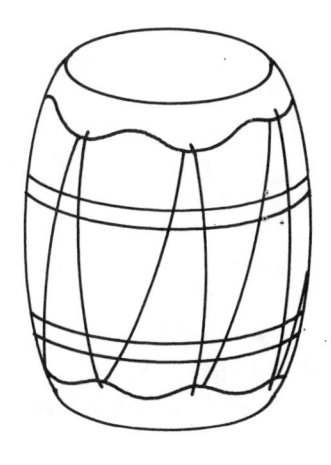

Figure 16-15. Drum

Item: *Bell bracelets.*
Materials: Coarse ribbon; bells (2 sizes); needle and thread
Directions: Sew bells on ribbon and join ribbon to form a bracelet.
Suggested Uses: Rhythmic activities.

Item: *Woodblocks.*
Materials: Blocks of wood; sandpaper; upholstery tacks; ribbon.
Directions: Cut wood to desired size. Tack sandpaper on bottom of blocks as well as on sides. Tack on ribbon, making sure that it's loose enough for children to put their hands through and grasp the block.
Suggested Uses: Rhythmic activities.

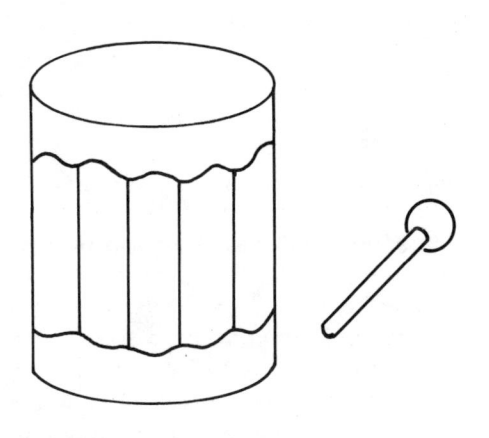

Figure 16-14. Drum

Item: Gutbucket.
Materials: Five gallon bucket or washtub; broom stick or short dowel; Bass string.
Directions: Turn tub or bucket upside down and drill a small hole in middle of bottom. Tie a knot in end of string and run through hole and attach to end of broom handle or dowel. Notch end of broom stick and attach to side of tub. Adjust tones by stretching the string and stroking the string with the other hand.
Suggested Uses: Rhythmic activities.

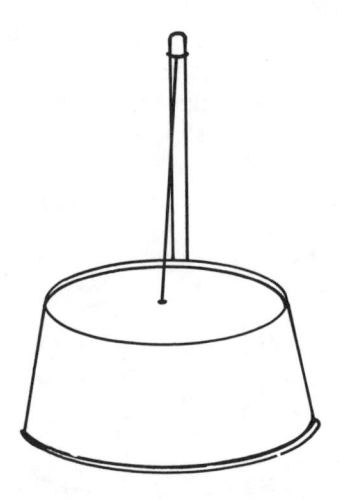

Figure 16-16. Gutbucket

Item: *Plastic bottle shaker.*
Materials: Empty plastic bottle; beans or peas; paint.
Directions: Empty plastic bottle and clean. Add beans and paint.
Suggested Uses: Rhythmic activities.

Item: *Old tires for obstacle courses.*
Materials: Tires that are not too worn out of different sizes and concrete.
Directions: Set the bottom of tire in concrete and then cover with at least two inches of dirt. Tires may be set in a row, randomly or in geometric figures of your choice.
Suggested Uses: Traveling in, through, over, and around tires in a variety of ways, i.e., locomotor movements, combination movements, on a variety of body parts. Vaulting, balancing, or as part of an obstacle course.

Item: *Isometric Exerciser.*
Materials: Two broomsticks and rope.
Directions: Tie *good* knots at varying distances along rope.

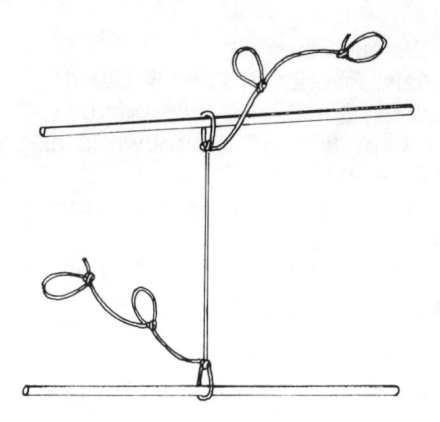

Figure 16-17. Isometric Exercise

Suggested Uses: May be used for isometric exercises, tug of war, combatives and other competitive activities.

Item: *High jump standards.*
Materials: Two 2" by 4" by 8' boards, package of finishing nails, bamboo pole.
Directions: Cut a five foot length off each 2" by 4" board and mount on the remainder of the board as in the figure. Put finishing nails every 2 inches.
Suggested Uses: High jumping, obstacle courses, and limbo games.

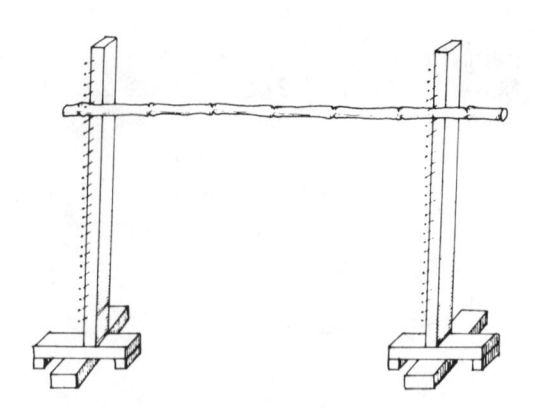

Figure 16-18. High jump

Item: *Wooden Markers.*
Materials: 4' by 8' by ½" plywood.
Directions: Cut plywood into 4" squares or circles with 4" diameters. They may then be painted a variety of colors with numbers and letters, and arrows can be painted on them.

Suggested Uses: Markers for courses, markers for a dribble maze, identification markers, number, color, and letter recognition.

Item: *Hurdle.*
Materials: Conduit pipe.
Directions: Bend the pipe to the shape of a hurdle at desired height. Be sure that the ends will not be exposed to the children for injury. This is done by putting a wooden dowel or union plug inside the two ends of the conduit and joining it together.
Suggested Uses: Hurdling, obstacle courses, over and under activities.

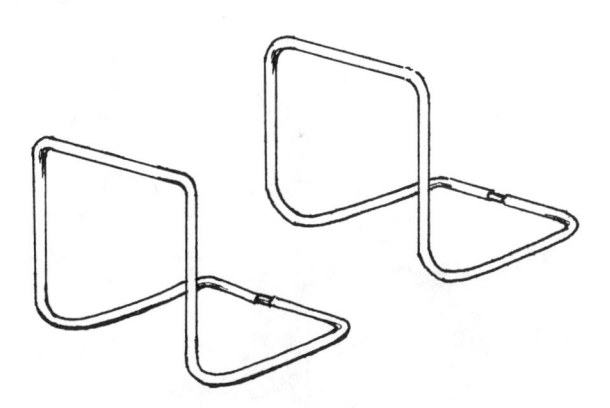

Figure 16-19. Hurdle

Item: *Wrist Roller.*
Materials: Broomstick, rope, brick.
Directions: Drill hole through broomstick to attach rope and rotate handle to raise the brick.
Suggested Uses: Development of muscular strength in the arms and shoulders.

Figure 16-20. Wrist roller

Equipment and supplies for elementary physical education are often found in the least likely places. The following are some additional ideas that may be useful:

— Varying lengths of logs, 6 inches or less, placed vertically side-by-side for climbing and jumping.
— Tires planted in the ground for obstacle courses and sand boxes.
— Logs and poles placed vertically with notches cut for climbing.
— Logs sawed into discs for stepping stones.
— Concrete culvert pipes as tunnels or mounted vertically with holes cut in them for climbing.
— Telephone poles and railroad ties mounted as low and high balance beams.
— Parallel bars made of pipes for swinging and gymnastic stunts.
— Manmade ramps of dirt, brick, concrete, wood, or blacktop for running up and down.
— Sand pits.
— Empty feedbags filled with straw, sand, or sawdust for bases.
— Bottle caps for target tossing games.
— Pieces of rope with strips of cloth dangling down three or four feet can form an excellent net.
— Net standards can be constructed by closing one opening of an old tire with plywood, pouring the tire full of cement, and inserting a metal pipe. By placing a horizontal spike through the pipe that is covered by cement, the standard will not work free.
— Old tires and tubes may be used for relay races.
— Two bicycle inner tubes linked together as you would rubber bands provide youngsters with a good "stretchy" tug-o-war.

This list of equipment and supplies is only a beginning and includes a few of the many possibilities open to the inventive educator of today. Take them, use imagination, modify and re-create! The challenge is yours!

380 *Equipment*

Figure 16-21. Varying arrangements of tires planted in ground

REFERENCES

1. Cochran, N.A. and Wilkinson, L.D. and Furlow, J.J. *A Teacher's Guide to Elementary School Physical Education.* Dubuque, Iowa: Kendall/Hunt Publishing Co., 1971.

2. Cochran, N.A. and Wilkinson, L.C., and Furlow, J.J. *Learning on the Move.* Dubuque, Iowa: Kendall/Hunt Publishing Co., 1975.

3. Dauer, V.P. and Pangrazi, R.P. *Dynamic Physical Education for Elementary School Children.* Minneapolis: Burgess Publishing Co., 5th Ed., 1975.

4. Fleming, G.A. Creative Rhythmic Movement. Englewood Cliffs, New Jersey: Prentice-Hall, Inc., 1976.

5. Gallahue, D.L. *Developmental Play Equipment for Home and School.* New York: John Wiley and Sons, Inc., 1975.

6. Kirchner, G. *Physical Education for Elementary School Children.* Dubuque, Iowa: William C. Brown Co., Publishers, 3rd Ed., 1974.

7. Murray, R.L. *Dance in Elementary Education.* New York: Harper and Row, Publishers, 3rd Ed., 1975.

8. Werner, P.H. and Simmons, R. A. *Inexpensive Physical Education Equipment for Children.* Minneapolis: Burgess Publishing Co., 1976.

APPENDICES

APPENDIX A
EVALUATING AND DEVELOPING FITNESS

The V.C.U. Fitness Test

For Whom: Children six to twelve years of age.

Norms: Norms are available for most test items, although more norms are needed for younger children. The test items are just as useful without such norms, however, since norms can be determined from data at individual schools or within a school system.

Ease: The test items are easy to administer and data is simple to interpret.

Validity: Each item has a validity of .90 or above unless otherwise specified.

Reliability: Reliabilities of .90 or above unless otherwise specified.

Objectivity: All tests have an objectivity of .90 or above.

Time: The entire test should not take more than one hour to administer.

Test Item 1: Flexed Arm Hang

Component: Upper body strength and endurance.

Equipment: Stopwatch and a horizontal metal or wooden bar approximately 1½ inches in diameter placed high enough for a student to maintain the flexed arm position with the chin over the bar and legs fully extended.

Procedure: Child is lifted to the flexed arm position. As soon as the support is removed, a stopwatch is started. The amount of time the child can maintain his or her chin over the bar is recorded. As soon as the chin drops below the bar, or touches the bar, the watch is stopped.

Scoring: The number of seconds the child held his or her chin over the bar is recorded.

Norms: Flexed Arm Hang (Girls 10-12)

(In Seconds)

Rating	Age — 10	11	12
Excellent	31	35	30
Good	18	17	15
Average	10	10	8
Poor	6	5	5

Flexed Arm Hang (Girls & Boys 6-9)

(In Seconds)

Rating	Age — 6	7	8	9
Excellent	30	45	55	60
Good	20	24	30	40
Average	9	12	13	14
Poor	2	5	7	7

Test Item 2: Sit-Ups

Component: Abdominal strength.

Equipment: A stopwatch and mats for testing indoors (Mats not needed if grass is available for outside testing).

Procedure: Children should be paired with one holding the other's feet. The child being tested lies on his back with knees bent so heels are six to eight inches from the buttocks. Arms are folded across the chest opposite hand to shoulder. The holder applies pressure on the other child's feet only. When the go signal is given, the child sits up, keeping the arms across the chest at all times.

Scoring: One point is given for each sit-up completed during a 60-second time period. A child in the up position when time is called gets credits for a completed sit-up.

Flexed arm hang

Flexed arm hang indoors using parallel bars

Test Item 3: Timed Runs

Component: Cardiovascular efficiency.

Equipment: a 100-meter tape, a stopwatch, numbered pinnies (10), and ten clip-type clothespins.

Procedures: a 100-meter tape is placed on the grass in an oval resembling a one-fourth mile track (it should be oval to reduce the sharpness of the turns). Each child is assigned a numbered pinnie and a numbered clip-type clothespin corresponding to the pinnie number. The clothespin can be clipped to the pinnie during the run. A form such as the one in Figure A-1 is used for recording. Ten students can be tested simultaneously by one tester who records the number of times each child crosses the start/finish line. Children ages six to nine run as far as they can in six minutes, while children ages ten to twelve run for nine minutes. At the end of the time, a whistle is blown and the children stop immediately and clip their clothespin to the tape. This is followed by a cool-down period consisting of walking. An *alternative testing procedure* is to pair children with one recording laps, while the other runs (this works only with 4-6 graders). Older children (fifth or sixth graders) can test the younger children using this pairing system.

Scoring: Scores are recorded to the nearest meter with a total determined by multiplying the number of laps by 100 and adding the nearest meter to where the child's pin was placed (remember, it has the same number as the pinnie) to get the total, i.e., Jimmy (#10) crossed the start/finish line 17 times giving him a score of 1700 meters; his pin was clipped closest to 27 meters, so his total run was 1727 meters.

Norms: Norms are presented for both the six-minute and nine-minute run. The validity of the six-minute run, however, has not been established although a reliability of .92 has been found using six-year-old children as subjects.

Sit-ups

Norms: Sixty-Second Sit-up Test

Age —	6	7	8	9
Rating				
Excellent	26	28	29	34
Good	20	23	25	28
Average	16	17	19	24
Poor	8	9	10	12

Age —	10	11	12
Rating			
Excellent	40	44	45
Good	35	36	39
Average	26	26	29
Poor	13	15	17

Six-Minute Run
(In meters)

Age —	6	7	8	9
Rating				
Excellent	1100	1150	1200	1250
Good	950	1000	1050	1100
Average	860	870	880	890
Poor	650	700	750	800

Nine-Minute Run

Age —	10	11	12
Rating			
Excellent	1900	2000	2050
Good	1600	1700	1750
Average	1200	1500	1600
Poor	800	900	950

Ready to run

100-meter track

Figure A-1
Scoring Sheet for Timed Distance Run

No.	1	2	3	4	5	6	7	8	9	10	11	12	13	14	15	16	17	18	19	20	21	22	23	24	25	Total
1																										
2																										
3																										
4																										
5																										
6																										
7																										
8																										
9																										
10																										

1 _____   6 _____
2 _____   7 _____
3 _____   8 _____
4 _____   9 _____
5 _____   10 _____

Figure A-2

Tricep Skinfold of Children by Sex and Age

Sex and age	Mean	Standard Deviation	5th	10th	25th	50th	75th	90th	95th
			\multicolumn{7}{c	}{In Millimeters}
Boys, 6-11 yrs	9.4	4.28	5.0	5.5	7.0	8.0	11.0	15.0	18.0
6 years	8.1	2.79	5.0	5.0	6.0	8.0	9.0	12.0	13.0
7 years	8.4	3.17	4.5	5.0	6.0	8.0	9.5	12.0	14.0
8 years	9.0	3.77	4.5	5.0	6.5	8.0	11.0	13.5	17.0
9 years	10.0	4.96	5.0	6.0	7.0	8.5	12.0	16.0	20.0
10 years	10.1	4.43	5.0	6.0	7.0	9.0	12.0	16.0	20.0
11 years	11.0	5.32	5.0	6.0	7.0	9.5	14.0	19.0	22.0
Girls, 6-11 yrs.	11.5	4.61	6.0	7.0	8.0	10.0	14.0	18.0	21.0
6 years	9.7	3.39	5.5	6.0	7.0	9.0	11.0	14.0	16.0
7 years	10.4	3.61	6.0	6.5	8.0	10.0	12.0	16.0	17.0
8 years	11.4	4.43	6.0	6.5	8.0	10.5	13.5	18.0	20.0
9 years	12.3	4.84	6.0	7.0	9.0	11.0	14.5	19.0	22.0
10 years	12.6	5.12	6.0	7.0	9.0	12.0	15.0	20.0	23.0
11 years	12.6	5.19	6.0	7.0	9.0	12.0	15.0	20.0	23.0

Test Item 4: Skinfold Measurement

Component: Percentage of body fat.
Equipment: A Large Skinfold Caliper (approximately $180) or a plastic caliper (cost $4).
Procedure: Only the tricep skinfold will be used. Locate a point midway between the elbow and shoulder joints. Gather all the skin on the back of the arm. The child then bends the arm to a 90 degree angle and the measurement is taken just below the thumb and first finger.
Scoring: Results are recorded in millimeters.
Norms: See Figures A-2 and A-3.

Test Item 5: Sit and Reach Test*

Component: Flexibility of back and hamstring muscles.
Equipment: Yardstick and tape.
Procedures: A yardstick is taped to the floor and the child sits so the 15 inch mark on the yardstick is even with his heels. The child then bends forward and touches the yardstick as far down toward or beyond his feet as possible. The child's score is recorded to the closest inch he was able to reach.
*No norms available for elementary children.

Figure A-2, continued

Tricep Skinfold of Children by Race, Sex, and Age

Race, Sex, and Age	Mean	Standard Deviation	5th	10th	25th	50th	75th	90th	95th
						In Millimeters			
WHITE Boys, 6-11 yrs.	9.8	4.33	5.0	6.0	7.0	8.5	11.0	15.5	19.0
6 years	8.3	2.82	5.0	6.0	6.5	8.0	9.5	12.0	13.0
7 years	8.7	3.20	5.0	6.0	7.0	8.0	10.0	12.0	14.5
8 years	9.3	3.80	5.0	6.0	7.0	8.0	11.0	14.0	17.0
9 years	10.4	5.06	5.0	6.0	7.0	9.0	12.0	17.0	21.0
10 years	10.5	4.41	5.5	6.0	7.5	9.5	13.0	16.0	20.0
11 years	11.5	5.32	5.5	6.0	8.0	10.0	14.0	19.0	22.0
Girls, 6-11 yrs.	11.8	4.55	6.0	7.0	8.5	11.0	14.0	18.0	21.0
6 years	10.0	3.39	6.0	6.5	8.0	10.0	11.0	14.0	16.0
7 years	10.8	3.47	6.5	7.0	8.0	10.0	12.5	16.0	18.0
8 years	11.7	4.34	6.0	7.0	9.0	11.0	14.0	18.0	20.0
9 years	12.7	4.83	7.0	8.0	9.0	11.5	15.0	20.0	22.5
10 years	13.0	5.08	6.0	7.0	9.0	12.0	16.0	20.0	23.0
11 years	12.9	5.07	7.0	7.5	9.0	12.0	16.0	20.1	22.0
BLACK Boys, 6-11 yrs.	7.2	3.13	4.0	4.0	5.0	6.5	8.0	11.0	13.0
6 years	7.0	2.25	4.0	5.0	5.5	7.0	8.0	10.0	11.0
7 years	6.4	2.14	4.0	4.0	5.0	6.0	7.0	9.0	10.0
8 years	7.1	2.98	4.0	4.0	5.0	6.5	8.0	12.0	13.0
9 years	7.2	2.99	4.0	4.0	5.0	6.5	8.0	11.0	14.0
10 years	7.6	3.49	4.0	4.0	5.5	7.0	9.0	11.0	13.0
11 years	8.1	4.32	4.0	4.0	6.0	7.0	9.0	12.0	18.0
Girls, 6-11 yrs.	9.5	4.50	5.0	5.5	6.5	8.0	11.0	15.0	20.0
6 years	7.9	2.84	5.0	5.0	6.0	7.0	9.0	11.0	14.0
7 years	8.3	3.68	5.0	5.0	6.0	7.0	9.0	12.0	16.0
8 years	9.6	4.59	5.0	5.0	6.5	8.0	11.0	14.0	20.0
9 years	10.2	4.45	5.0	6.0	7.0	9.0	12.5	15.5	19.0
10 years	10.3	4.74	5.0	6.0	7.0	9.0	12.0	20.0	20.2
11 years	10.9	5.58	4.0	6.0	7.0	10.0	12.0	20.0	25.0

Figure A-3

Skinfold Measures for Obesity*

Age	Tricep Skinfold Thickness Indicating Obesity (In Millimeters)	
	Males	*Females*
5	12	14
6	12	15
7	13	16
8	14	17
9	15	18
10	16	20
11	17	21
12	18	22

*Caucasian Americans

Figure A-4
Physical Fitness Report Card

Test Explanation: The physical fitness test components included here are those directly related to the health of your child. Most fitness tests emphasize motor fitness components such as speed, agility, power, etc., which have little relationship to a child's well being. The data from this test should aid you in evaluating your child's health needs. A brief explanation of the test items follows:

1. Running. The child tries to see how far he or she can run in a given time, six minutes for grades 1-3 and nine minutes for grades 4-6. The test is used to estimate cardiovascular efficiency which is considered to be the most important fitness component.

2. Sit-ups. This test is used to measure abdominal strength and endurance. The child lies on his or her back with the knees bent and hands behind the head. The number of sit-ups which can be completed in 60 seconds is recorded.

3. Percentage of Body Fat. This test is used to estimate the child's percentage of body fat. Since excess fat is considered a health hazard, maintenance of a low percentage is desirable. The estimate is made by measuring the skinfold at the back of the arm.

4. Bar Hang. This test is used to measure upper body strength and endurance. The child is lifted into a flexed arm position (pull-up) with the chin over a horizontal bar. Upon being released, the child tries to keep the chin over the bar as long as possible. The time is recorded in seconds.

5. Sit and Reach Test. This test is used to determine the flexibility of the back and hamstring (back of the leg) muscles, The child is asked to sit on the floor and reach as far as possible toward or beyond his feet if possible. Scores are recorded in inches.

Score Interpretation: Three pieces of information are recorded on the following pages: (1) your child's raw score, (2) the percentile rank of that score, and (3) a classification of your child based on his or her performance.

The percentile rank is based on your child's score compared with other children his or her age at (name of school) or with national norms. National norms are available for percentage of body fat, bar hang for girls ten years of age and older, The nine-minute run for boys and girls, and sit-ups for boys and girls ten years of age and above. All other percentiles are comparison of (name of school) children only. A percentile rank of 63, for example, means your child scored better than 62 percent of the children taking the test.

The four-point classification system is: 1 = Excellent, 2 = Good, 3 = Average, 4 = Needs Improvement. The ratings are for information only, not as a means of grading students.

The main concern is to see improvement, so fall and spring scores will be color-coded and placed on the same chart for easy comparison. Fall scores will be in blue and spring in red. The test will be given at the beginning and end of the school year.

Test Data

Fall Test Date _____ (Blue)   Spring Test Date _____ (Red)

Percentiles

Percentile	Abdominal Strength	% of Body Fat	Upper Body Strength	Cardiovascular Efficiency	Flexibility
100					
90					
80					
70					
60					
50					
40					
30					
20					
10					
0					

Test Data, Continued

	Sit-ups (Abdominal Str.)		Percent of Body Fat	
	Fall	Spring	Fall	Spring
Your child's score				
Percentile rank				
Classification				

	Bar Hang (Upper Body Str.)		Running (Cardiovascular Eff.)	
	Fall	Spring	Fall	Spring
Your child's score				
Percentile rank				
Classification				

	Flexibility	
	Fall	Spring
Your child's score		
Percentile rank		
Classification		

RUNNING FOR LIFE

Anyone who has been reading either the professional or the popular literature is aware of the new interest in health related fitness. The new AAHPERD Youth Fitness Test reflects that interest. Gone are the motor fitness items, and in their place are cardiovascular efficiency, body composition, muscular strength and endurance, and flexibility. The test spells out clearly how one can assess each item. Assessment, however, is only a beginning. Educators and parents must then seek ways to improve weaknesses in the children. Two traditionally weak areas in children are cardiovascular efficiency and body composition. Inactivity due to modern living and television are quickly producing a situation where overweight, out of shape children are becoming the norm. A program to alter that trend is Running for Life.

Running for Life is a program designed to increase children's fitness while improving their knowledge of academic subjects. The fitness components most affected are cardiovascular efficiency and body composition. The major cognitive component is geography, although math, reading, and science can be incorporated into the program.

There are a number of ways to approach Running for Life. The most popular is low level competition between teams which can be organized in a variety of ways. The teams provide the motivation for the program's exercise component. Competition can be conducted within a particular grade level or the entire student population can be divided into teams. The latter method is accomplished by organizing each class into three or more color teams, i.e., red, white, and blue. Each team will have children from every grade level. By having equal numbers on each team from each class, classes who cannot participate because of trips, teacher apathy, and/or weather will affect each team equally. This multigrade team approach, however, does not provide as much motivation as the intragrade competition. Running for Life does not have to be schoolwide. Individual grade levels or even specific classes could use Running for Life as a fitness motivation and for learning geography.

Whichever method is used, however, the exercise is the same. After a preconditioning period of at least three weeks, children are supervised by the classroom teacher for daily 20-minute periods during which time they attempt to see how many laps they can complete running, walking, or a combination of the two. Wheelchair bound students can wheel themselves or be pushed by a classmate with both pusher and wheeler getting credit for each lap. To count laps, a token can can be given to the child as he or she crosses the start/finish line. The distance around the "track" can be any length as long as it remains constant for every child participating in the program. After 20 minutes, each child records his laps. The class' total laps are used to calculate the distance traveled.

The laps are converted to meters which are used to plot progress on a map. The conversion is done by dividing the total team laps by a number selected by the program director. The magnitude of the number is determined by how fast he wants the teams to progress. A large number will cause teams to move slowly and vice versa. The same number must be applied to all teams. An illustration:

There are three teams, Red, White, and Blue. The total weekly laps for each team are:

Red	=	345
White	=	283
Blue	=	240

The conversion number, 15, is selected. Each team total is divided by 15 with the following results:

Red	=	23 meters
White	=	19 meters
Blue	=	16 meters

Progress would then be appropriately marked on a map. If the director wished to move the teams more quickly, a lower divisor (conversion number) would be used. The same divisor must always be used in recording any weekly total but can be changed from week to week during the program to speed up or slow down all teams' progress.

Although the program director is usually a physical educator, the program is conducted by the classroom teacher, but not during the physical education time taught by a specialist. Since the program requires a minimum of three workouts per week and physical educators traditionally only see children once a week, it would not be possible for the specialist to supervise the running. It should also be emphasized that fitness is only one aspect of physical education and other appropriate physical education activities should be taught by both the specialist and the classroom teacher.

Geography is the classroom focus of Running for Life. Although any aspect of geography can be used, as will be seen later, let us first focus on the United States. A large 4' by 6' map of the United States is made and displayed in a prominent area of the school. The starting point for the "race" can be the children's hometown or they can begin on one side of the country and progress across it. Map tape is used to mark progress (determined by converting laps to meters). As teams cross into states of time zones, various subjects such as terrain, weather, or information about a particular state can be discussed. Math can also be integrated into the discussion by having the children calculate average speed, distance traveled, and/or other simple addition and subtraction problems. If Running for Life is a schoolwide program, a K-5 geography curriculum should be developed to avoid redundancy over the years.

Some innovative ideas have been generated by those who have already participated in Running for Life. At one school, children got pen pals from their ultimate destination and discussed their progress through an exchange of letters. In another instance, teachers shared vacation slides from various states with all participants at certain grade levels. Fruit became the focus of another program where children ran to states famous for various fruits, i.e., Georgia peach. No matter which team arrived in the state first, everyone went to the cafeteria to have a piece of the fruit. This fruit idea was done yearly in the fourth grade.

The classroom component can also be varied by changing the map from the United States to the world or perhaps the universe. Then opportunities for discussions about oceans, tides, rivers, cities of the world, etc. would be possible. Music, art, dance, and creativity could be incorporated by discussing and participating in the cultural activities of people from other countries. Overall program variety would keep children's interest over the years and avoid repetition.

Running laps can get boring; so to keep interest, goals must not be too long term. Around Thanksgiving, children can run to Massachusetts and then have their Thanksgiving meal. From Thanksgiving to Christmas, children can run to the North Pole. The cross country run seems to work best in the spring and can last six to eight weeks (not including the three weeks of preconditioning) without losing the participants' interest.

To avoid lap running, credit can be given for a certain amount of aerobic activity such as aerobic dance, rope jumping, and/or continuous running or vigorous walking anywhere around the playground. Progress then can be determined by converting aerobic points to meters as was done with laps. A name for the program would be The Lifetime Aerobics Program or Aerobicing Along.

No matter which organization pattern is selected, the goal is improved children's fitness. Developing positive attitudes toward and participation in aerobic activities is essential to the health of all youth. The research literature is quite clear on the positive effects of reasonable exercise on the growth and development of children, but the attitudinal effects of any one exercise program must be evaluated to determine its value. Running for Life has been studied to determine the attitude of participants toward the various components. A researcher using an anonymous questionnaire found that all three groups, children, teachers, and administrators, expressed very positive attitudes toward all aspects of the program.

APPENDIX B
EVALUATION INSTRUMENTS
FOR THE AFFECTIVE DOMAIN

AFFECTIVE DOMAIN

Figure B-1

Body Image Assessment

Instructions: Have the child draw a picture of himself or herself on a plain 8½" x 11" piece of paper. Score one point for each body part drawn (pairs such as eyes get one point). Instrument can be individually or group administered although children should not be able to see each other's drawings during group assessment. Drawings of two typical five-year-old children are included below: (Also see Affective Domain, Chapter 5)

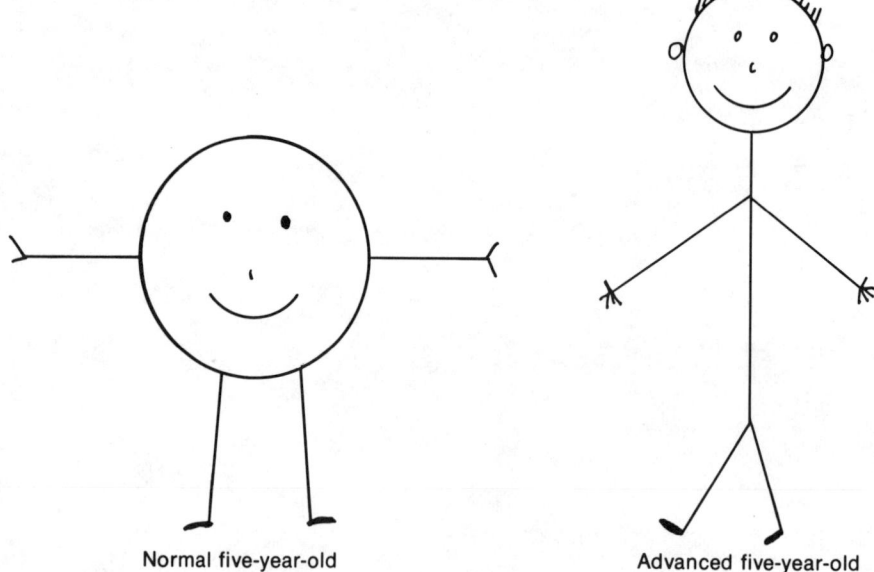

Normal five-year-old

Advanced five-year-old

Figure B-2

Attitude Questionnaire for Kindergarten and First Grade

Instructions

Have the children place an X on the face which best reflects their feelings regarding the various statements. The three faces on the answer sheet should be randomly placed for each question. The question mark face should be X'ed if a child does not understand the question.

Most children can follow using the numbers to the left of each set of faces, but familiar objects may be used (book, tree, spoon) in place of numbers for non-readers.

Practice: Check children's answers to be sure they understand.
_____ a. When I get ice cream, I am . . .
_____ b. When I hurt myself, I am . . .

Questions
_____ 1. When I know we are going to physical education, I am . . .
_____ 2. When (teacher's name) is not in school, I am . . .
_____ 3. When we dance, I am . . .
_____ 4. When we tumble, I am . . .
_____ 5. When we have to play with partners, I am . . .
_____ 6. When (teacher's name) gets mad, I am . . .
_____ 7. When I have to sit out of activity, I am . . .

Kindergarten Questionnaire Answer Sheet

KEY: Happy / Sad / Do not understand

Practice.
a. ☺ ☹ ?
b. ☹ ? ☺

Questions.
1. ☺ ☹ ?
2. ? ☹ ☺
3. ☹ ? ☺
4. ☺ ☹ ?
5. ? ☺ ☹
6. ☹ ? ☺
7. ☺ ☹ ?

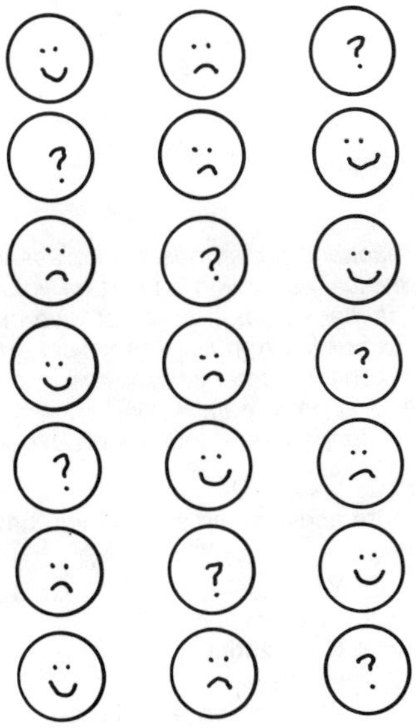

Figure B-3

Attitude Questionnaire for Seven to Nine-Year-Old Children

This questionnaire will help me design a better physical education program for you. Please do not put your name on the questionnaire.

Section One

Instructions. Look at the scale below and place the *number* corresponding to the word or phrase which best indicates your feelings about the statement. Place the number on the line to the left of each statement.

Scale
1. Agree
2. Disagree
0. Do not understand statement

Examples:
a. Ice cream tastes good.
b. I like to fall down and hurt my knees.

Questions.
___ 1. Physical education is fun.
___ 2. (Teacher's name) likes me.
___ 3. I do not like physical education.
___ 4. I like to dance in physical education.
___ 5. (Teacher's name) makes me feel good.
___ 6. I like to do things with a partner.
___ 7. (Teacher's name) praises me when I do well.
___ 8. I do not like tumbling and gymnastics.
___ 9. (Teacher's name) gets mad too easily.
___10. I do exercises at home.
___11. I like (teacher's name).

Section Two

Questions.
1. My favorite activity is _____
2. My least favorite activity is _____
3. The game I like to play the most is _____

Figure B-4

Attitude Questionnaire for Ten and Eleven-Year-Olds

This questionnaire will help me design a better physical education program for you. Please read each statement carefully before responding. Do not put your name on the questionnaire.

Section One

Instructions. Look at the scale below and place the number corresponding to the word or phrase which best reflects your feelings about the statement. Place the number on the line to the left of each statement.

Scale
1. Strongly agree
2. Agree
3. Disagree
4. Strongly disagree
0. Do not understand statement

Examples:
___ a. Ice cream tastes good.
___ b. I would like to fall and break a leg.

Questions.
___ 1. Physical education is an important part of the curriculum.
___ 2. (Teacher's name) likes me.
___ 3. We do too many exercises in physical education.
___ 4. I do a lot of physical fitness activities at home.
___ 5. I enjoy working in groups during physical education.
___ 6. I like to dance in physical education.
___ 7. (Teacher's name) yells too much.
___ 8. (Teacher's name) has embarrassed me in class.
___ 9. Physical education should be voluntary.
___10. (Teacher's name) does not give me much attention in c
___11. I do not learn much in physical education.
___12. (Teacher's name) praises me in physical education.
___13. Playing on a team is fun.
___14. (Teacher's name) is fair with everyone.

Section Two

Give a one (1) to the activity you like the most, a two (2) to your next favorite activity, and so until you have given a number to each activity.

___Football   ___Tennis   ___Volleyball
___Dance   ___Basketball   ___Rhythmics
___Track & Field   ___Fitness Activities ___Gymnastics
___Softball   ___Hockey
___Tumbling   ___Small group activities

Section Three

Respond to the following questions in the space provided or use the back of the paper:
1. What do you like most about (teacher's name)?
2. What could (teacher's name) do to be a better teacher?
3. What would be a way to improve the physical education program?

APPENDIX C
THE COGNITIVE DOMAIN

Although there are a multitude of tests for cognitive ability, few if any are useful to physical educators. The best way to obtain cognitive data is to question students in those areas which seem important to physical education. These areas include safety, health and fitness knowledge. Questioning should be done periodically on a random basis. The random technique will give an overall picture of cognitive ability without requiring a paper-pencil test. Since such questioning seeks specific knowledge, children should be questioned individually rather than in front of peers to avoid embarrassment should they not know the answer. Questions can be asked during individual learning situations when each child is occupied with a task. The following questions would seem appropriate:

Why is there no sliding on the floor?
Why should you stay inside the lines?
When should you brush your teeth?
Why is being fit important?

Additional questions can be developed from information in each of the curriculum chapters 7-10.

APPENDIX D
RECORD SOURCES

Methodist World of Fun Series. Audiovisual Services. United Methodist Board of Education, P.O. Box 871, Nashville, Tenn. 37202

Honor Your Partner Series. Square Dance Records. Educational Activities, Inc. Freeport, N.Y. 11520

Dances Without Partners. Educational Activities, Inc.

Creative Movement and Rhythmic Expression by Hap Palmer. Educational Activities, Inc.

Movin' by Hap Palmer. Educational Activities, Inc.

Rhythms Today. Silver Burdett Co., Morristown, N.J.

Square Dance Fun for Everyone. Kimbo Records, Box 246, Deal, N.J. 00723. Also Available from Educational Activities, Inc.

Parachute Play — Available from both Kimbo and Educational Activities.

INDEX

Ability grouping, 66
Abnormal development, 19-20
Accident reports, 345-346
Aerobic dance, 87
Anxiety, 31
Attitude questionnaire:
  non-reader, 9
  upper elementary, 10, 392-394
Auditory perception, 27

Balance, 100, 132, 175, 244, 327
Balance beam activities, 132, 209, 244
Baseball — softball, 211
  objectives and activities, 235-236, 255
Basketball, 211
  objectives and activities, 238-239, 255
Behavior modification, 324-325
Behavioral objectives, 61, 64
  programmed test, 77-79
Bloom, B., 3
Body build, 30
Body image, 13, 211
  activities, 146-147, 177, 214, 328
Bowling, 211
Bulletin boards, 48
Buros' *Mental Measurement Yearbook*, 4

Catching, 168, 201, 203, 235
Circuit training, 87, 361
Communication skills, 26
  non-verbal, 45-46
Competition, 351-354
Creativity, 140-143, 149-150, 172-173, 206-207, 213, 249-250
Critical learning periods, 31
Curriculum design, 61
  systematic approach, 61

Dance:
  aerobic, 87
  folk and square, 247
  skills and activities, 268-316
Demonstrations, 27-28, 31
Discipline, 51-52, 54, 57, 212
Draw-a-Person Test, 8

Educational domains, 3
  Affective, 3, 6
    goals and objectives, 7
    evaluation, 7, 392-394
  Cognitive, 3
    goals and objectives, 4
    testing, 4, 395
  Psycho-motor, 3, 4
    goals and objectives, 5
    evaluation, 5
Educational gymnastics, 13, 43
Eye-foot coordination, 122, 168, 201-204
Eye-hand coordination, 122, 161, 167, 197, 201, 203, 329-330

Fartlek training, 86
Football:
  objectives and activities, 237-238, 255

Games:
  defined, 113
  cognitive, 360-365
  value of, 113-115
  rating of, 115
  kindergarten, 151-155
  first and second grade, 181-187
  third and fourth grade, 215-221
  fifth and sixth grade, 254-257
Goals of physical education, 5

Hockey, 211
  objectives and activities, 238, 255
Humphrey, T., 45, 111, 359

Individualized Education Plan (IEP), 320-323, 334
Infant Olympics, 352
Integrated activities, 147-150, 177-180

Jump ropes, 168, 206, 249, 251

Kicking, 168, 201
Kinesthetic awareness, 13
Kinesthetic perception, 27
Kinesthetic and proprioceptive activities, 137, 169

Learning:
  defined, 17
  principles, 20-22
Legal liability, 339
Lesson planning, 72-73
Likert Scale, 7
Little League elbow, 352
Locomotor activities, 127-128

Manipulative skills, 130-131, 167
  activities, 202
Motivation, 30, 100, 354
Motor fitness attributes:
  speed, 100
  agility, 100
  balance, 100, 132, 327
  power, 100
Motor learning process, 25-26
Movement education, 13

Negligence, 340, 344
Non-locomotor activities, 129-130
Nutrition, 19, 353

Parallel bar activities, 210, 243
Physical attributes:
  strength, 84, 104
    evaluation of, 93
    developing, 93-98, 325-327
  cardiovascular, 84
    evaluation of, 85
    developing, 85-88, 100
  body composition, 84
    evaluation of, 98
    reducing body fat, 98
  flexibility, 88, 104
    evaluation of, 88-89
    developing, 90-92
Physical fitness:
  defined, 83-84
  objectives and activities, 134-135, 175-177, 207-208, 246
  myth(s) about, 87-88, 96
Perceptual-motor, 13, 19
Permission slips, 345
Piaget, T., 18, 359
Posture, 101-102, 161, 230
Public law 94-142, 320
Purdue Perceptual-Motor Survey, 5

Rhythmics, 135-139, 170-172, 204-206, 247
Running for Life Programs, 390-391

Safety, 73, 124-125, 147, 165, 177, 199, 215, 233, 251, 340-344
Self-concept, 6, 13, 30, 144, 212, 251
Self-instructional materials, 67
Soccer, 204, 211
  objectives and activities, 236-237, 257
Supervision, defined, 342

Tactile perception, 27
Task analysis, 323-324
Teaching styles, 42-43
Tennis, 211
  objectives and activities, 244-245
Throwing, 167, 203
Track and field,
  objectives and activities, 245-246
Tumbling and gymnastics, 132-134, 173-175, 208-210, 241-244

Unit planning, 68

Vaulting box activities, 134, 175, 209, 242
VCU Fitness Test, 384-390
Visual aids, 28
Visual perception, 27
Volleyball:
  objectives and activities, 239-240, 256

Warm-up, 32

Competition

physical & psycho. aims —

```
   80
   82
   97
  259
   90
  349       86
      ┌────────
    3 │ 259
        24
        ───
        19
        18
        ──
         1
```

```
   80
   82
   97
   90
```

```
       87
      ┌────
    4 │ 349
        32
        ───
        29
        28
```